General Principles
of English Law

General Principles of English Law

P W D Redmond LLM
Barrister, formerly Senior Lecturer in Law at the City of London College

and

Peter Shears BA, LLB, LLM
Director of Legal Studies, University of Plymouth

Seventh Edition

THE M & E HANDBOOK SERIES

Pitman Publishing
128 Long Acre, London WC2E 9AN

A Division of Longman Group UK Limited

First published 1964
Second edition 1966
Third edition 1970
Fourth edition 1974
Fifth edition 1979
Sixth edition 1990
Seventh edition 1993

© Macdonald & Evans Ltd 1964, 1966, 1970, 1974, 1979
© Longman Group UK Ltd 1990, 1993

A CIP catalogue record for this book is available from
the British Library.

ISBN 0 7121 0858 0

Founding Editor: P W D Redmond

Typeset by FDS Ltd, Penarth, South Glamorgan
Printed and bound in Singapore

Contents

Preface to the seventh edition   *ix*
Table of cases   *xi*
Table of statutes   *xxviii*

Part one   The English legal system

1   Nature and history of English law   **3**
Nature of law; History of common law; History of equity;
Subsidiary systems of law; The Judicature Acts 1873–75

2   Sources of English law   **19**
Principal sources; Custom; Legislation; Case law

3   The judicial system   **36**
Introduction; The House of Lords; The Judicial Committee of
the Privy Council; The Court of Appeal; The High Court;
Inferior civil courts; Inferior criminal courts; The judiciary;
Special courts; The legal profession; Legal aid; Arbitration

4   The law of persons   **66**
Legal personality; Nationality and domicile; Marriage; Infants
or minors; The Crown

Part two   The law of contract

5   Formalities and consent   **91**
Introduction; Formalities; Intention to create legal relations;
The offer; The acceptance; Termination of offer

6   Consideration, privity and capacity   **105**
Consideration; Privity; Capacity

7 **The terms of a contract**   **118**
General considerations; Standard form contracts; Exclusion
clauses

8 **Invalidity**   **129**
Introduction; Mistake; Misrepresentation; Duress; Undue
influence; Void and illegal contracts; Contracts in restraint of
trade; Competition law

9 **Discharge of contracts**   **147**
Introduction; Discharge by performance; Discharge by
agreement; Discharge by operation of law; Discharge by
frustration; Discharge by breach; Proper law; Limitation;
Remedies

10 **Quasi-contract**   **160**
The main features of quasi-contract

11 **Agency**   **165**
Introduction; Creation; Termination; Duties of principal and
agent; The authority of the agent

12 **Mercantile law**   **178**
Assignment; Negotiable instruments; *Nemo dat quod non habet*;
Sale of goods; Supply of goods and services; Gifts; Bailment;
Hire purchase; Liens

Part three The law of torts

13 **Nature of tortious liability**   **201**
Tort; Tortious liability

14 **Capacity and defences in tort**   **211**
Capacity in tort; Capacity — specific instances; Vicarious
liability; General defences in tort

15 **Trespass and nuisance**   **224**
General; Trespass to the person; Trespass to land; Wrongful
interference with goods; Nuisance

16 Negligence   **239**
The tort of negligence; Occupiers' liability

17 Strict liability   **253**
Meaning and scope of strict liability; The rule in *Rylands* v.
Fletcher; Liability for fire; Liability for animals; Statutory torts

18 Defamation   **261**
General requirements and definitions; Defences

Part four The law of property

19 Real and personal property   **271**
Introduction; Kinds of property; The 1925 legislation

20 Estates and interest in land   **280**
Tenure and estates; Legal estates in land; Co-ownership;
Legal interests; Equitable interests; Strict settlements and
trusts for sale

21 Leases, covenants and servitudes   **292**
Leases; Covenants in a lease; Restrictive covenants; Easements
and profits

22 Securities   **302**
Securities generally; Mortgages of land; Mortgages of
personalty

Part five Equity and trusts

23 Equity and trusts   **317**
Equity; Equitable doctrines; Equitable remedies; Trusts;
Express private trusts; Express public trusts (charities);
Purpose trusts; Resulting trusts; Constructive trusts; Variation
of trusts; Appointment and retirement of trustees; Duties and
powers of trustees

Part six Law of succession

24 **Law of succession**   347
Requisites of a valid will; Property that may be disposed of by
will; Revocation of wills; Maintenance of dependants; Personal
representatives; Intestacy; Bankruptcy

Part seven Criminal law

25 **Criminal liability**   367
Crime and criminal liability

26 **Limitations on criminal responsibility**   379
Types of limitation and how they relate to criminal
responsibility

27 **Offences against the person**   387
Fatal offences; Non-fatal offences

28 **Offences against property**   395
Theft Acts 1968 and 1978; Other offences

29 **Offences against state security and public order**   407
Offences against state security; Offences against public order

Appendices   415
1 Bills of exchange and cheques for banking students;
2 Examination technique

Index   435

Preface to the seventh edition

It makes me sad to have to report here that since the last edition of this book Mr Redmond has died. Not only was this work his idea, but so was the whole Handbook series.

The law marches on, however, with or without us, and I have tried in this new edition to track its progress. Particular strides have been taken with the implementation of the new Children Act and the Courts and Legal Services Act, but there have also been changes large and small across much of the vast area covered by this book.

I would like to register my gratitude to Inger Curtis, of the University of Nebraska, whose careful scholarship eased the production of this, the seventh edition.

The book is intended to be of use to students of the law at every level and to those who are following courses leading to a variety of professional examinations. Further, it is designed to be useful to those who simply want to know some law!

I have stated the law as I believe it to be in the wet winter of 1992–93.

Peter Shears

Table of cases

Abbott v. The Queen [1977] A.C. 755; [1976] 3 All E.R. 140 *384*

Adam v. Ward [1917] A.C. 309 *266*

Adams v. Ursell (1913) 1 Ch. 269 *236*

Adams and Kensington Vestry, *Re* (1884) 27 Ch.D. 394 *326*

Addis v. Crocker [1961] 1 Q.B. 11; [1960] 2 All E.R. 629 *266*

Alcock & Others v. Chief Constable of the South Yorkshire Police (1991) 4 All E.R. 907 *247*

Aldred's Case (1610) 9 Rep. 57 B; 5 Co. Rep. 102 *256*

Alec Lobb (Garages) Ltd v. Total Oil GB Ltd (1985) 1 All E.R. 303 *143*

Alexander v. Railway Executive [1951] 2 K.B. 882; [1951] 2 All E.R. 442 *190, 191*

Alexander v. Rayson [1936] 1 K.B. 169 *139, 141*

Aliakmon, The, (1986) 2 W.L.R. 902 *205, 242*

Allcard v. Skinner (1887) 36 Ch.D. 145 *138*

Allen v. Greenwood (1979) 2 W.L.R. 187 *300*

Allen v. Whitehead [1930] 1 K.B. 211 *381*

Allsop v. Church of England Newspapers Ltd [1972] 2 Q.B. 161; [1972] 2 All E.R. 26 *262*

Aluminium Industrie BV v. Romalpa Aluminium Ltd [1976] 2 All E.R. 552 *187*

Amalgamated Investment v. John Walker & Sons (1976) 3 All E.R. 509 *151*

Andrews v. Director of Public Prosecutions [1937] A.C. 576; [1937] 2 All E.R. 552 *390, 393*

Anns v. London Borough of Merton (1977) A.C. 728 *29, 244*

Anton Piller KG v. Manufacturing Processes Ltd (1976) Ch. 55; (1976) 2 W.L.R. 162 *47, 323*

Arenson v. Arenson [1973] Ch. 346; [1973] 2 All E.R. 235 C.A. [1977] A.C. 405; [1975] 3 All E.R. 901 H.L. *243*

Armory v. Delamirie (1722) 1 Str. 505 *232*

Ashbury Railway Carriage Co. v. Riche (1875) L.R. 7 H.L. 653 *114, 170*

Associated Japanese Bank v. Credit Du Nord (1988) N.L.J., L.R. 109 *130*

Associated Leisure Ltd v. Associated Newspapers [1970] Q.B. 450; [1970] 2 All E.R. 754 *264*

Astor's Settlement Trusts, *Re* [1952] Ch. 534; [1952] All E.R. 1067 *332*

Atlas Express Ltd v. Kafco (1989) 1 All E.R. 641 *137*

Attia v. British Gas PLC (1987) 3 All E.R. 455 *247*

Attorney-General v. Guardian Newspapers [1987] 1 W.L.R. 1248 *408*

Attorney-General v. Guardian Newspapers (No. 2) [1988] 3 W.L.R. 766 *408*

Attorney-General for Northern Ireland v. Gallagher [1963] A.C. 349; [1961] 3 All E.R. 299 *383*

Attorney-General's Reference No. 1 (1989) I.L.R., 1 August 1989 *41*

Attwood v. Lamont [1920] 3 K.B. 571 *142*

Avery v. Bowden (1856) 6 E. & B. 953; 5 E. & B. 714 *151, 152, 154*

Baden, *Re, see* McPhail v. Doulton

Baker v. Bolton (1808) 1 Camp. 493 *214*

Baker v. Hopkins [1959] 1 W.L.R. 996; [1959] 3 All E.R. 225 *219*

Baker v. Willoughby [1970] A.C. 467;
[1969] 3 All E.R. 1528 *207*

Balfour v. Balfour [1919] 2 K.B. 571
94

Balfour v. Barty-King [1957] 1 Q.B.
496; [1957] 1 All E.R. 156 *218, 255*

Ballett v. Mingay [1943] K.B. 281;
[1943] 1 All E.R. 143 *213*

Bamford v. Turnley (1862) 3 B. & S. 62
236

Bank of England v. Vagliano [1891]
A.C. 107 *419*

Banning v. Wright [1972] 1 W.C.R. 972;
[1972] 2 All E.R. 987 *109*

Bannister v. Bannister [1948] 2 All E.R.
133 *335*

Barker v. Herbert [1911] 2 K.B. 633
235

Barkway v. South Wales Transport Co.
[1950] A.C. 185; [1950] 1 All E.R. 392
245

Barnes, the Goods of (1926) 43 T.L.R.
71 *348*

Bartlett v. Barclay's Bank Trust Co. Ltd
(No. 1) (1980) 1 All E.R. 139, *340*

Baxendale v. Bennett (1873) 3 Q.B.D.
525 *419*

Beard v. London General Omnibus
Company [1900] 2 Q.B. 530 *218*

Beaulieu v. Finglam (1401) Y.B. 2 Hen
4, 18, pl. 6 *255*

Bebee v. Sales (1916) 32 T.L.R. 413
213

Bell v. Lever Bros. [1932] A.C. 161
131

Bernstein v. Pamsons Motors (1987) 2
All E.R. 220 *187*

Berry v. Berry [1929] 2 K.B. 316 *150*

Beswick v. Beswick [1968] A.C. 58;
[1967] 2 All E.R. 1197 *120*

Bettini v. Gye (1876) 1 Q.B.D. 183 *120*

Biggs v. Hoddinott [1898] 2 Ch. 307
309

Bird v. Holbrook (1828) 4 Bing. 628
251

Bird v. Jones (1845) 7 Q.B. 742 *226*

Birkmyr v. Darnell (1704) 1 Salk. 27
94

Blackburn v. Attorney-General [1971]
1 W.L.R. 1037; [1971] 2 All E.R. 1380
62

Black Clawson International Ltd v.
Papierwerke Waldhof-Aschaffenburg A.G. [1975] A.C. 591; [1975]
1 All E.R. 810 *33*

Blackwell v. Blackwell [1929] A.C. 318
335

Blackpool Marton Rotary Club v.
Martin [1988] S.T.C. 823 *69*

Blyth v. Birmingham Waterworks Co.
(1856) 11 Ex. 781 *239*

Bolton Partners v. Lambert (1889) 41
Ch.D. 295 *170*

Bolton v. Madden (1873) L.R. 9 Q.B. 55
106

Bolton v. Stone [1951] A.C. 850; [1951]
1 All E.R. 1078 *241*

Bonsor v. Musicians' Union [1955] A.C.
104; [1955] 3 All E.R. 518 *56*

Boston Deep Sea Co. v. Farnham
[1957] 1 W.L.R. 1051; [1957] 3 All
E.R. 204 *170*

Boulton v. Jones (1857) 2 H. & N. 564
97

Bourhill v. Young [1943] A.C. 92;
[1942] 2 All E.R. 396 *240*

Bowman v. Secular Society [1917] A.C.
406 *412*

Box v. Jubb (1879) 4 Ex. D. 76 *255*

BP Exploration Co. (Libya) v. Hunt
(No. 2) [1979] 1 W.L.R. 783 *153*

BP Exploration v. Hunt (No. 2) (1983)
2 A.C. 352 *153*

Bradbury v. Morgan (1862) 1 H. & C.
249 *102*

Bradford (Mayor) v. Pickles [1895] A.C.
587 *204, 205, 235-6, 284*

Brady v. Todd (1861) 9 C.B. (N.S.) 592
165

Bratty v. Attorney-General for
Northern Ireland [1963] A.C. 386;
[1961] 3 All E.R. 523 *382*

Bridle v. Ruby (1988) 3 W.L.R. 191
299

Brinkibon v. Stahag Stahl GmbH
(1983) 2 A.C. 34 *100*

British Celanese v. Hunt (1969) 2 All
E.R. 1252 *237, 254*

British Concrete Co. v. Schelff [1921] 2
Ch. 563 *143*

British Movietonews Ltd v. London
and District Cinemas Ltd [1952] A.C.
166; [1951] 2 All E.R. 617 *152*

British Museum v. Attorney-General
(1984) 1 All E.R. 337 (1984) 1 W.L.R.
418 *340*

British Railways Board *v*. Herrington [1972] A.C. 877; [1972] 1 All E.R. 749 *251*

British Russian Gazette Ltd *v*. Associated Newspapers Ltd [1933] 2 K.B. 616 *109*

Broadway Approvals Ltd *v*. Odhams Press [1965] 1 W.L.R. 805; [1965] 2 All E.R. 523 *265*

Brocklehurst, *Re* [1978] Ch. 14; [1978] 1 All E.R. 767 *138*

Brooke *v*. Bool [1908] 2 K.B. 578 *215*

Brown *v*. Lewis (1896) 12 T.L.R. 455 *69*

Browne *v*. Brandt [1902] 1 K.B. 696 *192*

Buckoke *v*. Greater London Council [1971] Ch. 655; [1971] 2 All E.R. 254 *384*

Buckpitt *v*. Oates [1968] 1 All E.R. 1145 *219*

Bucks Constabulary Fund (No. 2), *Re* 1979 1 W.L.R. 936 *333*

Buffery *v*. Buffery (1987) The Times 10 December *79*

Bulmer *v*. Bollinger (1974) 2 All E.R. 1226 *32*

Bunge Corporation *v*. Tradax (1981) 2 All E.R. 513 *123*

Bunker *v*. Brand [1969] 2 Q.B. 480; [1969] 2 All E.R. 59 *248, 250*

Burge *v*. Ashley & Smith Ltd [1900] 1 Q.B. 744 *140*

Burnett *v*. British Waterways Board [1973] 1 W.L.R. 1329; [1973] 2 All E.R. 1353 *219*

Burns *v*. Bidder [1967] 2 Q.B. 227; [1966] 3 All E.R. 29 *373*

Burt *v*. Claude Cousins & Sons Ltd (1971) 2 Q.B. 426 (1971); 2 All E.R. 611 *168*

Bute (Marquess) *v*. Barclays Bank Ltd [1955] 1 Q.B. 202; [1954] 3 All E.R 365 *429*

Butler Machine Tool Co. *v*. Ex-Cell-O Corporation [1979] 1 W.L.R. 401; [1979] 1 All E.R. 965 *101, 125*

Butterfield *v*. Forrester (1809) 11 East 60 *246*

Byrne *v*. Boadle (1863) 2 H. & C. 722 *245*

Byrne *v*. Van Tienhoven (1880) 5 C.P.D. 344 *99, 103*

Cambridge Water Company *v*. Eastern Counties Leather PLC (1991) The Times, 23 October, *254*

Campbell *v*. Spottiswoode (1863) 3 B. & S. 769 *265*

Candlewood Navigation Corporation *v*. Mistui OSK Lines (1985) 2 All E.R. 935 *244*

Caparo Industries *v*. Dickman (1990) 1 All E.R. 568, *244*

Capital and Counties Bank *v*. Henty (1882) 7 App. Cas. 741 *261*

Carlill *v*. Carbolic Smoke Ball Co. [1893] 2 Q.B. 484 *97, 99, 122*

Carslogie, The [1952] A.C. 292; [1952] 1 All E.R. 20 *208*

Carstairs *v*. Taylor (1871) L.R. 6 Exch 217 *254*

Cassidy *v*. Daily Mirror [1929] 2 K.B. 331 *262*

Cassidy *v*. Minister of Health [1951] 2 K.B. 343; [1951] 1 All E.R. 574 *216*

Castle *v*. St Augustine's Links (1922) 3 T.L.R. 615 *235*

Cattle *v*. Stockton Waterworks Co. (1875) L.R. 10 Q.B. 453 *242*

Cavanagh *v*. Ulster Weaving Co. Ltd [1960] A.C. 145; [1959] 2 All E.R. 745 *241*

Central London Property Trust *v*. High Trees House Ltd [1947] K.B. 130; [1956] 1 All E.R. 256 *109*

Century Insurance Co. *v*. Northern Ireland Road Transport Board [1942] A.C. 509; [1942] 1 All E.R. 491 *217*

Chadwick *v*. British Transport Commission [1967] 1 W.C.R. 932; [1967] 2 All E.R. 945 *219, 247*

Chandler *v*. DPP [1964] 3 All E.R. 142 *407*

Chandler *v*. Webster [1904] 1 K.B. 493 *153*

Chapelton *v*. Barry Urban District Council [1940] 1 K.B. 532; [1940] 1 All E.R. 356 *126*

Chaplin *v*. Leslie Frewin (Publishers) Ltd [1966] Ch. 71; [1965] 3 All E.R. 764 *115*

Chapman *v*. Chapman [1954] A.C. 429; 1 All E.R. 798 *336*

Chappell & Co. Ltd v. Nestlé Co. Ltd
[1960] A.C. 87; [1959] 2 All E.R. 701
105
Chatterton v. Secretary of State for
India [1895] 2 Q.B. 189 *266*
Chaudhry v. Prabhakar (1988) 3 All
E.R. 718 *172*
Cheese v. Lovejoy (1877) 2 P.D. 251
352
Chic Fashions (West Wales) v. Jones
[1968] 2 Q.B. 299; [1968] 1 All E.R.
229 *229*
Chillingworth v. Chambers [1896] 1 Ch.
685 *343*
Christie v. Davey [1893] 1 Ch. 316 *236*
Christoforides v. Terry [1924] A.C. 566
173
Cinnamond v. British Airports
Authority (1980) 1 W.L.R. 582 *229*
City Equitable Fire Insurance Co. Ltd,
Re [1925] Ch. 407 *342*
Clarke v. Dunraven [1897] A.C. 59 *96*
Clayton's Case (1816) 1 Mer. 572 *149*
Clayton v. Woodman [1962] 2 Q.B. 533;
[1962] 2 All E.R. 33 *243*
Cleary v. Booth [1893] 1 Q.B. 465 *227*
Cohen v. Daily Telegraph [1968] 1
W.L.R. 916; [1968] 2 All E.R. 407
265
Cole v. Turner (1704) 6 Mod. 149 *226*
Collen v. Wright (1857) 8 E. & B. 647
174
Collins v. Renison (1754) 1 Sayer 138
227
Colls v. Home and Colonial Stores
[1904] A.C. 179 *235*
Combe v. Combe [1951] 2 K.B. 215;
[1951] 1 All E.R. 767
110
Comet Group PLC v. British Sky
Broadcasting (1991) T.L.R. 211
165
Commissioners of Income Tax v.
Pemsel [1891] A.C. 531 *328*
Commissioners of Taxation v. English,
Scottish and Australian Bank Ltd
[1920] A.C. 683 *429*
Condon v. Basi (1985) 2 All E.R. 453;
(1985) 1 W.L.R. 866 *219*
Condor v. Baron Knights (1966) 1
W.L.R. 87 *152*
Consolidated Co. v. Curtis [1892] 1
Q.B. 495 *233*

Cook v. Beal (1697) 1 Ld Raym. 176
227
Cook v. Sqaure D. Ltd (1991) The
Times, 23 October, *215*
E. Coomes (Holdings) Ltd v. Shields
[1979] 1 All E.R. 456 *63*
Cooper v. Phibbs (1867) L.R. 2 H.L. 149
130
Cope v. Sharp (1912) 1 K.B. 496 *221*
Coppen v. Moore [1898] 2 Q.B. 306
381
Corbett v. Corbett [1971] P. 83; [1970]
2 All E.R. 33 *76*
Corcoran v. Anderton (1980) 71 Cr.
App. Rep. 104 *398*
Costa v. E.N.E.L. 6/64 (1964) *29*
Coutts v. Browne-Lecky [1947] K.B.
104; [1946] 2 All E.R. 207 *115*
Coventry, *Re* (1980) Ch. 461 *354*
Craddock Bros. v. Hunt [1923] 2 Ch.
136 *124*
Craig, *Re* [1971] Ch. 95; [1970] 2 All
E.R. 390 *137*
Craven-Ellis v. Canons Ltd [1936] 2
K.B. 403; [1936] 3 All E.R. 1066
163
Crowhurst v. Amersham Burial Board
(1878) 4 Ex. D. 5 *254*
Cumming v. Ince (1847) 11 Q.B. 112
137
Cummings v. Grainger (1976) 2 Q.B.
397; [1977] 1 All E.R. 104 *207, 257*
Cunard v. Antifyre [1933] 1 K.B. 551
236
Cundy v. Lindsay (1878) 3 App. Cas.
459 *95*
Curran v. Northern Ireland
Co-Ownership Housing Association
(1987) 2 All E.R. 13 *244*
Currie v. Misa (1875) L.R. 10 Exch. 153
105
Curtis v. Chemical Cleaning and Dyeing
Co. [1951] 1 K.B. 805; [1951] 1 All
E.R. 631 *126*
Cutler v. United Dairies (London) Ltd
[1933] 2 K.B. 297 *219*

Dakin v. Lee [1916] 1 K.B. 566 *163*
D & C Builders v. Rees (1965) 3 All
E.R. 837 *108*
D & F Estates v. Church Commis-
sioners [1988] 3 W.L.R. 368 *245*

Dann v. Hamilton [1939] 1 K.B. 509;
[1939] 1 All E.R. 59 *218*

Daulia Ltd v. Four Millbank
Nominees Ltd [1978] Ch. 231; [1978]
2 All E.R. 557 *103*

Davies v. Benyon-Harris (1931) 47
T.L.R. 424 *115*

Davies v. Director of Public
Prosecutions [1954] A.C. 378; [1954]
1 All E.R. 507 *375*

Davis v. Johnson (1978) 1 All E.R. 841
30, 32, 40

Davis v. Johnson [1979] A.C. 264;
[1978] 1 All E.R. 1132

Davis Contractors Ltd v. Fareham
Urban District Council [1956] A.C.
696; [1956] 2 All E.R. 145 *151, 152*

Dearle v. Hall (1828) 3 Russ. 1 *179,
180*

De Lasala v. De Lasala [1979] 2 All
E.R. 1146 *39*

De Mattos v. Benjamin (1894) 63
L.J.Q.B. 248 *140*

Denley's Trust Deed, Re [1969] 1 Ch.
373; [1968 3 All E.R. 65 *332*

Department of the Environment v.
Bates (1989) 1 All E.R. 1075 *245*

Derry v. Peek (1889) 14 App. Cas. 337
135, 243

Dickinson v. Dodds (1876) 2 Ch.D. 463
103

Dimskal Shipping Co. v. International
Transport Workers Federation (1991)
4 All E.R. 871 *137*

Diplock, Re, Ministry of Health v.
Simpson [1951] A.C. 251; [1950] 2 All
E.R. 1137 *343*

Director of Public Prosecutions v.
Majewski [1977] A.C. 443; [1976] 2
All E.R. 142 *383, 384*

Director of Public Prosecutions v.
Morgan [1976] A.C. 182; [1975] 2 All
E.R. 347 *385, 391*

Director of Public Prosecutions v.
Newbury [1977] A.C. 500; [1976] 2 All
E.R. 365 *390*

Director of Public Prosecutions v.
Stonehouse (1978) A.C. 55; (1977) 2
All E.R. 909 *376*

Docker v. Somes (1834) 2 My. & K. 655
341

Donoghue v. Stevenson [1932] A.C. 562
29, 203, 240, 247, 248, 434

Doughty v. Turner Manufacturing Co.
Ltd [1964] 1 Q.B. 518 [1964] 1 All
E.R. 98 *209*

Douglas-Menzies v. Umphelby [1908]
A.C. 224 *347*

Downshire's Settled Estates, Re [1953]
Ch. 218; [1953] 1 All E.R. 103 *336*

Doyle v. White City Stadium Ltd
[1935] 1 K.B. 110 *115*

Dufour v. Pereira (1769) Dick 419 *353*

Dulieu v. White [1901] 2 K.B. 669 *247*

Dungate v. Dungate [1965] 1 W.L.R.
1477 *155*

Dunlop Pneumatic Tyre Co. Ltd v.
New Garage and Motor Co. Ltd
[1915] A.C. 79 *157*

Dunlop Pneumatic Tyre Co. Ltd v.
Selfridge & Co. Ltd [1915] A.C. 847
106, 107

Durance, In the Goods of (1872) L.R. 2
P. & D. 406 *352*

Dutton v. Bognor Regis Urban
District Council [1972] 1 Q.B. 373;
[1972] 1 All E.R. 462 *244*

Earl of Oxford (1615) *11*

Eastham v. Newcastle United Football
Club [1964] Ch. 413; [1963] 3 All E.R.
139 *142*

Edmunds v. Wallingford (1855) 14
Q.B.D. 811 *160*

Edwards v. Toombs (1983) Crim L.R.
43 *401*

Egger v. Chelmsford (Viscount) [1965]
1 Q.B. 248; [1964] 3 All E.R. 406
267

Electrochrome Ltd v. Welsh Plastics
Ltd [1968] 2 All E.R. 205 *204*

Ellenborough Park, Re [1956] Ch. 131;
[1955] 3 All E.R. 667 *298*

Ellis v. Loftus Iron Co. (1874) L.R. 10
C.P. 10 *228*

Entores Ltd v. Miles Far East
Corporation [1955] 2 Q.B. 327; [1955]
2 All E.R. 493 *100*

Esso Petroleum Co. Ltd v.
Commissioners of Custom and
Excise [1976] 1 W.L.R. 1; [1976] 1 All
E.R. 117 *95*

Esso Petroleum Co. Ltd v. Harpers
Garage (Southport) Ltd [1968] A.C.
269; [1976] 1 All E.R. 699 *143, 309*

Esso Petroleum Co. Ltd *v.* Mardon
[1976] Q.B. 801; [1976] 2 All E.R. 5
244

Esso Petroleum Co. Ltd *v.* Southport
Corporation (1955) 3 All E.R. 864
221

Eurymedon, The, see New Zealand
Shipping Co. Ltd *v.* Satterthwaite
(1975) *96, 107, 111*

The Eugenia (1964) *152*

Farrant *v.* Barnes (1862) 11 C.B. (N.S.)
553 *248*

Fay *v.* Prentice (1845) 1 C.B. 828 *234*

Felthouse *v.* Bindley (1862) 11 C.B.
(N.S.) 869 *99*

Fibrosa Spolka Akcyjna *v.* Fairbairn
Lawson Combe Barbour Ltd [1943]
A.C. 32; [1943] 2 All E.R. 122 *153*

Financings Ltd *v.* Stimson [1962] 1
W.L.R. 1184; [1962] 3 All E.R. 386
102

Finnemore (dec'd), in Re (1991) 1
W.L.R. 793 *352*

First National Securities *v.* Jones
(1978) C.A. 2 All E.R. 221 *92*

Fisher *v.* Bell [1961] 1 Q.B. 394; [1960]
3 All E.R. 731 *98*

Fitch *v.* Dewes [1921] A.C. 158 *142*

Fitzleet Estates *v.* Cherry [1977] 1
W.L.R. 1345; [1977] 3 All E.R. 996
29

Fletcher *v.* Ashburner (1779) 1 Bro. C.C.
497 *320*

Foakes *v.* Beer (1884) 9 App. Cas. 605
108, 109

Foley *v.* Classique Coaches Ltd [1934]
2 K.B. 1 *101*

Foster *v.* Driscoll [1929] 1 K.B. 470
141

Fox *v.* Mackreth (1788) 2 Cox. Eq. 320
341

Froom *v.* Butcher [1976] Q.B. 286;
[1975] 3 All E.R. 520 *246*

Fullard, *Re* (1982) Fam. 42 *354*

Fullwood *v.* Hurley [1928] 1 K.B. 498
173

Gadd *v.* Houghton (1876) 1 Ex. D. 357
175

Galloway *v.* Galloway (1914) 30 T.L.R.
531 *130*

Garbett *v.* Hazell, Watson & Viney Ltd
[1943] 2 All E.R. 359 *261*

Garland *v.* British Rail Engineering
(1982) I.R.L.R. 257 *19*

Garnac Grain Co. *v.* Faure &
Fairclough Ltd [1968] A.C. 1130;
[1967] 2 All E.R. 353 *168*

General Cleaning Contractors *v.*
Christmas [1953] A.C. 180; [1952] 2
All E.R. 1110 *250*

Gibson, In the Estate of, [1949] P 434
[1949] 2 All E.R. 90 *349*

Gibson *v.* Manchester City Council
[1979] 1 W.L.R. 294; [1979] 1 All E.R.
972 *98*

Gilbert & Partners *v.* Knight [1968] 2
All E.R. 248 *163*

Gillingham Borough Council *v.*
Medway (Chatham) Dock Ltd (1991)
unreported *234*

Gilmour *v.* Coats [1949] A.C. 426;
[1949] 1 All E.R. 848 *329*

Gissing *v.* Gissing [1971] A.C. 886;
[1970] 2 All E.R. 780 *318*

Goldman *v.* Hargrave [1967] A.C. 645;
[1966] 2 All E.R. 989 *207, 255*

Goldsmith *v.* Pressdram Ltd [1977] Q.B.
83; [1977] 2 All E.R. 557 *411-12*

Goldsmith *v.* Sperrings Ltd (1977) 1
W.L.R. 478 *264*

Gordon's Will Trusts, *Re* [1978] Ch.
145; [1978] 2 All E.R. 969 *320*

Gore *v.* Gibson (1845) 13 H. & W. 623
113

Gorris *v.* Scott (1874) L.R. 9 Exch. 125
258

Goss *v.* Lord Nugent (1833) 5 B. & Ad.
58 *119*

Gough *v.* Thorne [1966] 1 W.L.R. 1387;
[1966] 3 All E.R. 398 *213*

Gouriet *v.* Union of Post Office
Workers [1978] A.C. 435; [1977] 3 All
E.R. 70 *323*

Government Stock Co. Ltd *v.* Manila
Railway Co. Ltd [1897] A.C. 81 *312*

Grainger *v.* Gough [1896] A.C. 325 *98*

Grant *v.* Australian Knitting Mills
[1936] A.C. 85 *248*

Gray *v.* Jones [1939] 1 All E.R. 798 *262*

Great Northern Railway *v.* Swaffield
(1874) Exch. 132 *169*

Green *v.* Chelsea Waterworks Co.
(1894) 70 L.T. 547 *255*

Greenock Corporation *v.* Caledonian Railway [1917] A.C. 556 *221*

Greer *v.* Sketchleys Ltd (1979) I.R.L.R. 445 *143*

Gregory *v.* Fearn [1953] 2 All E.R. 559 *33*

Grist *v.* Bailey [1967] Ch. 532; [1966] 2 All E.R. 875 *131*

Groves *v.* Matthews [1910] 2 K.B. 401 *170*

Groves *v.* Wimborne [1898] 2 Q.B. 402 *215, 258*

Guinness PLC *v.* Saunders (1988) B.C.C. 377 *341*

Gulbenkian's Settlement Trusts, *Re* [1970] A.C. 508; [1968] 3 All E.R. 785 *331*

Guthing *v.* Lynn (1831) 2 B. & Ad. 232 *98*

Hadley *v.* Baxendale (1854) 9 Exch. 341 *156*

Haigh *v.* Brooks (1839) 10 Ad. & El. 309 *106*

Hall *v.* Brooklands Auto Racing Club [1933] 1 K.B. 205 *219*

Hambrook *v.* Stokes (1925) 1 K.B. 141 *247*

Hamilton, *Re* [1895] 2 Ch. 370 *326*

Hampstead Guardians *v.* Barclays Bank (1923) 39 T.L.R. 229 *429*

Hansa Nord, The, (Cehave NV *v.* Bremer Handelsgesellschaft) [1976] Q.B. 44; [1975] 3 All E.R. 739 *121, 122*

Hardman *v.* Chief Constable of Avon & Somerset (1986) Crim L.R. 330 *405*

Hardwick Game Farm *v.* Suffolk Agricultural Producers' Association [1969] 2 A.C. 31; [1968] 2 All E.R. 444 *126*

Harlington and Leinster Enterprises *v.* Christopher Hull Fine Art (1990) 1 All E.R. 737 *185*

Harris *v.* Nickerson (1873) L.R. 8 Q.B. 286 *98*

Harris *v.* Wyre Forest District Council (1990) *127*

Hart *v.* O'Connor (1985) 2 All E.R. 880 *113*

Hartley *v.* Ponsonby (1857) 7 E. & B. 872 *107*

Harvela Investments *v.* Royal Trust Co. of Canada (1986) A.C. 207 *100*

Harvey *v.* Facey [1893] A.C. 552 *98*

Haseldine *v.* Daw [1941] 2 K.B. 343; [1941] 3 All E.R. 156 *249*

Hatzteldt-Wildenburg *v.* Alexander [1912] 1 Ch. 284 *100*

Haynes *v.* Harwood [1935] 1 K.B. 146 *219*

Heald *v.* Kenworthy (1855) 10 Exch. 739 *176*

Hedley Byrne & Co. Ltd *v.* Heller & Partners Ltd [1964] A.C. 465; [1963] 2 All E.R. 575 *243*

Helby *v.* Matthews [1895] A.C. 471 *190*

Hemmings *v.* Stoke Poges Golf Club [1920] 1 K.B. 720 *230*

Herd *v.* Weardale Steel Co. [1915] A.C. 67 *226*

Hermann *v.* Charlesworth [1905] 2 K.B. 123 *140*

Herman *v.* Jeuchner (1885) 15 Q.B.D. 561 *141*

Herne Bay Steamboat Co. *v.* Hutton [1903] 2 K.B. 740 *152*

Heron II, The, *see* Koufos *v.* Czarnikow Ltd

Hickman *v.* Maisey [1900] 1 Q.B. 752 *228*

High Trees, *see* Central London Property Trusts Ltd *v.* High Trees House Ltd *109*

Hill *v.* Baxter (1958) 1 Q.B. 277 *373* *382*

Hill *v.* William Hill (Park Lane) Ltd [1949] A.C. 530; [1949] 2 All E.R. 452 *140*

Hillas *v.* Arcos (1932) 147 LT 503 *101*

Hinds *v.* Sparks [1964] Crim. L.R. 717 *264*

Hirachand, Punamchand *v.* Temple (1911) 2 K.B. 330 *109*

Hochster *v.* De la Tour (1853) 2 E. & B. 678 *153*

Hodgson *v.* Marks [1971] Ch. 892; [1971] 2 All E.R. 684 *138*

Hoenig *v.* Isaacs [1952] 2 All E.R. 176 *148*

Hollins *v.* Fowler (1875) L.R. 7 H.L. 757 *233*

Holwell Securities *v.* Hughes [1974] 1 W.L.R. 155; [1974] 1 All E.R. 161 *99*

Honeywill & Stein Ltd v. Larkin [1934]
1 K.B. 191   *218, 259*
Hong Kong Fir Shipping Co. Ltd v.
Kawasaki Kisen Kaisha Ltd [1962] 2
Q.R. 26; [1962] 1 All E.R. 47   *122–3*
Hopkins Will Trusts, *Re* [1965] Ch. 669;
[1964] 3 All E.R. 46   *328*
Horrocks v. Lowe [1975] A.C. 135;
[1974] 1 All E.R. 662   *266*
Horsfall v. Thomas (1862) 1 H. & C. 90
134
Household Fire Insurance v. Grant
(1879) 4 Exch. D. 216   *99*
Howard v. Sheward (1866) L.R. 2 C.P.
148   *165*
Howe v. Lord Dartmouth (1802) 7 Ves.
137   *340*
Hudson v. Parker (1844) 1 Rob. Ecc. 14
349
Hughes v. Lord Advocate [1963] A.C.
837; [1963] 1 All E.R. 705   *209*
Hulton v. Jones [1910] A.C. 20   *263*
Hummeltenberg, *Re* [1923] 1 Ch. 237
328
Huth v. Huth [1915] 3 K.B. 40   *263*
Hyde v. Hyde (1866) L.R. 1 P. & D. 130
76
Hyde v. Wrench (1840) 3 Beau. 334
100

ICI v. Shatwell [1965] A.C. 656; [1964] 2
All E.R. 999   *218, 219, 259*
Imperial Loan Co. v. Stone [1892] 1
Q.B. 599   *113*
Inche Noriah v. Shaik Allie Bin Omar
[1929] A.C. 127   *138*
Incorporated Council of Law
Reporting v. Attorney-General [1972]
Ch. 73; [1971] 3 All E.R. 1029   *329*
Ingram v. Little [1961] 1 Q.B. 31; [1960]
3 All E.R. 332   *132–3*
Inland Revenue Commissioners v.
Baddeley [1955] A.C. 572; [1955] 1 All
E.R. 525   *329*
Inland Revenue Commissioners v.
Bullock (1976) 3 All E.R. 353   *72*
Inland Revenue Commissioners v.
Glasgow City Police Athletic
Association [1953] A.C. 380; [1953] 1
All E.R. 747   *329*

J.M. v. Runeckles [1984] 79 Cr. App.
Rep. 255   *82*

Jackson v. Hopperton (1864) 16
C.B.(N.S.) 829   *267*
James, *ex parte* (*Re* Condon) (1874) L.R.
9 Ch. App. 609   *161*
James McNaughton Paper Group v.
Hicks Anderson & Co. (1991) 1 All
E.R. 134   *244*
Jarvis v. Swan Tours [1973] Q.B. 233;
[1973] 1 All E.R. 71   *157*
Jenner v. Ffinch (1879) 5 P.D. 106   *349*
Jewsbury v. Newbold (1857) 26 Lj. Ex.
247   *168*
Joachimson v. Swiss Bank Corporation
[1921] 3 K.B. 110   *429*
Joel v. Morrison (1834) 6 C.P. 501   *217*
Johnson v. Diprose [1893] 1 Q.B. 512
310
Johnstone v. Pedlar [1921] 2 A.C. 262
72
Jolly v. Rees (1863) 15 C.B.N.S. 628
168
Jon Beauforte Ltd, *Re* (1953) Ch. 131,
113
Jones v. Northampton Borough
Council (1990) The Times, 21 May
69
Jones v. Livox Quarries [1952] 2 Q.B.
608   *246*
Jones v. Wright (1991) 3 All E.R. 88
247
Joscelyne v. Nissen [1970] 2 Q.B. 86;
[1970] 1 All E.R. 1213   *124*
Julia, The, (1860)   *40*
Junior Books v. Veitchi (1982) 2 W.L.R.
477   *244–5*

Kay v. Butterworth [1945] 173 L.T. 191
383
Keech v. Sandford (1726) Sel. Cas. Ch.
61   *334, 341*
Keightley Maxted & Co. v. Durant &
Co. [1901] A.C. 240   *169*
Kelsen v. Imperial Tobacco Co. [1957]
2 K.B. 334; [1957] 2 All E.R. 343
228
Kemble v. Farren (1829) 6 Bing. 141
157
Kemsley v. Foot [1952] A.C. 345; [1952]
1 All E.R. 501   *265*
Kennaway v. Thompson (1980) 3 All
E.R. 329   *237*
Kennedy v. Thomassen [1929] 1 Ch. 426
102

Kepitigalla Rubber Estates Ltd v. National Bank of India [1909] 2 K.B. 1010 *429*

Keppel v. Wheeler [1927] 1 K.B. 577 *172*

Kerr v. Kennedy [1942] 1 K.B. 409; [1942] 1 All E.R. 412 *262*

Kier v. Whitehead Iron & Steel Co. [1938] 1 All E.R. 591 *102*

Kirk v. Gregory (1876) 1 Ex. D. 55 *233*

Knightsbridge Estates Trust Ltd v. Byrne [1939] Ch. 441; [1938] 4 All E.R. 618 *309*

Knupffer v. London Express [1944] A.C. 116; [1944] 1 All E.R. 495 *263*

Koeppler's, Re (1986) Ch. 423 *329*

Koppel v. Koppel (1966) 2 All E.R. 187 *311*

Kores Manufacturing Co. Ltd v. Kolok Manufacturing Co. Ltd [1959] Ch. 108; [1958] 2 All E.R. 65 *142*

Koufos v. Czarnikow Ltd (The Heron II) [1969] 1 A.C. 350; [1967] All E.R. 686 *156*

Kreglinger v. New Patagonia Meat Co. [1914] A.C. 25 *308*

Krell v. Henry [1903] 2 K.B. 740 *151*

Kubach v. Hollands [1937] 3 All E.R. 907 *248*

Lacy (William) Ltd v. Davis [1957] 1 W.L.R. 932; [1957] 2 All E.R. 712 *162*

Lakeman v. Mounstephen (1874) L.R. 7 H.L. 17 *94*

Lampleigh v. Braithwaite (1615) Hob 105 *108*

Larner v. London County Council [1949] 2 K.B. 683; [1949] 1 All E.R. 964 *161*

Latham v. Johnson & Nephew Ltd [1913] 1 K.B. 398 *249*

Leach, Re (1985) 3 W.L.R. 413 *354*

Leaf v. International Galleries [1950] 2 K.B. 86; [1950] 1 All E.R. 693 *136*

Leakey v. National Trust (1980) 1 All E.R. 17 *207*

Leigh & Sullivan v. Aliakmon Shipping, The Aliakmon, (1986) 2 W.L.R. 902 *242, 244*

Lemmon v. Webb [1894] 3 Ch. 1 *237*

Leslie v. Sheill [1914] 3 K.B. 607 *115, 213*

L'Estrange v. Graucob [1934] 2 K.B. 394 *126, 133*

Letang v. Cooper [1965] 1 Q.B. 232; [1964] 2 All E.R. 929 *226*

Lewis v. Averay [1972] 1 Q.B. 198; [1971] 3 All E.R. 907 *132*

Lewis v. Daily Telegraph [1964] 2 Q.B. 601; [1964] 1 All E.R. 705 *263*

Liesbosch Dredger v. Edison [1933] A.C. 449 *208*

Lilly v. Smales [1892] 1 Q.B. 456 *174*

Limpus v. London General Omnibus Co. (1862) 1 H. & C. 526 *217*

Lipinski's Will Trusts, Re [1976] Ch. 235; [1977] 1 All E.R. 33 *332*

Liverpool City Council v. Irwin [1976] Q.B. 319; [1976] 2 All E.R. 39 *120*

Lloyd v. Grace, Smith & Co. [1912] A.C. 716 *217*

Lloyds Bank v. Cooke [1907] 1 K.B. 794 *419*

Lochgelly Iron & Coal Co. v. M'Mullan [1934] A.C. 1 *239*

Locker's Settlement, Re (1977) 1 W.L.R. 1323 *325*

London Artists Ltd v. Littler [1969] 2 Q.B. 375; [1968] 1 All E.R. 1075 *265*

London Joint Stock Bank v. Macmillan [1918] A.C. 777 *428, 429*

Long v. Lloyd (1958) 2 All E.R. 402 *135*

Long v. Millar (1879) 4 C.P.D. 450 *96*

Luxor (Eastbourne) Ltd v. Cooper [1941] A.C. 108; [1941] 1 All E.R. 33 *171, 173*

Lynch v. Knight (1861) 9 H.L.C. 577 *261*

Lysaght, Re [1966] Ch. 191; [1965] 2 All E.R. 888 *330*

M'Pherson v. Daniels (1829) 10 B. & C. 263 *264*

Macdonald v. Green [1951] 1 K.B. 594; [1950] 2 All E.R. 1240 *140*

McKay v. Essex Area Health Authority (1982) 2 All E.R. 771 *211*

McKew v. Holland, Hannen & Cubitts [1969] 3 All E.R. 1621 *208*

McLoughlin *v.* O'Brien (1981) 2 All
E.R. 298 *247*

McPhail *v.* Doulton (Baden) [1971]
A.C. 424; [1970] 2 All E.R. 228
325,327

McWilliams *v.* Sir William Arrol & Co.
[1962] 1 W.L.R. 295; [1962] 1 All E.R.
623 *258*

Manchester Diocesan Council for
Education *v.* Commercial & General
Investments Ltd [1970] 1 W.L.R. 241;
[1969] 3 All E.R. 1593 *99*

Mareva Companies Naviera SA *v.*
International Bulk Carriers SA
(1975) 2 Lloyds Rep. 509 *47, 323*

Marsh *v.* Joseph [1897] 1 Ch. 213
170

Martell *v.* Consett Iron Co. Ltd [1955]
Ch. 363; [1955] 1 All E.R. 489 *141*

Martin-Baker Aircraft Co. *v.* Canadian
Flight Equipment [1955] 2 Q.B. 556;
[1955] 2 All E.R. 722 *170*

Maskell *v.* Horner [1915] 3 K.B. 106
137

Mason *v.* Levy Auto Parts Ltd [1967] 2
Q.B. 530 [1967] 2 All E.R. 62 *256*

Mason *v.* Provident Clothing Co.
[1913] A.C. 724 *142*

Meering *v.* Grahame-White Aviation
Co. [1919] 122 L.T. 44 *226*

Mendelssohn *v.* Normand Ltd [1970] 1
Q.B. 177; [1969] 2 All E.R. 1215 *119*

Merritt *v.* Merritt [1970] 1 W.L.R. 1121;
[1970] 2 All E.R. 760 *95*

Mersey Docks *v.* Coggins & Griffiths
[1947] A.C. 1; [1946] 2 All E.R. 345
216

Metropolitan Asylum District *v.* Hill
(1881) 6 App. Cas. 193 *222*

Metropolitan Water Board *v.* Dick,
Kerr & Co. Ltd [1918] A.C. 119 *152*

Mihalis Angelos, The, [1970] 1 Q.B.
164; [1970] 3 All E.R. 125 *121*

Miles *v.* Forest Rock Granite Co.
(1918) 34 T.L.R. 500 *254*

Miller *v.* Jackson (1977) 3 All E.R. 338
237

Mitchell, George *v.* Finney Lock Seeds
(1983) 2 A.C. 803 *127*

Mitchil *v.* Alestree (1676) 1 Vent. 695
239, 256

Mogul Steamship Co. *v.* McGregor,
Gow & Co. [1892] A.C. 25 *204*

Monson *v.* Tussauds [1894] 1 Q.B. 671
261

Montefiore *v.* Motor Components Ltd
[1918] 2 K.B. 241 *141*

Moody *v.* Stevenson (1991) The Times,
30 July, *354*

Moorcock, The, (1889) 14 P.D. 64 *120*

Moore *v.* King (*Re* Olding) (1842) 3
Curt. 243 *349*

More *v.* Weaver [1928] 2 K.B. 520
266

Morgan Crucible PLC *v.* Hill Samuel
(1991) 1 All E.R. 148, *244*

Morgans v. Launchbury [1973] A.C.
127; [1972] 2 All E.R. 606 *216*

Morice *v.* Bishop of Durham (1804) 9
Ves. 399; (1805) 10 Ves. 522
327, 331

Morris *v.* Baron & Co. [1918] A.C. 1
150

Morris *v.* Redland Bricks Ltd. [1970]
A.C. 652; [1969] 2 All E.R. 576 *323*

Morriss *v.* Marsden (1952) 1 T.L.R. 947
213

Multiservice Bookbinding *v.* Marden
[1978] 2 W.L.R. 535 *308*

Murphy *v.* Brentwood District Council
(1990) 2 All E.R. 908, *29, 244*

Murray *v.* Harringay Arena (1951) 2
All E.R. 320 *219*

Musgrove *v.* Pandelis [1919] 2 K.B. 43
255

Nash *v.* Inman [1908] 2 K.B. 1 *114*

National Anti-Vivisection Society *v.*
Inland Revenue Commissioners
[1948] A.C. 31; [1947] 2 All E.R. 217
329

National Carriers Ltd *v.* Panalpina Ltd
(1981) 1 All E.R. 161 *151, 152*

National Westminster Bank *v.* Morgan
(1985) 1 All E.R. 821 *138*

Neville Estates Ltd *v.* Madden [1962]
Ch. 832; [1961] 3 All E.R. 769
329, 332

New, *Re* [1901] 2 Ch. 534 *336*

Newstead *v.* London Express
Newspapers Ltd [1940] 1 K.B. 337;
[1939] 4 All E.R. 319 *263*

Newton v. Clarke (1839) 2 Curt. 320
349
New Zealand Shipping Co. Ltd v.
Satterthwaite (The Eurymedon)
[1975] A.C. 154; [1974] 1 All E.R.
1015 *96, 107, 111*
Nichols v. Marsland (1875) L.R. 10 Ex.
255; (1876) 2 Ex. D. 1 *221, 255*
Nicolene Ltd v. Simmonds [1953] 1 Q.B.
543; [1953] 1 All E.R. 822 *101*
Noakes & Co. Ltd v. Rice [1902] A.C. 24
309
Noble v. Harrison [1926] 2 K.B. 332
237
Nordenfelt v. Maxim-Nordenfelt Co.
[1894] A.C. 535 *142, 143*
Norfolk's (Duke of) Settlement Trusts
Re, [1979] Ch. 37; [1978] 3 All E.R.
907 *341*
North and South Trust Co. v. Berkeley
[1971] 1 W.L.R. 470; [1971] 1 All E.R.
980 *168*
North Ocean Shipping v. Hyundai
[1979] 1 Lloyds Rep. 89; [1978] 3 All
E.R. 1170 *107, 137*

O'Brien, *Re* (1946) 175 L.T. 406 *350*
Ocean Frost, The, (1986) 1 Lloyds Rep.
1 *174*
Ocean Tramp Tankers Corporation v.
V/O Sovfracht, The Eugenia [1964] 1
All E.R. 161 *152*
O'Connor v. Swan & Edgar (1963) 107
Sol. Jo. 215 *250*
Oldcastle's Case (1419) 1 Hale P.C. 50
384
Olding, *Re, see* Moore v. King (1842)
349
Olley v. Marlborough Court Hotel
[1949] 1 K.B. 532; [1949] 1 All E.R.
127 *126, 193*
Oppenheim v. Tobacco Securities
Trust Co. Ltd [1951] A.C. 297; [1951]
1 All E.R. 31 *329*
Ormrod v. Crosville Motor Services
[1953] 1 W.L.R. 1120; [1953] 1 All
E.R. 753 *217*
O'Shea, *Re* [1911] 2 K.B. 981 *140*
Ottaway v. Norman [1972] Ch. 698;
[1971] 3 All E.R. 1325 *335*

Ough v. King (1967) 3 All E.R. 859
300
Overseas Tankship (UK) v. Morts
Dock, *see* The Wagon Mound (No. 1)
209
Overton v. Bannister (1844) 3 Hare
503 *318*
Oxford's (Earl of) Case (1615) 1 Co.
Rep. 1 *11*

Pannett v. McGuinness [1972] 2 Q.B.
599; [1972] 3 All E.R. 137 *251*
Pao On v. Lau Yiu Long (1980) A.C.
614 *137*
Paradine v. Jayne (1647) Aleyn 26 *152*
Paris v. Stepney Borough Council
[1951] A.C. 367; [1951] 1 All E.R. 42
241
Parker v. Clark [1960] 1 W.L.R. 286;
[1960] 1 All E.R. 93 *95*
Parker v. South Eastern Railway Co.
(1877) 2 C.P.D. 416 *126*
Paul v. Contance [1977] 1 W.L.R. 527
[1977] 1 All E.R. 195 *326*
Payne v. Cave (1789) 3 Term. Rep. 148
98
Payne v. Maple Leaf Gardens Ltd
(1949) 1 D.L.R. 369 *219*
Pearce v. Brooks (1866) L.R. 1 Exch.
213 *141*
Penny v. Northampton Borough
Council (1974) 118 Sol. J.6 628 *251*
Percival Ltd v. London County Council
Asylums, etc. Committee (1918) 87
L.J.K.B. 677 *102*
Perry v. Kendricks Transport Ltd
[1956] 1 W.L.R. 85; [1956] 1 All E.R.
154 *255*
Peters v. Prince of Wales Theatre Ltd
[1943] K.B. 73; [1942] 2 All E.R. 533
255
Pharmaceutical Society v. Boots Cash
Chemists (Southern) Ltd [1952] 2
Q.B. 795; [1952] 2 All E.R. 456;
[1953] 1 Q.B. 401; [1943] 1 All E.R.
482 *98*
Pharmaceutical Society v. Storkwain
(1986) 1 W.L.R. 903 *374*
Philco Radio Ltd v. Spurling [1949] 2
All E.R. 882 *208*

Phillips *v.* Brooks [1919] 2 K.B. 243
132–3, 136, 183

Phipps *v.* Pears [1964] 1 Q.B. 76 *298*

Photo Production *v.* Securicor (1980)
A.C. 827 *127*

Pickard *v.* Sears (1837) 6 Ad. & E. 469
183

Pilcher *v.* Rawlins (1872) 7 Ch. App. 259
319

Pinnel's Case (1602) 5 Co. Rep. 117
108, 109

Pitts *v.* Hunt (1990) 3 All E.R. 344,
220

Planché *v.* Colburn (1831) 8 Bing. 14
163

Pledge *v.* White [1896] A.C. 187 *307*

Plummer *v.* I.R.C. (1988) 1 All E.R. 97,
72

Polemis, *Re* [1921] 3 K.B. 560 *208–9*

Pontardawe Rural District Council *v.*
Moore-Gwyn [1929] 1 Ch. 655 *254*

Porter *v.* Freudenberg [1915] 1 K.B. 857
113

Poussard *v.* Spiers and Pond (1876) 1
Q.B.D. 410 *120*

Prescott *v.* Barker (1874) 9 Ch. App. 174
349

Price *v.* Easton (1833) 4 B. & Ad. 433
112

Printing & Numerical Registering Co.
v. Sampson (1875) L.R. 19 Eq. 462
139

Quinn *v.* Leathem [1901] A.C. 495 *30*

R. *v.* Allen (1985) A.C. 1029 *401*

R. *v.* Ashbee [1989] 1 W.L.R. 109 *400*

R. *v.* Bailey (1800) 168 All E.R. 657
385

R. *v.* Bainbridge [1960] 1 Q.B. 129;
[1959] 3 All E.R. 200 *375*

R. *v.* Banks (1873) 12 Cox. C.C. 393
377

R. *v.* Betty [1963] 3 All E.R. 602;
(1963) 48 C.A.R. 6 *375*

R. *v.* Betty and Ridley (1930) 22 C.A.R.
148 *375*

R. *v.* Bonner [1970] 1 W.L.R. 838;
[1970] 2 All E.R. 97 *396*

R. *v.* Boyle [1964] 1 Q.B. 292; [1954] 2
All E.R. 721 *399*

R. *v.* Brain (1834) 6 C. & P. 349 *387*

R. *v.* Brown (1841) Car. & M. 314 *73*

R. *v.* Bruce [1975] 1 W.L.R. 1252;
[1975] 3 All E.R. 277 *398*

R. *v.* Bullock [1955] 1 W.L.R. 1; [1955]
1 All E.R. 15 *375*

R. *v.* Burgess (1991) 2 W.L.R. 1206
382

R. *v.* Byrne [1960] 2 Q.B. 396; [1960] 3
All E.R. 1 *390*

R. *v.* Caldwell (1981) 2 W.L.R. 509
374, 384

R. *v.* Camplin [1978] 2 All E.R. 168
389

R. *v.* Chief Metropolitan Stipendiary
Magistrate, *ex parte* Choudhury
(1991) 1 Q.B. *412*

R. *v.* Civil Service Appeal Board, *ex
parte* Cunningham (1991) 4 All E.R.
310, *85*

R. *v.* Clarke [1949] 2 All E.R. 488; 33
C.A.R. 216 *392*

R. *v.* Collins [1973] Q.B. 100; [1972] 2
All E.R. 1105 *399*

R. *v.* Coney (1882) 8 Q.B.D. 534; 15
Cox. C.C. 46 *375*

R. *v.* Davies [1975] Q.B. 691; [1975] 1
All E.R. 890 *389*

R. *v.* District Auditor, *ex parte* West
Yorkshire Metropolitan County
Council (1986) 26 R.V.R. 24
332

R. *v.* Ditta (1988) Crim. L.R. 42, *384*

R. *v.* Dudley and Stephens (1884) 14
Q.B.D.; 15 Cox. C.C. 624 *385*

R. *v.* Easom [1971] 2 Q.B. 315; [1971] 2
All E.R. 945 *398*

R. *v.* Ellames [1974] 1 W.L.R. 1391;
[1974] 3 All E.R. 130 *403*

R. *v.* Feely [1973] Q.B. 530; [1973] 1 All
E.R. 314 *400*

R. *v.* Gibbins & Proctor (1918) 82 J.P.
287 *373*

R. *v.* Gold & Schifreen (1987) 3 All E.R.
618 *403*

R. *v.* Gomez (1991) Cr. App. R. 156
396

R. *v.* Gorrie (1918) 83 J.P. 136 *380*

R. *v.* Gotts (1992) 1 All E.R. 832 *384*

R. *v.* Gould [1968] 2 Q.B. 65; [1968] 1
All E.R. 849 *41, 393*

R. *v.* Hall [1973] Q.B. 126; [1972] 2 All E.R. 1009 *397*

R. *v.* Hancock and Shankland [1986] 1 All E.R. 641 *388*

R. *v.* Hayward (1833) 6 C. & P. 157 *389*

R. *v.* Higgins (1801) 2 East. 5 *377*

R. *v.* HM Treasury, *ex parte* Smedley (1985) Q.B. 657 *26*

R. *v.* Holden (1991) Crim. L.R. 478 *397*

R. *v.* Howe (1987) A.C. 417 *384*

R. *v.* Immigration Appeals Tribunal, *ex parte* Joyles (1972) 3 All E.R. 213 *26*

R. *v.* Immigration Appeals Adjudicator, *ex parte* Crew (1982) The Times 26 November *33*

R. *v.* Jackson [1891] 1 Q.B. 671 *227*

R. *v.* Jackson (1983) 147 J.P. 715 *401*

R. *v.* Jones and Smith [1976] 1 W.L.R. 672; [1976] 3 All E.R. 54 *399*

R. *v.* Jordan (1956) 40 C.A.R. 152 *388*

R. *v.* Kemp [1957] 1 Q.B. 399; [1956] 3 All E.R. 249 *382*

R. *v.* Kowalski (1988) Crim. L.R. 124 *394*

R. *v.* Larsonneur (1933) 24 C.A.R. 74 *372*

R. *v.* Latimer (1886) 17 Q.B.D. 359; 16 Cox. C.C. 70 *386*

R. *v.* Laverty [1970] 3 All E.R. 432; [1971] R.T.R. 124 *400*

R. *v.* Lawrence [1971] 2 All E.R. 1253 *400*

R. *v.* Lemon [1979] 2 W.L.R. 281; [1979] 1 All E.R. 898 *412*

R. *v.* Lipman [1970] 1 Q.B. 152; [1969] 3 All E.R. 410 *383*

R. *v.* Lord Chancellor's Department, *ex parte* Nangle (1991) I.R.L.R. 343 *85*

R. *v.* Lowe [1973] Q.B. 702; [1975] 1 All E.R. 805 *390*

R. *v.* M'Naghten (1843) 10 Cl. & Fin. 200 *381*

R. *v.* McInnes (1971) 3 All E.R. 295 *84*

R. *v.* Mahal (1991) Crim. L.R. 632 *390*

R. *v.* Martin [1989] 1 All E.R. 652 *385*

R. *v.* Meredith (1973) Crim. L.R. 253 *396*

R. *v.* Miller [1954] 2 Q.B. 282; [1954] 2 All E.R. 529 *392*

R. *v.* Modupe (1991) Crim. L.R. 530 *401*

R. *v.* Moloney (1985) A.C. 905 *373*

R. *v.* Morris (1984) A.C. 320 *395, 396*

R. *v.* Mutters (1864) Le. & Ca. 491; 10 Cox. C.C. 6 *411*

R. *v.* P. & O. European Ferries (Dover) Ltd (1991) 93 Cr. App. R. 72, *381*

R. *v.* Pittwood (1902) 19 T.L.R. 37 *373*

R. *v.* Purdy (1946) 10 J. of Crim. L. 182 *384*

R. *v.* Quick [1973] Q.B. 910; [1973] 3 All E.R. 347 *373*

R. *v.* R. (1991) 2 All E.R. 257, *392*

R. *v.* Robinson (1977) Crim. L.R. 173 *398*

R. *v.* St George (1840) 9 C. & P. 483 *225*

R. *v.* Secretary of State for Foreign and Commonwealth Affairs, *ex parte* Trawnik (1986) The Times 21 February *212*

R. *v.* Secretary of State for Health, *ex parte* United States Tobacco International Inc. (1991) 3 W.L.R. 529 *26*

R. *v.* Shivpuri (1986) 2 W.L.R. 988 *376*

R. *v.* Sloggett [1972] 1 Q.B. 430; [1971] 3 All E.R. 264 *403*

R. *v.* Smith [1959] 2 Q.B. 35; [1959] 2 All E.R. 193 *388*

R. *v.* Stone and Dobinson [1977] Q.B. 354; [1977] 2 All E.R. 341 *373, 390*

R. *v.* Stones [1989] 1 W.L.R. 156 *399*

R. *v.* Taaffe (1984) A.C. 539, *376*

R. *v.* Tandy (1987) The Times, 23 December *390*

R. *v.* Tolson (1889) 23 Q.B.D. 168; 16 Cox. C.C. 629 *385, 393*

R. *v.* Turner (No. 2) [1971] 1 W.L.R. 901; [1971] 2 All E.R. 441 *396*

R. *v.* Whiteley (1991) 93 Cr. App. R. 25 *405*

R. *v.* Whybrow (1951) 35 C.A.R. 141 *376*

R. *v.* Whyte (1987) 3 All E.R. 416 *84*

R. *v.* Woodrow (1846) 15 M. & W. 404 *385*

R. *v.* York (1748) Fost. 70 C.C.R. *82*

Race Relations Board *v.* Applin [1975]
A.C. 259 84; [1974] 2 All E.R. 73   *377*

Raffles *v.* Winchelhaus (1864) 2 H. & C.
906   *131*

Ramsgate Victoria Hotel Co. *v.*
Montefiore (1866) L.R. 1 Ex. 109
102

Read *v.* J Lyons & Co. Ltd [1947] A.C.
156; [1946] 2 All E.R. 471   *241, 254*

Reading *v.* Attorney-General [1951]
A.C. 507; [1951] 1 All E.R. 647   *161*

Ready Mixed Concrete (South East)
Ltd *v.* Minister of Pensions [1968] 2
Q.B. 497; [1968] 1 All E.R. 433   *216*

Reardon-Smith Line *v.* Hansen-
Tangen [1976] 1 W.L.R. 989; [1976] 3
All E.R. 570   *122, 123*

Reid *v.* Metropolitan Police
Commissioner (1973) 2 All E.R. 97;
(1973) Q.B. 551   *183*

Rhodes *v.* Forwood (1876) 1 App. Cas.
256   *173*

Rickards *v.* Lothian [1913] A.C. 263
254

Rickards *v.* Oppenheim [1950] 1 K.B.
616; [1950] 1 All E.R. 420   *148*

Ricketts *v.* Tilling [1915] 1 K.B. 644
218

Rigby *v.* Chief Constable of
Northamptonshire (1985) 2 All E.R.
985   *221*

River Wear Commissioners *v.* Adams
(1877) 2 App. Cas. 743   *31*

Robinson *v.* Davison (1871) L.R. 6 Ex.
269   *152*

Robinson *v.* Graves [1935] 1 K.B. 579
184

Robinson *v.* Kilvert (1889) 41 Ch. D. 88
236

Robinson *v.* Post Office (1974) 2 All
E.R. 737   *209*

Roe *v.* Minister of Health [1954] 2 Q.B.
66; [1954] 2 All E.R. 131   *242*

Rogers *v.* Parish (1987) 2 All E.R. 232
187

Roles *v.* Nathan [1963] 1 W.L.R. 1117;
[1963] 2 All E.R. 908   *250*

Rondel *v.* Worsley [1969] 1 A.C. 191;
[1967] 3 All E.R. 993   *58, 243*

Roscorla *v.* Thomas (1842) 3 Q.B. 234
108

Rose *v.* Ford [1937] A.C. 826; [1937] 3
All E.R. 359   *213*

Rose *v.* Miles (1815) 4 M. & S. 101
234, 235

Rose *v.* Plenty [1975] I.C.R. 430; [1976]
1 All E.R. 97   *217–8*

Rose and Frank Co. *v.* Crompton Bros
[1925] A.C. 445   *95*

Ross *v.* H.M. Advocate (1991) S.L.T.
564,   *383*

Ross *v.* London County Bank [1919] 1
K.B. 678   *429*

Roswell *v.* Prior (1701) 12 Mod 635
236

Rouse *v.* Squires [1973] Q.B. 889;
[1973] 2 All E.R. 903   *207*

Routledge *v.* Grant (1828) 4 Bing. 653
103

Royscot Trust Ltd *v.* Maidenhead
Honda Centre (1991) 3 W.L.R. 57,
134

Rutter *v.* Palmer [1922] 2 K.B. 87   *126*

Ryan *v.* London Borough of Camden
(1982) The Times 16 December   *251*

Rylands *v.* Fletcher (1868) L.R. 1 Ex.
265; L.R. 3 H.L. 320   *202, 206, 207,*
218, 221, 253–4, 255–6, 259

Saif Ali *v.* Sydney Mitchell [1978] 3
W.L.R. 849; [1978] 3 All E.R. 1033
58, 243

Salford Corporation *v.* Lever [1891] 1
Q.B. 168   *173*

Salisbury *v.* Woodland [1970] 1 Q.B.
324; [1969] 3 All E.R. 863   *237*

Salomon *v.* Salomon & Co. Ltd [1897]
A.C. 22   *66, 68*

Saunders *v.* Anglia Building Society
[1971] A.C. 1004; [1970] 3 All E.R.
961   *133*

Saunders *v.* Vautier (1841) 4 Beav. 115
331, 336, 337

Scammell *v.* Ouston [1941] A.C. 251;
[1941] 1 All E.R. 14   *101*

Scarf *v.* Jardine (1882) 7 App. Cas. 345
169

Scarisbrick, *Re* [1951] Ch. 622; [1951] 1
All E.R. 822   *328*

Schebsman, *Re* [1944] Ch. 83; [1943] 2
All E.R. 768   *112*

Scholfield *v.* Londesborough [1896] A.C. 514 *421*

Schroeder Music Publishing Co. Ltd *v.* Macaulay [1974] 1 W.L.R. 1308; [1974] 3 All E.R. 616 *125, 143*

Schuler *v.* Wickham Machine Tool Sales Ltd [1974] A.C. 235; [1973] 2 All E.R. 39 *121*

Scorer *v.* Seymour-Johns [1966] 1 W.L.R. 1419; [1966] 3 All E.R. 349 *142*

Scott *v.* Avery (1856) 5 H.L.C. 811 *125*

Scott *v.* Coulson [1903] 2 Ch. 249 *130*

Scott *v.* Shepherd (1773) 2 W.B.I. 892 *208*

Scriven *v.* Hindley [1913] 3 K.B. 564 *132*

Scruttons Ltd *v.* Midland Silicones Ltd [1962] A.C. 446; [1962] 1 All E.R. 1 *111*

Sedleigh-Denfield *v.* O'Callaghan [1940] A.C. 880; [1940] 3 All E.R. 349 *236*

Seymour *v.* Bridge (1885) 14 Q.B.D. 460 *171*

Seymour *v.* Pickett [1905] 1 K.B. 115 *149*

Shaw *v.* Symmons [1917] 1 K.B. 799 *191*

Shepherd & Co. Ltd *v.* Jerrom (1986) Q.B. 301 *152*

Shiffman *v.* Order of St John [1936] 1 All E.R. 557 *254*

Sigsworth, *Re* (1935) Ch. 89 *31*

Sim *v.* Stretch [1936] 2 All E.R. 1237 *261*

Simaan General Contracting *v.* Pilkington Glass (1988) 2 W.L.R. 761 *244*

Simkiss *v.* Rhondda Borough Council (1983) 31 L.G.R. 460 *251*

Simms *v.* Leigh R.F.C. (1969) 2 All E.R. 923 *219*

Simona, The, (1988) 2 All E.R. 742 *154*

Simpkins *v.* Pays (1955) 3 All E.R. 10 *95*

Sinclair v. Brougham [1914] A.C. 398 *160*

Sinclair, *Re* (1985) Ch. 446 *353*

Six Carpenters' Case (1610) 8 Co Rep. 146a *229*

Sky Petroleum *v.* VIP Petroleum (1974) 1 All E.R. 954 *322*

Smart *v.* Saunders (1848) 5 C.B. 895 *171*

Smith *v.* Baker [1891] A.C. 325 *219*

Smith *v.* Bush and Harris *v.* Wyre Forest District Council (1990) 1 A.C. 831, *127, 243*

Smith *v.* Cox [1940] 2 K.B. 558; [1940] 3 All E.R. 546 *148*

Smith *v.* Leech Brain (1961) 3 All E.R. 1159 *209*

Smith *v.* London and South Western Railway Co. (1870) L.R. 6 C.P. 14 *222*

Snelling *v.* J. G. Snelling Ltd [1973] Q.B. 87; [1972] 1 All E.R. 79 *112*

Soar *v.* Ashwell [1893] 2 Q.B. 390 *334, 335*

Sochacki *v.* Sas [1947] 1 All E.R. 344 *255*

Solle *v.* Butcher [1950] 1 K.B. 671; [1949] 2 All E.R. 1107 *131*

Sorrell *v.* Finch [1977] A.C. 728; [1976] 2 All E.R. 371 *166*

Southerden, in the estate of (1925) P. 177 *352*

Sowden *v.* Sowden (1785) 1 Bro. C.C. 582 *320*

Spartan Steel and Alloys Ltd *v.* Martin [1973] Q.B. 27; [1972] 2 All E.R. 557 *242*

Spector *v.* Ageda [1973] Ch. 30; [1971] 3 All E.R. 417 *140*

St Helen's Smelting Co. *v.* Tipping (1865) 11 H.L.C. 642 *235*

Stanley v. Powell [1891] 1 Q.B. 86 *206, 221, 226*

Steel *v.* Wellcome Trustees Ltd (1988) 1 W.L.R. 167 *340*

Stein *v.* Henshall [1976] VR 612 *396*

Stephens *v.* Taprell (1840) 2 Curt. 459 *352*

Stewart *v.* Casey [1892] 1 Ch. 104 *108*

Stilk *v.* Myrick (1809) 2 Camp. 317 *107*

Strathcona *v.* Steamship Co. *v.* Dominion Coal Co. [1926] A.C. 108 *112*

Stratheden and Campbell (Lord), *Re* [1894] 3 Ch. 265 *330*

Strong v. Bird (1874) L.R. 18 Eq. 315
190

Sturges v. Bridgeman (1879) 11 Ch. D.
852 237

Sugden v. Lord St Leonards (1876) 1
P.D. 154 352

Suisse Atlantique Société d'Armement
Maritime SA v. NV Rotterdamsche
Kolen Centrale [1967] 1 A.C. 361;
[1966] 2 All E.R. 61 127

Sumpter v. Hedges [1898] 1 Q.B. 673
147, 163

Sweet v. Parsley [1970] A.C. 132; [1969]
1 All E.R. 347 374

Sweeting, Re (1988) 1 All E.R. 1016
320

Tarry v. Ashton (1876) 1 Q.B.D. 314
218, 237

Taylor v. Caldwell (1863) 3 B. & S. 826
151

Taylor v. Laird (1856) 25 L.J. Ex. 329
98

Telnikoff v. Matusevitch (1991) 3
W.L.R. 952 265

Theaker v. Richardson [1962] 1 W.L.R.
151; [1962] 1 All E.R. 299 263

Thomas v. Bradbury, Agnew & Co.
Ltd [1906] 2 K.B. 627 265

Thompson v. L.M.S. Railway [1930] 1
K.B. 41 126

Thorne v. Motor Trade Association
[1937] A.C. 797; [1937] 3 All E.R. 157,
323 402

Thornton v. Shoe Lane Parking [1971]
2 Q.B. 163; [1971] 1 All E.R. 686
96, 126

Tito v. Waddell (No. 2) [1977] Ch. 106;
[1977] 3 All E.R. 129 322

Tiverton Estates v. Wearwell [1975] Ch.
146; [1974] 2 All E.R. 209 95

Torkington v. Magee [1902] 2 K.B. 427
178

Townley v. Sherbourne (1634) J. Bridge
35 342

Trimmer v. Danby (1856) 25 L.J. Ch.
135 189

Trollope & Colls Ltd v. N.W.
Metropolitan Regional Hospital
Board [1973] 1 W.L.R. 641; [1973] 2
All E.R. 260 119

Tulk v. Moxhay (1848) 2 Ph. 774
296, 297

Turberville v. Savage (1669) 1 Mod
Rep. 3 225

Tweddle v. Atkinson (1861) 1 B. & S.
393 112

Underwood Ltd v. Martins Bank
[1924] K.B. 775 429

United Dominions Trust v. Eagle
Aircraft Services Ltd [1968] 1 W.L.R.
74; [1968] 1 All E.R. 104 122

United Dominions Trust v. Western
(1976) Q.B. 513 133

Valentini v. Canali (1889) 24 Q.B.D. 166
115

Vandervell v. Inland Revenue
Commissioners [1967] 2 A.C. 291;
[1967] 1 All E.R. 1 333

Van Duyn v. Home Office [1975] Ch.
358; [1974] C.M.L.R. 347; [1974] 3 All
E.R. 178 75

Victoria Laundry (Windsor) Ltd v.
Newman Industries Ltd [1949] 2 K.B.
528; [1949] 1 All E.R. 997 156

Vizetelly v. Mudies Select Library Ltd
[1900] 2 Q.B. 170 264

Wagon Mound, The, (No. 1) [1961] A.C.
388; [1961] 1 All E.R. 404 209

Wagon Mound, The, (No. 2) [1967] A.C.
617; [1966] 2 All E.R. 709 209

Walford v. Miles (1992) 1 All E.R. 453,
101

Walsh v. Holst [1958] 1 W.L.R. 800;
[1958] 3 All E.R. 33 245

Walsh v. Lonsdale (1882) 21 Ch. D. 9
287, 293, 305, 318

Walters v. Lunt [1951] 2 All E.R. 645; 35
C.A.R. 94 380

Ward v. Hobbs (1878) 4 App. Cas. 13
134

Ward v. Tesco Stores Ltd [1976] 1
W.L.R. 810; [1976] 1 All E.R. 219
245

Warner Bros. v. Nelson [1937] 1 K.B.
209; [1936] 3 All E.R. 160 323

Watmore v. Jenkins [1962] 2 Q.B. 572;
[1962] 2 All E.R. 868 373

Watson, Re (1973) 3 All E.R. 678, 329

Watson *v*. Prager (1991) 1 W.L.R. 726
142

Watteau *v*. Fenwick [1893] 1 Q.B. 346
174

Watt *v*. Longsdon [1930] 1 K.B. 130
266

Welch *v*. Bank of England [1955] Ch.
508; [1955] 1 All E.R. 811 *428*

Weller *v*. Foot and Mouth, etc. Institute
[1966] 1 Q.B. 569; [1965] 3 All E.R.
560 *242*

Wells *v*. Cooper [1958] 2 Q.B. 265;
[1958] 2 All E.R. 527 *241*

Wenhak *v*. Morgan (1888) 20 Q.B.D.
635 *263*

Wenlock (Baroness) *v*. River Dee Co.
(1887) 10 App. Cas. 354 *67*

Wettern Electric Ltd *v*. Welsh
Development Agency (1983) 2 All
E.R. 629 *120*

Westerton, *Re* [1919] 2 Ch. 104 *179*

Weston's Settlements, *Re* [1969] 1 Ch.
234; [1968] 3 All E.R. 338 *337*

West Sussex Constabulary's Fund
Trusts, *Re* [1971] Ch. 1; [1970] 1 All
E.R. 544 *333*

Wheat *v*. Lacon & Co. Ltd [1966] A.C.
552; [1966] 1 All E.R. 582 *248*

Whitby *v*. Mitchell (1890) 44 Ch. D. 85
277

White *v*. Blackmore [1972] 2 Q.B. 651
[1972] 3 All E.R. 158 *220*

White *v*. Bluett (1853) 23 L.J. Ex. 36
106

White *v*. City of London Brewery
(1889) 42 Ch. D. 237 *305*

White and Carter *v*. McGregor (1961)
3 All E.R. 1978 *154*

Whitley Partners, *Re* (1886) 32 Ch. D.
337 *165*

Wilchick *v*. Marks [1934] 2 K.B. 56
236

Wilcox *v*. Jeffrey [1951] 1 All E.R. 464
375

Wilkes *v*. Allington [1931] 2 Ch. 104
189

Wilkinson *v*. Downton [1899] A.C. 86;
[1897] 2 Q.B. 57 *247*

William Lacey Ltd *v*. Paris (1957) *162*

Williams *v*. Fawcett (1985) 1 All E.R.
787 *30*

Williams *v*. Linnett [1951] 1 K.B. 565
[1951] 1 All E.R. 278 *192*

Williams *v*. Roffey Bros (1990) 2 W.L.R.
1153, *107*

Wilson *v*. Carnley [1908] 1 K.B. 729
141

Wilson & Meeson *v*. Pickering [1946]
K.B. 422; [1946] 1 All E.R. 394
420, 424

Wilson *v*. Pringle (1986) 2 All E.R. 440,
226

Wilsons & Clyde Coal Co. *v*. English
[1938] A.C. 57; [1937] 3 All E.R. 628
215

Wingham, *Re* [1949] P. 187; [1948] 2 All
E.R. 908 *348*

Winkfield, The [1902] P. 42 *232*

Wood *v*. Smith (1991) 3 W.L.R. 514
348

Woodward *v*. Mayor of Hastings [1945]
K.B. 174; [1944] 2 All E.R. 565 *250*

Wringe *v*. Cohen [1940] 1 K.B. 229;
[1939] 4 All E.R. 241 *237*

Yonge *v*. Toynbee [1910] 1 K.B. 215
172, 174

Young *v*. Bankier Distillery Co. [1893]
A.C. 691 *235*

Young *v*. Bristol Aeroplane Co. [1944]
K.B. 718; [1944] 2 All E.R. 293;
[1946] A.C. 163; [1946] 1 All E.R.
98 *29*

Yuen Kun Yeu *v*. Attorney-General of
Hong Kong (1987) A.C. 175 *244*

Table of statutes

Abortion Act 1967 *385, 390–1*
   s. 1 *390*
Accessories and Abettors Act 1861 *374*
   s. 8 *374*
Act of Settlement 1701 *51*
Administration of Estates Act 1833 *276*
Administration of Estates Act 1925 *277, 355, 357, 359*
   s. 7 *355*
Administration of Estates Act 1971 *357*
Administration of Justice Act 1960 *84*
   s. 15 *84*
Administration of Justice Act 1969 *38*
Administration of Justice Act 1970 *17, 24, 36, 82*
Administration of Justice Act 1982 *214, 347*
   s. 17 *348*
   s. 18 *352–3*
   s. 19 *351*
   s. 20 *347*
Administration of Justice Act 1985 *59, 267*
   s. 57 *267*
Adoption Act 1926 *81*
Adoption Act 1976 *81*
Animals Act 1971 *206, 256*
   s. 1 *230, 256*
   s. 2 *256*
   s. 3 *257*
   s. 4 *257*
   s. 4(2) *257*
   s. 5(1) and (2) *256*
   s. 5(3) *257*
   s. 6 *256*
   s. 8 *257*
   s. 10 *257*
   s. 11 *257*
Appellate Jurisdiction Act 1876 *16, 37*

Arbitration Act 1950 *61, 62*
   s. 24 *62*
Arbitration Act 1979 *61, 62*

Betting and Loans (Infants) Act 1892 *115*
Bill of Rights 1689 Art.9 *83, 266*
Bills of Exchange Act 1882 *21, 23, 28, 139, 140, 180, 181, 417*
   s. 3(1) *93, 180, 417, 419*
   s. 10 *426*
   s. 14(1) *420*
   s. 15 *421*
   s. 17 *420*
   s. 20 *419*
   s. 20(1) *419*
   s. 22 *115*
   s. 24 *426*
   s. 27 *108, 181*
   s. 29 *183, 424*
   s. 30 *425*
   s. 32 *423*
   s. 33 *424*
   s. 34 *424*
   s. 35 *424*
   s. 39 *421*
   s. 41 *421*
   s. 44 *421*
   s. 45 *421*
   s. 46 *422*
   s. 54 *426*
   s. 55 *426*
   s. 60 *428*
   s. 73 *417, 426*
   s. 80 *428*
Bills of Rights 1689 *83, 266*
   Article 9 *266*
Bills of Sale Act 1878 and 1882 *311*
British Nationality Act 1948 *23*
British Nationality Act 1981 *73*
Building Societies Act 1986 *59*

Business Names Act 1985 *70*

Chancery Amendment Act (Lord Cairns' Act) 1858 *16*
Charitable Uses Act 1601 *328*
Charitable Uses Act 1960 *328*
Charities Act 1960 *330–1*
  s. 13 *330*
  s. 14 *330*
Charities Act 1985 *330*
Cheques Act 1957 *149, 181, 418*
  s. 1 *428*
  s. 3 *149*
  s. 4 *428*
Cheques Act 1992 *181, 427*
Children and Young Persons Act 1969 *380*
  s. 16 *380*
Children Act 1989 *48, 81, 82*
Civil Aviation Act 1982 *228*
Civil Evidence Act 1968 *264*
  s. 13 *264*
Civil Liability (Contribution) Act 1978 *215*
Coal Industry Nationalisation Act 1946 *67*
Code Napoleon *23*
Code of Practice *370*
Common Law Procedure Act 1852 *202*
Common Law Procedure Acts 1852–54 *16*
Commonwealth Immigration Act 1962 *74*
Commonwealth Immigration Act 1968 *74*
Companies Act 1985 *67, 68, 70, 71, 114*
  s. 35 *69*
  s. 36(4) *170*
  s. 67 *136*
  s. 396 *312*
Companies Act 1989 *69, 113, 114*
Competition Act 1980 *144*
Congenital Disabilities (Civil Liability) Act 1976 *212*
Consumer Credit Act 1974 *24, 46, 193, 302, 311–12*
  Part III, ss. 21–42 *193*
  Parts V and VI, ss. 55–86 *194*
  s. 56 *194*
  s. 61 *194*
  s. 90 *195*
  ss. 99 and 100 *194*
  ss. 114–121 *312*
Consumer Protection Act 1987 *248*
  Part I *248*
Contagious Diseases (Animals) Act 1869 *258*
Contracts of Employment Act 1963 *52*
Conveyancing Act 1881 *276*
Copyright Act 1956 *105*
  s. 8 *105*
Copyright, Designs and Patents Act 1988 *46*
Coroners Act 1988 *49*
County Courts Act 1846 *45*
County Courts Act 1984 *45, 60, 159*
  s. 69 *157*
Court of Probate Act 1857 *13*
Courts Act 1971 *17, 24, 36, 44, 51*
Courts and Legal Services Act 1990 *24, 41, 45, 46, 59, 60*
  s. 8 *40*
  s. 62 *58*
  s. 71 *52*
Court Martial (Appeals) Act 1968 *56*
Criminal Appeal Act 1907 *17, 37*
Criminal Attempts Act 1981 *376, 377*
  s. 1(1) *377*
  s. 1(2) *377*
Criminal Courts Act 1973 *45*
  s. 22 *45*
Criminal Damage Act 1971 *404*
  s. 2 *405*
  s. 10(1) *405*
Criminal Justice Act 1925 *384*
  s. 47 *384*
Criminal Justice Act 1948 *37, 41*
Criminal Justice Act 1982 and 1988 *48*
Criminal Justice Act 1987 *378*
Criminal Justice Act 1991 *49*
Criminal Law Act 1967 *24, 369, 384, 410*
  s. 1 *369*
  s. 3 *84, 384*
  s. 4 *375*
  s. 5 *375–6*
  s. 5(2) *410*
Criminal Law Act 1977 *45, 230, 374, 377, 410*
  s. 1 *377*
  s. 1(1) *377*

s. 2   *377*
s. 3   *377*
s. 5(1)   *377*
s. 5(2)   *378*
s. 6   *231*
s. 6(1)   *411*
s. 6(3)   *231*
s. 7   *231*
s. 7(6)   *411*
Criminal Procedure (Insanity) Act
   1964   *382*
s. 1   *382*
s. 6   *382*
Criminal Procedure (Insanity) Act
   1991   *382*
Crown Proceedings Act 1947   *23, 85,
   212*

Dangerous Dogs Act 1991   *258*
Defamation Act 1952   *261, 262, 264,
   266*
s. 1   *261*
s. 2   *262*
s. 4   *263, 267*
s. 5   *264*
ss. 7–9 and schedules   *266*
Defective Premises Act 1972   *251–2*
Dentists Act 1984   *56*
Diplomatic Privileges Act 1964   *212,
   380*
Divorce Reform Act 1969   *79*
Domestic Proceedings and Magistrates'
   Courts Act 1978   *78, 82*
Domicile and Matrimonial Proceedings
   Act 1973   *72*

Ecclesiastical Licenses Act 1533   *77*
Education (No. 2) Act 1986   *227*
Employers Liability (Defective
   Equipment) Act 1969   *258*
Employment Act 1980 and 1988   *56, 70*
Employment Act 1982   *70, 212*
Employment Act 1988   *212*
Employment Act 1990   *52, 70, 212*
Employment Protection (Consolidation)
   Act 1978   *52, 85*
Enduring Powers of Attorney Act
   1985   *166, 172*
Equal Pay Act 1970   *20, 71, 75*
Estate Agents Act 1979   *168*
s. 13   *168*

European Communities Act 1972   *19,
   62*
ss. 2 and 3   *19, 63*
European Community Treaty
   Article 48   *75*
   Article 85 and 86   *145*
European Convention on Human
   Rights 1950   *63, 84*

Factories Act (1961)   *215*
Factory and Workshop Act 1878   *258*
Factors Act 1889   *166*
s. 1(1)   *166*
s. 2   *166*
ss. 1 and 2   *183*
Family Law Reform Act 1969   *82*
s. 1(1)   *80*
s. 9   *80*
Family Law Reform Act 1987   *80, 81*
Fatal Accidents Act 1846   *214*
Fatal Accidents Act 1976   *214, 222*
s. 1(1)   *214*
s. 1(3)   *214*
Fires Prevention (Metropolis) Act
   1774   *255*
Football (Offences) Act 1991   *85*
Forgery and Counterfeiting Act 1981
   395, 403
s. 1   *403*
ss. 4 and 5   *404*
s. 5   *404*
s. 8   *403*
s. 9   *404*
s. 10   *404*

Gaming Act 1835   *140*
Gaming Act 1892   *140*
Gaming and Wagering Acts
   1845–1968   *140*
Guard Dogs Act 1975   *257*
s. 1   *257*
s. 5   *258*
Guardianship of Minors Acts 1971 and
   1973   *44*

Health and Safety at Work, etc., Act
   1974   *215*
Hire-Purchase Act 1964   *183*
s. 27   *183*
Homicide Act 1957   *382, 389*
s. 2   *382, 389*

s. 3   *389*
s. 4   *389*
Hotel Proprietors Act 1956   *192*
  s. 1   *192*
Housing Act 1988   *53*
Human Fertilisation and Embryology
  Act 1990   *44*

Immigration Act 1971   *74*
  s. 2   *74*
Immigration Act 1988   *74, 75*
In Consimili Casu 1285   *7, 224*
Industrial Relations Act 1971   *212*
Infanticide Act 1938   *390*
  s. 1   *390*
Infant Life (Preservation) Act 1929   *390*
  s. 1   *390*
Infants Relief Act 1874   *115*
  s. 1   *115*
Inheritance (Provision for Family and
  Dependants) Act 1938   *349, 353*
Inheritance (Provision for Family and
  Dependants) Act 1975   *353–4*
  s. 1   *354*
  s. 3   *355*
  s. 6   *355*
  s. 25   *355*
Innkeepers Liability Act 1878   *192, 195*
Insolvency Act 1985   *359*
Insolvency Act 1986   *326, 360*
  s. 27   *360*
  ss. 267–277   *360*
  s. 268   *360*
  s. 274   *360*
  s. 279   *362*
  s. 326   *361*
  s. 328   *361*
  s. 339   *326*
  s. 356–362   *360*
Intestates Estates Act 1952   *353*

Judicature Act 1873   *12, 36, 272*
Judicature Act 1873–75   *9, 12, 15–17,*
  23, 28
Judicial Trustees Act 1896   *339*

Land Charges Act 1925   *277*
Land Charges Act 1972   *277*
  s. 4   *309*
Landlord and Tenant Act 1927   *295*
  s. 19   *295*

Land Registration Act 1925   *277*
Land Registration Act 1988   *277*
Land Transfer Act 1897   *276*
Larceny Acts 1827, 1861 and 1916
  395, 404
Latent Damage Act 1986   *222*
Law Commissions Act 1965   *24*
Law of Property Act 1922   *276*
Law of Property Acts 1922–25   *28*
Law of Property Act 1925   *69, 273,*
  276, 277, 304
  s. 1   *282, 287, 288, 292*
  s. 40   *93, 167*
  s. 51   *303*
  s. 52   *274, 293, 303, 334*
  s. 53   *304*
  s. 53(1)   *327*
  s. 54   *168*
  s. 60   *283, 292*
  s. 62   *299*
  s. 84   *297*
  s. 85   *304*
  s. 87   *305*
  s. 88   *305*
  s. 93   *307*
  s. 94   *307*
  s. 97   *309*
  s. 101   *309, 310, 311*
  s. 103   *306*
  s. 136   *178, 179, 180, 274*
  s. 146   *294*
Law of Property Act 1989   *92*
Law of Property (Miscellaneous
  Provisions) Act 1989   *92, 93*
Law Reform (Contributory Negligence)
  Act 1945   *24, 246*
  s. 1(1)   *246*
Law Reform (Enforcement of
  Contracts) Act 1954   *24*
Law Reform (Frustrated Contract) Act
  1943   *24, 153*
Law Reform (Husband and Wife) Act
  1962   *78, 211, 213*
Law Reform (Married Women and
  Tortfeasors) Act 1935   *71, 213*
  s. 6   *215*
Law Reform (Miscellaneous Provisions)
  Act 1934   *214*
Law Reform (Miscellaneous Provisions)
  Act 1970   *141*
  s. 1   *141*

Leasehold Reform Act 1967 and 1969 *293*

Legal Aid Act 1988 *60*

Legal Aid and Advice Act 1949 *24*

Legitimacy Act 1976 *80*

Libel Act 1843 *267*
  s. 6 *412*

Limitation Act 1980 *108, 155, 221, 267, 343, 379, 429*
  s. 4(a) *267*
  s. 5 *155*
  s. 6 *155*
  s. 8 *155*
  s. 17 *308*
  s. 18 *320*
  s. 20 *308*
  s. 28 *155*
  s. 29(5) *155*
  s. 29(6) *155*
  s. 29(7) *155*
  s. 32 *155*

Limited Partnership Act 1907 *71*

Local Land Charges Act 1975 *277, 300*

Local Government Act 1974 *86*

Magistrates Courts Act 1980 *371, 379*
  Schedule 1 *371*
  ss. 16–23 *371*
  s. 16 *371*
  s. 19–23 *372*

Magna Carta 1215 *8, 22, 37, 83*

Malicious Damage Act 1861 *404*

Marriage Act 1949 *76, 77, 78*
  1st Schedule *76*

Marriage Act 1983 *77, 78*

Marriage (Prohibited Degrees of Relationship) Act 1986 *76*

Married Women's Property Act 1882 *71*
  s. 17 *78, 213*

Matrimonial and Family Proceedings Act 1984 *47, 80*

Matrimonial Causes Act 1857 *13*

Matrimonial Causes Act 1973 *78, 79, 336*
  s. 11 *78*
  s. 12 *79*
  s. 13 *78*

Matrimonial Courts Act 1973 *393*
  s. 19 *393*

Matrimonial Homes Act 1983 *78*

Medicines Act 1968 *374*
  s. 58(2) *374*

Mental Health Act 1983 *79*
  s. 1(2) *113*
  s. 96 *348*

Medical Act 1983 *56*

Mercantile Law Amendment Act 1856 *94*

Metropolitan Police Act 1859 *381*

Minors' Contracts Act 1987 *114*
  s. 2 *116*

Misrepresentation Act 1967 *134, 321*
  s. 1 *134*
  s. 2 *134*
  s. 2(1) *135*
  s. 2(2) *321*
  s. 3(2) *135*

Motor Vehicles (Compulsory Insurance) Act 1971 *219*

Murder (Abolition of Death Penalty) Act 1965 *388*

Occupiers Liability Act 1957 *248, 249–50*
  s. 2(1) *249*
  s. 2(2) *249*

Occupiers Liability Act 1984 *220, 251*

Offences Against the Person Act 1861 *23, 226, 372, 391*
  s. 18 *391*
  s. 20 *391*
  s. 37 *391*
  s. 38 *391*
  s. 45 *226, 227*
  s. 47 *391*
  s. 57 *372, 392*

Official Secrets Act 1911 *45, 407*
  s. 1 *407*
  s. 2 *408*

Official Secrets Act 1911–20 and 1989 *407*

Official Secrets Act 1989 *407*

Opticians Act 1958 *56*

Parliament Act 1911 (amended in 1949) *22, 23*

Parliamentary and Health Service Commissioner Act 1987 *86*

Parliamentary Commissioner Act 1967 *86, 266*
  s. 10 *266*

Parliamentary Commissioner (Consular Complaints) Act 1981 *86*

Partnership Act 1890 *70, 71*
  s. 1 *70*

Perjury Act 1911 *408*
  s. 1 *408*

Perpetuities and Accumulations Act 1964 *288*

Police and Criminal Evidence Act 1984 *227, 369–70*
  s. 24 *227*
  s. 24–25 *369*

Powers of Attorney Act 1971 *171*
  s. 4(1) *171*

Practice Declaration 1987 *44*

Prescription Act 1832 *299*

Prevention of Terrorism (Temporary Provisions) Act 1989 *410*

Prosecution of Offenders Act 1985 *60*

Protection from Eviction Act 1977 *410*
  s. 1(1) and (3) *410*

Provisions of Oxford 1258 *7, 10, 11, 22, 224*

Public Order Act 1936 *408*
  ss. 5 and 5(a) *408*
  s. 5 *408*

Public Order Act 1986 *75, 85, 231, 408, 409, 410*
  s. 1 *409*
  s. 2 *409*
  ss. 4–5 *409*
  s. 4 *409*
  s. 5 *409*
  s. 31 *410*
  s. 39 *231, 411*
  Part III *75*

Public Trustee Act 1906 *338*

Race Relations Act 1976 *46, 52, 75*

Redundancy Payments Act 1965 *52*

Reform Act 1832 *23*

Rehabilitation of Offenders Act 1974 *264*
  s. 4(1) *265*
  s. 8(3) *265*

Rentcharges Act 1977 *286*
  s. 2 *286*
  s. 3 *286*

Resale Prices Act 1964 *55*

Resale Prices Act 1976 *144*

Restrictive Trade Practices Act 1956 *55*

Restrictive Trade Practices Act 1976 *55, 144*

Rights of Light Act 1959 *300*

Road Traffic Act 1988 *220, 393*
  s. 34 *385*
  s. 149 *220*

Road Traffic Act 1991 *393*

Sale of Goods Act 1893 (amended until consolidated in 1979) *23, 28, 123, 184, 187*

Sale of Goods Act 1979 *101, 120, 123, 184, 185, 187, 188, 195*
  s. 3 *113, 114*
  s. 6 *130*
  s. 8(2) *96*
  s. 10–15 *121*
  s. 10 *148*
  s. 11 *187*
  s. 11(3) *121*
  s. 12 *185*
  s. 13 *185*
  s. 14 *185*
  s. 15(2) *186*
  s. 17 *185*
  s. 18 *185*
  s. 22(1) *183*
  s. 25 *183*
  s. 44 *196*
  s. 52 *322*
  s. 57(2) *98*

Scandalum Magnatum 1275 *411*

Settled Land Act 1882 *276*

Settled Land Act 1925 *190, 276, 289, 336*
  s. 27 *190*
  s. 64 *336*

Sex Discrimination Act 1975 *52, 71, 75*

Sex Discrimination Act 1986 *75*

Sexual Offences Act 1956 *392*
  s. 2 *392*
  s. 4(1) *392*
  s. 6 *392*
  ss. 14 and 15 *392*
  s. 23(1) *392*

Sexual Offences Act 1967   *392*
  s. 1   *392*
Sexual Offences (Amendment) Act
  1976   *385, 391*
  s. 1   *385*
Shops Act 1950   *140*
Slander of Women Act 1891   *262*
Solicitors Acts 1839–1974   *58*
Solicitors Act 1974   *56*
State Immunity Act 1978   *212, 380*
Statute Law Revision Acts 1948 etc.   *24*
Statute of Forcible Entries 1381   *230*
Statute of Frauds 1677   *94*
  s. 4   *94*
Statute of Treasons 1351   *407*
Statute of Westminster II 1285   *8, 10,*
  22
Sunday Observance Act 1677   *33*
Supply of Goods and Services Act
  1982   *184, 187*
  ss. 2–5   *187*
  ss. 7–10   *188*
  s. 13   *188*
  s. 14   *188*
  s. 15   *188*
Supply of Goods (Implied Terms) Act
  1973   *184*
Supreme Court Act 1981   *12, 36, 37,*
  42, 43, 44, 82, 157, 357
Supreme Court of Judicature Act 1873
  12

Theatres Act 1968   *261*
  s. 4   *261*
Theft Act 1968   *78, 395, 404*
  s. 1(1)   *395, 397*
  s. 2(1)   *400*
  s. 2(2)   *397*
  s. 3   *397*
  s. 4(1)   *396*
  s. 4(2)   *396*
  s. 5(1)   *396*
  s. 5(2)   *397*
  s. 5(3)   *397*
  s. 5(4)   *397*
  s. 6   *400*
  s. 7   *395*
  s. 8(1)   *398*
  s. 9   *399*
  s. 10   *399*
  s. 11   *398*

  s. 12   *398*
  s. 12(5)   *398*
  s. 13   *398*
  s. 15   *397, 399*
  s. 15(1)   *400*
  s. 15(2)   *400*
  s. 15(3)   *400*
  s. 16   *395, 399, 400*
  s. 17   *401*
  s. 21   *402*
  s. 21(3)   *402*
  s. 22(1)   *402*
  s. 23   *403*
  s. 24(3)   *403*
  s. 24(4)   *402*
  s. 25   *403*
  s. 25(1)   *403*
  s. 25(2)   *403*
  s. 27(3)   *403*
  s. 30   *403*
  s. 34(2)   *402*
Theft Act 1978   *395, 399, 400, 404*
  s. 1(1)   *401*
  s. 1(2)   *401*
  s. 1(1)   *401*
  s. 2(1)   *401*
  s. 2(2)   *401*
  s. 2(3)   *401*
  s. 3(1)   *401*
  s. 19   *401*
  s. 20   *402*
Torts (Interference with Goods) Act
  1977   *195, 231, 434*
  s. 1   *231*
  s. 2   *232, 233*
  s. 3   *233*
  s. 7   *234*
Town and Country Planning Act 1990
  283
Trade Descriptions Act 1968   *379*
Trade Disputes Act 1906   *212*
Trade Union Act 1871   *69*
Trade Union Act 1984   *70, 212*
Trade Union and Labour Relations Act
  1974   *95, 212*
  s. 18   *95*
Trading with the Enemy Act 1939
  140, 141
Transport Act 1962   *67*
Treason Act 1795   *407*
Treason Felony Act 1848   *407*

Treaty of Rome *19*
  Article 119 *19*
Tribunals and Inquiries Act 1958 *27, 54*
Tribunals and Inquiries Act 1971 *53–4*
Trustee Act 1925 *277, 336, 340*
  s. 8 *341*
  ss. 13 and 16 *342*
  ss. 14 and 34 *338*
  s. 15 *342*
  s. 19 *342*
  s. 23 *341*
  s. 27 *341*
  s. 28 *341*
  s. 30(1) *342*
  s. 30(2) *341*
  s. 31 *342*
  s. 32 *342*
  s. 33 *337*
  s. 34 *285*
  s. 36 *339*
  s. 39 *339*
  s. 41 *339*
  s. 53 *336*
  s. 57 *336*
  s. 58 *339*
  s. 61 *343*
  s. 68 *338*
Trustee Investments Act 1961 *340, 342*

Unfair Contract Terms Act 1977 *127, 135, 184, 186, 220*
  s. 1(3) *220*
  s. 2 *220, 243, 249*
Uniform Laws of International Sales Act 1967 *100*
Unsolicited Goods and Services Act 1971 *99, 191*

Vagrancy Act 1824 *392*
  s. 4 *392*
Variation of Trusts Act 1958 *336, 337*
Veterinary Surgeons Act 1966 *56*

War Crimes Act 1991 *23*
Wills Act 1837 *347*
  s. 3 *348, 349*
  s. 7 *348*
  s. 9 *348*
  s. 11 *348*
  s. 15 *349*
  s. 18 *352*
  s. 18(a) *353*
  s. 20 *351*
  s. 32 *351*
Wills Act 1937 *351*
  s. 33 *351*
Wills Act 1968 *349*
  s. 1 *349*
Wills (Soldiers and Sailors) Act 1918 *348*

Part one

The English legal system

1
Nature and history of English law

Nature of law

1. The meaning of 'law'

A law, in the widest sense, means a rule to which actions conform or should conform. Law therefore suggests a real or desired conformity. One can thus speak loosely of the laws of science, economics, logic, psychology, etc., as well as of the laws of nations.

2. Law in the strict sense

This book is concerned with law in the strict sense of the word, that is, rules of conduct imposed by a state upon its members and enforced by its courts. Such rules of conduct constitute the law of the land (or 'municipal law'), the object of which is to enforce certain standards of behaviour among citizens in the interests of peace and good order.

3. Law and morality

Apart from the laws laid down by the state and enforced by the courts, there are also certain customary rules of behaviour called rules of morality. These are not enforced by the courts and depend for their effect solely on the force of public opinion, though many rules of morality may well be given the status of rules of law, by statutes etc., and thereby become enforceable in the courts. There is no necessary correlation between law and morality. The crucial difference between rules of law and rules of morality lies in the method of their enforcement.

4. Public and private law

Law can be divided into two main areas:

(a) Public law is that part of the law which governs the relations of citizens with the state and of one state with another (public international law). Public law thus includes criminal law, constitutional law, administrative law and international law.

(b) Private or civil law is that part of the law of a country which governs the relations of citizens among themselves. It therefore includes the law of property, the law of persons, the law of contract and the law of torts (civil wrongs).

This book is concerned mainly with private law, and also with criminal law and constitutional law.

5.   English and Roman law

In most parts of Europe, and in many other parts of the world, two main systems of law are now in force.

(a) *Modern Roman law*, derived from the ancient laws of the Roman Empire, as modernised and applied in France, Spain, Italy, most other European countries, South Africa, South America, certain parts of Canada (e.g. Quebec) and the United States (e.g. Louisiana).

(b) *English common law*, which is a native product of Britain that has absorbed only a few rules of Roman law and today is applied in most parts of the Commonwealth and of the United States.

6.   Common law and equity

English law consists of two main and complementary components.

(a) *Common law*, comprising ancient customs, judicial precedents and enacted laws, and so called because it was made common to the whole of England and Wales after the Norman Conquest (1066). Prior to this time there was no common system of law for the whole country.

(b) *Equity*, comprising principles laid down in the court of Chancery before 1873 and intended to supplement the common law by providing new rights and new remedies, and by softening the common law where this was too rigid and inflexible (*see* 23: **1**).

7.   Substantive law and procedure

A distinction is drawn by lawyers between:

(a) the rules of law themselves; and

(b) the procedural rules by which the law is enforced in the courts.

Substantive law means law in the strict sense. Procedural or adjectival law governs the machinery by which substantive law is applied, i.e. the rules of evidence and procedure in civil and criminal courts.

Example ──

If a man kills another it is a question of substantive law as to whether the appropriate charge is murder (killing with malice aforethought) or manslaughter (unintentional or mitigated killing). Once he has been charged with either of these crimes, the rules of procedure will then govern: (1) the method by which his guilt should be proved; (2) the evidence that should be admissible at his trial; and (3) the manner in which such evidence should be presented in court.

───

8. Law and fact

Lawyers always distinguish between the law involved in a case and the facts the court has to consider in reaching its decision.

Thus, if a man is charged with murder, it is a question of law as to what is the precise meaning of murder and whether the accused's conduct amounts to murder in the eyes of the law. But it will be the business of the prosecutor to put before the court such facts as show:

(a) that a murder has been committed; and
(b) that the accused was the person who committed the murder.

Wherever a case is tried by a judge and a jury, the judge decides on points of law and the jury decides on matters of fact. The jury will then decide the case, in terms of the law contained in the judge's direction. Even where a judge tries a case without a jury (as in the vast majority of civil cases), a distinction will be made between findings of fact and declarations of law.

History of common law

9. Anglo-Saxon law (pre-1066)

Before the Norman Conquest, England was only loosely united under the Crown. The central government was weak and inefficient, the local areas largely governed themselves and had their own systems of courts and local laws based on ancestral customs.

10. The Norman Conquest (1066)

William I conquered England after winning the Battle of Hastings, which he regarded as a 'trial by battle' that decided the issue of the disputed ownership of England. In accordance with medieval ideas, he claimed to become the owner of every inch of English soil. Relying on this claim, he:

(a) established the feudal system of land tenure, under which all persons who possessed land did so merely as tenants or sub-tenants of the king; and
(b) established a strong central government and a national judicial system.

11. The feudal system

During the Middle Ages, land was the principal form of wealth, and government in all parts of Western Europe was largely based on this fact. By introducing a highly efficient form of feudal land tenure, the Normans were able to establish an efficient central government and a common law, i.e. law common to all parts of England, and later, Wales.

The feudal system of land tenure involved the following points:

(a) all land belonged absolutely to the Crown;
(b) all persons holding land did so merely as tenants ('feudatories') of the Crown;
(c) tenants paid for their occupation of land by rendering services to the Crown and its government, e.g. by providing and equipping soldiers (though from about 1166, money payments known as 'scutage' were made instead);
(d) sub-tenants rendered similar feudal services to their immediate landlords ('mesne' lords), e.g. tilling the landlord's fields;
(e) feudatories holding land directly from the king were called tenants in chief ('tenants *in capite*') and comprised most of the lords and barons, who constituted the King's Grand Council (Curia Regis), which was the precursor both of the king's courts and of Parliament;
(f) between tenants in chief and the lowest class of sub-tenants were several intervening ranks of sub-tenants, all owing feudal duties to their immediate mesne landlord;
(g) the lowest class were called villeins or serfs:
    (*i*)   they were tied to the land on which they lived and worked;
    (*ii*)   they could be sold with the land (though not apart from it);
    (*iii*)   they could not marry without their lord's consent; and
    (*iv*)   they rendered menial services to their lord such as tilling fields, keeping cattle, providing produce for the lord's kitchen.

12. Development of common law

The feudal system of land tenure enabled the Norman kings to establish efficient administration, despite bad roads and communications. Under Henry I (1100–35) and Henry II (1154–89) a definite attempt was made to establish a common legal system for the whole country. Royal judges were sent regularly to all parts of the country to settle disputes (mainly relating to possession of land) in the king's name. Gradually these itinerant judges (justices *in eyre*) extended their jurisdiction to criminal matters after the Assizes of Clarendon (1166) and Northampton (1176), so laying the foundations of a common law of property and of crime.

13. The writ system

To begin an action in a royal court, a plaintiff had to obtain a writ, i.e. a written command issued by the Lord Chancellor in the King's name, ordering the defendant to appear in court and show cause why the plaintiff should not be given the relief he claimed.

There were many different writs, but if there was no appropriate writ to cover the type of claim the plaintiff was making, there could be no remedy. The rule was: no writ, no remedy (*ubi remedium, ibi jus*), so a new writ would be created, at a price.

At first there was no limit to the varieties of writ that the Royal Chancery would issue, but in an attempt to stop Royal courts competing with their own profitable feudal courts, the barons forced Henry III (1216–72) to forbid the issue of further new varieties of writ. This enactment, the Provisions of Oxford 1258, thus had the effect of restricting the growth of common law by tying it to the writs and remedies available before 1258.

14. The statute *In Consimili Casu* 1285

In order to nullify the most harmful restrictions imposed by the Provisions of Oxford 1258, Edward I (1272–1307) enacted the Statute of Westminster II 1285, which provided that new writs could be issued to cover new types of claim *if* the new claims were analogous to those recognised before 1258. In other words, new writs could be issued by the Chancery provided they were 'in like case' (*in consimili casu*) to those that could have been issued before the Provisions of Oxford.

This statute *In Consimili Casu* is of great importance because:

(a) it made possible the further development of common law; and
(b) it made future development extremely conservative and technical, as no revolutionary extensions could be made and new

claims were remedied only if they were analogous to those recognised before 1258.

15. Later development of common law

After 1285, the common law developed steadily along conservative lines. As the government became stronger, the Royal courts increased in importance and prestige, and gradually took away all business from the barons' feudal or seignorial courts.

Consisting originally of criminal law and the law of property, the common law was expanded during the later Middle Ages to include a law of contract and a law of torts (civil wrongs not amounting to crimes). Because of the need to base all extensions of common law on writs existing before 1258, both contract and tort had to be developed with great subtlety, mainly from the ancient writ of trespass (*see* 23: **2**).

16. Medieval courts

There were four main types of court in the Middle Ages:

(a) *Communal courts*, applying local customary law, e.g. shire or county courts, and hundred or parish courts. These declined in importance as common law spread.

(b) *Seignorial courts*, held by feudal landlords for their tenants, e.g. baronial courts and manorial courts. These also decayed as the common law expanded. Fines levied by these courts went largely into the landlords' pockets. The landlords therefore bitterly resisted the competition and expansion of common law; their concern to maintain their interests is apparent in the Magna Carta (particularly chapter 17, which fixed the location of some of the courts at Westminster).

(c) *Ecclesiastical courts*, dealing with the discipline of the clergy, matrimonial and testamentary matters. These courts diminished in importance after the Reformation (*circa* 1535) and matrimonial and testamentary jurisdiction was taken from them and given to the High Court in 1857.

(d) *Royal courts*, including courts of common law and equity (*see* **17**).

17. Common law courts

The Curia Regis (King's Grand Council) originally had judicial as well as governmental functions, but, during the Middle Ages, the judicial powers were gradually deputed to various subsidiary courts:

(a) *Courts of Assize* (e.g. Assizes of Clarendon and Northampton)

These dealt mainly with criminal matters, from the reign of Henry II (1154–89) onwards. They toured the country and the itinerant judges derived their authority from various Royal commissions, i.e. oyer and terminer ('to hear and determine' more serious criminal questions), general gaol delivery (a commission to clear the prisons of persons awaiting trial), and Trailbaston (a commission to deal with abuses of justice).

(b) *The Court of King's Bench* This separated from the Curia Regis in the thirteenth century. It had wide criminal jurisdiction, mainly appellate, and dealt also with civil actions in which the Crown was involved. This particularly meant jurisdiction in actions of trespass. This civil jurisdiction was gradually extended to cover all kinds of civil action.

(c) *The Court of Common Pleas* This separated from the Curia Regis in the thirteenth century and dealt with all civil actions between subjects, particularly with actions relating to land — in other words, matters that did not touch the king's own rights, or peace.

(d) *The Court of Exchequer* This was the first branch of the Curia Regis to establish itself as a separate court. It dealt mainly with revenue matters, but also had a restricted civil jurisdiction.

(e) *The Court of Exchequer Chamber*. There have been several successive courts of this name set up to deal with appeals 'in error' from the other common law courts. The last court of this name was abolished in the nineteenth century, when the present appellate system was established (*see* 3: **2, 3, 10**).

18. The Judicature Acts 1873–75

In the nineteenth century Parliament made extensive reforms to the judicial system and the administration of the law, culminating in the passing of the Judicature Acts. These ended many anachronisms in common law and merged its administration with that of its sister system, equity (*see* 1: **37**). Only the administration was merged, not the systems.

19. Modern common law

Common law is still the basis of modern English law and is constantly developing by means of the doctrine of precedent (*see* 2: **19–22**).

Common law is said to be 'unwritten law' because no complete codification has ever been made, so that today it may be necessary for a lawyer to consult many statutes, judgments and books of authority to ascertain the principles of common law applicable to a particular case.

The modern law of property, contracts, torts and crimes is all based on ancient common law, though legislation has, now of course, added considerably to most of these.

History of equity

20. Origins of equity

From the thirteenth century, all appeals against decisions of the Royal judges were made direct to the king, who was regarded as the 'fountain of justice' and was, therefore, head of the judicial system. Later, pressure of business forced the kings to pass these appeals to the principal Royal official, the Lord Chancellor.

The Lord Chancellor was both:

(a) the king's chief secretary; and
(b) his chaplain, or, 'keeper of the king's conscience'.

As a priest, he tended to decide cases on the basis of morality or natural justice (i.e. equity) rather than in accordance with narrow and technical rules of law. Equity, in its earliest or most primitive sense, means 'fairness' or natural justice.

21. Development of equity

Because it refused to be bound by technicalities, and was not restricted by the writ system, the Chancellor's court eventually became extremely popular. Vice-Chancellors were appointed to deal with litigation and a permanent Court of Chancery was established in London, which dealt with:

(a) matters where the common law provided no remedy; and
(b) matters where, although a remedy was available at common law, it was either insufficient or not forthcoming in the particular case.

This led the Court of Chancery to offer remedies of its own to supplement the common law, such as specific performance and the injunction, and also to recognise rights that were unrecognised by the common law, e.g. the rights of beneficiaries of uses (trusts).

The restrictions imposed on the expansion of common law by the Provisions of Oxford 1258 and the Statute of Westminster II 1285 caused equity to increase in importance and the Court of Chancery and common law courts began to come into conflict.

22. Competition with common law

The great popularity of equity led to harmful competition with the common law courts. The dispute became increasingly bitter during the latter part of the sixteenth century, with Chancery and common law judges sometimes issuing contradictory verdicts.

To terminate the dispute, which reached its peak in the *Earl of Oxford's Case* (1615), James I (1603–25) forced Lord Chancellor Ellesmere and the head of the common law system, Lord Chief Justice Coke, to present the matter to the Attorney-General, Sir Francis Bacon, to arbitrate. On Bacon's recommendation, James I then ordered that, in cases of conflict with common law, equity should prevail.

The King's ruling was never completely accepted by the common law courts and some competition continued until the administration of equity and common law was fused by the Judicature Acts 1873–75.

23. Advantages and defects of equity

These are as follows:

(a) Equity had the following advantages:
  (*i*) it was less formal and technical than the common law;
  (*ii*) its expansion was not restricted by the Provisions of Oxford 1258 as it did not depend on writs;
  (*iii*) it would enforce entirely new claims, which the common law did not recognise, e.g. trusts (*see* 23: **8**).

(b) The chief disadvantage of equity was its flexibility. As decisions were not based on rigid rules, they might vary from Chancellor to Chancellor, depending upon the views of each. Thus, although its flexibility was originally an advantage, as equity grew in importance, it became a defect.

By the seventeenth century, the fluctuations and uncertainty of equity had become a major reproach and John Selden, an eminent jurist, summed up the position by saying that 'Equity varies with the length of the Chancellor's foot'.

24. Formalisation of equity

In order to achieve uniformity and stifle criticism, Lord Nottingham (Lord Chancellor 1673–82), sometimes called the 'father of modern equity', attempted to alter the vague rules of equity to produce a formal system. This work was carried on by his successors, notably Lord Hardwicke (Lord Chancellor 1736–56) and, by the nineteenth century, equity had become a system as rigid and formal as the common law itself.

As a result of the process of formalisation, the word equity had, by the nineteenth century, acquired two distinct meanings:

(a) natural justice, or fair play (the original meaning);
(b) the system of rules administered by the Court of Chancery before 1873, when the Judicature Act of that year amalgamated the administration of equity and common law.

25. Importance of equity

The great importance of equity is that it introduced many new ideas into English law, mainly in the form of:

(a) new rights, such as trusts and the equity of redemption (*see* 22: **11**);
(b) new remedies, such as injunctions and specific performance (*see* 23: **6, 7**).

Equity is, therefore, a valuable supplement to the common law. Lawyers have always maintained that equity is not a completely separate system of law, but is intended merely to fill in gaps in the legal system: 'Equity is a gloss on the common law', Frederic W. Maitland (1850–1906).

26. The Judicature Acts 1873–75

As part of a general process of reform of the law in the nineteenth century, the Judicature Acts were passed to abolish all existing courts and substitute a unified court structure, consisting eventually of the House of Lords and the Supreme Court of Judicature (*see* 3). The Judicature Acts laid down that:

(a) equity and common law should in future be administered side by side in all courts;
(b) where there is any conflict between a rule of equity and a rule of common law, the rule of equity shall prevail, as given in the Supreme Court of Judicature Act 1873 (now re-enacted in the Supreme Court Act 1981 —*see* 23: **1–7** for a more detailed analysis of modern equity).

Subsidiary systems of law

27. Multiplicity of systems

In addition to common law and equity, there were, in medieval England, other parallel and competing systems. The most important of these were ecclesiastical or canon law, the law merchant (mercantile law) and, later, the conciliar courts.

28. Ecclesiastical law

Before the Reformation in the sixteenth century, the laws of the Roman Catholic Church were applied in England by ecclesiastical courts, claiming sole jurisdiction in certain spiritual and moral matters.

The Reformation severed the English Church's link with Rome and made the king the head of the Church of England. In legal matters, the effect of this was to bring the ecclesiastical courts increasingly under the control of the state and, gradually, much of their jurisdiction was handed over to the common law courts.

29. Ecclesiastical courts

These had jurisdiction primarily over the following matters:

(a) Discipline of the clergy. Bishops' consistory courts and Archbishops' provincial courts still have jurisdiction to punish clergy of the Church of England for moral offences, but criminal matters are dealt with by the ordinary common law courts. (There are today two provincial courts, the Court of Arches in the archdiocese of Canterbury, and the Chancery Court of York in the archdiocese of York.)

(b) Matrimonial causes, e.g. divorce, nullity and legitimacy. This jurisdiction was transferred to a new civil court for divorce by the Matrimonial Causes Act 1857.

(c) Testamentary matters, i.e. the administration of the estates of deceased persons and the proving of wills. This jurisdiction was transferred to a new Court of Probate by the Court of Probate Act 1857.

30. The law merchant

Much of the commerce of the Middle Ages was conducted by travelling merchants who moved from fair to fair throughout the country. It was their custom to set up temporary informal courts at each fair or market to settle trading disputes.

The law administered by these informal courts was customary and international in character. It consisted of:

(a) international trade usages, based largely on the Roman *jus gentium* (that part of Roman law developed to meet the needs of merchants throughout the Roman Empire);

(b) maritime law, based largely on the ancient Rhodian Sea Laws of the Greeks; and

(c) police regulations for the conduct of the fair or market.

31. Courts merchant
Courts that administered the law merchant were as follows:

(a) Informal courts ('pie powder' courts). These were the commonest merchants' courts, being set up informally at each fair or market to administer rough-and-ready justice. Professional lawyers were contemptuous of such courts, complaining that the merchant judges came on to the bench with travel-stained and dusty feet. Consequently they called such courts *pieds poudres*, or, 'dusty feet' courts; the two French words were commonly mispronounced by the English as 'pie powder'.

(b) Formal courts established by the Crown for the settlement of important commercial disputes. The most important of these were the courts of staple, set up in major trading centres to encourage foreigners to trade in England by giving them favourable and understanding tribunals.

The High Court of Admiralty, established by Edward III (1327–77), was another formal court charged with the task of punishing pirates and settling international disputes connected with shipping and sea-trading.

32. Decline of courts merchant
These courts gradually declined in importance and their jurisdiction was taken over by the common law courts. Reasons for the decline were:

(a) increased efficiency and centralisation of the common law courts;

(b) statutory limitations imposed from 1477 onwards upon the jurisdiction of the courts merchant.

33. Absorption by common law
By the middle of the eighteenth century, the common law courts had taken over nearly all the jurisdiction of the pie powder and staple courts. Lord Mansfield, Lord Chief Justice, established the principle that recognised mercantile customs should be enforced at common law, thus obviating the need for separate courts merchant.

The High Court of Admiralty survived as a separate court until the nineteenth century when it was merged into the High Court by the Judicature Acts 1873–75. Its work is now carried on in the Admiralty Court of the Queen's Bench Division of the High Court.

34. Conciliar Courts

While the Royal courts (common law and equity) all sprang from the King's Council after the twelfth century, the king nevertheless continued to exercise a 'residuary' jurisdiction (as well as law-making capacity) through his Council (Curia Regis). These notions have persisted in the form, for example, of Orders in Council (*see* 2: **15**) and in the jurisdiction of the Privy Council.

Under the Tudors and early Stuart monarchs, the Council was used as an instrument of law enforcement and, indeed, creation.

The main organs of the Council thus involved were:

(a) *Court of Star Chamber* Developed from the Council in the fifteenth century, under the reign of Edward IV, to 'punish divers misdemeanours', the work of the Star Chamber judges resulted in a large number of criminal offences being introduced, including conspiracy attempts, forgery and perjury. All of these have been assimilated into the common law, though not always in the form of misdemeanours.
(b) *Court of Requests* Developed by Lord Chancellor Wolsey during the sixteenth century, it started life much earlier as a court of the Council, which heard petitions from the poor.
(c) *Local councils* These were set up to maintain order, particularly in the borders between England and Wales and Scotland.

The conciliar courts were similar to the Court of Chancery in that they did not rely on common law writs and procedure. Under James I (1603–25) and Charles I (1625–49) they were used oppressively; the Long Parliament accordingly abolished the Star Chamber and local councils in 1641, and the Court of Requests lapsed at about the same time.

The Judicature Acts 1873–75

35. Need for reform

By the nineteenth century, the British legal system had become archaic and too unwieldy to meet the requirements of modern society. The continued separation of law and equity was a particular handicap. Under the influence of several thinkers, notable Jeremy Bentham (1748–1832), Parliament launched a programme of reform.

36. Preliminary reforms

One of the principal defects of the existing system was that a plaintiff seeking several simultaneous remedies might have to bring expensive proceedings in several courts to obtain them. In an action for breach of contract, for instance, he might have to bring a common law action for damages plus a further action in equity to obtain an order for specific performance, commanding the defendant to perform his bargain.

To prevent this need for multiple actions, legislation was passed to make both common law and equitable remedies available in all the principal courts:

(a) The Common Law Procedure Acts 1852–54, gave common law courts power to award certain equitable remedies in addition to or as alternatives to the ordinary remedy of damages, e.g. injunctions and discovery of documents. Also a defendant was to be allowed to raise certain discretionary defences previously available only in the Court of Chancery.

(b) Chancery Amendment Act (Lord Cairns' Act) 1858 gave the Court of Chancery a discretion to award the common law remedy of damages as an alternative to the normal equitable remedies of injunction, specific performance, etc. (for equitable remedies generally, *see* 23: **5–7**).

37. Judicature Act 1873

This completely reorganised the judicial system by establishing a unified Supreme Court in place of the multiplicity of common law and equity courts existing previously *see* 3: **1–17**).

The objects of the Act were:

(a) to fuse the administration of common law and equity, which therefore are now applicable side by side in all courts today;

(b) to simplify procedure;

(c) to establish a unified Supreme Court of Judicature consisting of a Court of Appeal and a High Court (*see* 3: **10–17**);

(d) it was thought expedient to abolish the judicial powers of the House of Lords also, as its members were not, of course, judges; in 1876, however, the House was reconstituted, with special Lords of Appeal in Ordinary (law-lords), sitting together as the highest court of appeal: Appellate Jurisdiction Act 1876.

38. Effect of the Judicature Acts

These were as follows:

(a) the Supreme Court of Judicature was established, consisting of a Court of Appeal (in place of the old Court of Exchequer Chamber) and a High Court, divided into three divisions — the Queen's Bench Division, the Chancery Division and the combined Probate, Divorce and Admiralty Division;

(b) the old common law courts of Queen's Bench, Common Pleas and Exchequer were merged into the Queen's Bench Division of the High Court;

(c) the Court of Probate, the court for divorce, and the High Court of Admiralty were merged in the Probate, Divorce and Admiralty Division of the High Court;

(d) the Chancery Court of Equity became the Chancery Division of the High Court;

(e) the House of Lords was established as the supreme appellate tribunal for Great Britain (though it remained outside the Supreme Court);

(f) later, a Court of Criminal Appeal was established, leaving the Court of Appeal to deal with appeals in civil cases (Criminal Appeal Act 1907) but in 1966, the Court of Criminal Appeal was abolished and replaced by a Division of the Court of Appeal specifically established to hear criminal appeals.

39. Recent reforms
Further rationalisation of the judicial system has taken place in recent years. Thus:

(a) the old Court of Criminal Appeal was abolished in 1966; now there is one general Court of Appeal which has a civil division, and a criminal division;

(b) the Probate, Divorce and Admiralty Division was reorganised in 1971 and renamed the Family Division: Administration of Justice Act 1970 (*see* 3: **17**);

(c) assizes and quarter sessions were abolished in 1971 and replaced by the Crown Court, as specified in the Courts Act 1971.

Progress test 1

1. Distinguish between: (a) law and morality and between (b) public and private law.   (**3, 4**).

2. How did the feudal system influence the development of

English law? Explain the significance of the Provisions of Oxford 1258 and the statute *In Consimili Casu* 1285.   **(10–15)**

3.   Describe: (a) the types of court existing in the Middle Ages and (b) the common law courts that developed from the Curia Regis. **(16–17)**

4.   Why is common law said to be unwritten?   **(19)**

5.   What is meant by the statement that equity is 'a gloss on the common law'?   **(20–25)**

6.   Assess the advantages and defects of equity and explain how the system gradually became formalised.   **(23, 24)**

7.   What is the importance of equity in the development of English law?   **(22, 25, 26)**

8.   Explain what is meant by: (a) ecclesiastical law; (b) the law merchant and (c) the conciliar courts and outline their respective jurisdictions.   **(28–34)**

9.   What courts existed in England before the passing of the Judicature Acts 1873–75 and how did these Acts change the judicial system?   **(17, 36, 37, 38)**

10. What were the objects of the Judicature Acts 1873–75?   **(37)**

11. Summarise the most recent statutory reforms of the judicial system.   **(39)**

2
Sources of English law

Principal sources

1. General
The principal sources of English law are statute law (legislation), case law and custom.

While these are the principal sources, others do, in fact, exist:

(a) For instance, it is normal, in the absence of one of the above, or to elucidate a difficult point, to resort to the writings of the more important textwriters.

(b) Since 1972, certain laws made by the institutions of the European Communities may be applicable in the United Kingdom as a consequence of the European Communities Act 1972, ss. 2 and 3. Such laws may take the form of Regulations and Directives from the European Commission and Council of Ministers and decisions of the European Court of Justice, which our courts are 'bound to take notice of'. As a member state of the European Community, the United Kingdom has, to a very limited extent, subordinated its legal system to that of the Community. This contradicts the accepted doctrine of Parliamentary sovereignty (*see* 2: **8**).

Nevertheless, Community law is undoubtedly a source of English law. This is particularly true of directly applicable Community law, such as the provisions of Article 119 of the Treaty of Rome, which provides for equal pay for work of equal value, irrespective of sex. In a series of cases, this principle has been held to apply to the UK. The courts have been careful, however, to construe this principle as existing over and above British legislation on the subject, rather than contrary to it, thus preserving, as far as possible, the supremacy of the British Act concerned. In *Garland* v. *British Rail Engineering* (1982), for example, the House of Lords held that Community law, in effect, conferred greater rights upon a woman than did English law. That did not make them incompatible, however, and the British statute (the Equal Pay Act 1970) could, and indeed should, be interpreted (*see* 2: **26**) so as to allow these greater rights to be granted.

Custom

2.   Customary origin of law

Most legal systems have their origins in ancient customs of a nation or tribe, e.g. Roman law. English common law was originally based on oral customs of the Anglo-Saxons, which the Norman judges welded into a formal system of law in the medieval Royal courts.

Custom is, therefore, the oldest source of English law. Most of the more important national or general customs were absorbed into the common law very early and, by the fourteenth century, custom had ceased to be the mainspring of common law development and had been replaced by judicial precedent.

3.   Kinds of custom

These are of two main kinds:

(a) *General custom.* This means a custom recognised and obeyed throughout the country even before it was enforced by the courts. General custom is the foundation of common law. All major general customs have been absorbed into the law already. It is unlikely that new ones could arise to create new law today.

(b) *Local custom.* This means a rule or tradition regularly obeyed by the inhabitants of a particular locality, e.g. a customary right of way used by the inhabitants of a village across neighbouring land. Such customs may be recognised and enforced by the courts and so become part of common law, though applicable only within a particular district. Local customs do still sometimes create new law, though rarely (*see* 2: **4, 5**).

4.   Validity of local customs

In order to gain recognition and enforcement by the courts, a local or particular custom must be:

(a)   reasonable;
(b)   not contrary to any statute or any fundamental principle of law;
(c)   observed as of right, i.e. *nec vi, nec clam, nec precario* (not by force, nor secretly, nor subject to permission);
(d)   exercised from 'time immemorial', i.e. since 1189 (*see* 2: **5**);
(e)   definite in nature and scope;

(f) exercised continuously and without interruption;

(g) recognised as binding by those who are affected by it.

5. Time immemorial

In order to gain recognition from the courts, a custom must, in theory, have been in force from 'time immemorial', i.e. from the end of Henry II's reign in 1189. In practice, however, it is generally sufficient to show that the custom has existed as long as any living person can remember, i.e. 'beyond living memory'. If this is proved, the court will presume that the custom has been in force since 1189.

The presumption can be rebutted by showing that, for some reason, it was impossible for the custom to have existed in 1189 or subsequently, e.g. where a right of way is claimed across land known to have been under water some time since the reign of Henry II.

6. Conventional usages

In addition to general and local customs as sources of law, particular trades or groups of people may have their own professional customs or usages that may be recognised and enforced by the courts, provided they are of sufficiently long standing, definite and recognised as obligatory by the persons to whom they apply.

Thus the Bills of Exchange Act 1882, is largely based on the customs previously existing among bankers regarding cheques and other bills of exchange.

Legislation

7. Meaning of legislation

Legislation means enacted law, that is, law laid down by a body constituted for the purpose, e.g. the British Parliament. Enacted laws of this kind are called statutes.

Legislation may be direct or indirect. Direct legislation means laws enacted by the legislature itself, e.g. Acts of Parliament. Indirect or delegated legislation means rules or laws laid down by a body or person to whom the legislature has delegated power to make such rules, e.g. regulations laid down by a minister under power given him by an Act of Parliament.

8. Sovereignty of Parliament

In Britain today, Parliament is the supreme legislative body. Therefore:

(a) Parliament can enact any law it chooses; and
(b) its enactments are absolutely binding on the courts and all citizens.

By virtue of this supremacy, or sovereignty, Parliament can delegate legislative power to subordinates and the delegated or subordinate legislation laid down by such persons is also binding on the courts.

If, however, a person or body to whom legislative power has been delegated exceeds the scope of its powers, laws laid down in excess of power (*ultra vires*) are void and can be so pronounced by the courts. This *ultra vires* doctrine enables the courts to assert some control over delegated legislation. The same doctrine can also be invoked to prevent a company or corporation exceeding its legal powers.

9. Early legislation

Before the fifteenth century, legislation was not an important source of law. Statutes were enacted by the king and Grand Council, a body consisting of the chief men of the realm, e.g. the barons and the aldermen of the City of London, who, together, forced King John to pass the Magna Carta 1215, which stated the constitutional rights of English people.

In this early period, statutes were comparatively infrequent and dealt mainly with matters of national importance, e.g. the Provisions of Oxford 1258 and the Statute of Westminster II 1285 (*see* 1:**13, 14**).

10. The rise of Parliament

During the thirteenth and fourteenth centuries, the Grand Council was divided into two bodies (the Lords and Commons) and began to be called Parliament (from 'parley', to discuss). For some time the king continued to legislate independently of Parliament, but the Civil War in the middle of the seventeenth century established the principle that, in future, all statutes had to have the consent of Parliament. From this time on, therefore, statute law consists of Acts of Parliament.

Parliament consists of three essential components: the Sovereign, the House of Lords and the House of Commons. Proposals for legislation must be put before both Houses in the form of bills. If approved by both Houses, a bill is then placed before the Sovereign and does not become an Act of Parliament until it receives the Royal assent (which, by convention, is not refused). Since 1911 (Parliament Act 1911 as amended in 1949) it has been possible for the Commons to send 'public' bills up for Royal assent even if the Lords oppose them; the Lords are permitted to delay a bill for two consecutive parliamentary sessions only. For example, the War Crimes Act 1991 was sent for Royal assent despite having been defeated twice by the House of Lords.

It is also a convention of the constitution that matters of national importance should be initiated in the House of Commons and financial bills must be so initiated (Parliament Act 1911).

11. Importance of legislation since 1832

The Reform Act 1832 made the House of Commons a genuinely democratic body representing the population as a whole and thereby increased its importance as the means of expressing the national will. From this date onwards legislation became increasingly important as a source of law.

12. Nineteenth-century legislation

The Emperor Napoleon had reformed and codified French law by the Code Napoléon 1805 and Britain, profiting by the French example, increasingly used legislation as an agency for the reform of English law.

During the nineteenth century, Acts of Parliament:

(a) reorganised the judicial system, e.g. by the Judicature Acts 1873–75 (*see* 1: **37, 38**);

(b) reformed judicial procedure, e.g. by abolishing archaic procedures that had fallen into disuse since the Middle Ages, such as trial by battle;

(c) codified confused sections of the common law — for example, the Sale of Goods Act 1893 (much amended, and finally consolidated in 1979), the Bills of Exchange Act 1882 and the Offences Against the Person Act 1861.

13. Twentieth-century reforms

In this century, legislation has been used increasingly for the reform of the law, for example:

(a) the property legislation of 1922–25 reformed the law of property (see 29: **15–18**);

(b) the Crown Proceedings Act 1947 made the Crown liable for the first time for torts committed by its servants;

(c) the British Nationality Act 1948 defined British nationality and the position of Commonwealth citizens;

(d) the Legal Aid and Advice Act 1949 made provision for financial assistance for parties in civil and criminal cases;

(e) the Statute Law Revision Acts 1948, etc., repealed archaic statutes that had fallen into disuse;

(f) the Lord Chancellor's Law Revision Committee was established in 1932 to advise regularly on reform of the law and the reports of this Committee resulted in many reforming Acts of Parliament, e.g. the Law Reform (Frustrated Contracts) Act 1943, the Law Reform (Contributory Negligence) Act 1945 and the Law Reform (Enforcement of Contracts) Act 1954;

(g) the Law Commission was established in 1965 to promote law reform (*see* the Law Commissions Act 1965). Its members are salaried and appointed by the Lord Chancellor from among holders of high judicial office, experienced barristers and solicitors and academic lawyers. The Commissions' duty is to review all of English law with a view to systematic reform and codification, elimination of anomalies and obsolete laws, etc. — the commissioners' recommendations resulted in the Criminal Law Act 1967 and the Commission has proposed the codification of the law of contract and the criminal law;

(h) the Administration of Justice Act 1970 re-allocated work between various branches of the High Court;

(i) the Courts Act 1971 restructured the court system by abolishing the assizes and quarter sessions and substituting a Crown Court staffed by High Court judges, circuit judges, recorders (part-time judges) and justices of the peace;

(j) the Courts and Legal Services Act 1990 enacted widespread reforms in such areas as civil court proceedure, the provision of legal services (particularly advocacy, litigation, conveyancing and probate services), judicial offices and pensions, various reforms concerning solicitors, arbitration and a number of other miscellaneous matters.

14. Delegated or subordinate legislation

By virtue of its sovereign position, Parliament can delegate some of its legislative powers (by 'parent' or 'enabling' legislation), usually to Ministers of the Crown, local councils, etc. For example, the Secretary of State for Trade possesses delegated power to regulate the licensing of those involved in the consumer credit industry under the Consumer Credit Act 1974.

Delegated or subordinate legislation has become increasingly important in recent years as a source of new law, for the following reasons.

(a) *lack of Parliamentary time* — Parliament has insufficient time to debate in detail all the day-to-day measures needed for efficient government;

(b) *technicality* — Parliament does not always have the specialised or local knowledge necessary to debate all matters in full;

(c) *urgency* — Parliamentary procedure is necessarily too slow to cope with sudden emergencies and these cases may, in any event, arise while Parliament is not in session;

(d) *elasticity* — An Act of Parliament can be overruled only by another Act of Parliament, while a ministerial rule or regulation can be rescinded by the minister who issued it, if it proves impracticable or becomes outdated.

15. Types of delegated legislation
These include the following:

(a) *orders in Council* — these are orders made by the Queen and Privy Council either under statutory authority or by virtue of the residual powers of the Crown (called the Royal prerogative) and do not usually require to be confirmed by Parliament;

(b) *statutory instruments* — these must be put before Parliament for approval, the procedure being laid down by the parent Act, e.g.:

    (*i*) negative procedure: the regulation comes into force at once and will remain in force unless annulled by resolution of either House of Parliament within 40 days;

    (*ii*) affirmative procedure: the regulation must be laid before Parliament for 40 days and will not come into force unless approved during the period;

(c) *by-laws of local authorities* — these rules of law are restricted in operation to the area for which the local authority is responsible, e.g. by-laws of the city of Liverpool.

16. Criticism of delegated legislation
The increase of delegated legislation has been severely criticised on the ground that it gives to non-elected persons a legislative power that should rightly be restricted to the nation's elected representatives (Lord Hewart, *The New Despotism*).

A further criticism is that Parliament exercises too little control over the issue of delegated legislation. The following controls, however, do exist:

(a) Parliament retains power to rescind any delegated power;

(b) the courts can declare an exercise of delegated power *ultra vires* and void (but this judicial safeguard can be expressly excluded by the Act delegating the power);

(c) public inquiries are sometimes required to be held before a piece of delegated legislation becomes effective, so as to give the public an opportunity to object, but the findings of such inquiries can sometimes legally be ignored by the body to whom power is delegated;

(d) a select Committee of the House of Commons (the 'Scrutiny Committee') was set up in 1944 to examine ministerial rules and orders and report to Parliament any such measure that seems unreasonable, excessive or unduly expensive.

17. Control of delegated legislation

While delegating minor legislative functions to subordinate bodies, Parliament retains overall control by:

(a) reserving authority to debate (and, if necessary, to veto) requests for delegated legislative power;

(b) appraising delegated legislation by requiring it (where appropriate) to be put before Parliament for review (after which either House may resolve on annulment within 40 days);

(c) the Scrutiny Committee of the House of Commons examining all statutory instruments and deciding whether any should be brought to the attention of the House for appraisal. Some statutory instruments require actual confirmation by Parliament before becoming effective;

(d) the courts, though subordinate to Parliament and unable to question the legality of the delegation of power by Parliament (*see R. v. Immigration Appeals Tribunal, ex parte* Joyles (1972), and compare *R. v. HM Treasury ex parte Smedley* (1985)) nevertheless act as watchdogs to ensure that the delegated authority is properly exercised and scrutinise not the granting but the use of delegated legislative power. They can declare *ultra vires* and void any such exercise if it offends against the following presumptions, i.e. it is presumed that the enabling Act does not give power (unless expressly stated otherwise):

  (*i*)   to make unreasonable or uncertain rules; nor
  (*ii*) to allow sub-delegation; nor
  (*iii*) to levy taxes; nor
  (*iv*) to infringe basic constitutional rights, such as freedom of
          speech and personal liberty.

Example ───

In *R.* v. *Secretary of State for Health, ex parte* United States Tobacco

International Inc. (1991) a set of regulations banning the sale of oral snuff in the form of 'Skoal Bandits' was quashed because they were a disproportionate response to the health danger and the Secretary of State had conducted inadequate consulations before making them.

---

18. Administrative law

In some countries, e.g. France, there is a separate branch of law dealing with the power of ministers and government departments, and the control of such powers. This is called administrative law (in French, *droit administratif*).

In Britain there is no clearly separate administrative law as yet, although many jurists believe that it is necessary and is beginning to develop spontaneously. Generally, however, control of the executive (government) is left entirely to the ancient common law and, in particular, to the doctrine of *ultra vires*. Also, since 1967, the Parliamentary Commissioner for Administration has been empowered to investigate complaints arising from maladministration in a government department, even when this is done within the power allowed it.

Administrative tribunals exist to enforce delegated legislation and to examine its application and misuse. These tribunals have been criticised as being arbitrary and tending to diminish the right of citizens to appeal to the courts. These criticisms led to the passing of the Tribunals and Inquiries Act 1958, which aimed at bringing administrative tribunals under more effective control and securing properly qualified chairmen by giving the Lord Chancellor supervisory powers over the membership of tribunals (*see* 3: **42–45**).

Case law

19. The doctrine of precedent

The most outstanding characteristic of English law is that it is largely 'judge made'. That is, the bulk of common law and equity has not been enacted by Parliament, but has been developed through the centuries by the judges applying established or customary rules of law to new situations and cases as they arise. The principle behind the doctrine of precedent is that, in each case, the judges apply *existing* principles of law; that is, they follow the example, or precedent, of earlier decisions. Thus the law develops, case by case, by analogy with earlier cases.

20. Declaratory and original precedents

When a judge applies to a case an existing rule of law, without extending it, his decision is a declaratory precedent.

Where the case to be decided is one *without* precedent, however, i.e. unlike any previous case, the judge must decide it according to general principles of law. By so doing he lays down an original precedent that judges will follow in future if they encounter a similar case.

21. Geldart's criticisms of the doctrine

Professor Geldart described the advantages of the system of precedent as:

(a) *certainty*;
(b) *flexibility* and *aptitude for growth*;
(c) *greater detail* than is possible in a purely enacted system of law;
(d) *practicality*.

He also listed the disadvantages as:

(a) *rigidity*, as the discretion of every judge is restricted by the rule that he must follow the decisions of his predecessors;
(b) *over-subtlety*, which sometimes results from the need in a particular case to find a logical excuse for not following an existing precedent where it would cause hardship to do so;
(c) *bulk and complexity*, as much of English law is contained in multitudinous reports of cases dating back to the Middle Ages and these reports have to be consulted by lawyers to ascertain what rules of law are applicable to new cases.

> NOTE: This has led to much agitation for the complete codification of English law along Continental lines, but no general codification has yet been made, though individual Acts of Parliament have codified particular sections of the law, e.g. the Law of Property Acts 1922–5, the Sale of Goods Act 1893 and the Bills of Exchange Act 1882.

22. History of the doctrine

The doctrine began to develop in the Royal courts after the reign of Henry II (1154–89) and in the equity courts rather later, but it did not become firmly established until the eighteenth century, though it had been widely adhered to before then. It did not take its modern form, however, until a hierarchy of courts was established by the Judicature Acts 1873–75. It had its origin in the desire of the medieval judges to create a system of law common to the whole country and the consequent need to secure uniformity in their decisions.

Furthermore, the doctrine in its modern form depends upon a reliable system of law reporting (*see* 2: **33**).

23. The hierarchy of precedent: *stare decisis*

Some courts have greater authority than others and this affects the importance of the precedents laid down by each. The most powerful court in Britain is the House of Lords, then comes the Court of Appeal and then the High Court. It must be borne in mind, however, that the European Court of Justice, which sits in Luxembourg, has the very last word in matters involving European Community law. Where domestic law conflicts with Community law, domestic law loses: 'the member states have limited their sovereign rights, albeit within limited fields and have thus created a body of law which binds both their nationals and themselves' in *Costa* v. *E.N.E.L.* (1964). So the precedents from the European Court of Justice bind all domestic courts in all member states.

The general rule governing the standing of judicial decisions (known as the doctrine of *stare decisis*) is that a decision made by a higher court must be followed by a lower court (i.e. it 'binds' that lower court). Thus:

(a) *The House of Lords* (HL) binds all lower courts. Until 1966, the HL was bound by its own previous decisions and, ever since that time, the House has determined that they should only stray from previous decisions where there is good reason to do so, such as a 'material change in circumstances': *Fitzleet Estates* v. *Cherry* (1977). This might take the form of a marked change in social conditions, although in *Murphy* v. *Brentwood District Council* (1990), the House openly overruled their earlier decision in *Anns* v. *London Borough of Merton* (1977) because they thought it was wrong. When the HL decides on a point of Scots law, its decision is not binding on English courts, unless the point of law involved is equally relevant to England, as in *Donoghue* v. *Stevenson* (1932).

(b) *The Court of Appeal* (CA) is bound by the HL; it also binds itself (since 1944, due to *Young* v. *Bristol Aeroplane Co.* (1944)) subject to the following exceptions:

- (*i*) the CA may choose one or other of two previous decisions that conflict with one another;
- (*ii*) the CA must follow a HL decision, where that conflicts with its own previous decision;
- (*iii*) the CA may decline to follow a previous CA decision if that was made *per incuriam* (i.e. where a statute or other binding

rule of law was not considered by the court in reaching that previous decision, thus making it unsound).

Unlike the HL, the CA cannot revoke its decision to bind itself and certainly not since the HL decision in *Davis* v. *Johnson* (1978), where the HL confirmed that the CA was bound by its own previous decisions (but consider *Williams* v. *Fawcett* (1985) where the liberty of the individual and the unlikelihood of an appeal to the House of Lords were central issues).

(c) *Divisional courts* of the High Court are bound by their own decisions and by decisions of the HL and CA.

(d) *The High Court* is bound by the HL and CA, as well as by decisions of its own divisional courts. High Court decisions bind inferior courts such as county courts. High Court judges are not bound by decisions of their predecessors or colleagues, but will rarely depart from them if:

    (*i*) the decision is of long standing; or

    (*ii*) they were laid down by judges of high repute.

(e) *The Crown Court, county courts, magistrates' courts, etc.*, are bound by decisions of all superior courts, but do not themselves lay down binding precedents.

24. *Ratio decidendi: obiter dicta*

When a judge delivers his judgment, he will normally begin by giving a résumé of the facts of the case and then go on to give his decision and the reason for his decision (*ratio decidendi*). It is the *ratio decidendi* of a judgment that creates a precedent for the future. If there are several reasons, or *rationes*, for the one judgment, these may create several precedents. 'A case is only authority for what it actually decides': said Lord Halsbury, LC in *Quinn* v. *Leathem* (1901).

Any general comments on law made 'by the way' (*obiter dicta*) in the course of a judgment are disregarded when considering what part of the judgment constitutes the precedent.

25. Overruling and distinguishing precedents

If it would lead to injustice in the particular case before him, a judge may refuse to apply an earlier precedent. If the precedent is one laid down by an inferior court, he may overrule it. If, however, it was laid down by a superior court (so that in theory he should follow it), he will have to evade the precedent by distinguishing between the case he is deciding and the one in which the precedent was laid down.

When one of the parties to a case appeals to a higher court against the decision of the lower, the appeal court may reverse the decision of the lower court or confirm it.

26. Interpretation of statute law

As Parliament is the sovereign legislative body, the courts cannot challenge the validity of an Act of Parliament, but they can influence the effect of an Act by the way in which they interpret it when called upon to apply it in a case. The interpretation of statutes is increasingly important as the bulk of legislation increases and, indeed, a large body of case law has developed as the courts have laid down precedents in their interpretation of Acts of Parliament.

27. Rules governing interpretation of statutes

There are three differing (and inconsistent) approaches to the problem of interpretation and, in applying one of these, the courts will have recourse to various principles and rules. The three differing approaches, which will generally suit different circumstances, are known as:

(a) the literal rule (*see* 2: **28**);
(b) the golden rule (*see* 2: **29**);
(c) the mischief rule (*see* 2: **30**).

28. The literal rule

Where the words of a statute are clear and unambiguous, as Lord Esher said, 'you must follow them, even though they lead to an absurdity. The court has nothing to do with the question whether the legislature has committed an absurdity'. Thus, if the words are clear, no 'interpretation' as such can take place.

29. The golden rule

Where the words of a statute are not clear, then the court must apply this (or the mischief rule) to ascertain the intention of Parliament. The golden rule was expressed by Blackburn, J, in *River Wear Commissioners* v. *Adams* (1877) as involving that 'we take the whole statute together, and construe it altogether, giving the words their ordinary meaning' unless to do so would result in 'some inconsistency, absurdity, inconvenience or repugnance'. The natural meaning is, therefore, preferred, but this rule enables the courts to depart from it occasionally. For example, in *Re Sigsworth* (1935), the statute that governed the distribution of an intestate's estate to the next of kin was held not to benefit the next of kin who had murdered the lady in question, his mother.

30. The mischief rule

This rule applies where a statute purports to remedy a particular 'mischief' that, hitherto, had gone without remedy. It may be used, therefore, to expedite the intention of Parliament in providing such a remedy. This, incidentally, reflects the approach taken by the European Court of Justice, that the context and wording are regarded as subsidiary to purpose — *see Bulmer* v. *Bollinger* (1974).

31. General rules and principles of interpretation

Whenever the courts are concerned to give their interpretation to a statute, they observe the following principles (this is, of course, unnecessary where the literal rule can be followed):

(a) the courts must always and only attempt to ascertain, and give effect to the intention of Parliament;

(b) the courts may not look into the 'background' of a statute (*travaux préparatoires*) to assist them; they cannot, therefore, refer to Parliamentary debates (*see Davis* v. *Johnson* (1978)), though in order to establish the mischief the statute seeks to remedy, they may look at such things as reports of commissions, like the Law Commission — *see Black Clawson International Ltd* v. *Papierwerke Waldhof-Aschaffenburg A.G.* (1975).

(c) penal statutes should be interpreted favourably for persons accused of crimes so as not to conflict with their common-law rights;

(d) a major constitutional change, or a major change in the common law, can be effected only by clear and positive words; in the absence of such words, the courts will presume that no such change is intended;

(e) words should be added or subtracted no more than is absolutely necessary;

(f) ambiguities as to particular words may be resolved by the following rules of construction:

   (i) *ejusdem generis*: where a number of words, all of similar meaning, are followed by one of doubtful meaning, then that word should be interpreted as having a similar meaning to the others;

Example _____

'No tradesman, artificer, workman, labourer *or other person whatsoever*.' It was held in *Gregory* v. *Fearn* (1953) that an estate agent was not included, as being different from 'workmen, labourers, etc.' (Sunday Observance Act 1677).

(*ii*) *Expressio unius est exclusio alterius*: the mention of one word in itself rules out a contrary meaning.

Example ————————————————————————————————

It is an offence to have an unlicensed *motor* vehicle; clearly, any vehicle that is propelled *other* than by a motor is not included — *see R*. v. *Immigration Appeals Adjudicator ex parte Crew* (1982) where a statute included the word 'mother' and was thus interpreted as having excluded the word 'father').

---

32. Influence of jurists

The writings of famous lawyers may influence the development of case law and so constitute an indirect source of law. Generally the writings of jurists long dead have more authority than those of living writers, though today the tendency of the courts is to permit citation of long-approved opinions of living jurists on difficult points of law, e.g. Cheshire, *Private International Law*.

The influence of jurists was greater before law reporting became highly developed in the nineteenth century (*see* 2: **33**). Several famous books have had considerable influence in the development of the common law, e.g.:

(**a**) Bracton, *De Legibus et Consuetudinibus Angliae* (Concerning the Laws and Customs of the English), thirteenth century;
(**b**) Lord Chief Justice Coke, *Institutes and Commentaries*, and his Reports, seventeenth century;
(**c**) Blackstone, *Commentaries*, 1765.

33. Development of law reporting

The efficient working of the doctrine of precedent depends largely on the existence of accurate reports of cases and decisions. To meet this need the Incorporated Council of Law Reporting was established in 1865. The Council publishes detailed reports of cases heard in the superior courts, the reports being made by specially trained barristers and sometimes revised by the judges presiding in the case. In addition, several private firms publish similar series of reports, e.g. the All England Law Reports.

The earliest existing reports were informal notes made by students from the time of Edward I (1272–1307) to Henry VIII (1509–47) and published in a famous unofficial series of Year Books.

These reports are written mainly in Anglo-French and are haphazard and inaccurate. Although interesting historically, they are not now much cited in the courts as containing precedents.

From the sixteenth century onwards, the Year Books were super-seded by a series of reports of varying accuracy published by private reporters, e.g. Lord Chief Justice Coke's Reports (1572–1616) and Sir George Burrow's Reports (1756–72). Reports of this kind, are from time to time, consulted by present-day lawyers and may be cited in court to support legal arguments.

Progress test 2

1. State briefly what you consider to be the chief sources of English law. **(1, 7, 19)**

2. 'Custom is the mother of substantive law.' Discuss this statement. How far can custom be regarded as a living source of law today? **(1–6)**

3. Explain what is meant by the 'sovereignty of Parliament'. How does this doctrine accord with the increase of delegated legislation? **(7, 8, 11, 14)**

4. Summarise some of the chief reforms of the law by legislation during the nineteenth and twentieth centuries and explain what machinery exists for reform today. **(12, 13)**

5. Explain what is meant by subordinate or delegated legislation, and state what advantages or disadvantages you consider this type of legislation possesses. **(14–16)**

6. 'The doctrine of precedent is the cornerstone of English law.' Discuss this statement and explain what is meant by the doctrine of precedent. **(19–25)**

7. How far is it true to say that English law is 'judge made'? **(19–31)**

8. What is the importance of *stare decisis* in the doctrine of precedent? Explain what is meant by: (a) *ratio decidendi* and (b) *obiter dicta*. **(23, 24)**

9. Summarise the rules that govern the interpretation of statutes. **(27–31)**

10. In what ways have eminent jurists influenced the development of English law? **(32)**

3
The judicial system

Introduction

1. General

The judicial system today is organised in the form of a pyramid, with the House of Lords at the apex, the Supreme Court of Judicature below it (consisting of the Court of Appeal, the High Court and the Crown Court) and then the inferior civil and criminal courts (the county courts and magistrates' courts).

The present organisation of the judicial system is based partly on the Judicature Act 1873, and later statutes, and was greatly reformed by the Administration of Justice Act 1970 and the Courts Act 1971. This rationalised the structure overall (as dealt with below) and also abolished various obsolete courts, e.g. the assize courts, quarter sessions, the Bristol Tolzey and 'pie powder' court and the Liverpool Court of Passage, some of which were survivals from the Middle Ages. In addition the old County Palatine Courts of Lancaster and Durham have been merged with the Chancery Division of the High Court.

The 1970 Act was repealed and replaced, and the 1971 Act partly so, by the Supreme Court Act 1981 as amended, which now governs the structure of the Supreme Court. Furthermore, the accession of the United Kingdom to the European Community has meant that in certain limited ways the European Court of Justice is the final court of appeal in some cases (*see* 3: **66**).

The House of Lords

2. Before 1873

In the Middle Ages, the House of Lords had supreme appellate jurisdiction with respect to decisions of the Court of King's Bench as well as some jurisdiction in civil and criminal matters as a court of first instance, as follows:

(a) *civil cases*: after the seventeenth century, the only civil cases decided by the House of Lords at first instance were disputes about peerages and about the privileges of the House (this jurisdiction survives today, but is rarely invoked);

(b) *criminal cases*: the Magna Carta 1215 provided that every free man was entitled to trial by his equals or 'peers', so, a member of the House of Lords charged with a serious criminal offence was entitled to be tried by the Lords and by no other court; this privilege was abolished by the Criminal Justice Act 1948.

3. Appellate Jurisdiction Act 1876

This made the House of Lords Appeals Committee the supreme civil appeal court and, in 1907, it was also made the supreme criminal appeal court by the Criminal Appeal Act 1907.

Jurisdiction today covers:

(a) *civil appeals* to hear appeals from the Scottish Court of Session, the Supreme Court of Northern Ireland and the English Court of Appeal (Civil Division); appeal lies to the House of Lords with leave of the Court of Appeal or of the House of Lords itself.

(b) *criminal appeals* to hear appeals from the Criminal Division of the Court of Appeal, submitted to the Lords with leave of the CA or the House of Lords itself at the insistence of defendant or prosecutor on a point of law of general public importance and, while the House of Lords is the final court of appeal for England and Northern Ireland in criminal matters, the equivalent in Scotland is the Scottish Court of Criminal Appeal.

4. Composition of the court

As one of the three divisions of Parliament, the House consists of hereditary peers, certain bishops of the Church of England and the archbishops, life peers and peeresses, and 11 Lords of Appeal in Ordinary (the 'law lords'), as defined in the Supreme Court Act 1981.

When sitting as a court, however, only the law lords are entitled to participate in the Appeals Committee, together with the Lord Chancellor, the Lord Chief Justice, the Master of the Rolls and any other peer who holds or has held high judicial office, e.g. a former Lord Chancellor. A quorum is any three of these. (Law lords are appointed from among barristers of at least 15 years' standing, and judges of the Supreme Court of at least 2 years' standing and usually they are promoted from amongst the Lords Justices of Appeal — the judges in the Court of Appeal.)

5. Effect of decisions

Decisions of the House of Lords Appeals Committee are absolutely binding on all other courts in the United Kingdom (except the Judicial Committee of the Privy Council) (*see* 2: **23**).

Subject to what was noted above (2: **23**) concerning the European Court of Justice, a decision of the House of Lords can be overruled only by:

(a) an Act of Parliament; or
(b) a subsequent decision of the House of Lords itself.

6. Administration of Justice Act 1969

This Act provided a new right of appeal direct from the High Court to the House of Lords (sometimes referred to as 'leapfrogging') where:

(a) the parties agree and the trial judge grants a certificate;
(b) the trial judge certifies that the case involves a point of law of general public importance that:
    (*i*) relates to the construction of an enactment; or
    (*ii*) is one in respect of which the judge is bound by a precedent laid down by the HL or CA; and
(c) the House of Lords gives leave to appeal.

The Judicial Committee of the Privy Council

7. The Privy Council

This is a remnant of the Royal Council (Curia Regis) of the Middle Ages. Until the seventeenth century it wielded most of the governmental powers now possessed by the Cabinet. Today its duties are largely formal and advisory. It is composed mainly of cabinet ministers and ex-ministers and the law lords and is led by a member of the Cabinet called the Lord President of the Council.

The Privy Council is also a minor source of delegated legislation in the form of Orders in Council. In addition, it issues Royal proclamations by virtue of the Crown's residual prerogative powers, e.g. appointing a Council of Regency to act for the Queen when she is overseas.

8. The Judicial Committee

This consists of the Lord President of the Council (who rarely, in fact, participates), the Lord Chancellor, and a number of Privy

Councillors who hold or have held high judicial office, e.g. the law lords (a quorum is three). The Judicial Committee is the supreme court of appeal:

(a) for Colonies and certain Commonwealth nations that have chosen to preserve this link with London, such as New Zealand, and for appeals from Malaysia;
(b) for the English ecclesiastical courts of the Church of England;
(c) for appeals from medical tribunals; and
(d) for appeals from the Admiralty Court of the QBD on 'prize' matters (captured vessels).

9. Effect of decisions
   A decision of the Judicial Committee is binding on all courts in the territory from which the particular appeal was remitted.
   Its decisions are not binding:

(a) upon territories other than the one from which the appeal came; nor
(b) upon British courts.

This said, its decisions always have great persuasive influence in every Commonwealth country, especially in Britain (as its members are largely the same judges as constitute the House of Lords Appeals Committee — *see De Lasala* v. *De Lasala* (1979)).

The Court of Appeal

10. The Court of Appeal (CA)
   This Court ranks next below the House of Lords in the domestic structure (the JCPC being mainly concerned with Commonwealth matters).
   The CA now has two divisions:

(a) the Civil Division, which hears civil appeals from:
   (*i*) all divisions of the High Court; and
   (*ii*) the county courts;
(b) the Criminal Division, which hears appeals from the Crown Court (*see* 3: **19**).

11. The Civil Division
   The Court is staffed by the Master of the Rolls (MR) and 28 Lords Justices of Appeal (LJJ). In addition, the Lord Chancellor (and former

Lord Chancellors), the Lord Chief Justice, the President of the Family Division and the law lords are *ex officio* members of the court. Also, the Lord Chancellor has power to co-opt High Court judges from time to time. A Court usually consists of three judges, although, under the Supreme Court Act 1981, it is possible for only two to sit. In important cases, a 'full court' may consist of five. A full court is nevertheless bound by previous CA decisions, even if those decisions were reached by only three judges — *see Davis* v. *Johnson* (1978) (2: 23).

Lords Justices are appointed from among High Court judges or eminent barristers of at least 15 years' standing. The jurisdiction of the Civil Division is as follows:

(a) appeals from the High Court (and county courts) on matters of law and of fact (evidence on appeal usually consists of a transcript of that evidence, though fresh evidence may be admitted where deemed appropriate, and the Court may allow or disallow an appeal in whole or in part);

(b) appeals from miscellaneous courts, e.g. the Court of Protection (dealing with mental patients), the Restrictive Practices Court and certain tribunals (such as the Lands Tribunal).

The Court of Appeal will rarely overturn a trial judge's findings of fact. As was stated in *The Julia* (1860), 'we must, in order to reverse, not merely entertain doubts whether the decision below is right, but be convinced that it is wrong'. An award of damages can be overturned where the trial judge is shown to have been wholly erroneous in his assessment. Section 8 of the Courts and Legal Services Act 1990 empowers the Court to make rules permitting the Court of Appeal to substitute damages where a civil jury (e.g. in a defamation action) has awarded an excessive or inadequate sum.

12. The Criminal Division

The Court is composed of the Lord Chief Justice (LCJ) and Lords Justices of Appeal, but the LCJ (in consultation with the Master of the Rolls) may, from time to time, require judges of the Queen's Bench Division of the High Court to join the Court. Decision is by majority vote. A Court usually consists of three judges, sometimes two, and, in certain cases, such as granting leave to appeal, a single Lord Justice may sit.

Grounds for appeal to the CA. include:

(a) on any ground involving a point of law;

(b) by leave of the CA or (rarely) of the trial judge on any ground;
or

(c) against sentence, with leave of the CA only.

The powers of the CA include being able to:

(a) dismiss the appeal; or

(b) allow it or quash the conviction; or

(c) order a new trial where there is new evidence (this last power was provided by the Criminal Justice Act 1948, as amended, and further, according to the 1988 incarnation of the Act, the court can increase the severity of a sentence on a reference from the Attorney General — for example, Attorney General's Reference No. 1, 1989, where a three-year sentence for incest was doubled);

(d) the Attorney General can refer a case for an opinion on a point of law arising from a charge that resulted in an acquittal.

An appeal to the HL is only allowed where:

(a) the CA certifies that a point of law of general importance is involved; and

(b) either the CA or the HL grant leave to appeal (either the accused or the prosecution may appeal).

Decisions made by the CA bind all lower courts and the court will usually abide by its own earlier decisions, unless this would impair civil liberty generally — *see R. v. Gould* (1968). A full court of the criminal division can overrule its own previous decisions.

The Home Secretary can, but rarely does, refer cases to the court of Appeal where other avenues have been exhausted and new evidence has arisen, e.g. concerning the 'Birmingham Six' in 1987 and again in 1991.

The High Court

13. Composition of the High Court
It consists of three divisions:

(a) the Queen's Bench Division;

(b) the Chancery Division; and

(c) the Family Division.

The Courts and Legal Services Act 1990 has considerably affected the distribution of work between the High Court and its inferior, the county court (*see* **21** below).

The Court is staffed by about 80 puisne judges (pronounced 'puny'), appointed from among barristers of at least 10 years' standing as specified in the Supreme Court Act 1981. In addition, the Lord Chancellor may co-opt, when necessary, circuit judges or recorders from time to time.

14. The Queen's Bench Division

The QBD consists of the Lord Chief Justice and about 50 puisne judges.

Its jurisdiction is as follows:

(a) *original jurisdiction* — The QBD is the largest and busiest division of the High Court, with the widest jurisdiction, exercised by several departments:

- (*i*) the 'ordinary court', which deals with all classes of litigation not assigned expressly to other divisions, e.g. actions in tort and contract;
- (*ii*) the Admiralty court, which deals with shipping matters such as salvage and 'prize' disputes (relating to seizure of vessels), as given in the Supreme Court Act 1981;
- (*iii*) the Commercial Court, which deals with certain specialised commercial disputes assigned to it including insurance, banking and the interpretation of mercantile documents such as bills of lading;

(b) *appellate jurisdiction* — 'divisional court' of the QBD (consisting of two or three QBD judges) hears appeals from inferior courts on matters not catered for by the CA (*see* 3: **28**) and, in addition, a single QBD judge may hear appeals from certain administrative tribunals (*see* 3: **45**);

(c) *supervisory jurisdiction* — by means of prerogative orders (*see* 3: **15**).

15. Prerogative orders of the QBD

These are used to ensure control over inferior courts and administrative tribunals and other public bodies exercising judicial or quasi-judicial powers, by way of Judicial Review. This must be specifically applied for under RSC Ord. 53. The orders include the following:

(a) *mandamus* — this is a discretionary order commanding performance of a positive duty rather than a mere discretionary power, e.g. where a tribunal has improperly refused to accept jurisdiction over a case that it is under a legal duty to hear and, although it is not available against the Crown, it may issue to compel a minister to carry out a statutory duty;

(b) *prohibition* — this is an order forbidding an inferior court or tribunal or official from exceeding its jurisdiction and is available against the Crown;

(c) *Certiorari* — this is an order commanding an inferior court or tribunal to bring before the High Court a matter decided or pending in the inferior court or tribunal, so that the High Court may satisfy itself:

(*i*) that no excess of jurisdiction occurs;

(*ii*) that natural justice has not been denied; or

(*iii*) that there is no error on the face of the record;

(d) the QBD may also issue the writ of *habeas corpus*, to secure a prisoner's presence before the court (*see* 4: **47**);

(e) *an award of damages* — this may be made to an applicant for judicial review as well as or instead of the prerogative orders (RSC Ord. 53, r. 7).

16. The Chancery Division

This consists of the Lord Chancellor (who rarely participates) and about 13 puisne judges. (A Vice-Chancellor has now been appointed to control the day-to-day working of the Division, as deputy for the overworked Lord Chancellor under the Supreme Court Act 1981.)

Its jurisdiction is principally over the following matters:

(a) the administration of estates of deceased persons, and contentious probate matters;

(b) partnerships;

(c) mortgages;

(d) trusts;

(e) rectification and cancellation of written instruments;

(f) specific performance of contracts relating to land;

(g) bankruptcy;

(h) most company matters;

(i) revenue matters.

The Chancery Division also has appellate jurisdiction as:

(a) a Divisional Court to hear appeals from county courts on bankruptcy and certain other matters; and

(b) a single Chancery judge hearing appeals from the Commissioners of the Inland Revenue on certain tax matters.

The Chancery Division therefore includes a jurisdiction in those matters that, until its abolition in 1873, were exclusively dealt with in the old Court of Chancery, but, unlike that court, does not administer, exclusively, the 'system' of equity. Wherever necessary, the rules of the common law are used.

17. The Family Division

This consists of the President and about 17 puisne judges whose jurisdiction covers:

(a) non-contentious or formal probate matters;
(b) matrimonial causes, i.e. divorce, nullity, separation, etc;
(c) adoption, legitimacy and guardianship of minors;
(d) cases arising under the Human Fertilisation and Embryology Act 1990.

Appellate jurisdiction covers appeals from:

(a) county courts and magistrates' courts under the Guardian- ship of Minors Acts 1971 and 1973;
(b) juvenile courts in adoption cases.

The full list of the matters dealt with is contained in the Supreme Court Act 1981.

18. The former assize courts

Until they were abolished by the Courts Act 1971, the assizes exercised High Court jurisdiction in criminal and certain civil matters. England and Wales were divided into seven circuits, each of which were toured by two or more judges of the Queen's Bench Division and Probate, Divorce and Admiralty Division three or four times a year. The assizes had equal status in civil and criminal matters with the High Court.

19. The Crown Court

The Courts Act 1971 abolished the old quarter sessional and assize courts, which formerly dealt with indictable offences, and transferred this jurisdiction to the new Crown Court. This consists of a jury and a judge appointed from among High Court judges, circuit judges and recorders (who are barristers or solicitors of at least ten years' standing, acting as part-time judges). Offences dealt with by the Crown Court are divided into four classes, as per the Practice Declaration 1987.

(a) *Class one offences* require to be tried by a High Court judge, i.e. any offence carrying the death penalty, misprision of treason, murder, certain offences under the Official Secrets Act 1911 or any attempt, incitement or conspiracy to commit any of the above;

(b) *Class two offences* are triable by a High Court judge also, but can be released for adjudication by an inferior judge, e.g. manslaughter, infanticide, child destruction, abortion, rape, incest, sedition or any attempt, incitement or conspiracy to commit any of the above;

(c) *Class three offences* can be tried on indictment by a High Court judge, circuit judge or recorder, and include those offences not listed in classes one, two or four. (this is the residuary class);

(d) *Class four offences* are normally tried by a circuit judge or recorder though they may be tried on indictment by a High Court judge, and include wounding, robbery, offences relating to forgery, theft and incitement or conspiracy to commit any of these, as well as all offences triable either way (*see* 25: **8**).

> NOTE: By the powers of the Criminal Courts Act 1973, s.22, where a sentence of two years or less is imposed by any court it may be suspended for a period between one and two years, i.e. the prisoner is released but warned that if he is convicted of another offence during the operational period he may be sentenced for that offence and imprisoned for the earlier offence in respect of which the suspended sentence was awarded. It is also possible to suspend part of a sentence under the Criminal Law Act 1977, as amended.

Inferior civil courts

20. The county courts

These have existed since the Middle Ages, but fell into decay until they were modernised and revived by the County Courts Act 1846, which simplified their procedure and stipulated that county courts must in future be presided over by a judge who should be a barrister of at least seven years' standing, appointed by the Lord Chancellor. These courts are now governed by the County Courts Act 1984, the Courts and Legal Services Act 1990, the High Court and County Courts Jurisdiction Order 1991 and the County Court Rules.

As a result of reorganisation, county court judges have been replaced by circuit judges, each of whom may serve several county courts and may (where necessary) move from one circuit to another. Circuit judges also sit in the Crown Court (*see* 3: **19**). Also CA or High Court judges (and recorders) may act as circuit judges when directed by the Lord Chancellor.

There are now about 300 county courts in England and Wales,

each court being served by a circuit judge (or a deputy). They are distributed around the country on the same principle as post offices — there should be one within relatively easy reach.

Each judge is assisted by a District Judge, appointed by the Lord Chancellor from solicitors of at least seven years' standing. The registrar has, himself, limited judicial authority (where not more than £1,000 is involved). This is particularly important in the 'small claims' arbitration procedure which is increasingly important in the settlement of disputes, such as consumer grievances, of up to £1000.

21. Jurisdiction of the county courts
This covers the following:

(a) actions founded on contract or tort (except defamation);

(b) equity matters, e.g. trusts, mortgages;

(c) actions for recovery of land and questions as to title to land;

(d) probate matters;

(e) bankruptcies (in most courts outside the Metropolitan area);

(f) winding up companies;

(g) supervision of the adoption and guardianship of minors;

(h) some county courts have Admiralty jurisdiction, i.e. those situated in large ports;

(i) some county court judges have authority to act as special commissioners of divorce hearing undefended divorce petitions (for matrimonial causes *see* 3: **22**);

(j) patents: under the Copyright, Designs and Patents Act 1988, certain county courts are designated patent county courts with a view to handling the lesser patent cases without incurring the vast costs involved in High Court litigation;

(k) additional matters remitted by the High Court and matters arising under various statutes, e.g. the Race Relations Act 1976, the Consumer Credit Act 1974 — there are 59 items of such 'special jurisdiction' as this listed in *County Court Practice*.

Between 1985 and 1988, the Lord Chancellor conducted a Civil Justice Review. Many of the recommendations contained within the resulting report have been put into effect by the Courts and Legal Services Act 1990. One important aspect considered was the distribution of the workload of civil cases between the High Court and the county court. There are certain 'criteria' that are taken into account:

(a) the financial substance of the action;

(b) the importance of the action (i.e. to outsiders or to the general public);
(c) the complexity of the facts;
(d) the legal issues;
(e) the remedies or the procedutres involved in the matter;
(f) whether a transfer of the case to the county court is likely to speed up the handling of the case.

Subject to these criteria:

(a) the county court should try any action worth less than £25,000, all personal injury claims under £50,000 and all probate and equity matters under £30,000;
(b) the High Court should handle all matters above £50,000, all applications for judicial review and all applications for *Anton Piller* and *Mareva*-type injuctions;
(c) cases involving claims between £25,000 and £50,000 should be allocated according to the criteria, and, if the High Court thinks that a case should have been brought before the lower court, then a costs penalty can be imposed.

22. Divorce county courts

Under the Matrimonial and Family Proceedings Act 1984, a county court designated by the Lord Chancellor as a 'divorce county court' has jurisdiction in undefended divorce actions. All divorces are now started in the county courts; defended actions are transferred to the Family Division, and even undefended actions may be so transferred.

Divorce county courts also have jurisdiction in ancillary matters, such as variation and enforcement of maintenance agreements and protection of children.

23. Appeals from county courts

In matters of ordinary jurisdiction, appeal lies to the CA on points of law or the admission or rejection of evidence. Bankruptcy appeals go to a Divisional Court of the Chancery Division.

24. Magistrates' and youth courts

Although mainly concerned with criminal matters (*see* 3: **25**), these courts also exercise some civil jurisdiction.

Magistrates courts deal with:

(a) matrimonial (or 'domestic') proceedings concerning separation, maintenance and custody of children;

(b) guardianship of minors;
(c) domestic violence;
(d) enforcement of debts in certain cases; and
(e) licensing matters.

Youth courts deal with adoption and care of minors under 17 years, under the Children Act 1989 and the Criminal Justice Acts 1982 and 1988. (Jurisdiction also extends to criminal offences, excluding homicide.)

Inferior criminal courts

25. Summary and indictable offences

In criminal law, less serious offences are dealt with summarily (at once) by the magistrates in the magistrates courts (known formerly as 'petty sessions'). Where the offence is too serious to be tried summarily in this way, however, the magistrates commit the offender to the Crown Court for trial by a judge and jury. It is then the duty of the magistrates to draw up an indictment stating the charge against the offender and to submit this to the higher court at the trial.

Because of the procedural differences in the method of treatment, less serious offences are called summary offences and more serious ones are called indictable offences. (As to the meaning of 'arrestable offences' *see* 25: 8.)

26. Magistrates courts

These are presided over:

(a) by two or more of the 29,000 or so unpaid lay magistrates ('justices of the peace'), appointed by the Lord Chancellor and assisted by a legally qualified clerk of the court; or
(b) by one stipendiary magistrate appointed by the Lord Chancellor from among solicitors and barristers of at least seven years' standing.

The popularity of the TV character, *Rumpole of the Bailey* has fixed an impression of the nature of criminal proceedings in the public mind. However, the magistrates court is the only court the average individual is likely to be involved with. Over 95 per cent of criminal trials take place there. Well over half of those sent to prison are sent by magistrates.

Magisterial jurisdiction is of two kinds.

(a) *initiatory*, e.g. taking depositions for indictable offences and deciding whether there is a prima-facie case to justify committing the accused upon indictment to the Crown Court (*see* 3: **25**);

(b) *summary*, i.e. deciding upon sentences for petty offences where, in most cases, the maximum penalty is up to a £5,000 fine or 6 months' imprisonment.

There is also a limited civil jurisdiction over matrimonial and domestic disputes, e.g. awarding maintenance to a deserted wife under an order for judicial separation (*see* 3: **24**).

27. Youth courts

These are separate courts presided over by three specially qualified lay magistrates to deal with young offenders, i.e. persons under 17 years. The three are not usually all of the same sex. The public are excluded from proceedings, and the court has summary jurisdiction over all offences by youths, except homicide. The press are also heavily restricted. Also, the Criminal Justice Act 1991 provides for hearings to take place outside normal hours (evenings, Saturdays) when the relevant parent or guardian's employment might be threatened by having to attend at the usual time.

28. Appeals from magistrates courts

Appeals may be made to two higher courts:

(a) *the Crown Court* — in criminal cases against conviction and/or sentence, the local Crown Court will hear the appeal without a jury.
(b) *the Divisional Court of the QBD* — this is done by way of the case being stated on a point of law arising in domestic or criminal proceedings.

29. Coroners' courts

These date from 1194 and are governed largely by the Coroners Act 1988, and are presided over by a specially qualified coroner (sometimes a barrister or solicitor and/or doctor), assisted by a jury. The function of the court is to inquire into the causes of any death where these were not immediately apparent or where the death was violent and unnatural or took place in one of the places listed in the Act, e.g. prison.

The court also holds inquests into the ownership of treasure trove, i.e. coins, bullion or manufactured gold or silver found buried in any land where the owner of such valuables cannot be ascertained or where the ownership is disputed.

30. Justices of the peace

Unpaid magistrates have been a feature of the English legal system since the Middle Ages. Originally they had wide administrative powers as well as judicial functions, e.g. regulating wages and administering the poor law. In the nineteenth century most of these administrative duties were taken from them and conferred instead on local authorities. The JPs' duties are now largely confined to acting as magistrates in the courts described above.

Justices, who may be of either sex, are appointed by the Lord Chancellor, acting on the advice of local committees.

The judiciary

31. The Lord Chancellor (LC)

The Lord Chancellor is appointed by the Crown on the advice of the Prime Minister and is a government minister, speaker of the House of Lords and head of the Judiciary.

As head of the judicial system, the LC is President of the Court of Appeal and of the Chancery Division of the High Court, as well as chairperson of the House of Lords Appeals Committee. He or she is responsible for the appointment of JP's and advises the Crown on the appointment of High Court judges. The position includes a variety of other duties too, e.g. making ecclesiastical appointments.

32. The Lord Chief Justice (LCJ)

The LCJ is appointed by the Crown on the advice of the Prime Minister. He or she is the head of the Court of Appeal (Criminal Division) and of the QBD and is a member of the House of Lords.

33. The Master of the Rolls (MR)

The MR is appointed by the Crown on the advice of the Prime Minister. He or she is the Lord Chancellor's deputy, acting as head of the C.A.. He or she controls the admission of solicitors to the Rolls of the Supreme Court (such admission being necessary before any solicitor can practise).

34. The Lords of Appeal in Ordinary

The Law Lords are appointed by the Crown on the advice of the Prime Minister from among barristers of at least 15 years' standing or from among the existing ranks of judges of at least 2 years' standing. They are life peers and members of the House of Lords and the Judicial Committee of the Privy Council.

35. The President of the Family Division
The President of the Family Division is appointed by the Crown on the advice of the Prime Minster and is head of the Family Division and a member of the Court of Appeal.

36. The Lords Justices of Appeal (LJ, plural LJJ)
They are appointed by the Crown on the advice of the Prime Minister and are judges of the Court of Appeal.

37. Puisne judges of the High Court (J, plural JJ)
They are appointed by the Crown on the advice of the Lord Chancellor, from among barristers of at least ten years' standing, and are assigned to a division of the High Court.

38. Circuit judges
They are appointed by the Crown on the advice of the Lord Chancellor, from among barristers of at least 10 years' standing or recorders of three years' standing.

39. Length of appointment
All judges are appointed *quamdiu se bene gesserint* ('for so long as they are of good behaviour') as per the Act of Settlement 1701. They can be removed from office only for misconduct, by the Crown, upon the advice of both Houses of Parliament in a joint address. Since the Courts Act 1971, judges of the High Court and circuit judges retire at 72 (though the LC may extend this period to 75 in exceptional cases). Circuit judges may be removed from office by the Lord Chancellor for misconduct or incompetence.

40. Judicial immunity
Judges of the High Court and all other superior courts are immune from liability in civil proceedings for anything said or done by them in court.

Special courts

41. Nature of special courts
In addition to the ordinary law courts, there are now a number

of administrative tribunals and domestic tribunals that exercise judicial or quasi-judicial powers.

42. Administrative tribunals

These assist in the administration of Acts of Parliament and delegated legislation and in determining disputes arising from the operation of such legislation. There are now about 2,000 such tribunals. They deal with six or seven times the workload of the civil courts, but the individual rarely has a choice between approaching a court or a tribunal with his or her case. Usually the work has been allocated by Parliament.

Examples

Social Security tribunals Disputes over claims to benefit under the social security legislation, including unemployment benefit, are dealt with, in the first instance, by a local adjudication officer, who will review the decision of the local social security officer. If payment is still refused, the matter can be referred to the local Social Security Appeal tribunal. This consists of three members: one lawyer and two laymen. Further appeals can be made, although leave is required, to a Social Security Commissioner, who is a solicitor or barrister (of at least ten years' standing) appointed by the Crown (*see* the Courts and Legal Services Act 1990, s.71). From the Commissioner, with leave, there is an appeal route to the Court of Appeal and on to the House of Lords.

National Health Service Tribunals A dissatisfied patient can apply to the service committee of his area Family Health Service Authority (FHSA), which will investigate and report with recommendations to the central FHSA. If the committee's decision is to do less than remove the practitioner in question from the service, then both sides have a right to appeal to the minister. If removal is the verdict, then the National Health Service Tribunal will hear the case. There are three members: a lawyer (for at least 10 years), a practitioner and a layman. If the Tribunal agrees with the decision to remove, then an appeal lies to the minister. If it does not, the decision is final. Thus the minister can reverse in favour of a practitioner, but not against him. In fact, although over 2,000 cases are dealt with each year by the Committees, only half a dozen or so reach the Tribunal.

Industrial tribunals Set up to deal with disputes arising under the Contracts of Employment Act 1963 and Redundancy Payments Act 1965, their jurisdiction has increased considerably since the Race Relations Act 1976 and the Sex Discrimination Act 1975 (*see* 4: **28**) as well as the Employment Protection (Consolidation) Act 1978 and a series of other measures including the Employment Act 1990.

The Lands Tribunal This deals with disputes over the valuation of land compulsorily purchased by local authorities and appeals against assessments of the rateable value of property. The Tribunal has a President, who must be a barrister of at least seven years' standing or a person who has held high judicial office; the other eight members must be barristers or solicitors of equal standing or persons with special experience in valuation of land. Appeal lies to the CA on points of law.

Special Commissioners of Income Tax The Commissioners hear appeals against income tax assessments.

Rent Assessment Committees (in some circumstances called Rent Tribunals) assess rents for certain statutorily controlled tenancies, and 'assured tenancies' under the Housing Act 1988.

43. Advantages of administrative tribunals

These were established mainly to save the ordinary courts from unnecessary additional work, to save cost to the citizen, and to provide specialised arbitrators for disputes of a technical nature. The advantages of this are:

(a) expert knowledge is available where needed;
(b) quickness and cheapness of their proceedings;
(c) informality;
(d) wide discretion enables the tribunals to avoid rigid adherence to technicalities.

44. Disadvantages of administrative tribunals

They have been much criticised on the same grounds as the delegated legislation they have been set up to administer (*see* 2: **15**). Their disadvantages include:

(a) unpredictability, arising from the flexibility that is one of their advantages;
(b) secrecy — the public is sometimes excluded from their hearings;
(c) reasons are not always given for their decisions;
(d) there is no legal aid available for representation by professional lawyers in most cases;
(e) appeal facilities are inadequate in some cases;
(f) bias is feared in cases where the members of the tribunal are on the staff of a ministry that may be a party to the dispute before the tribunal (although in fact there is very little evidence of bias in the vast majority of such cases).

45. The Tribunals and Inquiries Act 1971

Because of severe criticism, the Franks Committee was set up to investigate the operation of administrative tribunals and the publication of the committee's report in 1957 led to the passing of an Act to reform some of the more obvious defects.

The Tribunals and Inquiries Act 1958 made the following provisions:

(a) A Council on Tribunals was established, with members to be nominated by the Lord Chancellor. Its function is to examine the personnel and workings of tribunals covered by the Act and such other matters relating to the tribunals as the Lord Chancellor may refer to it from time to time.

(b) Appeal from tribunals to the High Court on points of law was established and cannot be ousted (save by a later Act of Parliament). The High Court can also exercise jurisdiction of a supervisory nature by means of prerogative orders (*see* 3: 15).

(c) Tribunals must give reasons for decisions.

(d) Members of tribunals covered by the Act can be dismissed only with the approval of the Lord Chancellor, thus giving members greater freedom from fear of dismissal.

(e) Chairmen of some tribunals must be appointed by the minister from a panel of suitably qualified persons appointed by the Lord Chancellor.

The 1958 Act and later amendments have now been incorporated into the Tribunals and Inquiries Act 1971.

46. Judicial control of tribunals

By means of prerogative orders, the QBD exercises a general supervisory jurisdiction over tribunals. The court's prime concern is to see that the principles of natural justice have been observed.

These principles of natural justice are vague, but can roughly be stated as follows, insofar as they relate to administrative bodies in general, and tribunals in particular:

(a) no man should be a judge in his own case, as he may be biased in his own favour (this rule covers cases where a minister appoints judges for a tribunal to decide a dispute between himself and a citizen, the courts viewing such appointments with caution);

(b) *audi alterem partem* (hear both sides), i.e. both sides must be given a fair chance to state their views, orally or in writing (depending on the requirements of the particular tribunal);

(c) there must be full investigation of facts.

(d) the tribunal should, wherever possible, give reasons for its decisions (this is now compulsory in many cases under the Tribunals and Inquiries Act 1971).

NOTE: Of these principles, only the first two are usually stated to be 'rules of natural justice' of general application.

47. The *ultra vires* doctrine

A further ground for interference by the courts is that the tribunal has acted beyond its powers (*ultra vires*).

This doctrine also covers the following situations:

(a) excess of authority by any government department or minister;
(b) excess of delegated powers by any local authority or other public body;
(c) a limited company or other corporation exceeding the powers granted to it (but *see* 4: **10**).

Wherever an act is *ultra vires*, it is void and the court may so declare.

48. The Restrictive Practices Court

This was established for the purpose of suppressing such restrictive practices as agreements between suppliers of goods for the maintenance of prices: Restrictive Trade Practices Act 1956, and Resale Prices Act 1964. These Acts have now been consolidated into the Restrictive Trade Practices Acts 1976, as amended.

The court consists of three High Court judges, one judge of the Scottish Court of Session, one judge of the Supreme Court of Northern Ireland, and not more than ten other persons appointed by the Crown on the advice of the Lord Chancellor by reason of their special knowledge. A hearing is presided over by one judge and two of the lay members. The court has the same status as a division of the High Court and appeal lies to the Court of Appeal.

The court hears cases referred to it by the Director General of Fair Trading, with whom all such agreements as fall within the scope of the Act must be registered for scrutiny by the court. If not so registered, all such agreements are void. Once registered, they will be examined by the court and pronounced void unless they appear to be in the public interest.

49. Other special courts

These include ecclesiastical courts, e.g. the Consistory and Provincial Courts of the Church of England (*see* 1: **29**) and courts martial, which enforce discipline in the armed services by applying a special body of military law.

Courts martial consist of military officers advised on points of law by a barrister employed by the office of the Judge Advocate General. Appeal lies to the Courts Martial Appeal Court, which is governed by the Courts Martial (Appeals) Act 1968. Further appeal lies to the House of Lords.

50. Domestic tribunals

These maintain discipline among members of particular trades or professions. Some such tribunals are set up by agreements among the members of an association (e.g. trade union tribunals) and others are established by law (e.g. Solicitors Disciplinary Tribunal (solicitors), and the Disciplinary Committee of the General Medical Council).

The Solicitors Disciplinary Tribunal consists of nine solicitors specially appointed by the Master of the Rolls to deal with complaints of unprofessional conduct by solicitors usually referred to it by the Solicitors Complaints Bureau. The Tribunal normally sits as a panel of three. It may order a solicitor to be 'struck off' the Rolls or suspended from practice for a time or may impose fines. Proceedings are usually private, although, since 1985, it has been able to sit in public. Appeal lies to the Divisional Court of the QBD and thereafter to the CA and the House of Lords as specified in the Solicitors Act 1974.

The Medical Act 1983 gives the Professional Conduct Committee of the General Medical Council power to suspend, make conditional or even erase the registration of a medical practitioner. Here the grounds would be serious professional misconduct or criminal offences. If the complaint concerns fitness for practice in a physical or mental sense, then the Health Committee possesses similar powers. There is, for both of these committees, a Preliminary Committee.

Similar committees exist for dentists as per the Dentists Act 1984; opticians, under the Opticians Act 1958; and vets under the Veterinary Surgeons Act 1966.

Disciplinary tribunals of trade unions are not set up under legal authority, but derive their authority solely from agreement of the members of the union. Their jurisdiction is fixed by the union, and usually includes power to expel a member from the union or impose fines. In *Bonsor* v. *Musicians' Union* (1955) it was established by the House of Lords that if a member is wrongfully expelled he may obtain damages against his union in compensation for any loss sustained as a result of the expulsion. He may even have a statutory right of redress, as given under the Employment Acts 1980 and 1988.

The legal profession

51. Membership of the profession
Judges, barristers and solicitors constitute the three main branches of the profession, although, over the past 30 years or so, legal executives have become increasingly important within the profession and, more recently, licensed conveyaners have appeared. Judges are usually selected from among the higher ranks of barristers, and cannot practise as barristers after their appointment to the judicial bench.

52. Barristers
In the Middle Ages several Inns of Court were established for the training of barristers, i.e. lawyers who conduct and argue cases in court. In 1852 a Council of Legal Education was set up to regulate standards of professional education and this body is today responsible for conducting barristers' qualifying examinations.

Students begin their training by registering in one of the four remaining Inns of Court, i.e. Gray's Inn, Lincoln's Inn, Middle Temple, Inner Temple, and thereafter by passing their Professional exams and then being 'called to the Bar' of their own Inn of Court by the senior members (or 'Benchers') of the Inn. There is a 'dining' requirement, which means that a student must eat dinner at his Inn on at least three occasions during eight 'law terms' of which there are four in a year. This is an outdated burden that reflects those days when students who received little or no formal education while training for the Bar were said to 'eat their way' to becoming barristers.

53. Queen's Counsel (QC)
Since the end of the seventeenth century, the practice has developed of appointing senior barristers as King's Counsel, so as to have a body of eminent barristers available to advise the Crown on law. Appointment as QC (or 'silk') is made by the Lord Chancellor upon the application of the aspirant, on the grounds of seniority and eminence in his or her profession.

Before 1920, QC's could not appear in cases against the Crown without special leave, but this is no longer necessary. The advisory duties of the QC's to the Crown are also largely non-existent today.

In court, QC's are usually assisted by a junior barrister, though in 1977 it was decided that QC's may appear alone. Judges are usually appointed from among QC's.

54. Junior barristers

All barristers other than QCs are called juniors. They are entitled to commence practice as soon as they have been called to the Bar of their Inn, subject to a year's pupillage with a senior barrister (pupil master).

55. Conditions of barristers' work

These are as follows:

(a)   Barristers have exclusive right of audience in the House of Lords, CA, the High Court and JCPC and share with solicitors a concurrent right of audience in all other courts. It has recently been proposed that their exclusive right of audience in the higher courts be removed.

(b)   Barristers cannot sue for fees owing to them because traditionally they were regarded as 'gentlemen' and not in need of payment — although there has always been a pocket (called a 'fee bag') in the back of a barrister's gown, intended for the use of grateful clients. Instructing solicitors pay barrister's fees. Since the decision in *Rondel* v. *Worsley* (1967) HL, barristers have enjoyed an immunity from liability to actions in negligence brought by their clients. However, this immunity is strictly confined to work that 'is intimately connected with the conduct of the case in court' — *see Saif Ali* v. *Sydney Mitchell* (1978) HL. This immunity at common law has now been embodied in statute form in the Courts and Legal Services Act 1990, s.62.

(c)   A barrister can only be briefed by a solicitor or, for non-court business, a patent agent. This rule may soon be relaxed. Generally the solicitor is entitled to be present at any interview between the barrister and the client.

56. Solicitors

The ancient professions of attorneys, proctors and solicitors were unified and regulated by a succession of Solicitor's Acts 1839–1974. These Acts established solicitors as officers of the Supreme Court, and set up a Law Society, which supervises their training and discipline.

Training is commenced by the student becoming articled to a practising solicitor for a period of between two and five years, depending upon initial qualifications. In fact, most students are graduates. The majority are law graduates and they will serve for two years after having completed and passed the examination of the Legal Practice Course. A graduate in an area other than law will need to complete the 'academic stage' by means of a common professional examination or a diploma in law. Then the aspiring solicitor will be admitted to the Rolls of the Supreme Court and receive his licence to practise.

57. Position of solicitors
This is as follows:

(a) unlike barristers, they are officers of the court;

(b) unlike barristers, they do not generally appear as advocates in the superior courts, although under the Courts and Legal Services Act 1990 they will have the right to; they are frequently seen in the inferior courts, i.e. county and magistrates courts, and also in the Crown Courts in some matters.

(c) they can sue for their fees and are liable for actions for professional negligence by their clients;

(d) solicitors are primarily con- cerned with office work, e.g. drafting documents and advising generally; barristers are primarily concerned with advocacy in cases in court, but, in practice, many solicitors specialise in advocacy in cases in the inferior courts and some barristers specialise in paperwork, drafting documents, etc. (there are around 70,000 soliciotrs and 7,000 barristers);

(e) until recently, professional solicitors enjoyed a monopoly over the professional conveyancing of property, but the combined effect of the Administration of Justice Act 1985 and the Building Societies Act 1986 has been to create a new profession — that of the licensed conveyancer, and under the Courts and Legal Services Act 1990, this is extended further to 'authorised conveyancing practitioners'.

58. Discipline of the profession
Discipline of solicitors is in the hands of the Solicitors Disciplinary Tribunal (*see* 3: **50**).

Discipline of barristers is in the hands of the Senate of the four Inns of Court, which is appointed from among judges and senior barristers, and the Disciplinary Tribunal. (The Bar is less regulated by statute than the solicitorial side of the profession, e.g. Bencher's tribunals have no statutory constitution.)

59. Institute of Legal Executives
The Institute was established in 1963 to give professional status to solicitors' clerks who are not themselves admitted solicitors, but who bear responsibility in advising clients for their solicitor employers. Admission to the Institute is by examination, leading first to Associateship, and then to Fellowship. Fellows of the Institute have been granted certain (restricted) rights of audience in open court in

county courts under the County Courts Act 1984. These are widened under the Courts and Legal Services Act 1990.

Legal aid

60. Legal advice and assistance

Preliminary legal advice and assistance can be obtained by persons with low incomes under the Legal Aid Act 1988. This scheme is known as the 'Green Form Scheme'. In 1987 a new scheme of advice was created. It is called the Accident Legal Aid Scheme, but it is known as ALAS. Here, victims of accidents of all kinds may consult a solicitor free of charge for advice as to whether it is worth pursuing a claim. This is a voluntary scheme. The Law Society hope that the business it creates as a consequence of such free consultations will pay for them!

61. Legal aid in civil cases

Assistance is available under the Legal Aid Act 1988 to enable a party to bring civil proceedings to court. The system is administered by the Legal Aid Board and local Legal Aid Committees consisting of solicitors and barristers. Eligibility for legal aid depends on the applicant's disposable income and capital, and funds are provided by the Treasury through the Legal Aid Fund.

Legal aid will not be granted unless the Committee thinks the applicant has a reasonable case in law.

62. Legal aid in criminal cases

Legal aid is available now for all criminal proceedings, from the magistrates court to the House of Lords. As in civil proceedings, the applicant may be called on to provide some of the costs himself, as per the Legal Aid Act 1988.

NOTE: **Dock Briefs** By an ancient tradition, a prisoner in the dock could choose any barrister robed and present in the Crown Court to defend him. The barrister so chosen was bound to accept the brief at a nominal fee. This system was abolished in 1980.

63. The Crown Prosecution Service

The Prosecution of Offenders Act 1985 created a Crown Prosecution Service for England and Wales. It had been felt for a long time that there should be such a service, independent of the police, who had hitherto been responsible for bringing the bulk of prosecutions to court, as well as investigating offences and generally enforcing the law. The service is headed by the Director of Public Prosecutions (DPP). Below him are Chief Crown Prosecutors, each responsible for a designated area, and then other Crown Prosecutors. They are solicitors or barristers.

Arbitration

64. Arbitration

Commercial agreements now frequently contain an 'arbitration clause', under which in the event of any dispute arising between the parties to the contract (rather than go to the expense of suing each other in court) the dispute is to be referred to one or more arbitrators for informal settlement under the Arbitration Acts 1950 and 1979.

Arbitrators may be appointed from any suitable persons selected by the disputants at the time (or nominated in advance in the contract) or by a particular statute authorising arbitration as the appropriate way of settling particular types of dispute.

The advantages of arbitration as a way of settling disputes are:

(a) cheapness (by comparison with litigation in the courts);
(b) informality;
(c) speed and accessibility;
(d) privacy (particularly important for large business concerns).

Any person can be an arbitrator, if acceptable to the disputants, but in practice arbitrators are usually selected from among lawyers or other professionals (who are chosen for their specialised knowledge in the field of the dispute) and are frequently members of the Institute of Arbitrators (a body composed of professional arbitrators). Ordinary judges may act as arbitrators, e.g. a judge of the Commercial Court of the QBD.

65. Conduct of arbitrations

Reference to arbitration under the Arbitration Act 1950 may be made either by a court order, by a particular statute or by agreement of the disputants. A court will not usually entertain proceedings in connection with any matter covered by an 'arbitration agreement' unless:

(a) the dispute is outside the scope of the agreement; or
(b) there are grounds to believe that arbitration would operate

unfairly, as per the Arbitration Act 1950, s. 24, as amended by the Arbitration Act 1979.

The Arbitration Act 1950 (as amended) implies the following clauses into arbitration agreements, unless expressly excluded:

(a) reference is to a single arbitrator, unless otherwise stated (if reference is to two arbitrators, they must appoint an umpire to decide between them by a casting vote);

(b) examination on oath — parties to arbitration must be prepared to submit to examination on oath and must produce necessary documents, etc., as in judicial proceedings and witnesses may also have to submit to examination on oath;

(c) the arbitrator's award is final and binding so the courts will not set it aside unless bias or fraud can be proved, or some other exceptional cause;

(d) arbitrators can order specific performance, except in relation to contracts concerning land;

(e) the parties may alter the arbitration agreement by mutual consent, but the arbitrator cannot do so on his own;

(f) time for making the award may be fixed by the agreement, but otherwise a reasonable time is implied;

(g) death or bankruptcy of any party to an arbitration does not affect the validity of the agreement or the arbitrator's authority;

(h) an arbitration agreement may be revoked by the court if the arbitrator shows bias or there is any question of fraud in the dispute.

66. The European Court of Justice

The accession of the United Kingdom to the European Community on 1 January 1973 has necessitated consideration of the European Court in the context of the English legal system.

Two separate issues are involved:

(a) *The Treaty* As this was a purely executive act, our courts are not bound by the Treaty's provisions as such: 'we take no notice of treaties until they are embodied in laws enacted by Parliament', Lord Denning, MR, in *Blackburn* v. *A-G* (1971).

(b) *European Communities Act 1972* The passing of this statute meant that 'all rights, powers, liabilities, obligations and restrictions . . . under the Treaties, and all remedies and procedures under the Treaties . . . are to be given legal effect in the United Kingdom'. By virtue of this statute:

(*i*) certain provisions become part of, and even prevail over, English law — *see Coomes* v. *Shields* (1978);

(*ii*) matters relating to the meaning or effect of the Treaties, or of any other Community instrument must be referred to the European Court, or, if not, decided in accordance with the principles laid down in that court, which is stated in s.3(1).

Thus, in matters with a 'European element', the decisions of the European Court of Justice should be followed by United Kingdom courts; in any case, European law is enforced by the English courts.

The European Court will not, however, hear an action that is not referred to it by a national court; though under Article 177 of the Treaty, a court 'against whose decisions there is no judicial remedy' *must* refer questions such as those given above to the European Court. As this is a 'procedure provided under the Treaty', then it is within the scope of the Act, s. 2(1).

67. Constitution of the European Court

The Court has 13 judges and 6 Advocates-General:

(a) the judges are appointed every six years (one judge tends to come from each of the member states, plus one extra so as to avoid an equally divided court) and all judges in the Court are eligible for the highest judicial office in their respective countries, though they need not have actually sat as judges in domestic courts or are jurisconsults (legal advisers);

(b) Advocates-General are similarly qualified to judges; their job, however, differs in that they give opinions, which are meant to state the issue and viewpoint of the point of European law involved in a case;

(c) in 1989 a first instance court was set up to deal with staff disputes and certain competition matters and its purpose is to reduce the heavy workload on the European Court, although an appeal route lies to that Court from the new one.

68. The European Convention on Human Rights 1950

Under this international convention a Commission and Court of Human Rights was established. These are not to be confused with the institutions of the EC and are quite separate.

The work of the Commission and of the Court depends upon the acceptance, on the part of states, of their jurisidiction. The United Kingdom has recognised their jurisdiction and, therefore, an individual who alleges a breach of the terms of the Convention (which safeguards human rights) on the part of the British government or its agents can apply to the Commission to bring his case before the Court, whose rulings will be accepted in Britain.

Progress test 3

1. State the composition and jurisdiction of the following courts: (a) House of Lords, (b) Court of Appeal, (c) Judicial Committee of the Privy Council and (d) Chancery Division of the High Court. **(3, 4, 8, 11, 12, 16)**

2. Explain briefly the original and appellate jurisidiction of the Queen's Bench Division of the High Court. **(14, 15)**

3. Explain the binding effect of decisions of: (a) the House of Lords, (b) the Court of Appeal and (c) the judicial Committee of the Privy Council. **(5, 9, 11, 12)**

4. Outline the jurisdiction of the Family Division of the High Court. **(17)**

5. Distinguish between summary and indictable offences and explain the functions of the magistrates' courts. **(25, 26)**

6. State what you know about the following: (a) Lord Chancellor, (b) Lord Chief Justice, (c) Master of the Rolls and (d) law lords. **(31–34)**

7. What is meant by saying that judges are appointed *quamdiu se bene gesserint*? **(39, 40)**

8. What were the main provisions of the Tribunals and Inquiries Act 1971? **(45)**

9. What do you understand to constitute the main principles of natural justice? **(46)**

10. Explain briefly the *ultra vires* doctrine. **(47)**

11. Explain the composition and functions of the Restrictive Practices Court. **(48)**

12. What is meant by a domestic tribunal? Give examples. **(50)**

13. Summarise the differences between barristers, solicitors and legal executives. **(51–59)**

14. Outline the jurisdiction and constitution of the European Court of Justice. **(67, 68)**

4

The law of persons

Legal personality

1. Meaning of legal personality

A person in law means any entity accepted by the law as having certain defined rights and obligations. Such persons may be natural (human beings) or artificial (corporations).

2. Corporations

A corporation is an artificial person composed of one or several natural persons. The corporation is recognised by the law as having a separate personality from its human members — *see Salomon* v. *Salomon and Co. Ltd* (1897) HL.

3. Kinds of corporation

A corporation sole is one that consists of one human member only at any one time or of the successive holders of certain offices, e.g. bishops, the Crown, the Public Trustee.

Corporations aggregate consist of many members simultaneously, e.g. limited companies. Corporations aggregate are of three kinds, classified according to the method of their creation:

(a) chartered or common law corporations (*see* 4:4);
(b) statutory corporations (*see* 4: 5);
(c) registered corporations (companies) (*see* 4: 6).

4. Chartered corporations

These are incorporated by the grant of a Royal Charter, creating the corporation and setting out its objects etc., e.g. the Chartered Institute of Secretaries, the Hudson's Bay Company.

This kind of corporation was the earliest known to the law but is increasingly rare because cheaper and easier methods of incorporation now exist.

The *ultra vires* doctrine (*see* 4: 10) does not apply to chartered corporations, but, if such a corporation exceeds the powers granted in its charter this may be grounds for withdrawal of the charter. Procedure in such cases is for the Attorney General to issue a writ of *scire facias* ('to know why you are doing . . .') demanding to know why the corporation has acted in the way complained of. Failing a satisfactory answer, the charter may be withdrawn by the Crown — *see Baroness Wenlock* v. *River Dee Co.* (1887).

5. Statutory corporations

These are incorporated by special Act of Parliament, a method largely used during the nineteenth century for the incorporation of railway companies but now increasingly rare. This method of incorporation today is used to set up public utilities and controlling bodies for the nationalised industries, e.g. the National Coal Board (set up by the Coal Industry Nationalisation Act 1946) and the British Railways Board (set up by the Transport Act 1962).

(The *ultra vires* doctrine does apply to statutory corporations.)

6. Registered companies

These are incorporated merely by registration in the manner laid down by the Companies Act 1985 (or one of the earlier similar Acts). Registration is effected by depositing certain documents at the office of the Registrar of Companies, e.g.:

(a) the memorandum of association, which sets out the capital and objects of the company;
(b) the articles of association, which set out the rules governing the relations of the members among themselves and of the company to the members;
(c) various declarations by persons concerned in the promotion or direction of the proposed company to the effect that the statutory requirements have been complied with.

The vast majority of companies incorporated today are registered companies and, of these, most are limited by shares (*see* 4: **7**(*a*)). There are now the best part of a million companies registered under the Companies Acts.

(The *ultra vires* doctrine does not apply to registered companies.)

7. Kinds of registered companies

These are as follows:

(a) *limited companies*, i.e. companies in which the liability of members to pay the debts of the company is limited:

(*i*) to the amount unpaid on their shares, if any (companies limited by shares); or

(*ii*) to the amount guaranteed by the members as their contribution towards the company's debts and payable if the company is wound up (companies limited by guarantee) — guarantee companies are comparatively rare and, where they exist, they frequently also have a share capital;

(b) *unlimited companies*, i.e. companies in which the liability of the members to pay the debts of the company is unlimited — these companies are rare nowadays and are formed mainly in cases where the company is intended to be non-trading, non-profit-making, e.g. companies formed for furtherance of artistic or educational purposes.

8.   Public and private companies

Under the provisions of the Companies Act 1985 (as amended) the minimum number of people who may form a company is two, although there is a EC Directive permitting single-member companies. There are two main classes of companies: public and private. A company will be private unless:

(a) its memorandum of association states that it is to be public, and includes 'public limited' (or PLC) in the company name; and

(b) the nominal value of its allotted share capital is at least £50,000 with 25 per cent of the nominal value and the whole of any premium paid up. The Registrar of Companies must certify his satisfaction of this capitalisation before the company can begin to trade.

9.   Consequences of incorporation

These are:

(a) the corporation or company can then be sued in its own name, and can sometimes be prosecuted for criminal offences, e.g. tax evasion, and similarly, it can sue in its own name;

(b) once incorporated, the company forms a legal personality, separate and distinct from the personalities of its members, whom it can therefore sue and who can sometimes sue it and with whom it can make contracts, etc. — *see Salomon* v. *Salomon & Co. Ltd* (1897);

(c) the corporation can, within the limits of its powers, trade like an ordinary individual;

(d) the corporation can make contracts in its own name, in any form, through human agents;

(e) the corporation can generally own and dispose of property like an ordinary individual.

10. The *ultra vires* doctrine

This doctrine runs throughout the law. It is important in constitutional and administrative law (*see* 3: **47**).

In the context of company law it indicates that an action taken by a company lies 'beyond the powers' given to it by the incorporating statute or registered within its memorandum of association. However, the Companies Act 1985, s. 35, as amended by the Companies Act 1989 has radically altered the position (*see* 6:**9**).

11. Unincorporated associations

These differ from corporate bodies in that they do not have a legal personality distinct from the members of the association. They include trade unions and most societies and clubs (*see*, e.g., *Blackpool Marton Rotary Club* v. *Martin* (1988).)

12. Legal position

The law generally disregards the association and treats it as simply a group of persons, who are thus individually responsible for the association's actions — *see Brown* v. *Lewis* (1896) and *Jones* v. *Northampton Borough Council* (1990).

Exceptions:

(a) where a large number of persons have the same common interest in one case in court, the court or they may depute one or some of their numbers to sue or be sued on behalf of all of them — as given in the Rules of the Supreme Court, Order 15, r. 12;

(b) since the Law of Property Act 1925 forbids more than four people to own land together, such associations must nominate four of their number to hold land as trustees on behalf of the association and the trustees are then the legal owners of the land and can sue or be sued on behalf of the association.

(c) the association may, by express or implied contract, delegate powers to a committee to govern the association as a whole and, for instance, to hold a domestic disciplinary tribunal, e.g. the Stewards of the Jockey Club.

13. Trade unions

These were unlawful until legalised by the Trade Union Act 1871 and permitted to register an association name. They can sue or be sued in their own name. Trade unions were once largely immune from actions in tort. However, under the Employment Act 1982 (as amended by the Employment Act 1990), when a claim lies for inducing or threatening breach of contract or conspiring to commit a tort, then the union could, in certain circumstances, face liability in tort.

Furthermore, immunity is removed if no ballot is held before calling a strike, as per the Trade Union Act 1984; and the ballot should be postal, as stated in the Employment Act 1988. Under the Employment Act 1990, virtually all secondary action (i.e. not against the employer) is illegal, exposing the trade union to tortious liability.

14. Partnerships

A partnership is, according to s. 1 of the Partnership Act 1890, 'the relationship which subsists between persons carrying on a business in common with a view of profit'. A firm, or partnership, has no separate legal personality distinct from its members.

Rules governing partnerships are laid down by the Partnership Act 1890.

Examples

(1) Partners are agents for the firm in furthering the partnership business. The firm is therefore legally liable upon contracts made or torts committed by a partner on its behalf.

(2) For convenience, partners may sue or be sued in the firm's name.

(3) If a person who is not a partner allows outsiders to think he is a partner in a firm, he may be liable to such outsiders as though he were really a partner.

(4) If a firm trades under a name other than that of the partners who compose it (e.g. Smith & Jones trading as 'Smones & Co.'), that name cannot end with the word 'limited' (Companies Act 1985). Furthermore, the use of such 'business names' is controlled by the Business Names Act 1985. This generally requires the disclosure (on business premises and stationery) of the names of the partners.

(5) A firm is dissolved:
  (*i*)   by the expiry of any agreed period;
  (*ii*) by the completion of the particular undertaking for which it was formed;
  (*iii*) by death or bankruptcy of any partner;
  (*iv*) by mutual agreement; or
  (*v*)   by order of the court.

(6) Partners are jointly liable on the firm's contracts and jointly and severally liable for the firm's torts.

(7) Rights of the partners are governed by the partnership articles (if any)

or, if there are no articles, then by the Partnership Act 1890. Under the Act, partners are entitled to:

(*i*) share management;

(*ii*) invest equally and share profits equally; and

(*iii*) to settle disputes by majority vote.

Unless the articles expressly so provide, a partner is not entitled to receive remuneration for work done on behalf of the firm.

(8) A partner's liability may be limited to an agreed sum, if the other partners agree. A firm containing one or more partners whose liability for the firm's debts is limited in this way is a limited partnership and must be registered as such under the Limited Partnership Act 1907. Such a partnership must have at least one 'general' partner, i.e. one whose liability is unlimited. Limited partners cannot participate in the management of the firm without losing their limitation liability.

(9) Generally a firm will be limited to a maximum of 20 partners. Under the Companies Act 1985, however, solicitors, accountants and those making a market in the Stock Exchange can exceed 20 members. Further, regulations can enable other professional firms to exceed the limit, such as patent agents, actuaries, surveyors, auctioneers, estate agents and consulting engineers. Also, Partnerships (Unrestricted size) No. 9 Regulations 1992 extends the list to cover member firms of the International Stock Exchange.

Nationality and domicile

15. Status

The status of a person means his or her rank in society. In the Middle Ages there were many different ranks, from slave and serf up to peers of the realm; the duties and privileges of each rank were carefully defined. The tendency of the law has been towards the abolition of different grades of status. Now all adults have virtually equal status, but minors are still subject to certain incapacities intended for their protection.

Married women were formerly subject to similar incapacities to those of minors, on the supposition that they were incapable of protecting themselves, but these incapacities have been gradually abolished by the Married Women's Property Act 1882 and Law Reform (Married Women and Tortfeasors) Act 1935, for example.

Recent legislation has ensured that all women, married or single, may enjoy the same rights as men with regard to employment, etc., including the Equal Pay Act 1970 and Sex Discrimination Act 1975.

16. Nationality

This implies allegiance to a particular state. With the exception of some persons, who have become stateless because of some political upheaval in their own country, every person must owe allegiance to some state. The state to which the allegiance is owed is under a reciprocal duty to protect the subject, though a person who is temporarily in the UK, but who is not a national, owes what is known as 'local' allegiance, and is therefore owed protection — *see Johnstone* v. *Pedlar* (1921).

17. Domicile

This means the place where a person permanently resides, e.g. resides with *animus manendi* (intention of remaining), even for a short while. Thus, a French national who, with *animus manendi*, resides in Britain, may retain his French nationality while acquiring a British domicile. Note that length of residence is unimportant; it is the intention that matters. Thus, every person, even stateless persons, must have a domicile. However, an intention *eventually* to live and work in a particular country is not enough — *see Plummer* v. *I.R.C.* (1988).

18. Kinds of domicile

These include the following:

(a) *domicile of origin*, acquired at birth by a child. A legitimate child inherits his father's domicile and an illegitimate child his mother's. The law presumes that a person retains his domicile of origin all his life, until the contrary is proved.

(b) *domicile of choice*, acquired where an adult voluntarily relinquishes his domicile of origin by taking up residence in some other country with *animus manendi*.

(c) *domicile of dependence*, acquired by a child whose parents change their domicile by their own choice. Here the child's domicile changes with that of the parents.

Substantial changes in the modern law on this subject were made by the Domicile and Matrimonial Proceedings Act 1973.

19. Importance of domicile

It is important to discover a person's domicile in order to ascertain what system of law will govern certain matters. His *lex domicilii* (law of the domicile) governs:

(a) the jurisdiction of the courts in matters of divorce, the validity of his marriage and other aspects of everyday life such as taxation — *see I.R.C.* v. *Bullock* (1976);

(b) the legitimation of bastards;
(c) the validity of wills of movable property.

20. British Nationality Act 1981

For the purposes of defining issues relating to British nationality, the (extremely complicated) 1981 Act creates six classes. The first four are also included in the category 'Commonwealth citizens': British citizens, British Dependent Territories citizens, British Overseas citizens and British subjects. The other two classes make up the six: British Protected persons and certain citizens of the Republic of Ireland.

It follows that those who are neither Commonwealth citizens nor within these last two classes are aliens.

21. Acquisition of British citizenship

This can be acquired in the following ways:

(a) *by birth* within the United Kingdom to a British parent or to one who is ordinarily resident in the UK;
(b) *by adoption* by a British citizen;
(c) *by descent*, if the person is the child of a father who was a UK citizen himself (other than by descent), the child automatically acquires British nationality by descent, wherever born;
(d) *by registration* in accordance with the provisions of the 1981 Act, which include the restricted ability of an alien wife of a British citizen to obtain British citizenship by registration;
(e) *by naturalisation* which means, any adult may apply for a certificate of naturalisation as a British citizen to the Secretary of State, on condition that they take the oath of allegiance to the Crown and meet certain other detailed requirements.

22. Duties of British subjects

These are:

(a) to serve the state when required, e.g. as a juror;
(b) To assist the police in maintaining order and quelling disturbances (refusal to do so is a punishable offence — *see R* v. *Brown* (1841));
(c) to pay rates and taxes;
(d) to register births and deaths of members of their family;
(e) to see that children of the family attend school;
(f) to obey the general laws of the kingdom.

23. British nationality may be lost
This occurs in the following cases.

(a) *Declaration of renunciation* must be registered with the Secretary of State in order to be effective;

(b) *Deprivation of citizenship* by the Home Secretary in the case of citizens naturalised within the past five years, on the grounds of treasonous or seriously criminal conduct (where obtained by any process other than naturalisation, citizenship cannot be withdrawn in this way).

24. Immigration Acts
The social problems occasioned by unrestricted immigration from the Commonwealth led to the enactment of laws designed to limit immigration. Under the Acts of 1962 and 1968, the power to refuse admission to any Commonwealth citizen, except for those born in the UK or holding UK passports, was given to immigration officers.

Immigration officers were also given the power to impose conditions upon entry. The 1962 Act gave powers of deportation of Commonwealth citizens to the Home Secretary, and the 1968 Act made it an offence to land in Britain otherwise than in accordance with immigration regulations.

Immigration could not, however, be refused if the immigrant could show that:

(a) one of his parents or grandparents was born, naturalised or adopted in the United Kingdom (or, of course, if he himself was); or

(b) he is self-supporting; or

(c) he is going into employment approved by the Department of Employment.

The Commonwealth Immigration Acts 1962 and 1968 were repealed by the Immigration Act 1971. This Act is a comprehensive one and is now itself amended by the British Nationality Act 1981. It deals with the regulation of entry and stay in the United Kingdom of aliens as well as Commonwealth citizens. Section 2 of the Immigration Act refers to the 'right of abode'. Everyone having that right is free to live in, work in, and come and go freely from the UK; people who do not have that right are subject to control.

The Immigration Act 1988 addresses itself to wives within polygamous marriages. Woman within such marriages are denied a right to abode if there is another woman living who is the wife or widow of the same husband and who has been in the UK since the marriage or has been granted a certificate of entitlement to a right of abode.

25. Those lacking the right of abode (aliens)

Such people must obtain leave to enter the UK. If it is granted, conditions can be attached, such as duration, the right to work and the requirement to register with the police.

They can be deported for breach of such conditions, by a court if they commit an offence punishable with imprisonment, or simply because the Secretary of State deems deportation to be in the public interest. The family of a deportee can be deported with him (or her).

26. EC Nationals

It is necessary to consider nationals of European Community countries as a special category. Article 48 of the EC Treaty gives rise to the right of workers to migrate freely from one member state to another and such workers, as well as their families, may only be refused entry or deported from a state on grounds of the public interest. Public interest was held to have justified the refusal to admit a Dutch member of the Church of Scientology in *Van Duyn* v. *Home Office* (1975). The Immigration Act 1988 provides that, in general, the need for leave to enter or remain will be waived in the cases of those who do so using enforceable European Community rights.

27. Race relations and sex discrimination

The Race Relations Act 1976, the Equal Pay Act 1970 and Sex Discrimination Acts 1975 and 1986 saw the establishment of two Commissions, one for racial equality and the other for equal opportunities, whose function it is to enforce the Acts and promote equality of opportunity. The purpose of the Acts is to prevent discrimination on racial or sexual grounds and to ensure equal opportunities for all, irrespective of colour or sex, in such matters as employment and remuneration, as well as the obtaining of services, housing and education. The Sex Discrimination and Race Relations Acts are broadly similar, defining the remedies available in cases involving discrimination. Claims relating to employment should be made to an industrial tribunal and those relating to education, housing and comparable matters to the county court (*see* 3: **21**).

28. Public Order Act 1986

Under Part III of the 1986 Act there are a number of offences listed that refer to stirring up racial hatred, i.e. 'hatred against a group of persons in Great Britain defined by reference to colour, race, nationality (including citizenship) or ethnic or national origins'. These include the use of words or behaviour or the display of written material; the publishing or distribution of written material; the public performance of plays; the distribution, showing or playing of recordings; the broadcasting or inclusion of programmes in a cable service; and simply the possession of racially inflammatory material.

Marriage

29. Husband and wife

Marriage is 'the voluntary union for life of one man and one woman to the exclusion of all others', said Lord Penzance in *Hyde* v. *Hyde* (1866). Marriage in Britain is monogamous, but polygamous unions contracted overseas by foreign nationals may be recognised as valid by the British courts.

30. Capacity to marry

A party domiciled in England or Wales must have capacity according to English law, which requires the following:

(a) neither party must be under 16;

(b) neither party must be already married (unless the earlier marriage has been legally dissolved);

(c) neither party must have been certified insane at the time of marriage;

(d) one party must be male and the other female and the sex of a party is 'fixed at birth', so a man who undergoes a 'sex change' operation cannot marry a man — *see Corbett* v. *Corbett* (1971);

(e) neither party must be within the 'prohibited degrees', i.e. related so closely that the law forbids them to inter-marry, e.g. brothers and sisters (these 'prohibited degrees' are set out in the first Schedule to the Marriage Act 1949, as amended by the Marriage (Prohibited Degrees of Relationship) Act 1986).

31. Marriage by the Church of England

A marriage can be solemnised by the Church of England only where:

(a) a special licence has been issued by the Archbishop of Canterbury or other authorised person, specified by the Ecclesiastical Licences Act 1533; or

(b) a common licence has been issued by a bishop or his surrogate (deputy) for the marriages of persons residing within his diocese within three months of the issue of the licence, as given in the Marriage Act 1949; or

(c) a certificate has been issued by a superintendent registrar (*see* 4: **32**(*b*)) and such a certificate may be used, under the Marriage Act 1983, to permit the marriage of those who are housebound or in hospital or in prison;

(d) banns have been published (i.e. a public announcement made) on three successive Sundays preceding the marriage in a church authorised by the bishop for the purpose and for the celebration of marriages, in the parish in which one or both of the parties reside.

Church of England marriages must be solemnised in the presence of two or more witnesses in addition to the clergyman, between the hours of 8.00 a.m. and 6.00 p.m. as given in the Marriage Act 1949.

32. Marriage by other means

The following marriages may be solemnised on the authority of a superintendent registrar's certificate.

(a) a marriage in a registered building, in such form and ceremony as the parties see fit to adopt;

(b) a marriage in the office of the superintendent registrar;

(c) a marriage according to the usages of the Society of Friends (Quakers);

(d) a marriage between two professing Jews according to the usages of the Jewish religion;

(e) a marriage according to the usages of the Church of England (*see* 4: **31**).

In each case, the marriage must take place in the registrar's office or in a building approved by him. The registrar's certificate of authority to marry remains valid for three months. Two witnesses must be present at the ceremony and the marriage must be celebrated by a person licensed for the purpose or by the registrar, and the doors of the building must remain open throughout so as to allow public access, as specified in the Marriage Act 1949.

33. Legal consequences of marriage
These are chiefly as follows.

(a) The parties should co-habit unless separated by agreement or by a decree of judicial separation from a court.

(b) The husband must normally support the wife financially, in a style fitted to his income. She loses this right if she deserts her husband or if the marriage is dissolved or annulled. Her adultery is no longer an automatic bar (Domestic Proceedings and Magistrates Courts Act 1978), although it remains a factor to be taken into account. At common law a wife was under no obligation to support her husband, but now the wife may in certain circumstances, be bound to assist the husband financially (Matrimonial Causes Act 1973).

(c) Disputes as to property between spouses may be settled by the High Court or county court, as stated in the Married Women's Property Act 1882, s. 17. (Under the Matrimonial Homes Act 1983, the court may give a spouse a right of occupation of the matrimonial home, even if it belongs legally to the other spouse.)

(d) One spouse can now be prosecuted for stealing from the other under the Theft Act 1968.

(e) Spouses can now sue each other in contract and tort, though the court may stay any such tort action where it appears desirable (Law Reform (Husband and Wife) Act 1962).

34. Nullity
A marriage is null and void (i.e. regarded by the courts as never having taken place) where:

(a) one of the parties is already married;

(b) the parties are not respectively male and female (*see* 4: **30**);

(c) the requirements of the Marriage Acts 1949–1983 have not been complied with, which requirements relate to:

   (*i*) capacity (*see* 4: **30**); and

   (*ii*) formalities as to solemnisation (*see* 4: **31, 32**).

These provisions are contained in the Matrimonial Causes Act 1973, s. 11.

35. Voidable marriages
Whilst such marriages as were dealt with in **34** are absolutely void, voidable marriages remain valid until declared void by the court. The Matrimonial Causes Act 1973, s.13, provides, however, that a decree of nullity in the case of a voidable marriage must *not* be granted if:

(a) the court is satisfied that the petitioner, knowing he (or she) could have avoided the marriage, conducted himself (or herself) in a way suggesting that he or she would not do so; and
(b) to grant the decree would be unjust.

The Matrimonial Causes Act 1973, s.12, provides the following grounds for avoiding a marriage:

(a) non-consummation (whether due to refusal or incapacity);
(b) lack of consent;
(c) unfitness for marriage because of mental disorder, as given in the Mental Health Act 1983;
(d) where one party suffers from a communicable venereal disease; or
(e) where the respondent was pregnant by some person other than the petitioner.

36. Divorce under the Matrimonial Causes Act 1973

This Act re-enacted the provisions in the Divorce Reform Act 1969, thus affirming that 'irretrievable breakdown of marriage' is the sole ground for divorce. What constitutes breakdown will clearly depend on the circumstances of each case and, for the prevention of rash divorces, the Act makes provision for a reconciliation procedure which must be followed before any divorce can be granted.

To establish 'irretrievable breakdown' one party must establish one or more of the following five 'facts', although there need be no causal connection between the 'fact' and the 'irretrievable breakdown' — *see Buffery* v. *Buffery* (1987):

(a) that the respondent has committed adultery and the petitioner finds it intolerable to live with the respondent (both elements — adultery and intolerability — must be established. One need not follow from the other);
(b) that the respondent has behaved in such a way that the petitioner cannot reasonably be expected to live with the respondent;
(c) that the respondent has deserted the petitioner for a continuous period of at least two years immediately preceding presentation of the petition;
(d) that the parties have lived apart for a continuous period of at least two years immediately preceding presentation of the petition and the parties agree to divorce.
(e) that the parties have lived apart for a continuous period of at

least five years immediately preceding presentation of the petition (whether they agree to divorce or not).

NOTE: (1) There was a time when generally no petition could be brought for divorce during the first three years of marriage. This period has been reduced to one year in the Matrimonial and Family Proceedings Act 1984. (2) There is a waiting period of (usually) six weeks between a *decree nisi* and a *decree absolute*. During this time the marriage subsists. The divorce is granted unless (*nisi*) any cause can be established for not making it *absolute*.

37. Magistrates' jurisdiction

Magistrates courts have summary jurisdiction in domestic proceedings where a wife applies for maintenance from a deserting husband or an order for judicial separation on the grounds of persistent cruelty or adultery.

The magistrates may also order husband and wife to live apart and award custody of the children to either party, with provision of maintenance.

Infants or minors

38. Minority

A minor is given as a person under the age of 18 in the Family Law Reform Act (FLRA) 1969, s. 1(1). Minority was once referred to as 'infancy'. Cases, statutes and other materials may still use this term.

Under s. 9 of the Act, a minor (or 'infant') becomes an adult at the 'commencement of the relevant anniversary of the date of his birth', i.e. the first moment of his or her eighteenth birthday.

39. Legitimation

An illegitimate child, i.e. one born out of wedlock, can now be legitimated by and from the date of the subsequent marriage of its parents (legitimation *per subsequens matrimonium*) under the Legitimacy Act 1976. A child born of an adulterous association can now be legitimated in this way, also under the Legitimacy Act 1976. The common law presumption that only legitimate children could inherit on the intestacy of their parents has been abolished (Family Law Reform Act 1987).

A child born after artificial insemination where the donor was not the mother's husband, but who agreed to be the donor, is deemed to be the legitimate child of the married couple (Family Law Reform Act 1987).

40. Adoption of minors

Adoption was unknown to English law until 1926, when the first Adoption Act was passed. The legislation governing adoption has been consolidated into the Adoption Act 1976 and extensively amended by the Children Act 1989.

The legal effect of an adoption order is to terminate the existing legal relationship between natural parents and their child. It creates a new relationship of parent and child between the adopters and the adopted child. The only situation in which such an order can be revoked is where an illegitimate child is legitimated by the marriage of its parents.

Anyone who is under the age of 18, who has never been married and who lives in England or Wales may be adopted.

A couple may adopt a child if they are married and both at least 21 years old. It is also possible for single people to adopt a child. Even if the adopter is a parent of the child, a single person must be 21 or over.

Adoption is effected by court order. Before granting the order the court must be satisfied that:

(a) every person whose consent is necessary has in fact consented, i.e. parents, guardians, and the child, where possible;
(b) the infant has consented if he or she is of sufficient age to do so;
(c) no bribe has been made to any person in connection with the proposed adoption, but only such payments as are authorised by the court;
(d) the child has been in the probationary care of the adoptor for a specified period of time prior to the application.

41. Guardians

Every minor should have some adult to safeguard its interests. In the absence of parents, the court will appoint a guardian. A guardian stands *in loco parentis* to a child and, for most purposes, has the same rights and duties as a parent.

Guardians may be appointed by:

(a) the parents by will or by deed;
(b) the High Court, county court or magistrates where there is no one else to make an appointment, otherwise by the High Court only

where the minor has been placed under the care of the court, i.e. made a ward of court.

By the Administration of Justice Act 1970, jurisdiction in wardship was transferred from the Chancery Division to the Family Division of the High Court, which is charged with guardianship of wards of court. Interference with a ward of court is contempt of court, punishable by imprisonment. The court may appoint any person guardian of the minor, e.g. parents, under the supervision of the court. Consent of the court must be obtained before the minor can marry, leave the country, etc.

The law governing guardianship is now largely to be found in the Children Act 1989, the Domestic Proceedings and Magistrates' Courts Act 1978 and the Supreme Court Act 1981.

42. Incapacity of minors

The Family Law Reform Act 1969 gives the age of majority as 18. The law protects young people in a variety of ways, and as a corollary it restricts their capacity:

(a) They cannot own land, but they can own personal property.

(b) Before the age of majority they cannot vote, make a will (generally), make contracts which bind them (generally), get married without consent (of their parents or a court), see an 18-rated film at a cinema, order alcoholic drinks on licensed premises, enter a betting shop or a sex shop, be tattooed (except by a qualified medical practitioner) or (generally) work night shifts.

(c) Under 10, a child cannot be prosecuted for a crime (*doli incapax* — *see* 26: **3**), although care proceedings can be brought. Under 12 a child cannot be sold an animal as a pet. Under 13, they cannot generally be employed. Under 14 (but over 10) they can be criminally responsible with proof of knowledge of wrongdoing — *see R* v. *York* (1748), *J.M.* v. *Runeckles* (1984). Under 14, they cannot accept articles from rag dealers. Under 14, a boy cannot be convicted of any offence involving sexual intercourse. Under 15, a child cannot enter a knackers yard. Under 16, a child cannot buy liqueur chocolates or fireworks, education is compulsory (from 5) and restricted part-time employment is allowed. Under 17 a child cannot hold a pedlar's licence, nor can he buy or hire any firearm. There are a number of minimum ages for driving motor vehicles.

(d) There are no age requirements for liability in tort, except where some intent is required and the child is too young to have formed such an intent.

The Crown

43. Constitutional monarchy

A monarchy is a state in which all governmental power legally resides in one person, inheriting that power by birth, e.g. in Britain, the Queen.

However, the British monarch is not an absolute ruler, but must rule in accordance with the conventions and laws that together, compose the British constitution. Where the powers of a monarch are curtailed by a constitution in this way, a special form of limited or constitutional monarchy arises.

44. Unwritten constitution

The British constitution is said to be 'unwritten' because it is not contained like that, for example, of the United States of America or France, in one document or a connected series of documents. It is also said to be 'flexible', because it is possible for it to be changed by the normal law-making process of legislation.

The British constitution derives from:

(a) statutes, including certain celebrated statutes such as the Magna Carta 1215, and the Bill of Rights 1689, which are regarded with great esteem;
(b) rules of common law;
(c) customary rules, including those customs observed by Parliament itself; and
(d) constitutional conventions.

These are like customs in that they are not enforceable in the courts (i.e. are not rules of law), but are of considerable importance in that they are observed and therefore bind, not only Parliament but the Executive and the Queen herself. For example, the Queen may not refuse her assent to a Bill that has been passed in both Houses of Parliament.

45. Constitutional law

This is composed partly of statutes and conventions and regulates the powers of the government and Parliament and the relationship between government and citizens.

46. Rights of citizens: the rule of law

The rights of citizens under the state are protected in Britain by a doctrine called 'the rule of law'. Dicey, in his *Law of the Constitution* (1885), analysed the rule of law as depending on three propositions:

(a) the ordinary common law overrides and excludes the arbitrary exercise of governmental power;

(b) all classes of persons are equally subject to the law and the courts, including the government;

(c) the law of the constitution is not contained in any piece of legislation, but is derived from the rights of individuals, as declared by the courts.

47. Personal freedom

This is one of the basic rights of citizenship. A British subject can enforce his rights by means of the following remedies:

(a) *self-defence,* provided that if force is used it is only such as is proportionate to the harm threatened (*R.* v. *McInnes* (1971)) and is reasonably necessary to protect oneself or one's property from unlawful interference (Criminal Law Act 1967, s. 3. and *see R.* v. *Whyte* (1987)).

(b) *judicial protection*:

    (*i*) a civil action for damages for assault, false imprisonment, or malicious prosecution;

    (*ii*) criminal proceedings for assault or false imprisonment;

    (*iii*) a writ of *habeas corpus*, i.e. a QBD writ ordering a person who is detaining another to produce the prisoner in court and show why he should not be released (a single judge can order release; there is no appeal against his decision to order release in criminal cases, though appeals are possible in civil cases under the Administration of Justice Act 1960, s. 15.)

(c) *European Convention 1950* — the UK has undertaken, under this convention, to guarantee basic human rights. Enforcement of the convention is carried out by the Commission and the Court of Human Rights in Strasbourg (*see* 3: **68**).

48. Freedom of speech

This is the right to speak or write freely on any matter, subject to a number of limitations including:

(a) a civil action for libel or slander for the publication of any false and defamatory matter (*see* 18: **1, 2**);

(b) prosecution for criminal libel (*see* 29: **17**);

(c) prosecution for blasphemy, obscenity or sedition (*see* 29: **5, 18**);

(d) prosecution for 'stirring up racial hatred' under the Public Order Act 1986 (*see* 4:**28**);

(e) chanting in an indecent or racist manner at designated football matches (as well as throwing things and invading the pitch) under the Football (Offences) Act 1991.

49. Freedom of assembly

The right to hold meetings freely is now extensively curtailed by the laws against riots and disorder (*see* 29: **6–10**).

50. 'The Queen can do no wrong'

Although the government and its agents are basically subject to the same law as everybody else, the sovereign, being regarded as 'the fountain of justice', cannot legally be made liable to the jurisdiction of the courts, which themselves exist only by virtue of their authority from the sovereign. (This is a necessary principle dictated by logic in any monarchy.) The maxim 'The Queen can do no wrong' is today limited in application to the sovereign personally, i.e. the Queen in her personal capacity cannot be sued in any British court. However, the government, and other agents of the Crown, can now generally be freely sued, as stated in the Crown Proceedings Act 1947 (*see* 4:**51**).

51. Crown Proceedings Act 1947

This provides that the Crown can now be made liable like an ordinary person for:

(a) torts committed by its servants or agents;

(b) breaches of duties imposed on occupiers or owners of property;

(c) breaches of duties owed by an employer to his servants or employees;

(d) breaches of contracts (but note that the Crown is still not bound by contracts it makes with its own servants and cannot be sued on such contracts, although in *R*. v. *Lord Chancellor's Department, ex parte Nangle* (1991), an action was successfully brought under the Civil Service Pay and Conditions of Service Code. Civil servants, but not military personnel, however, now have a statutory right to resist unfair dismissal under the Employment Protection (Consolidation) Act 1978 (*see R.* v. *Civil Service Appeal Board, ex parte Cunninghame* (1991)).

The effect of the Crown Proceedings Act 1947 is that a citizen can now sue a Government department or minister for wrongs committed by employees or government servants, but cannot sue the

Queen personally (although the department or minister theoretically derives its authority from the Queen).

52. The Parliamentary Commissioner ('Ombudsman')

Under the Parliamentary Commissioner Act 1967, the Ombudsman's function is to investigate complaints of governmental administrative oppression or unfairness. He or she cannot, however, commence investigations unless first asked to do so by a Member of Parliament on behalf of the complainant. His or her jurisdiction is limited and does not extend to local government matters, nor to central government actions if correct procedure was followed by the department or ministry concerned (even though this may have produced harsh or unfair results). On the other hand, the effects of subsequent legislation, such as the Parliamentary Commissioner (Consular Complaints) Act 1981 and the Parliamentary and Health Service Commissioner Act 1987 have extended the Ombudsman's remit.

The reform of local government occasioned by the Local Government Act 1974 saw the creation of special commissions for local government, based on the model of the Ombudsman. The Parliamentary Commissioner is, in fact, an *ex officio* member of these commissions, though complaints relating to local government go not to him but to local commissioners for investigation.

This idea has been extended beyond the governmental area. There is now a similar officer to be found in banking, insurance, building societies, the health service, legal services, pensions, corporate estate agents, investment and even within the Stock Exchange.

Progress test 4

1. What kinds of personality are recognised by English law?
(1–3)

2. How can corporations be formed? How far are corporations subject to the *ultra vires* doctrine?   **(2–7, 10)**.

3. Distinguish: (a) incorporated and unincorporated associations, (b) public and private companies and (c) a partnership and a limited company.   **(8, 9, 11, 12, 14)**

4. Define and distinguish nationality, domicile and status. **(15–17)**

5. How can British nationality: (a) be acquired; and (b) be lost? **(20, 21, 23)**

6. Define what is meant by 'marriage'. **(29)**

7. Summarise the legal consequences of marriage. **(33)**

8. Summarise the grounds on which a divorce may be obtained. **(36)**

9. What is a minor or infant? At what age did infancy cease before 1970? Summarise the chief incapacities of minors. **(38, 42)**

10. Why is the British constitution said to be unwritten? What are the basic rights of British citizens and how are these protected? **(44–49)**

11. Summarise and explain the main provisions of the Crown Proceedings Act 1947. **(51)**

Part two

The law of contract

5
Formalities and consent

Introduction

1. A simple contract

A contract is a legally binding agreement, that is, an agreement imposing rights and obligations on the parties that will be enforced by the courts.

Y is a newsagent. Z goes into his shop and offers him 30p. Y accepts the money and gives Z his newspaper. We have here the elements of a contract:

(a) the *offer* (*see* 5: **10–12**);
(b) the *acceptance* (*see* 5: **13–17**); and
(c) the 30p, which is called the *consideration* (*see* 6: **1–5**).

It is a simple contract, imposing straightforward rights and obligations.

Suppose, though, Z only has a £5 note. Y has no change; Y says 'You can owe it to me,' and hands over the newspaper: Z then has an obligation to pay 30p.

Suppose, instead, Z opens the paper and finds that the printing has missed the inside pages: Z then has a right to return the incomplete paper and to be given a complete copy or, if Y has sold out, to be returned his 30p.

A right enjoyed by one party implies an obligation owed by the other. We can express the same thing either way round.

After he has bought his newspaper, Z gets on the bus to go to work. This time he is accepting an implied offer by the bus company. Z must pay the fare to the conductor (as agent for the bus company — *see* 11: **1**) in return for being taken to his destination. That is the consideration.

Formalities

2. Formal requirements

As we have seen, Z enters into a series of binding contracts as he walks down the street, buying a newspaper and travelling in the bus, without any formalities. Z enters into these contracts orally and they are therefore called parol contracts. Most contracts can be made in any way — orally, in writing, by telephone, telex or using a fax machine.

A few contracts require a particular form, usually to provide better evidence of the terms and so to prevent disputes. Some contracts must be:

(a) under seal (before 1989) (*see* 5: **3**);

(b) in writing (*see* 5: **4**);

(c) evidenced by writing (*see* 5: **5–7**).

3. Contract under seal

A contract under seal is called a deed or a specialty contract. A document becomes a deed if it is:

(a) *signed*;

(b) *sealed* — sealing was usually effected by affixing a disc or wafer of red paper at the bottom of the deed and, in many cases, it was not vital for the seal actually to be used, provided it was *intended* that a deed should be made — *see First National Securities* v. *Jones* (1978) CA; furthermore, since from s. 1(1)(b), the implementation of the Law of Property (Miscellaneous Provisions) Act 1989, it is now clear that a seal is no longer necessary for the valid execution of an instrument as a deed by an individual;

(c) *delivered* — delivery is largely a matter of intention, and a deed may be delivered (by constructive delivery) even though it remains in the possession of the maker (a deed by a corporation does not need to be delivered).

When a deed is signed, sealed and delivered it is executed. An *escrow* is a deed executed subject to a condition that it is not to become operative until a certain contingency is satisfied, for example the occurrence of a certain event or the expiry of a period of time.

Deeds are of two kinds:

(a) a *deed poll*, to which there is only one party, for example a deed or gift; or

(b) an *indenture*, to which there are two or more parties.

A deed does not need to be supported by consideration and can, therefore, be sued to make a gratuitous promise binding. A deed *must* be used:

(a) to confer or create certain legal interests in land (*see* 19: **22**);
(b) to transfer a British ship or any share in a British ship.

If a deed is not used, the contract is void.

A deed is subject to a longer period of limitation (*see* 9: **11**) and makes certain additional defences available:

(a) *non est factum* (*see* 8: **6**);
(b) estoppel by deed (*see* 9: **5**);
(c) merger (*see* 9: **6**).

4. Contracts in writing

Some contracts are required to be in writing. The consequences if they are not in writing vary.

Contracts that are *void* if not in proper written form include:

(a) a bill of sale (*see* 22: **15**); and
(b) a hire-purchase or other regulated consumer credit agreement (*see* 12: **23**) if not in the statutory written form (*see* 12: **24**).
(c) contracts for the sale or other disposition of land — until its repeal in 1989, s. 40 of the Law of Property Act 1925 required that such contracts as this needed only to be evidenced (rather than made) in writing, but the Law of Property (Miscellaneous Provisions) Act 1989 specifies that such contracts can *only* be made in writing and that the writing must contain all that has been agreed between the parties and both their signatures so that without the writing the contract is void.

On the other hand there are such contracts as a bill of exchange (*see* 12: **5**), which is defined by the Bills of Exchange Act 1882, s. 3(1), as an 'unconditional order in writing'. If it is not in writing it still takes effect as a simple contract.

5. Contracts evidenced by writing

Some contracts are required to be evidenced in writing. If there is not sufficient evidence, then the contract will not be enforced in the courts. Since the 1989 Act, the only important example is the contract of guarantee (*see* 5: **6**).

6.   Contracts of guarantee

There is an important distinction between a guarantee and an indemnity:

(a) a guarantee is a contract 'to answer for the debt, default, or miscarriage of another' under the Statute of Frauds 1677, s. 4, the primary liability;

(b) an indemnity is itself the assumption of a primary liability:

> 'If two come to a shop and one buys, and the other, to gain him credit, promises the seller,'If he does not pay you, I will'; this is a collateral undertaking. But if he says, "Let him have the goods, I will be your paymaster", or "I will see you paid", this is an undertaking as for himself'. Hold, CJ, in *Birkmyr* v. *Darnell* (1704), the first is a guarantee; the second an indemnity — *see Lakeman* v. *Mountstephen* (1874).

Being a primary obligation, an indemnity does not need to be evidenced in writing. A guarantee requires a written memorandum (*see* 5: **5**) with two exceptions:

(a) the consideration need not be stated in the memorandum, as under the Mercantile Law Amendment Act 1856;

(b) there is no need for a memorandum where the guarantee is part of a larger transaction, for example a guarantee given by a *del credere* agent (*see* 11: **2**).

Intention to create legal relations

7.   Intention to create legal relations

For an agreement to be enforceable as a binding contract it must have been the intention of the parties to create legal relations. There is no exhaustive list of situations in which there is no such intention, but they mainly fall into three categories:

(a) *Social and domestic arrangements* Atkin LJ, in *Balfour* v. *Balfour* (1919) said, 'There are agreements between parties which do not result in contracts within the meaning of that term in our law. The ordinary example is where two parties agree to take a walk together, or where there is an offer and acceptance of hospitality. Nobody would suggest in ordinary circumstances that those agreements result in what we know as a contract, and one of the most usual forms of agreement which does not constitute a contract appears to me to be the arrangements which are made between husband and wife'.

This presumption may be rebutted. A husband's agreement to pay money to his wife may be a contract if the parties are separated — *see Merritt* v. *Merritt* (1970). An agreement between relatives to share a house may be a contract if one party has, in consequence, sold her own house — *see Parker* v. *Clark* (1960). A joint entry in a competition can be a contract — *see Simpkins* v. *Pays* (1955).

(b) *Intention to create legal relations expressly denied* The presumption that a contract is intended in a commercial agreement may be expressly rebutted:

    (*i*) by a clause stating that the agreement 'shall not be subject to legal jurisdiction in the law courts' — *see Rose and Frank* v. *Crompton Bros* (1925);

    (*ii*) by the words 'subject to contract' on an agreement for the sale of land — *see Tiverton Estates* v. *Wearwell* (1975).

(c) *Collective agreements.* A collective agreement between a trade union and an employer under the Trade Union and Labour Relations Act 1974, s.18, is not legally enforceable unless:

    (*i*) it is in writing; and

    (*ii*) it states that the parties intend it to be binding.

The trivial nature of an agreement is not relevant to whether it is intended to be binding — *see Esso Petroleum Co. Ltd* v. *Commissioners of Customs and Excise* (1976). Nevertheless, the courts tend to treat the presence of consideration (*see* 6: 1) as an indication that a legal obligation is intended.

8. *Consensus ad idem*

The consent of the parties is necessary for a contract to be enforceable.

The classical nineteenth-century view was that there must be a *consensus ad idem*: the minds of the parties must meet and agree. In *Cundy* v. *Lindsay* (1878), Alfred Blenkarn ordered a consignment of handkerchiefs from P. Alfred signed himself 'A. Blenkarn & Co. of 37 Wood Street'. P. knew the respectable firm 'W. Blenkiron & Sons of 123 Wood Street'. Believing Alfred to be this firm, they sent the handkerchiefs to him as 'Messrs. Blenkiron & Co. of 37 Wood Street'. Alfred did not pay for the handkerchiefs but sold them to D. The House of Lords, as Lord Cairns LC observed, had 'to determine as between two parties, both of whom are perfectly innocent, upon which of the two the consequences of a fraud practised upon both must fall'. Lord Cairns resolved the problem by applying the consensus test. Was it in P's mind to enter into a contract with Alfred? 'Of him they knew nothing, and of him they never thought. With him they never intended to deal. Their minds never, even for an instant of time, rested upon him and as between him and them there was no consensus of mind which could lead to any agreement or any contract whatever.'

This approach works admirably where a man sells something to another man. One man makes an offer; the other accepts; consideration changes hands. In modern life, however, contracts may arise in many other ways:

(a) *By conduct* A contract is concluded as soon as money is put into an automatic ticket machine. 'The offer is made when the proprietor of the machine holds it out as being ready to receive money. The acceptance takes place when the customer puts his money into the slot' — *see* Lord Denning , MR, in *Thornton* v. *Shoe Lane Parking* (1971). There is no *consensus* between the proprietor and the customer.

(b) *By operation of law* The Sale of Goods Act 1979 s.8(2) states that where there is a contract for the sale of goods (*see* 12: **9**) in which no price has been agreed the buyer must pay a reasonable price. This is one of many cases where the law intervenes and takes a matter out of the hands of the parties.

(c) *By inference* A famous example is *Clarke* v. *Dunraven* (1897). The yachts 'Satanita' and 'Valkyrie' were entered for a race, each owner undertaking to observe the yacht club rules. The yachts collided and the question arose as to whether the owners had entered into a contract with each other. The House of Lords decided that they had: 'The effect of their entering for the race, and undertaking to be bound by these rules to the knowledge of each other, is sufficient, I think to create a contractual obligation to discharge that liability', said Lord Herschell. The knowledge, of course, was that all competitors had undertaken to the yacht club to observe the rules; it does not follow that one competitor knew of the existence or identity of the others.

As Lord Wilberforce said in *The Eurymedon* (1975) case, 'The precise analysis of this complex of relations into the classical offer and acceptance, with identifiable consideration, seems to present difficulty, but this same difficulty exists in many situations of daily life, e.g. sales at auction; supermarket purchases; boarding an omnibus; purchasing a train ticket; tenders for the supply of goods; offers of reward; acceptance by post; warranties of authority by agents; manufacturer's guarantees; gratuitous bailments; bankers' commercial credits. These are all examples which show that English law, having committed itself to a rather technical and schematic doctrine of contract, in application takes a practical approach, often at the cost of forcing the facts to fit uneasily into the marked slots of offer, acceptance and consideration.'

With this warning we will now consider the classical elements of a contract:

(a) offer (*see* **10–12**);
(b) acceptance (*see* **13–17**);
(c) termination of offer (*see* **18, 19**);
(d) consideration (*see* 6: **1–5**).

The offer

9. Offeror and offeree

The offer, made by the offeror to the offeree, is the statement of a willingness to be bound on certain specified terms. The offer may be oral, written or implied from conduct.

Offers are of two kinds:

(a) A *specific* offer is made to a specific offeree. No one else can accept it. 'If you propose to make a contract with A, then B cannot substitute himself for A without your consent and to your disadvantage, securing to himself all the benefit of the contract' — *see* Pollock, CB, in *Boulton* v. *Jones* (1857).

(b) A *general* offer can be accepted by anyone, and usually without prior notification of acceptance. In *Carlill* v. *Carbolic Smoke Ball Co.* (1893), D were advertising their patent medicine in a newspaper during an epidemic of influenza. If anyone used it as directed for two weeks and contracted influenza the advertisement provided that D would pay £100. The sum of £1,000 was deposited in a bank, 'showing our sincerity in the matter'. P bought a smoke ball, used it as directed for two months, and then contracted influenza. Bowen, LJ, found that there was:

(*i*) 'an offer made to all the world';
(*ii*) 'to ripen into a contract with anybody who comes forward and performs the condition'; and that
(*iii*) 'as notification of acceptance is required for the benefit of the person who makes the offer, the person who makes the offer may dispense with notice to himself if he thinks it desirable to do so.'

10. Characteristics of the offer

A valid offer has certain characteristics:

(a) *Certainty* A promise to pay an extra £5 or to buy another horse if a horse 'proves lucky to me' is too vague to amount to an offer — *see Guthing* v. *Lynn* (1831).

(b) *Communication* An offer must be communicated to the offeree before it can be accepted.

Thus, if a seaman helps to navigate a ship home without informing the owners in advance, he cannot insist on payment, since the owners have not had notice of his offer, and, therefore, no opportunity to accept or reject it — *see Taylor* v. *Laird* (1856).

This has raised problems in the reward cases. Suppose there is an armed robbery and the insurance company offers a reward for information leading to the conviction of the robbers. Your suspicions are aroused by the diamonds you see through the window next door. You inform the police and your neighbour is ultimately convicted. Are you entitled to the reward if you did not know that it had been offered? This also raises difficulties with counteroffers (*see* 5: **15**).

11. Statements not amounting to an offer

A preliminary statement, on analysis, may turn out not to be an offer.

(a) *Invitation to treat* This is a statement that is intended to elicit an offer from someone else — *see Gibson* v. *Manchester City Council* (1979). It has no legal force: the offer it elicits can be accepted or not without obligation. There are many examples of invitations to treat:

 (*i*) An auctioneer's request for bids — *Payne* v. *Cave* (1789). The bid itself is the offer, which can be retracted at any time until the fall of the hammer signifies the auctioneer's acceptance (Sale of Goods Act 1979, s.57(2)).

 (*ii*) The display of goods in a shop window with prices marked on them — *see Fisher* v. *Bell* (1961).

 (*iii*) The display of priced goods in a self-service store — *see Pharmaceutical Society* v. *Boots* (1953).

 (*iv*) A catalogue or price list advertising goods for sale — *see Grainger* v. *Gough* (1896).

(b) *Statement of intention* The announcement of a forthcoming auction — *see Harris* v. *Nickerson* (1873).

(c) *Communication of information in the course of negotiations* A statement of the price at which one is prepared to consider selling a piece of land — *see Harvey* v. *Facey* (1893).

The acceptance

12. Manner and communication of the acceptance

Subject to the following qualifications, acceptance may be made in any manner provided it is communicated to the offeror:

(a) *Prescribed manner of acceptance* 'It may be that an offeror, who by the terms of his offer insists upon acceptance in a particular manner, is entitled to insist that he is not bound unless acceptance is effected or communicated in that precise way, although it seems possible that, even so, if the other party communicates his acceptance in some other way, the offeror may by conduct or otherwise waive his right to insist upon the prescribed method of acceptance' — Buckley, J, in *Manchester Diocesan Council for Education* v. *Commercial & General Investments Ltd* (1970).

(b) *Acceptance by positive conduct.* Acceptance must be active. An offer by letter containing the words 'If I hear no more, I shall consider the horse is mine' is incapable on its own of constituting its own acceptance; there must be some positive act by the offeree — *see Felthouse* v. *Bindley* (1862).

A recipient of unsolicited goods may treat them as a gift unless the sender takes possession of them within a limited period (Unsolicited Goods and Services Act 1971 — *see* 12: **19**).

(c) *Waiver of communication.* An offeror may waive the need for communication of the acceptance — *see Carlill* v. *Carbolic Smoke Ball Co.* (1893) (*see* 5: **10**).

(d) *Contracts by post.* Here acceptance is complete as soon as it is posted, provided it is properly stamped and addressed — *see Household Fire Insurance Co.* v. *Grant* (1879).

In such cases, therefore, it does not matter if the letter of acceptance is lost in the post and never reaches the offeror, the contract is complete as soon as the letter is posted — *see Byrne* v. *Van Tienhoven* (1880).

There are three exceptions to this rule:

(i) 'If, having regard to all the circumstances, including the nature of the subject-matter under consideration, the negotiating parties cannot have intended that there should be a binding agreement until the party accepting an offer or exercising an option had in fact communicated the acceptance or exercise to the other' — Lawton, LJ, in *Holwell Securities* v. *Hughes* (1974).

(ii) An offer by telex is not accepted until notice of the acceptance is received by the offeror — *see Entores* v. *Miles Far East Corporation* (1955). This case was approved by the House of Lords in *Brinkibon* v. *Stahag Stahl GmbH* (1983), in which the Lords also dealt with telex communications in some detail, including non-instantaneous messages (e.g. overnight and non-business day messages).

(*iii*)   Mere posting is not sufficient in contracts governed by the Uniform Laws of International Sales Act 1967.

13. Contents of the acceptance

The acceptance must be unqualified and must correspond in every detail with the terms of the offer — *see Harvela Investments* v. *Royal Trust Co. of Canada* (1968).

Sometimes an acceptance purports to be conditional: 'It appears to be well settled by the authorities that if the documents or letters relied on as constituting a contract contemplate the execution of a further contract between the parties, it is a question of construction whether the execution of the further contract is a condition or term of the bargain or whether it is a mere expression of the desire of the parties as to the manner in which the transaction already agreed to will in fact go through. In the former case there is no enforceable contract either because the condition is unfulfilled or because the law does not recognise a contract to enter into a contract. In the latter case there is a binding contract and the reference to the more formal document may be ignored' — Parker, J, in *Hatzfeldt-Wildenburg* v. *Alexander* (1912).

Two other problems may arise:

(**a**)   where the acceptance introduces new terms (*see* 5:**15**);
(**b**)   where the terms are uncertain (*see* 5:**16**).

14. Counter-offers

An acceptance that imposes new terms is a counter-offer, which rejects the original offer and causes it to lapse. Thus, where a house is offered for sale at £1,000 and the offeree offers £950 the offer lapses — *see Hyde* v. *Wrench* (1840).

A common and striking example of counter-offers is the 'battle of the forms' in which two firms exchange their standard forms (*see* 7: **10**). One firm makes an offer, enclosing its standard terms. The offeree firm accepts this offer, enclosing its own standard terms. The firms then perform the contract. Later a problem arises. Whose standard terms apply? Technically the offeree firm, by changing the terms, made a counter-offer that was accepted by performance.

Everything seems to depend on the circumstances of each case — *see Butler* v. *Ex-Cell-O* (1979).

15. Certainty of terms

It is for the parties to make their intentions clear in their contract. The courts will not enforce a contract the terms of which are uncertain.

Where the terms of a contract are too vague, the contract will fail for uncertainty, e.g. the sale of a van 'on hire-purchase terms is too vague, since there are several varieties of hire-purchase terms': *Scammell* v. *Ouston* (1941). Further, an agreement to negotiate is too vague to be enforceable — *see Walford* v. *Miles* (1992).

An agreement that is definite on the whole will be enforced, notwithstanding the addition of some meaningless or unnecessary words or phrases. The court in such a case will ignore the meaniningless words and enforce the contract without them — *see Nicolene Ltd* v. *Simmonds* (1953).

An agreement that at first sight appears to be too vague will be enforced if:

(a) the parties themselves have provided machinery in the contract for resolving the uncertainty, e.g. where no price was fixed for the sale of petrol, but the agreement provided that all disputes should be referred to arbitration, it was held that the arbitrator could fix the price and so resolve the uncertainty — *see Foley* v. *Classique Coaches Ltd* (1934); or

(b) the deficiency can be remedied by the court implying a term (*see* 7: **3**) either:

(*i*) from the course of dealing between the parties in the past — *see Hillas* v. *Arcos* (1932);

(*ii*) from trade usages; or

(*iii*) where certain terms are implied by statute in similar contracts, e.g. the Sale of Goods Act 1979.

16. Tenders and standing offers

A tender is a form of offer for the supply of goods or services, usually made in response to a request for tenders from several possible suppliers.

Tenders take the following forms.

(a) *single offer*, e.g. a tender to build a factory, and acceptance of such a tender constitutes a contract;

(b) *standing offer*, e.g. a tender to supply goods as and when required, and here, the tenderer must supply as and when agreed, whenever an order is made, but he cannot insist on any orders being made at all;

Example

P tendered to supply goods up to a certain amount to the LCC over a certain period. The LCC's orders did not come up to the amount expected and P sued for breach of contract. It was held that each order made a separate contract and P was bound to fulfil the orders made, but there was no obligation to make any orders at all — *see Percival Ltd.* v. *LCC* (1918).

(c) *sole supplier*, the person seeking the tender may agree to take all his requirements for certain goods from the tenderer, but this agreement does not oblige him to make any orders at all, though if he does require goods within the category agreed, he must take them from the tenderer — *see Kier* v. *Whitehead Iron Co.* (1938).

Termination of offer

17. Lapse of offer
An offer lapses:

(a) if either offeror or offeree dies before acceptance — *see Kennedy* v. *Thomassen* (1929) — but the death of the offeror may not invalidate subsequent acceptance provided:
  (*i*)   the offeree did not know of the death when he accepted; and
  (*ii*) the personality of the offeror is not vital to the contract — *see Bradbury* v. *Morgan* (1862);

(b) if it is not accepted within:
  (*i*)   the specified time (if any); or
  (*ii*) a reasonable time, if none is specified (what is a reasonable time depends on the facts. Five months has been held to be an unreasonable delay in accepting an offer to take shares in a company — *see Ramsgate Victoria Hotel Co.* v. *Montefiore* (1866);

(c) if the offeree does not make a valid acceptance, e.g. makes a counter-offer (*see* 5: **15**) or conditional acceptance (*see* 5: **14**);

(d) if the offer is subject to the fulfilment of a condition and that condition is not fulfilled, e.g. an offer to buy a car provided it is in working order — *see Financings Ltd* v. *Stimson* (1962).

An offer to keep an offer open for a specified time (an option) is *not* binding unless:

(a) made under seal; or
(b) supported by valuable consideration like any other simple contract — *see Routledge* v. *Grant* (1828).

18. Revocation
An offer may be revoked at any time before acceptance.

(a) revocation must be communicated because, until the offeree actually receives the revocation, he is entitled to accept — *see Byrne* v. *Van Tienhoven* (1880);
(b) indirect communication — the offeree learns of the revocation he cannot later accept, even though he hears of it only indirectly, e.g. where a prospective purchaser of land learned through a reliable third party that the offeror had already agreed to sell the land to another offeree — *see Dickinson* v. *Dodds* (1876) — or, in the case of a unilateral or general contract (*see* 5: **10** (*b*)) it seems that 'once the offeree has embarked on performance it is too late for the offeror to revoke his offer' — *see* Goff, LJ, in *Daulia* v. *Four Millbank Nominees* (1978).

Progress test 5

1. What contracts require to be made by deed and which must be wholly written? **(3, 4)**

2. What contracts are unenforceable unless evidenced in writing? What is meant by 'unenforceable' and 'evidenced' in this context? **(5)**

3. What is a contract of guarantee and how does it differ from an indemnity contract? **(6)**

4. Explain the doctrine of part performance and give examples of its operation. **(7)**

5. When is a contract unenforceable for want of an intention to create legal relations? **(8)**

6. Distinguish between a general and specific offer. **(10)**

7. Distinguish an offer from (a) an invitation to treat and (b) a statement of intention. **(12)**

8. Apply the rules of offer and acceptance to the following situations: (a) bidding at an auction, (b) putting a coin into a slot machine, (c) display of goods in a shop window with the price marked and (d) prices marked on goods in a catalogue. **(9, 12)**

9. How may an offer be revoked? **(19)**

10. What is a counter-offer? What is the effect of the phrase 'subject to contract' in a written agreement? **(8, 15)**

11. Comment on the statement that there cannot be a contract to make a contract. **(14)**

12. What forms are commonly taken by tenders? **(17)**

13. A borrowed £1,000 from B for use in his business, and said that if business was good, he would repay £1,200 in a month's time. He has a very profitable month, but refuses to honour his promise. Can B enforce it? **(11)**

14. Under a heading 'Articles for Sale' in a newspaper, A advertised as follows: 'Nearly new Mini, good condition, £500' and his name and address. B saw the advertisement and sent a cheque for £500, saying in his letter, 'If I don't hear to the contrary I shall assume the car is mine and will collect it tomorrow'. Is there a contract? **(10, 13, 18)**

6
Consideration, privity and capacity

Consideration

1. Meaning of valuable consideration

The courts will not enforce a simple contract unless it is supported by valuable consideration.

The classic definitions of consideration are in terms of benefit and detriment. As Lush, J, phrased it in *Currie* v. *Misa* (1875), 'A valuable consideration may consist either in some right, interest, profit or benefit accruing to one party, or some forbearance, detriment, loss or responsibility given, suffered or undertaken by the other'.

It is easier to think of the consideration as the price paid for the contract. It means the element of exchange in a bargain and, in order to satisfy the requirement of English law, it must be valuable, i.e. something that is capable of being valued in terms of money or money's worth, however slight.

An interesting example is *Chappell* v. *Nestlé* (1960). As an advertising gimmick, D offered a record of the tune 'Rockin' Shoes' to any member of the public who sent them three chocolate wrappers and 1s 6d (7½ p). D threw the wrappers away. Under the Copyright Act 1956, s. 8, D were required to pay P, as copyright owner, a royalty of 6¼ per cent 'of the ordinary retail selling price'. Were the wrappers part of this selling price? By a bare majority, the House of Lords decided that they were. The wrappers were part of the consideration. 'It is said that when received, the wrappers are of no value to Nestlé's. This I would have thought irrelevant. A contracting party can stipulate for what consideration he chooses. A peppercorn does not cease to be good consideration if it is established that the promisee does not like pepper and will throw away the corn. As the whole object of selling the record was to increase the sales of chocolate, it seems to me wrong not to treat the stipulated evidence of such sales as part of the consideration': *per* Lord Somervell of Harrow.

Consideration is of two kinds:

(a) *executed* consideration, i.e. where the act constituting the consideration is wholly performed;

(b) *executory* consideration, i.e. where the consideration consists of a promise to do something in the future.

Therefore, if X pays a shopkeeper now for goods that are to be delivered later, X is giving executed consideration and the shopkeeper is giving executory consideration, i.e. a promise to be executed in the future.

2.   Adequacy of consideration

Consideration must be real. That is it must not be vague, indefinite or illusory, e.g. a son's vague promise to 'stop being a nuisance' to his father — *see White* v. *Bluett* (1853).

Although the consideration must be real, it need not be adequate, i.e. it is up to the parties to fix their own prices and, provided there is some definite valuable consideration, the court will not set a contract aside merely because the price fixed is inadequate — *see Haigh* v. *Brooks* (1839).

'The adequacy of the consideration is for the parties to consider at the time of making the agreement, not for the court when it is going to be enforced' said Blackburn, J, in *Bolton* v. *Madden* (1873).

However, a ridiculously inadequate consideration may be prima-facie evidence of misrepresentation or coercion (see 8: **7–11, 13**).

3.   Characteristics of consideration

(a) *Consideration must be legal* (*see* 8: **14**).

(b) *Consideration must move from the promisee* and there are two rules that are similar but which can be distinguished, as they were by Lord Haldane in *Dunlop* v. *Selfridge* (1915):

    (*i*) 'Only a person who is a party to a contract can sue on it.' This is the doctrine of privity (*see* 5: **6**);

    (*ii*) 'If a person with whom a contract not under seal has been made is to be able to enforce it, consideration must have been given by him to the promisor or to some other person at the promisor's request.' This is the rule that consideration must move from the promisee.

In many cases the two rules lead to the same result, and *Dunlop* v. *Selfridge* (1915) is an example. D supplied goods to a wholesaler X.

In return for supplied goods X promised not to re-sell them below the price fixed by D. X re-sold the goods to S on the same terms, but S retailed them below the fixed price. Certainly X could have sued S for breach of contract. In this case, however, D sued S. There were two objections to this:

(*i*) there was no contract between D and S, and S was not privy to the contract between D and X;

(*ii*) S had promised not to re-sell the goods below the fixed price, but this promise was made to X — D had not given consideration and so could not enforce S's promise;

(c) *Consideration must be something beyond the promisee's existing obligation to the promisor* That is, the promisee must have undertaken to do something, for the person whose promise he is seeking to enforce, beyond what he was already bound to do either:

(*i*) as part of his public duty as a citizen; or

(*ii*) as part of any private contractual duty owed to the promisor. Thus, if a seaman deserts his ship — so breaking his contract — and is induced to return to his duty only by a promise of extra wages, he cannot sue for the additional sum, as he has only done what he had already contracted to do — *see Stilk* v. *Myrick* (1809). This case was considered and followed in *North Ocean Shipping Co.* v. *Hyundai Construction Co.* (1979) (*see* 8: **12**). Consider also *Hartley* v. *Ponsonby* (1857). The point has been further considered in the important recent case of *Williams* v. *Roffey Bros* (1990). Here a firm of subcontractors was paid extra to finish a job on time and thus free the main contractor from the liability he would otherwise have incurred under a penalty clause. This was held to amount to valuable consideration. The case seems to undercut *Stilk* v. *Myrick*, but the court said that the rule had only been refined. The law now seems to be that the performance of an existing contractual duty can be consideration enough to bind a promise of extra payment in the absence of duress or fraud and provided that the other party obtains some extra benefit from its performance.

There is also the question of an existing obligation owed to a third party. The old authority on this was accepted by the Privy Council in *The Eurymedon* (1975) (*see* 6:6). Lord Wilberforce, delivering the majority opinion, said, 'An agreement to do an act which the promisor is under an existing obligation to a third party to do, may quite well amount to valid consideration and does so in the present case: the promisee obtains the benefit of a direct obligation which he can enforce'.

(d) *Consideration must not be past* That is, a promise made in return for some past service is unenforceable, e.g. where, having bought a horse, the purchaser promised to give the seller an extra sum if the horse proved satisfactory: such a promise is unenforceable as it relates to a past sale already completed — *see Roscorla* v. *Thomas* (1842).

EXCEPTIONS: Past consideration is sufficient in the following cases.

(1) To revive a statute-barred claim, a mere written acknowledgement is enough without any fresh consideration, as given in the Limitation Act 1980 (For the limitation of claims generally, *see* 9: 11.)

(2) A bill of exchange can be supported by an antecedent debt or other past liability (Bills of Exchange Act 1882, s. 27).

(3) Where the past consideration was rendered in response to an earlier request — *see Lampleigh* v. *Braithwaite* (1615). Here the promisor's earlier request is held to imply a promise to pay a reasonable sum later, and the subsequent promise to pay merely fixes the sum to be paid — *see Stewart* v. *Casey* (1892).

Thus, where A asked B to use his influence with the King to obtain for A a Royal pardon for a crime and B did as he was asked so that A, in gratitude, subsequently promised to pay him £100, it was held that B could enforce the promise — *see Lampleigh* v. *Braithwaite* (1615).

4.   The rule in *Foakes* v. *Beer*

The case of *Foakes* v. *Beer* (1884) concerned a judgment debt. B had obtained judgment against F for £2,000. The parties agreed that F should pay £500 at once and the balance in instalments and this was done. B then claimed interest, on the basis that the agreement to accept a bare £2,000 was unsupported by consideration. The House of Lords accepted this, relying on *Pinnel's Case* (1602) where Brian, CJ, said that 'payment of a lesser sum on the day in satisfaction of a greater cannot be any satisfaction for the whole'.

The rule in *Foakes* v. *Beer* shows that payment of a smaller sum will not discharge liability to pay a larger. If A owes B £100 and B agrees to accept £50 in complete discharge of the debt, there is nothing to stop B later changing his mind and suing for the remaining £50 — *see D. & C. Builders* v. *Rees* (1965).

5.   Exceptions to the rule in *Foakes* v. *Beer*

Acceptance of part payment made by a third party will discharge the full debt — *see Hirachand, Punamchand* v. *Temple* (1911). Furthermore, contractual rights can be abandoned or *waived*. A right that is waived without consideration can again be enforced on giving proper notice — *see Banning* v. *Wright* (1972). In two cases the waiver is binding and operates as an exception to the rule in *Foakes* v. *Beer* (1884).

(a) *Accord and satisfaction* This exception, like the rule, dates back to Brian, CJ, in *Pinnel's Case* (1602), who went on to say, 'But the gift of a horse, hawk or robe, etc., in satisfaction is good. For it shall be intended that a horse, hawk, or robe, etc. might be more beneficial to the plaintiff than the money in respect of some circumstance, or otherwise the plaintiff would not have accepted it in satisfaction'.

The modern definition is by Scrutton, LJ, in *British Russian Gazette* v. *Associated Newspapers* (1933): 'Accord and satisfaction is the purchase of a release from an obligation, whether arising under contract or tort, by means of any valuable consideration, not being the actual performance of the obligation itself. The accord is the agreement by which the obligation is discharged. The satisfaction is the consideration that makes the agreement operative'.

(b) *Promissory estoppel* Estoppel is a rule of pleading and evidence, a device by which the court decides to estop someone from saying in court something that he would be entitled to say if the court did not prevent him. The only form of estoppel of real importance today is equitable estoppel.

Promissory estoppel is an estoppel that is raised by four circumstances:

(*i*)   there is a pre-existing legal relationship between the parties;
(*ii*) the plaintiff deliberately waived his legal rights against the defendant;
(*iii*) the defendant gave no consideration for the waiver;
(*iv*) the defendant altered his position in reliance on the waiver, so that it would be inequitable to allow the plaintiff to capitalise on the lack of consideration.

This is illustrated by the *High Trees* case (*Central London Property Trust* v. *High Trees House* (1947)).

A let property to B at a rent of £2,500 p.a., but agreed to accept half this sum during the war years, and B relied on his promise, making no attempt to raise the full rent. If later A went back on his promise and sued for the full amount owing during the war years, the court would exercise its equitable discretion and estop A from retracting his promise.

Two points should be noted:

(*i*)   a promisor can withdraw his promise on giving reasonable notice, provided the promisee is able to resume his position.
(*ii*) promissory estoppel is 'a shield and not a sword': W divorced H and before the divorce became absolute, H promised to

pay £100 p.a. by way of maintenance, but he failed to honour this agreement and W sued him, relying on equitable estoppel to remedy the lack of consideration, and it was held that the doctrine did not create a new cause of action and so consideration was still necessary. Equitable estoppel could be used only as a defence at the discretion of the court — *see Combe* v. *Combe* (1951).

Privity

6.   The doctrine of privity

A contract is a private relationship between the parties who make it and so no other person can acquire rights or incur liabilities under it.

Compare this doctrine with the separate rule that 'consideration must move from the promisee' (*see* 6: 3(*b*)). The two rules together mean that a person seeking to sue upon a contract must satisfy the court:

(a) that he is a party to the contract; and
(b) that he has given consideration for the promise he seeks to enforce (or that the contract is under seal) (*see* 6: 1).

Contrast a legal duty with a contractual duty. A legal duty is one that, if not performed, can be sued upon by any person injured thereby: actions for tort are actions for breach of this kind of duty. A contractual duty is one that is owed only to the other party to the contract and only that party can sue to enforce it.

The doctrine of privity has two aspects (*see* 6: 7):

(a) no one can acquire rights under a contract to which he is not a party;
(b) no one can incur liabilities under a contract to which he is not a party.

Example _____

B sold his business to C on condition that C should pay (a) £6.50 per week to B for life and (b) £5 per week for life to Mrs B after B's death. B died and C refused to pay Mrs B, as she was not a party to the contract. It was held (a) that Mrs B was not party to the contract and could not personally enforce it, but (b) as administratrix of her late husband's estate she could enforce the contract on behalf of the estate — *see Beswick* v. *Beswick* (1968).

In the area of mercantile law we will find two fundamental exceptions to the doctrine of privity:

(a) assignment (*see* 12: **1**);
(b) agency (*see* Ch. 11).

The position of agency and privity has been discussed in two major cases:

(a) *Scruttons* v. *Midlands Silicones* (1962) A shipping company P agreed to carry a drum of chemicals belonging to Q across the Atlantic. The Bill of Lading limited the liability of 'the carrier' to $500. In London, P employed stevedores R to unload the drum. R negligently dropped the drum, causing damage in excess of $500. The House of Lords decided that R could not rely on the bill of lading. There was nothing to indicate that P was contracting on behalf of R or that the Bill of Lading was intended to benefit R.

(b) *The Eurymedon* (1975) In this case the Privy Council considered the application to very similar facts of a very different bill of lading. The exemption from liability was for the benefit of the carrier and of 'all persons who are or might be his agents from time to time (including independent contractors)'. The stevedores were independent contractors (*see* 14: **17**) and a majority of the Privy Council held that 'the exemption is designed to cover the whole carriage, from loading to discharge, by whomsoever it is performed'. Lord Wilberforce analysed the transaction thus, 'The bill of lading brought into existence a bargain initially unilateral, but capable of becoming mutual, between the shippers and the stevedore, made through the carrier as agent. This became a full contract when the stevedore performed services by discharging the goods. The performance of these services for the benefit of the shipper was the consideration for the agreement by the shipper that the stevedore should have the benefit of the exemptions and limitations contained in the bill of lading.' (Lord Simon of Glaisdale's dissenting opinion should also be read for its interesting analysis.)

7. Acquisition of rights and liabilities

(a) *Rights* If A and B make a contract whereby B is to pay A to do something for X, X cannot sue A if he fails to do what he promised. X cannot sue even if:

    (*i*) he has given consideration — *see Price* v. *Easton* (1833);
    (*ii*) he is closely related to the promisee — *see Tweddle* v. *Atkinson* (1861).

Apart from assignment and agency (*see* 6: **6**) there are exceptions to this rule:

(*i*) *Constructive trust* Where B is regarded as a trustee for X, X may sue A (and join B as co-defendant) if the contract is broken.

This is a constructive trust (*see* 23: **20**). Nevertheless, as Du Parcq LJ, said in *Re Schebsman* (1944), 'unless an intention to create a trust is clearly to be collected from the language used and the circumstances of the case, I think that the court ought not to be astute to discover indications of such an intention'. A constructive trust is rarely found.

(*ii*) *Statutory exceptions* There are limited statutory exceptions to the doctrine of privity in connection with price maintenance, insurance and covenants over land.

(*iii*) *Third party joined in proceedings* In *Snelling* v. *J.G. Snelling Ltd* (1972) X, Y and Z were brothers and were co-directors of a family company. They agreed that if any one of them resigned he would forfeit all money due to him from the company. X resigned and brought an action against the company for money due to him. Ormrod, J, said that, 'In a case such as this where the promisees under the agreement and the party to be benefited by the agreement are all before the court and the promisees have succeeded against the plaintiff on their counterclaim, the right view is that the plaintiff's claim should be dismissed'.

(**b**) *Liabilities* A contract between A and B cannot impose liabilities on X . The two major exceptions to this are the following.

(*i*) Sale of ships. If X buys a ship from B which has previously been chartered by A he may be bound by the charter party if he has notice of its terms — *see Strathcona S.S.* case (1926).

(*ii*) Restrictive covenants affecting land. These may run with the land, i.e. X may be bound by a covenant in favour of A attaching to land that X purchases from B (*see* 21: **14**).

Capacity

8. Capacity
These are certain special rules relating to capacity to contract:

(**a**) *Aliens* They have full capacity, save that they cannot own or hold shares in British ships.

Aliens resident in countries at war with Britain are classed as enemy aliens. They cannot sue in British courts during war-time, but can be sued and, if sued, they can defend the action, appeal and lodge counter-claims in the normal way, either personally or through agents — *see Porter* v. *Freudenberg* (1915).

(b) *Foreign sovereigns and senior diplomats* They have diplomatic immunity and cannot be sued in British courts, unless they voluntarily submit to the jurisdiction.

(c) *Patients* These are persons who are suffering any of the disorders listed in the Mental Health Act 1983, s.1(2). A contract is valid unless the person can prove:

(*i*) that he was so insane as not to understand what the contract was about; and

(*ii*) that the other party was aware of this — *see Imperial Loan Co.* v. *Stone* (1892); *Hart* v. *O'Connor* (1985).

Mentally disordered persons are subject to the Sale of Goods Act 1979, s. 3 (*see* 6: **10**).

(d) *Drunken persons* These seem to be subject to the same rules as mentally disordered persons — *see Gore* v. *Gibson* (1845). They are also subject to the Sale of Goods Act 1979, s. 3 (*see* 6: **10**).

(e) *Corporations* (*see* 6: **9**).

(f) *Minors* (*see* 6: **10**).

9. Corporations

These can make any contracts within the powers granted to them at the time of their incorporation or later.

The powers of a statutory company are generally stated in the Act of Parliament that created the company. Those of a registered company are implied in its memorandum of association, which states the objects for which the company is formed; a registered company has such powers as are reasonably necessary to enable it to achieve its objects.

If a corporation acts beyond its powers (*ultra vires*) the contract used to be void as far as the corporation was concerned. However, the position was not always the same for the other party to the contract (*see* 4: **10**). Before the Companies Act 1989, if a contract was *ultra vires* a corporation, it could not be ratified in any circumstances, even if all the members unanimously voted to ratify it (*see Re Jon Beauforte Ltd* (1953)), nor could they change the objects clause of the memorandum of association to prevent the contracts being *ultra vires* — *see Ashbury Carriage Co.* v. *Riche* (1875).

The Companies Act 1989 has, broadly, amended the Companies

Act 1985 to the effect that the validity of an act by a company cannot be challenged as being beyond the capacity of the company. So, third parties are protected from the *ultra vires* rule and can enforce contracts. Companies can enforce them too, but shareholders can apply for injunctions to prevent *ultra vires* contracts being entered into. Members can ratify otherwise *ultra vires* acts by the directors. A company's objects can now be simply 'to carry on business as a general commercial company', considerably relaing the limits of *ultra vires*.

10. Minors

A minor (sometimes still called 'an infant') attains his majority at the first instant of his eighteenth birthday.

Minors' contracts are roughly divisible into three classes: binding, voidable and void:

(a) *Contracts binding on minors*

   (*i*) Executed contracts for 'necessaries', i.e. goods and services necessary to maintain the minor in the style to which he is accustomed, having regard to his social position. A married minor may be liable for necessaries supplied to his wife and children and for funeral and legal expenses, etc.

Concerning goods, a minor must pay a reasonable price for goods suitable to his condition in life and to his actual requirements at the time of sale, and delivery: Sale of Goods Act 1979, s. 3. Thus if a minor orders 11 fancy waistcoats, he cannot be made to pay for them, as so many waistcoats cannot be suitable to actual requirements, though a couple might be — *see Nash* v. *Inman* (1908). There is no liability for undelivered goods, but, under the Minors' Contracts Act 1987, a court can order the restitution of goods acquired under an unenforceable or repudiated contract.

   (*ii*) Beneficial contracts of service, i.e. contracts of benefit to the minor in his education or training for a career, such as apprenticeships. Such contracts are binding even if they contain one or two burdensome terms, provided they are beneficial on the whole.

A contract signed by a young boxer, which was intended to protect him from exploitation during his minority, contained a clause by which he was to forfeit his pay for a fight if disqualified for fouling. It was held that this clause was burdensome but was binding as the contract as a whole was beneficial — *see Doyle* v. *White City Stadium* (1935).

C contracted with a publisher to publish his autobiography, as his wife and child needed money. Later C tried to avoid the contract. It was held that it was binding, as beneficial in earning C a livelihood — *see Chaplin* v. *Leslie Frewin (Publishers) Ltd* (1966).

(b) *Contracts voidable by a minor* Contracts requiring express repudiation are those involving a continuing interest in property of a permanent nature. Such a contract becomes binding when the minor is 18 unless he expressly repudiates it before or within a reasonable time after that, e.g. leases, contracts to take shares in a company, partnerships and some marriage settlements.

In a lease, a minor must pay the agreed rent until he disclaims the lease and may be unable to disclaim unless he does so before or within a reasonable time after his eighteenth birthday — *see Davies* v. *Benyon-Harris* (1931).

(c) *Contracts void against minors* The following are absolutely void against a minor:

- (*i*) contracts for repayment of money lent or to be lent;
- (*ii*) contracts for goods supplied or to be supplied (other than necessaries);
- (*iii*) all accounts stated, e.g. IOUs and other admissions of indebtedness (Infants Relief Act 1874, s.1). The Betting and Loans (Infants) Act 1892 makes void any promise made by a person after he comes of full age to pay a loan contracted during minority.

Note also that:

(a) a minor incurs no liability by signing a bill of exchange, such as a cheque, as drawer, endorser or acceptor (Bills of Exchange Act 1882, s. 22);

(b) if a minor fraudulently obtains goods under a void contract he must return them, but he cannot be made to pay for them — *see Leslie* v. *Sheill* (1914);

(c) a minor can recover money or property he has transferred under a void contract only if he has received no benefit under the contract — *see Valentini* v. *Canali* (1889);

(d) if an adult guarantees a loan made to a minor, the guarantee is void as well as the contract of loan — *see Coutts* v. *Browne-Lecky* (1947) — but not guarantees undertaken since the implementation of the Minors Contracts Act 1987, s. 2 (1987);

(e) if a minor borrows money to buy necessaries, he must repay the loan as the lender is placed in the position of the seller of the necessaries, i.e. is 'subrogated' into the position of the seller.

Progress test 6

1. What is meant by valuable consideration?   **(1)**

2. What is meant by saying that consideration must be real but need not be adequate?   **(2)**

3. What is meant by saying that consideration must move from the promisee?   **(3)**

4. What is past consideration and when, if ever, will it suffice to support a simple contract?   **(3)**

5. State the rule in *Foakes* v. *Beer* (1884) and mention any exceptions to it.   **(4, 5)**

6. State the rules governing promissory estoppel, and explain why it is ' a shield and not a sword'.   **(5)**

7. Explain the doctrine of privity of contract.   **(6)**

8. Summarise the exceptions to the doctrine of privity of contract. **(6)**

9. When, if ever, will the contracts of an insane person be enforceable?   **(8)**

10. What types of corporation are covered by the *ultra vires* doctrine, and what is the effect of an *ultra vires* contract?   **(9)**

11. What is a minor? What contracts are binding on minors?   **(10)**

12. A minor is bound by executed contracts for necessaries. What is meant by necessaries here? Must the minor pay the full price asked?   **(10)**

13. What contracts are (a) void, and (b) voidable against a minor? **(10)**

7
The terms of a contract

General considerations

1. **The contents of a contract**
   There are three aspects of the contents of a contract that we need to consider.

(a) *What are the terms?* A contract is a bargain between the parties. The contents of the contract are therefore principally *express terms* — what the parties agreed orally or in writing (*see* 7: **2**). In strictly limited circumstances, the courts are prepared to imply terms (*see* 7: **3**).

(b) *What is the status of those terms?* Obviously not all terms are of equal importance. If you buy a car and find that it does not have, as advertised, a radio, then the seller is in breach of a term. It is not a very important term, and you will be satisfied if the seller gives you money with which to buy a radio. If you buy a car and find there is no engine then a far more important term is in breach. It may be that money will not be enough, you may want to repudiate the contract altogether. The more important terms of a contract are called *conditions* (*see* 7: **4**): less important terms are called *warranties* (*see* 7: **4**). Where the importance of a term is not apparent until it has been broken, the term is called *innominate* (*see* 7: **6**).

(c) *When do those terms come into effect?* Sometimes a term operates to suspend or terminate the contract. The term is then called a *condition precedent* or a *condition subsequent* (*see* 7: **7**).

2. **Express terms**
   As we have already seen (*see* 5: **2**) the terms of a contract may be wholly oral, wholly in writing or partly oral and partly in writing.

(a) *Terms wholly oral* This presents a pure question of fact. What did the parties actually say?

(b) *Terms wholly in writing* A contract that is wholly in writing is subject to the *parol evidence rule*. The rule is this: 'If there be a contract which has been reduced into writing, verbal evidence is not allowed to be given of what passed between the parties, either before the written instrument was made, or during the time that it was in a state of preparation, so as to add to or subtract from, or in any manner to vary or qualify the written contract' — Lord Denman in *Goss* v. *Lord Nugent* (1833). The parol evidence rule applies only to the express terms of the contract. It does not apply, for example, to:

(*i*)   the validity of the contract (whether there was a mistake, misrepresentation or absence of consideration);

(*ii*) implied terms (*see* 7: **3**);

(*iii*) the construction of ambiguities (*see* 7: **8**);

(*iv*) rectification (*see* 7: **9**).

(c) *Terms partly oral and partly in writing* Sometimes the actual agreement may be oral, for example an agreement to buy a ticket, but it may be subject to a set of written standard terms (*see* 7: **10**). In *Mendelssohn* v. *Normand* (1970), P left his car in D's garage. He was told by an attendant not to lock the car, so he gave the keys to the attendant, who agreed to lock the car when he had moved it. The attendant gave P a ticket. The ticket exempted D from liability for any loss or damage however caused. Later P found that his luggage was stolen. The Court of Appeal held that: D was liable for the loss of the luggage notwithstanding the exemption clause. As Phillimore, LJ, put it, 'If one has an express undertaking, as here, followed by printed clauses, the latter must fail in so far as they are repugnant to the express undertaking'.

3.   Implied terms

The general rule is that the parties are presumed to have expressed their intentions fully. Lord Pearson in *Trollope & Colls* v. *N.W. Metropolitan Regional Hospital Board* (1973) put it thus: 'An unexpressed term can be implied if and only if the court finds that the parties must have intended that term to form part of their contract. It is not enough for the court to find that such a term would have been adopted by the parties as reasonable men if it had been suggested to them. It must have been a term that went without saying, a term necessary to give business efficacy to the contract, a term which although tacit, formed part of the contract which the parties made for themselves'.

There are three situations in which the courts will imply terms into contracts:

(a) to give effect to the *clear intentions* of the parties;

(b) where *custom or statute* requires it (examples are found in the Sale of Goods Act 1979, *see* 12: **11**);

(c) where, in certain circumstances, it is necessary to give *business efficacy* to the contract — *see The Moorcock* (1889).

Lord Denning, MR, once suggested that a term should be implied where this would be reasonable as well as where it is necessary, but the House of Lords rejected this idea and restated the traditional position in *Liverpool City Council* v. *Irwin* (1976), a case that dealt with the obligations of local authority landlords towards their tenants in high rise or multistorey dwellings. The issue was whether there was an implied term that the council should maintain the stairs, lifts and other common parts of the tower block in question. The decision that it should was because stairs, lifts and lights were 'essentials of the tenancy, without which life in the dwellings, as a tenant, is not possible'. As Lord Wilberforce stated the test, 'Such obligation should be read into the contract as the nature of the contract implicitly requires, no more, no less; a test in other words of necessity'. The same reasoning was applied in *Wettern Electric Ltd* v. *Welsh Development Agency* (1983).

4.   Conditions and warranties

As we have seen (*see* 7: **1(b)**), the difference between a condition and a warranty is apparent on breach. The distinction is illustrated by two operatic cases reported in 1876:

(a) In *Poussard* v. *Spiers and Pond* (1876), a lady was engaged to perform in an opera from the first night. She fell ill and the producer was forced to employ a substitute. Although she recovered after ten days, the uncertainty entitled the producer to repudiate the contract. As Blackburn, J said,'Failure on the plaintiff's part went to the root of the matter and discharged the defendants'.

(b) In *Bettini* v. *Gye* (1876), a singer fell ill, but missed only part of the rehearsals and recovered in good time for the performance. This did not go to the root of the matter, it was only a breach of warranty giving rise to damages.

The breach of a condition gives the innocent party a choice:

(a) He can repudiate the contract, be free from his own future obligations and recover damages to compensate him for any obligations he has already performed, which is known as discharge by breach (*see* 9: **9**).

(b) He can affirm the contract and recover damages; to compensate him for the breach.

The breach of a warranty entitles the innocent party to nothing more than damages; he does not have the choice of repudiation.

How do we know whether a term is a condition or a warranty? Use of the word 'condition' is not decisive — *see Schuler* v. *Wickman Machine Tool Sales* (1974) — and nor is use of the word warranty (Sale of Goods Act 1979, s. 11 (3)). Sometimes a statute tells us which terms are conditions and which warranties. The Sale of Goods Act 1979, ss. 10–15, sets out the conditions and warranties implied in a contract for the sale of goods (*see* 12: **11**), but the Act does not cover all the terms in a contract for the sale of goods, nor does it apply to other types of contract. The law was discussed by the Court of Appeal in *The Hansa Nord* (1976) case. Two approaches have been followed in the modern cases. The courts have looked at:

(a) the status of the term at the time when the contract was made (*see* 7: **5**); and

(b) the consequences of the breach (*see* 7: **6**).

5. Conditions

The traditional approach of distinguishing the important terms as conditions at the time when the contract was made was used in *The Mihalis Angelos* (1970) case. This was a shipping case in which the Court of Appeal had to decide the status of the term 'expected ready to load' in a charterparty. The shipowner undertook that he expected his ship to be ready to load by about a certain date. It was not ready and the question, therefore, was whether or not the charterer could repudiate the contract. The Court of Appeal decided that the term in question was a condition and the charterer could repudiate, even though he could not establish that the breach had produced serious consequences. Megaw, LJ, gave several reasons for this approach.

(a) *certainty* there are obvious advantages in a predictable and uniform 'legal categorisation of a particular, definable type of contractual clause in common use';

(b) *justice* 'If a shipowner has chosen to assert contractually, but dishonestly or without reasonable grounds, that he expects his vessel to be ready to load on such and such a date, wherein does the grievance lie?';

(c) *consistency* with decisions on similar clauses contained in analogous documents.

This approach is useful in unilateral contracts. A unilateral contract is one in which one party's obligation only arises if the other party does something. The newsagent is obliged to give me a newspaper only if I give him the money first. The commonest contracts of this kind in English law are options for good consideration to buy or to sell or to grant or take a lease, competitions for prizes and such contracts as that discussed in *Carlill* v. *Carbolic Smoke Ball Co.* (*see* 5: **10**) and *United Dominions Trust* v. *Eagle* (1968) — Diplock, LJ. As there is no obligation to do anything in a unilateral contract, the courts will not look at the consequences of breach. The status of the obligations in a unilateral contract is defined at the time the contract is made.

6.   Innominate terms

Many contracts are not unilateral. They are, to use Lord Diplock's term, synallagmatic. A synallagmatic contract is one in which 'each party undertakes to the other to do or to refrain from doing something and, in the event of his failure to perform his undertaking, the law provides the other party with a remedy. The remedy of the other party may be limited to recovering monetary compensation for any loss which he has sustained as a result of the failure, without relieving him from his own obligation to do that which he himself has undertaken to do and has not yet done or to continue to refrain from doing that which he himself has undertaken to refrain from doing. Or it may, in addition, entitle him, if he so elects to be released from any further obligation to do or to refrain from doing anything' — Diplock, LJ, in *United Dominions Trust* v. *Eagle* (1968).

At the time when the contract is made, it is not clear which the law will do. The terms of the contract are *innominate*: that is, their status is not known until the consequences of the breach are apparent. The breach will justify repudiation if the effect of it is to 'deprive the party who has further undertakings still to perform of substantially the whole benefit which it was the intention of the parties as expressed in the contract that he should obtain as the consideration for performing those undertakings' — Diplock LJ in *Hong Kong Fir Shipping Co.* v. *Kawasaki Kisen Kaisha* (1962).

Some criticism of the stricter rules relative to the sale of goods (*see* 7: **4**) was expressed in *The Hansa Nord* (1976) case and by the House of Lords in *Reardon-Smith Line* v. *Hansen-Tangen* (1976). In the latter case, Lord Wilberforce, also speaking for other law lords, said that 'The general law of contract has developed along much more rational lines (e.g. *Hong Kong Fir*) in attending to the nature and gravity of a breach or departure rather than in accepting rigid categories which do or do not automatically give a right to rescind, and if the choice were between extending cases under the Sale of Goods Act 1893 [now re-enacted in the Sale of Goods Act 1979] into other fields, or allowing more modern doctrine to infect those cases, my preference would be clear'. The future of the innominate term approach seems assured, although where, as here, the law develops as the cases arise, there will always be variations in approach. This arises between judges and between cases decided by the same judge. *See*, for example, Lord Wilberforce again, but in *Bunge Corporation* v. *Tradax* (1981).

7. Terms defining the operation of a contract
There are three special kinds of conditions.

(a) *condition precedent* — a condition that the contract shall not bind one or both of the parties until such condition is fulfilled, e.g. 'this contract not to be binding until the war ends';
(b) *condition subsequent* — a condition under which the contract shall cease to be binding at the option of one party on the happening of a certain event, e.g. 'this contract shall cease to be binding if war breaks out' (this is called a *determinable contract* and is binding until the condition subsequent is satisfied; contrast a *voidable* contract *see* 8: **1**);
(c) *condition concurrent* — a condition under which performance by one party is made dependent on performance by the other at the same time, e.g. payment of price upon delivery of goods ordered.

8. Construction of terms
Every case or contract involves the construction of terms, but all we can do here is to summarise some of the rules as this is a huge subject in its own right:

(a) The language used must be construed as far as possible in such a way as to give effect to the *intentions* of the parties. As Lord Wilberforce said in *Reardon-Smith Line* v. *Hansen Tangen* (1976), 'When one speaks of the intention of the parties to the contract, one is speaking objectively — the parties cannot themselves give direct evidence of what their intention was — and what must be ascertained is what is to be taken as the intention which reasonable people would have had if placed in the situation of the parties'.
(b) Words must be presumed to have their *normal literal meaning*.
(c) Where there are *two possible meanings*, one legal and one illegal,

the legal meaning is to be preferred so as to render the contract enforceable. (Illegal contracts are void.)

(d) The contract is to be construed most strongly against the party who drew it up (the *contra proferentem* rule). This is particularly important in the construction of exclusion clauses (*see* 7: **13**).

(e) Contracts are to be construed according to their *proper law*, i.e. usually the law of the country where they were made. (*see* 7: 9: **10**).

(f) If the contract fails to express the undoubted intentions of the parties, the court will *rectify* it so as to make it express those intentions (*see* 7: **9**).

9.   Rectification

Rectification is an equitable remedy (*see* 23: **5**). The courts will rectify the written instrument embodying the contract, not the contract itself. The remedy is available where:

(a) the mistake to be rectified lies only in the words used;

(b) there is a completed contract with all terms finally agreed;

(c) there is convincing proof, based on oral or written evidence, of a common continuing intention of the parties, and that the instrument fails to express that intention — *Joscelyne* v. *Nissen* (1970);

(d) the mistake is common to both parties — *Craddock Bros* v. *Hunt* (1923).

Standard form contracts

10.   Standard form contracts

'Standard form contracts are of two kinds. The first, of very ancient origin, are those which set out the terms on which mercantile transactions of common occurrence are to be carried out. Examples are bills of lading, charterparties, policies of insurance, contracts of sale in the commodity markets. The standard clauses in these contracts have been settled over the years by negotiation by representatives of the commercial interests involved and have been widely adopted because experience has shown that they facilitate the conduct of trade.' The other kind 'is of comparatively modern origin. It is the result of the concentration of particular kinds of business in relatively few hands'. These are the contracts that 'have been dictated by that party whose bargaining power either exercised alone or in conjunction with others providing similar goods or services, enables him to say: If you want these goods or services at all, these are the only terms on which they are obtainable. Take it or leave it' — Lord Diplock in *Schroeder Music Publishing* v. *Macaulay* (1974).

(a) *Commercial contracts* It is inevitable that large firms should contract on standard terms. Two engineering firms, for example, will contract on their own standard terms or on terms provided by the Institute of Civil Engineers. They have no time to reconsider and renegotiate standard problems such as the details of delivery, when payment is to be made or who is to bear (and therefore insure against) predictable risks. The legal problem here is that where the parties exchange standard terms it may be hard to see *whose* terms define their contractual obligations. This is a question of fact in each case — *see Butler* v. *Ex-Cell-O* (1979).

(b) *Consumer contracts* There is an increasing tendency for an offeror dealing with consumers to write out the contract entirely himself and to demand that the offeree accept all the terms of the offer without modification. The offeror may state all his terms in one document or, as in the case of railway tickets, may simply incorporate by reference certain standard conditions contained in another document. These 'offers with terms annexed' are subject to special rules. They include railway tickets, air and steamship tickets, any printed leases and most contracts for the supply of gas and electricity.

Exclusion clauses

11. Exclusion clauses

Standard form contracts invariably contain exclusion or exemption clauses. These may be clauses which:

(a) exclude liability for certain kinds of damage;
(b) limit the amount of damages that can be recovered for breach of the contract (liquidated damages — *see* 9: **14**) and in shipping cases this is called a demurrage clause;
(c) exclude certain risks in an insurance contract;
(d) provide for disputes to be submitted to arbitration, which is called a *Scott* v. *Avery* (1856) clause.

There are two issues to consider regarding an exclusion clause:

(a) Is the clause incorporated as a term of the contract? (*See* 7: **12**)
(b) If incorporated, is the clause effective? (*See* 7: **13**)

12. Incorporation of exclusion clauses

These are:

(a) *Effect of signature* 'When a document containing contractual terms is signed, then, in the absence of fraud, or, I will add, misrepresentation, the party signing it is bound, and it is wholly immaterial whether he has read the document or not' — Scrutton, LJ, in *L'Estrange* v. *Graucob* (1934). Apart from fraud or misrepresentation (*Curtis* v. *Chemical Cleaning & Dyeing Co.* (1951)) the defence of *non est factum* may also be available (*see* 8: **6**).

(b) *Ticket cases* If the contract is unsigned, the offeree is bound by all the terms in the document or annexed to it, if:

  (*i*) a 'reasonable man' would assume the document to be contractual, e.g. not merely a receipt for money — *see Chapelton* v. *Barry UDC* (1940);

  (*ii*) reasonable care was taken by the offeror to bring the terms to his attention, e.g. by a notice 'for conditions see Company's rules and regulations' clearly displayed on the face of the ticket;

If the notice given is reasonable, it is immaterial whether the offeree actually reads the conditions — *see Parker* v. *SE Railway* (1877) — or even whether the offeree is illiterate and unable to read them — *see Thompson* v. *LMS Railway* (1930);

  (*iii*) notice of annexed conditions was precontractual. A hotel guest makes his contract with the hotel when he signs the visitors' book, and is not bound by conditions contained in a notice he does not see until he reaches his room — *see Olley* v. *Marlborough Court Hotel* (1949) and also *Thornton* v. *Shoe Lane Parking Ltd* (1971) (*see* 5: **9**).

(c) *Previous course of dealing* Even if an exclusion term is not part of the signed terms of the contract and has not been specifically brought to the offeree's attention, it may be effective if the parties have previously consistently relied on it — *see Hardwick Game Farm* v. *Suffolk Agricultural Producers' Association* (1969). The courts are more inclined to apply this rule to a contract between commercial men.

13. Restrictions on exclusion clauses

(a) *Strict construction* Under the *contra proferentem* rule exclusion clauses are narrowly construed, against the person who inserted them. As Scrutton, LJ, said in *Rutter* v. *Palmer* (1922), 'In construing an exemption clause certain general rules may be applied: first the defendant is not exempted from liability for the negligence of his servants unless adequate words are used; secondly, the liability of the defendant apart from the exempting words must be ascertained; then the particular clause in question must be considered; and if the only liability of the party pleading the exemption is a liability for negligence, the clause will more readily operate to exempt him'.

(b) *Fundamental breach* A fundamental breach is one that goes to the root of the contract. As Lord Reid said in *Suisse Atlantique* (1966), 'Where such a fundamental breach has been established, and the innocent party has elected to treat the breach as a repudiation, then the whole contract has ceased to exist, including the exclusion clause, and that clause cannot then be used to exclude an action for loss which will be suffered by the innocent party after it has ceased to exist'.

This idea has often been criticised. It is now generally accepted that there is no such general rule and that each case must be considered on its own merits. A modern and important illustration is the House of Lords' decision in *Photo Production* v. *Securicor* (1980). D undertook to provide a guard for P's factory. One thing he was to guard against was fire. Rather surprisingly, however, the guard deliberately lit a fire and the factory was burned down causing a £615,000 loss. D tried to rely on two exclusion clauses. The House of Lords held that this was perfectly acceptable *in the particular circumstances of the case*. It was perfectly clear in the contractual documentation that D was seeking a complete exemption from all liability, however caused. Between commercial men there was no reason to imply any clauses by way of 'safeguard', such as might be needed in consumer contracts. It was also said that, although the *Suisse Atlantique* case was still good law, it had to be read subject to the freedom of the parties who were bargaining on equal terms to apportion risks as they thought fit. In a clear case, therefore, even most flagrant breaches may be covered by an exclusion clause.

(c) *Statute* The Unfair Contract Terms Act 1977 renders invalid an exclusion clause relied on by a party in the course of business against a consumer except in so far as the clause is a fair and reasonable one in the circumstances. The Act sets out various 'guidelines' for determining whether any particular term is 'fair and reasonable'. In *Photo Production* v. *Securicor* (1980) it was pointed out that this Act should reduce the number of cases coming before the courts to decide whether a particular clause was an effective exclusion clause. *See*, for example, *George Mitchell* v. *Finney Lock Seeds* (1983) and, with reference to excluding liability for negligence, *Smith* v. *Bush* (1990) and *Harris* v. *Wyre Forest District Council* (1990).

Progress test 7

1. What is the parol evidence rule?   (2)

2. In what circumstances will terms be implied into a contract?   (3)

3. Distinguish between conditions and warranties.   (4)

4. How do the courts assess the consequences of the breach of a term?   (5, 6)

5. Distinguish between a condition precedent and a condition subsequent.   (7)

6. Outline the rules governing the equitable remedy of rectification.   (9)

7. What is a standard form contract?   (10)

8. When does an exclusion clause become incorporated into a contract?   (12)

9. Outline the restrictions on exclusion clauses.   (13)

8
Invalidity

Introduction

1. Invalid contracts

Now that we have established the necessary elements of a valid contract, we must look at the factors that will render a contract invalid. These factors are:

(a) mistake (*see* 8: **2–6**);
(b) misrepresentation (*see* 8: **7–11**);
(c) duress (*see* 8: **12**);
(d) undue influence (*see* 8: **13**);
(e) illegality (*see* 8: **14–17**).

It is not possible to categorise very precisely the kinds of invalidity that these factors will cause. There are, however, four broad categories of invalidity:

(a) a *void* contract is generally one that is deemed never to have existed at all; if property is transferred under a contract that is later held to be void then the property can usually be recovered on a quasi-contract (*see* 10);
(b) a *voidable* contract is one that exists but can be brought to an end by one party if he chooses;
(c) an *illegal* contract is one that contravenes a statute or rule of the common law;
(d) an *unenforceable* contract is one that, though perfectly valid in all other respects, lacks some technical requirement, e.g. some necessary written evidence — such a contract will not be enforced by the courts unless and until the defect is rectified.

Such contracts are not void, however, and if they have been performed and property has been transferred, the court will not intervene to set them aside.

Mistake

2.   Operative mistake

In general, a mistake made by one or both parties in making the contract has no effect on the validity of the contract. In some cases, however, a mistake will operate to render the contract either void or voidable. This is called an operative mistake.

(a)   *mistake of law* a mistake of law will only be operative in two cases:
 (*i*)   *mistake of foreign law*, as the law of a foreign country must be proved in an English court as a fact;
 (*ii*)   *mistake as to title* — a contract to lease land one already owns is apparently treated as a mistake of fact — *see Cooper* v. *Phibbs* (1867);

(b)   *mistake of fact* most operative mistakes are mistakes of fact and fall into three categories.
 (*i*)   *common mistake,* where both parties make the same mistake (*see* 8: **3**);
 (*ii*)   *mutual mistake,* where each party is making a different mistake and they are never *ad idem* (*see* 8: **4**);
 (*iii*)   *unilateral mistake,* where one party is mistaken as the other party knows or ought to know (*see* 8: **5, 6**).

3.   Common mistake

Common mistakes are of two kinds.

(a)   *Mistake as to the existence of the subject matter* If there is no subject matter, it follows that there can be no contract. This is partly a matter of construction — *see Associated Japanese Bank* v. *Crédit Du Nord* (1988); partly a statutory provision: 'Where there is a contract for the sale of specific goods, and the goods without the knowledge of the seller have perished at the time when the contract is made, the contract is void' (Sale of Goods Act 1979, s. 6).

(b)   *Fundamental mistake of fact* Where the parties contract under a fundamental misapprehension as to a state of affairs, or facts forming the basis of the contract, the contract is void. The contract will therefore be void if the life of a dead man is insured (*Scott* v. *Coulson* (1903)) or unmarried parties make a separation agreement (*Galloway* v. *Galloway* (1914)).

The mistake must relate to the *fundamental nature* of the subject matter, or its *identity*. Mere mistakes as to the *value or quality* of the subject matter, even though common to both parties, apparently do not make the contract void. In *Bell* v. *Lever Bros* (1932), L employed B as managing director of one of L's subsidiary companies at a salary of £8,000. After three years, L decided to close down B's company, and paid B £30,000 as compensation for loss of office. Later L discovered that B, unknowingly, had committed irregularities that would have entitled L to dismiss him without compensation. L sued for recovery of the £30,000 on the grounds of common mistake. It was held that there had been common mistake, but merely as to the *value* or quality of what was bought (i.e. discharge from B's service contract). The mistake was not operative, and so the contract could not be set aside.

Where there is a fundamental mistake that does not render the contract void at common law, equity may still give a remedy. Equitable remedies in connection with a contract that is not void include:

(a) *Rectification* (*see* 23: **5**).
(b) *Specific performance* (*see* 23: **6**). The limitations of this remedy are shown by the case where A agreed to buy a house from B, both parties mistakenly believing it to be rent-controlled (which greatly reduced the value). When the truth was discovered, A endeavoured to enforce the contract. It was held that this was a mistake as to value, not sufficient to render the contract void at law. However, as specific performance is an equitable remedy and 'he who comes into equity must come with clean hands', specific performance would be granted only on terms that a more realistic price should be paid — *see Grist* v. *Bailey* (1967);
(c) Rescission of the contract, where 'the mistake was fundamental and the party seeking to set it aside was not himself at fault' — *see* Denning, LJ, in *Solle* v. *Butcher* (1950).

4. Mutual mistake

Here the contract is void because the parties *misunderstand* each other as to the basis of the contract, i.e. each makes a *different* mistake. Thus there is no real concurrence of offer and acceptance; A is offering one thing, B accepting another.

The test applied by the courts is — what inference would a reasonable man draw from the parties' conduct?

Examples

(1) In *Raffles* v. *Wichelhaus* (1864), A and B contracted for the shipment of a cargo on the ship *Peerless* out of Bombay. Unknown to either party, there

were two ships of the same name in Bombay at the time, each leaving on different dates. A meant *Peerless* No. 1 and B meant *Peerless* No. 2. It was held that the purported contract was void, as the date of departure was fundamental to the contract.

(2) In *Scriven* v. *Hindley* (1913), A, an auctioneer, was offering flax for sale. B bid a high price, thinking that hemp was being sold. It was held that there was no contract. B offered one thing, A accepted another.

---

5. Unilateral mistake as to the identity of the person contracted with

A contract is voidable where:

(a) A contracts with B under the impression that he is contracting with C;

(b) before or at the time of contracting, B knew of this mistake;

(c) it was of fundamental importance to A that he should be contracting with C; and

(d) A took all reasonable steps to verify that he was contracting with C.

Where the parties contracted 'face to face' the presumption is that there can be no mistake as to identity — *see Phillips* v. *Brooks* (1919) and *Lewis* v. *Averay* (1971). This presumption can be rebutted, however, by clear evidence to the contrary — *see Ingram* v. *Little* (1960)(a heavily criticised case).

Contrast the following cases:

(a) In *Phillips v. Brooks* (1919), a rogue, X, entered a jewellers and offered to buy goods. His offer was accepted and he then offered to pay by cheque. The jeweller accepted the cheque but said delivery would be delayed until the cheque was cleared. The rogue then said that he was a well-known person and asked to take some of the jewels immediately. Deceived as to his identity, the jeweller let him take some of the goods. X then took jewels and sold them to a pawnbroker and the cheque proved worthless. It was held that the contract was made *before* the identity became important, therefore it was *not void* on the grounds of mistake. The contract was in fact merely *voidable* on the grounds of misrepresentation.

(b) In *Lewis* v. *Averay* (1971) CA, L advertised his car for sale and B, a rogue, answered, describing himself as a well-known film star. L was impressed and accepted B's cheque after B had produced a film-studio admission card as proof of identity. B then took the car and sold it to A, a bona fide purchaser. When L discovered the fraud, he sued A to recover the car. It was held that L intended to contract with the man he met 'face to face' and the contract was therefore *not* void for mistake, but merely *voidable* for misrepresentation.

(c) In *Ingram* v. *Little* (1960), a rogue, X, offered to buy a car from I and to pay by cheque. I refused the offer and the cheque, as she did not know X. X then convinced her that he was a well-known person and, being convinced, she accepted his cheque and let him take the car. He sold the car to L and the cheque proved worthless. It was held that the purported contract between X and I was *void* for mistake, as the mistake occurred during the negotiations and I would not have accepted X's offer if she had not been convinced of his identity. Consequently, X never had any right to the car and so could not lawfully sell it to L, so that in the action in court I was allowed to recover the car from L. (In *Phillips* v. *Brooks*, the jeweller was not allowed to recover the jewels from B, the pawnbroker, who had bought them in good faith from X, as X had a *voidable* title to the jewels.)

6. Unilateral mistake as to the nature of the contract signed

Generally a person who signs a contract is bound by it, even if he has not read it — *see L'Estrange* v. *Graucob* (1934) (*see* 7: **12**).

The defence of *non est factum* operates to avoid this rule in a very limited number of cases. The extent of the defence was discussed by the House of Lords in *Saunders* v. *Anglia Building Society* (1970). P, a lady aged 78, signed a document transferring her house to D. She did not read the document and signed it believing that she was giving her house to her nephew who would allow her to continue to live there. On the facts of the case P failed. To succeed, she would have needed to establish three things:

(a) that the document was radically different in type from what she thought she was signing;

(b) that she was not negligent in failing to know this;

(c) that she would not have signed had she known the true facts — 'There must be a heavy burden of proof on the person who seeks to invoke this remedy', said Lord Reid (*see*, for example, *United Dominions Trust* v. *Western* (1976).

Misrepresentation

7. Misrepresentation

A person who has entered into a contract as a result of a

misrepresentation may be entitled to rescind the contract or to be compensated by damages for all his loss — *see Royscot Trust Ltd.* v. *Maidenhead Honda Centre* (1991).

To amount to a misrepresentation, the statement must have the following characteristics:

(a) *It must be made by a party to the contract or his agent* A misrepresentation made otherwise than by a party to a contract may be actionable in tort (*see* 16: **10–11**).

(b) *It must be a positive statement* Except in the case of a contract *uberrimae fidei* (*see* 8: **11**), there is no general duty of disclosure. A buyer has no remedy against a seller who sells pigs 'with all faults' *knowing* that they had swine fever and *knowing* that the buyer was unaware of this. He did not positively represent the pigs as healthy — *see Ward* v. *Hobbs* (1878).

(c) *It must be false*, whether innocent or negligent (*see* 8: **8**) or fraudulent (*see* 8: **9**).

(d) *It must state an existing fact* In tort, a negligent expression of opinion may be actionable (*see* 16: **10–11**).

(e) *It must be material*, and not a mere advertising puff.

(f) *It must be relied upon* In *Horsfall* v. *Thomas* (1862), A sold a broken gun to B, and patched the barrel with clay to conceal a crack. B did not examine the gun, and so was not misled by the patch. It was held that the misrepresentation was not actionable, as it had no effect on B.

(g) *It must not be a term of the contract* If a misrepresentation is made during negotiations and is later incorporated as a term in the contract, the remedies of the injured party will be basically those for *breach of contract*. The remedies available will then depend on whether the term incorporating the representation is a *condition* or a *warranty* (*see* 7: **4**). The contract can, however, still be rescinded for misrepresentation (*see* 8: **8** (*a*)).

8. Misrepresentation Act 1967
The basis of the modern law is the Misrepresentation Act 1967. The Act has four main provisions.

(a) Section 1 permits rescission of the contract (*see* 8: **10**) even though:
    (*i*) the misrepresentation has become a term; or
    (*ii*) the contract has been performed.

(b) Section 2(1) permits damages to be recovered for loss suffered as a result of a misrepresentation made by a party to the contract unless the party making the misrepresentation proves that he had reasonable ground to believe, and did believe, up to the time that the contract was made that the facts represented were true. This is a negligent misrepresentation in the sense of innocent but careless. It differs from negligent misrepresentation (also known as negligent mis-statements) in tort (*see* 8: **10**) in two respects:

> (*i*) in tort there must be a special relationship; under the Act the representation must be made by a party to the contract.
>
> (*ii*) under the Act negligence is presumed; the tort depends on the reliance.

(c) Section 2(2) permits the court to declare the contract subsisting and to award damages even though the plaintiff is seeking rescission.

(d) Section 3 (as substituted by the Unfair Contract Terms Act 1977 (*see* 7: **13**)) provides that a term excluding liability for misrepresentation has no effect except in so far as it is reasonable; the party claiming the term is reasonable must prove that it is so. This differs from negligent misrepresentation in tort (*see* 16: **10–11**) where the parties can sometimes exclude liability by express agreement.

9. Fraudulent misrepresentation

A fraudulent misrepresentation is 'An untrue statement made knowingly, or without belief in its truth, or recklessly, careless whether it be true or false' — Lord Herschel in *Derry* v. *Peek* (1889) HL.

A person to whom a fraudulent misrepresentation can choose from two remedies:

(a) to affirm the contract and claim damages for the tort of deceit or fraud (*see* 16: **10**); or

(b) to repudiate the contract, or have it rescinded, with or without claiming damages for deceit.

10. Limits to the right of rescission

Although the misled party can generally have the contract rescinded (set aside), this right is lost in the following cases:

(a) *Affirmation* Where the injured party has expressly or impliedly affirmed the contract *after* learning of the misrepresentation — *see* *Long* v. *Lloyd* (1958).

(b) *Restitution impossible* Where the parties cannot be restored to their original position, i.e. *restitutio in integrum* (total restitution) is impossible.

(c) *Prejudice of third parties* Where an innocent third party has obtained an interest in the subject matter of the contract in good faith and for value — *see Phillips* v. *Brooks* (1919) (*see* 8: **5**).

(d) *Undue delay* Where, in a case of innocent misrepresentation the plaintiff delays unreasonably in seeking rescission, the court may refuse him the discretionary equitable remedy of rescission. In the case of *Leaf* v. *International Galleries* (1950), A bought a painting from B, which B described as being 'by Constable'. Five years later A discovered that the painting was not by Constable, and was worth less than he had paid for it. He sued for rescission. It was held that he might have been entitled to damages for breach of warranty (which he had not sought), but he was not entitled to rescission because of his delay.

11. Contracts *uberrimae fidei* ('of the utmost good faith')

Although there is no general duty of disclosure, in some exceptional contracts the law imposes a special duty to act with the utmost good faith, i.e to disclose all material information.

Failure so to disclose renders the contract *voidable* at the option of the other party.

Examples

(1) *Contracts of insurance* The insured must disclose all facts that would influence the judgment of a prudent insurer, whether to decline the risk or to increase the premium.

(2) *Contract of family arrangement*, for the settlement of family property, etc. Each member of the family must disclose any portions he or she has already received without the knowledge of other members of the family.

(3) *Company prospectuses* Directors or promoters must make full disclosure in any prospectus inviting the public to subscribe for shares in the company, as given in the Companies Act 1985, s. 67. (Failure to do so renders the contract voidable and makes the director etc. liable for damages.)

(4) *Contracts for sale of land* The vendor must disclose any defects in title. The duty does not extend to other matters, e.g. the physical quantities of the land.

(5) *Guarantee and partnership contracts* These contracts are not *uberrimae fidei* at their formation, but, once made, they impose a duty on the parties to disclose all matters coming to their knowledge subsequently and likely to influence the judgment of other parties.

Duress

12. Duress

It is well established that where a person enters into a contract by reason of actual or threatened violence, for example unlawful confinement or violence threatened to his wife, children or parents, then the contract is voidable for duress — *see Cumming* v. *Ince*. (1847).

The position is less clear where violence or restraint is threatened to the person's *property*. The traditional view is that this does not amount to duress, although money paid as a direct result of the restraint can be recovered — *see Maskell* v. *Horner* (1915). In recent years this traditional view has been criticised and a wider doctrine of 'economic duress' seems to be growing (*see Atlas Express Ltd* v. *Kafco* (1989)). In *North Ocean Shipping Co.* v. *Hyundai Construction Co.* (1979), Mocatta, J, surveyed the English and the American cases and reached three conclusions: 'First, I do not take the view that the recovery of money paid under duress other than to the person is necessarily limited to duress to goods falling within one of the categories hitherto established by the English cases. Second, from this it follows that the compulsion may take the form of "economic duress" if the necessary facts are proved. A threat to break a contract may amount to such "economic duress". Third, if there has been such a form of duress leading to a contract for consideration, I think that contract is a voidable one which can be avoided and the excess money paid under it recovered'. (*See also Pao On* v. *Lau Yiu Long* (1980) *and Atlas Express* v. *Kafco Importers* (1989)). An important illustration is *Dimskal Shipping* v. *Internatioanl Transport Workers Federation* (1991), where the ITF's 'blacking' of a ship in order to obtain new contracts was held to amount to duress.

Undue influence

13. Undue influence

Undue influence is an equitable doctrine under which a contract may be voidable if it derives from pressure or coercion short of duress. The test is whether free judgment has been exercised. Ungoed-Thomas J, defined this to be of two kinds in *Re Craig* (1971), 'There are two well established classes of undue influence. The first is where the donee stands in such a fiduciary relation to the donor that a presumption of undue influence arises which prevails unless rebutted by the donee; and secondly, where undue influence is established independently of such a presumption'.

(a) *Presumption of undue influence* Ungoed-Thomas, J, went on to say, 'What has to be proved to raise the presumption of undue influence is first a gift so substantial (or doubtless otherwise of such a nature) that it cannot, prima facie, be reasonably accounted for on the ground of the ordinary motives on which ordinary men act; and secondly, a relationship between donor and donee in which the donor has such confidence and trust in the donee as to place the donee in a position to exercise undue influence over the donor in making such a gift':

> (i) *the gift* — it is clear from *Re Brocklehurst* (1978) that the test is not objective. The court takes full account of the particular character and attitudes of the particular donor;
> (ii) *the relationship* — the presumption arises in contracts between, for example, parent and child, trustee and beneficiary, solicitor and client, doctor and patient, priest and communicant, teacher and pupil;

(b) *Rebutting the presumption* — 'It is necessary for the donee to prove that the gift was the result of the free exercise of independent will', said Lord Hailsham LC in *Inche Noriah* v. *Shaik Allie Bin Omar* (1929), and this can be shown by proving, for example, that:

> (i) full disclosure of all material facts was made;
> (ii) the consideration was adequate;
> (iii) the weaker party was in receipt of independent legal advice; or
> (iv) the gift was spontaneous — *see Re Brocklehurst* (1978).

(c) *Other cases of undue influence* Even where it is not presumed, undue influence may still be alleged. In such cases the plaintiff must prove:

> (i) that it existed; and
> (ii) that it was exerted — *see Hodgson* v. *Marks* (1971).

It has been emphasised that the jurisdiction is based on *undue influence*; mere inequality of bargaining power is not enough of itself to justify the intervention of the courts — *see National Westminster Bank* v. *Morgan* (1985) HL.

(d) *Right to relief lost* Relief for undue influence is discretionary, and the claim for avoidance of the contract may be refused where:

> (i) the plaintiff's conduct has been tricky or unfair; or
> (ii) the plaintiff has delayed unreasonably in seeking relief — *see Allcard* v. *Skinner* (1887).

Void and illegal contracts

14. Void and illegal contracts

As Jessel, MR, in *Printing & Numerical Co.* v. *Sampson* (1875) said, the courts 'have this paramount policy to consider — that you are not lightly to interfere with the freedom of contract'.

They will therefore declare a contract void or illegal only where:

(a) a *statute* clearly prohibits the contract; or

(b) a well-established common law rule makes such a contract illegal on the grounds of public policy. This legal presumption in favour of validity is expressed in Latin as *ut res magis valeat quam pereat* ('it is better to preserve than to destroy').

15. Consequences of illegality

Void and illegal contracts have slightly different consequences.

(a) *Ex turpi causa non oritur actio* ('From an evil cause, no action arises') Where a plaintiff seeking the court's protection must rest his claim on his own immoral or illegal act, his claim will fail.

In the *Alexander* v. *Rayson* (1936) case, A rented a flat to R at £1,200 p.a. To avoid tax, they agreed that the money should be paid as £450 for rent and £750 for 'services'. A sued R for unpaid sums for 'services'. It was held that the agreement was made by both parties to defraud the revenue authorities. A, the plaintiff, was equally guilty with R, therefore the contract would not be enforced, and he could not recover the money owing.

(b) *Severance* If a contract is illegal, it is *all* bad. If, however, it has valid aspects, then the void aspects may be severed, either:

    (*i*) by removing any void provision altogether; or

    (*ii*) by restricting the scope of any void provisions.

(c) *Money paid* under a void contract can, in some cases, be recovered on a quasi-contract (*see* 10: **5**), but a claim cannot be founded on illegality.

(d) *Negotiable securities*, such as cheques, exchanged by the parties are *void* as between them; however, an innocent third party who takes such a security in the ordinary course of business and for value may be a holder in due course, in which case he will be legally entitled to enforce the security under the Bills of Exchange Act 1882 (*see* Appendix 1).

16. Contracts void or illegal by statute

These include:

(a) *Gaming and wagering contracts* A wager is a promise to give or pay something on the ascertainment of an uncertain future event, e.g. a horse race. A bet is a wager upon the result of a game.

Such contracts are *void* under the Gaming and Wagering Acts 1845–1968. The position is complex, but the following basic rules apply.

(*i*) money earned as commission on bets and wagers is irrecoverable (Gaming Act 1892), so an agent cannot recover commission from his principal, but the principal can recover winnings from the agent — *see De Mattos* v. *Benjamin* (1894);

(*ii*) negotiable instruments given for a bet are given for an illegal consideration and are void (Gaming Act 1835), so a holder in due course may be protected under the Bills of Exchange Act 1882 (*see* 12: **7**));

(*iii*) money lent to a loser to pay his bets is recoverable (*Re O'Shea* (1911)), but not if the lender himself pays the winner, as he is then participating in the transaction — *see Macdonald* v. *Green* (1951);

(*iv*) the winner of a wager cannot sue the loser for his winnings, even though the loser later makes a fresh promise to pay, supported by fresh consideration — *see Hill* v. *William Hill Ltd* (1949);

(*v*) money paid to a stakeholder to retain pending the result of a wager can be recovered from him by the payer — *see Burge* v. *Ashley & Smith Ltd* (1900).

(b) *Contracts for trading or selling on a Sunday* Except those made lawful in accordance with the Shops Act 1950, under which shops can be licensed to open on Sundays. The issue of 'Sunday trading' has been a matter of heated debate for many years. Some argue in terms of morality, others of commerce, still others of individual liberties. The European Court has decided (*Stoke on Trent City Council* v. *B & Q* (1992)) that the Shops Act does not infringe Community Laws. The Government has announced its preparedness to modify the law. A consultation process began early in 1993.

(c) *Illegal contracts* Megarry J, in *Spector* v. *Ageda* (1971) said, 'Where statute has intervened to strike a transaction with illegality, the courts must give effect not only to the direct provisions of the statute but also to their necessary consequences'. (An example is the Trading with the Enemy Act 1939).

17. Contracts void or illegal at common law

These are:

(a) *Contracts to oust the jurisdiction of the courts*

(b) *Contracts prejudicial to the status of marriage* This includes:

    (*i*) *contracts affecting the freedom of marriage,* e.g. imposing a general restraint upon a person marrying, also marriage brokage contracts, i.e. contracts to arrange marriages for a reward — *see Hermann* v. *Charlesworth* (1905);

    (*ii*) *contracts tending to interfere with the sanctity of marriage,* e.g. a promise by a married man to marry another woman as soon as his wife is dead — *see Wilson* v. *Carnley* (1908).

Engagements to marry are no longer enforceable at law due to the Law Reform (Miscellaneous Provisions) Act 1970, s. 1.

(c) *Contracts to commit crimes or torts,* whether in Britain or in any friendly nation, e.g. a contract to smuggle goods into the United States of America — *see Foster* v. *Driscoll* (1929).

(d) *Sexually immoral contracts,* if a carriage proprietor hires a carriage to a woman knowing that it will be used for the purpose of prostitution, the contract is illegal, and he cannot recover hiring charges — *see Pearce* v. *Brooks* (1866).

(e) *Contracts involving trade with an enemy nation,* illegal at common law and also under the Trading with the Enemy Act 1939 (*see also* 8: **16** (*c*))

(f) *Contracts tending to impede the administration of justice,* e.g. a promise by an accused to indemnify a person who has stood bail for him — *see Herman* v. *Jeuchner* (1885). A contract is also illegal if it tends to maintenance or champerty. Maintenance means giving financial or other assistance to a party in a lawsuit, where the maintainer has no satisfactory legal or moral interest in the case. Champerty means maintenance with a view to sharing the proceeds of the action. A common commercial interest is sufficient to negative maintenance — *see Martell* v. *Consett Iron Co. Ltd* (1955).

(g) *Contracts tending to corrupt public life or to obtain an unfair benefit from the government,* e.g. a promise to use influence to obtain exemptions from legal duty — *see Montefiore* v. *Motor Components Ltd* (1918).

(h) *Contracts to defraud the Inland Revenue* — *see Alexander* v. *Rayson* (1936) (*see* 8: **15**(*a*)).

Contracts in restraint of trade

18. Restraint of trade

Any contract that restricts a person from freely exercising his trade or profession is a contract in restraint of trade. Such contracts are prima facie void, but may be enforced if:

(a) *they are reasonable as between the parties,* i.e. seek to protect a legitimate *proprietary interest,* such as trade secrets or business goodwill;

(b) *they are reasonable in the public interest* — *see Nordenfelt* v. *Maxim-Nordenfelt Co.* (1894).

The categories of restraint of trade are not closed, but the cases fall into three broad classes:

(a) restraints upon employees (*see* 8: **19**);
(b) restraints on the sale of a business (*see* 8: **20**);
(c) *solus* agreements (*see* 8: **21**).

19. Restraints upon employees

An employer may force an employee to sign a covenant promising not to injure the employer's interests after the employment ceases, e.g. by attracting away his former employer's clients.

Such restraints are viewed with distrust by the courts and will be enforced only if they satisfy the following rules:

(a) *The restraint is void unless* the employee has some real *capacity to damage* his former employer's business, e.g. some knowledge of trade secrets that he might impart to competitors or some real influence with his former employer's clients which he could use to seduce them into supporting some other firm.

Thus, the employee must generally be in some moderately confidential capacity, e.g. a solicitor's legal executive, but not a door-to-door salesman with no real influence over customers — *see Mason* v. *Provident Clothing Co.* (1913).

Similarly, a covenant aimed at merely restricting competition is void — *see Eastham* v. *Newcastle Utd* (1964) and *Watson* v. *Prager* (1991) where a boxer's contact with his manager was declared unreasonable. A covenant by a tailor's assistant not to open a competing business within 10 miles of his former employer's has been held ineffective — *see Attwood* v. *Lamont* (1920).

(b) *The restraint must be reasonable* having regard to:

    (*i*) the *type* of employment — *see Mason* v. *Provident Clothing*;
    (*ii*) the *period* of restraint — *see Kores Ltd* v. *Kolok Ltd* (1959);
    (*iii*) the *area* of the restraint, e.g. a solicitor's managing clerk (legal executive) covenanted not to open a competing

business within seven miles of his former employer's. It was held that this was reasonable — *see Fitch* v. *Dewes* (1921).

Example

In *Scorer* v. *Seymour-Jones* (1966), S an estate agent, had two offices at X and Y. J was employed by S and signed a covenant promising not to open a competing business within five miles of either office within three years of leaving S. J was employed only at the X office. It was held that the restraint was too wide, as J never worked at Y office. *See* also *Greer* v. *Sketchleys Ltd* (1979).

20. Restraints on the sale of a business

Restraints imposed by the purchaser of a business on the seller, preventing the latter from competing with the business sold *so as to damage the goodwill* sold, are enforceable if reasonable.

Restraints of this kind are more readily enforced than those between employer and employee, as they lack the element of compulsion that may exist between the parties in a contract of employment.

Examples

(1) In the case of *Nordenfelt* v. *Maxim-Nordenfelt Co.* (1894), N, an inventor of guns, sold his world-wide business to M and promised not to manufacture guns anywhere in the world for 25 years. It was held that this was reasonable and binding.

(2) In *British Concrete Co.* v. *Schelff* (1921), S sold his localised business to C (who had branches all over Britain) and promised not to open a competing business anywhere within ten miles of any of C's branches. It was held that this was void. The restraint was more than was necessary to protect the small local business purchased from S.

21. Solus agreements

The typical solus agreement is one between a garage proprietor and an oil company, under which the garage promises to sell only the petrol and oils provided by the oil company (usually in return for a loan of money). Such agreements are valid if reasonable, and void if not.

Example

In *Esso Petroleum Co. Ltd* v. *Harpers Garage (Stourport) Ltd* (1968), HL, a *solus* agreement contained a clause in which the garage proprietor promised that if he decided to sell his garage within 21 years, he would do so only to a buyer who would accept the same *solus* agreement. It was held that the restraint was unreasonable in the circumstances. (*See* also *Alec Lobb (Garages) Ltd* v. *Total Oil GB Ltd* (1985)).

This also applies to mortgages (*see* 22: **12**). By similar reasoning an exclusive right to publish songs may, if unreasonable and based on the abuse of superior power, constitute a restraint of trade — *see Schroeder Music Publishing Co.* v. *Macaulay* (1974).

Competition law

22. Competition law
Competition law falls into four categories:

(a) *Monopolies and mergers* are subject to the control of the Monopolies Commission.

(b) *Restrictive trading agreements* are controlled by the Restrictive Trade Practices Act 1976 (as modified by the Competition Act 1980). All agreements by which producers, suppliers or exporters of goods restrict the manufacture, supply or distribution of goods by collective agreements between themselves, usually by fixing prices, are void unless they are registered with the Director General of Fair Trading. Once registered, such agreements are submitted for consideration by the Restrictive Practices Court (consisting of one High Court judge and two lay members) (*see* 3: **48**) that may pronounce the agreement void as contrary to the public interest or valid.

All agreements between *two or more persons* carrying on business in the United Kingdom are registrable if they relate to:

(*i*) the prices to be charged, quoted or paid for goods, supplies, offered or acquired or for the application of any process of manufacture to goods;

(*ii*) the prices to be recommended or suggested as to the prices to be charged or quoted in respect of the resale of goods supplied;

(*iii*) the terms or conditions on or subject to which goods are to be supplied or acquired or any such process as it applies to goods;

(*iv*) the quantities or descriptions of goods to be produced, supplied or acquired;

(*v*) the process of manufacture to be applied to any goods or the quantities or descriptions of goods to which any such process is to be applied; or

(*vi*) the persons or classes of persons to, for or from whom, or the areas or places in or from which, goods are to be supplied or acquired, or any such process applied.

(c) *Resale price maintenance* is governed by the Resale Prices Act 1976. Price maintenance agreements are prohibited unless the Restrictive Practices Court considers them to be in the public interest. Only two exemptions have been made — books (1969) and ethical and proprietary drugs (1970).

(d) Agreements affecting trade between member states of the European Community are governed by the EC Treaty, particularly Articles 85 and 86.

Progress test 8

1. Distinguish between common, mutual and unilateral mistake and summarise the categories of operative mistake. (2)

2. A sold to B for £10,000 a painting that both believed to be by Rubens. Four years later B has discovered that the painting is by X, an unknown artist, and is worth only £100. What remedies has B? Would it make any difference to your answer if B discovered the mistake four months after the sale? (3)

3. What is meant by the defence *non est factum*? If A signs an agreement to sell his house, believing it to be merely a mortgage of the house, can he escape the contract? (6)

4. Explain the rules governing unilateral mistakes as to identity. (5)

5. What is a misrepresentation? (7)

6. What constitutes fraudulent misrepresentation? What are the remedies for fraudulent misrepresentation? (9)

7. The equitable remedy of rescission is not always available where misrepresentation is proved. Explain this statement. (10)

8. Define duress and undue influence and explain the distinction. When is undue influence presumed? (12, 13)

9. A joined an eccentric religious order and B, the head of the

order, persuaded A to give £5,000 to the order. Later, A left the order and three years thereafter sued for the return of the £5,000 on the grounds of undue influence. Discuss.   **(13)**.

10. Explain the doctrine of severance.   **(15)**

11. Define a wager and summarise the chief effects of a wagering contract.   **(16)**

12. Define champerty and maintenance and explain their effect. **(17)**

13. What is a contract in restraint of trade and what is the attitude of the courts to such contracts?   **(18)**

14. A owned three grocery shops in Liverpool, Manchester and Bolton. He sold them to B Ltd, a large national retailing company, with 400 branches throughout the United Kingdom. At the time of sale, A signed a covenant not to open a competing shop within one mile of any of B's businesses. Is the covenant enforceable? Would it make any difference to your answer if the covenant restricting A's opening of competing businesses was limited to Lancashire? **(20)**

15. Outline the extent of competition law.   **(22)**

9
Discharge of contracts

Introduction

1. Methods of discharge

Discharge brings the contract to an end. A contract may be discharged in any one of five ways:

(a) by performance (*see* 9: **2–4**);
(b) by agreement between the parties (*see* 9: **5**);
(c) by operation of law (*see* 9: **6**);
(d) by frustration (*see* 9: **7, 8**);
(e) by breach (*see* 9: **9**).

Discharge by performance

2. Complete performance

Performance must be complete and exactly in accord with the terms of the contract.

There are three circumstances in which performance may be partial and yet render the party performing able to be paid:

(a) *Instalments* If performance is to be by instalments, payment can be recovered for instalments actually completed (unless the intention of the parties is to the contrary).

(b) *Partial performance accepted* If the promisee voluntarily accepts less than complete performance where he had genuine freedom of choice, the promisor is entitled to claim payment on *quantum meruit* (*see* 10: **7**). In *Sumpter* v. *Hedges* (1898), A contracted to erect a building for B. When the work was half done, A abandoned the job. B had to complete the building himself, but A sued him for payment for work done on a *quantum meruit*. It was held that B need pay nothing, as he had not freely chosen to complete the building, but had no choice.

(c) *Substantial performance* of a contract for work or services, i.e. where performance is as complete as a reasonable man could expect. This is a question of fact: for example, in the case of *Hoenig* v. *Isaacs* (1952), A decorated B's flat for £750, but, because of faulty workmanship, B had to pay an extra £290 to complete the job. B refused to pay any money to A. It was held that A was entitled to recover £750 less the £290 paid to make good his defective workmanship.

3.   Manner of performance
This can take one of the following forms:

(a) *Tender* It is sometimes sufficient if the promisor merely *attempts* to perform. If performance is rejected, the promisor is discharged from further liabilities and may sue for breach of contract if he so wishes.

Tender of payment relieves the promisor from future liability to make further tenders, but does not discharge his liability to pay.

(b) *Time for performance or payment* Failure to perform or pay on time may be a breach of warranty, but is rarely a breach of condition, i.e. is rarely 'of the essence' of the contract:

 (i)   *time of payment* is not of the essence unless a contrary intention appears in the contract (this rule is statutorily applied to contracts for the sale of goods under the Sale of Goods Act 1979, s. 10.);

 (ii)   *time of performance* is not usually of the essence, but may be made so by agreement and this is usually done in mercantile contracts.

Example _____

In *Rickards* v. *Oppenheim* (1950), O waived the original delivery date, but stipulated a later date as final. It was held that this made the later date 'of the essence', i.e. a *condition* of the contract.

_____

(c) *Payment*:
 (i)   *payment of a smaller sum* will not usually discharge liability to pay a greater (*see* 6: **4**);
 (ii)   *payment to an agent* is usually a good discharge, if the agent is held out as having authority to receive money;
 (iii)   *payment by a third party* is not a good discharge, unless he pays as agent for the debtor — *see Smith* v. *Cox* (1940);
 (iv)   *payment to one joint creditor* discharges liability to the others;
 (v)   *payment by negotiable instrument* is conditional payment only,

until the negotiable instrument is cashed, or as otherwise
agreed;

(vi) *payment by post* is ineffective if the letter is lost in the post,
unless the creditor requested this method of payment
(contrast this with the rules relating to acceptance of offers
by post (*see* 5: **13**));

(vii) *payment by cheque* is now considered prima-facie evidence of
receipt, but a formal receipt can also be demanded (Cheques
Act 1957, s. 3.).

4. Appropriation of payments

Where there are several debts outstanding between the parties,
it is sometimes important to ascertain what payment has discharged
what debt. In the absence of express agreement to the contrary, the
following legal rules apply:

(a) *the debtor can appropriate any payment* to any debt, no matter which
is the longest outstanding;

(b) *if the debtor fails to appropriate* expressly, the *creditor* can
appropriate in any way he chooses, e.g. applying the money to pay
off a statute-barred debt — *see Seymour* v. *Pickett* (1905);

(c) *the rule in Clayton's case* (1816) If there is a *current account* between
the parties, subject to constant incomings and outgoings, then if
neither party appropriates any item expressly, the law *presumes* that
the first payment in discharges the earliest outstanding debt.

Discharge by agreement

5. Types of agreement

These take the following forms:

(a) *executory contracts*, i.e. those wholly unperformed by either side,
can be discharged by *simple waiver*, consideration for the waiver lying
in the exchange of promises not to sue to enforce the contract.

(b) *executed contracts*, i.e. those wholly or partly performed by one
party, the discharging of such contracts having to be supported by
consideration or be under seal.

There are three broad categories to consider:

(a) *Release* This can be:

(i) under seal;

(ii) supported by consideration, in which case it amounts to
accord and satisfaction (*see* 6: **5**).

(b) *Variation* This can be:
   (*i*)   supported by consideration;
   (*ii*) waiver, in which case it may constitute an estoppel (*see* 6: **5**);
   (*iii*) rescission by mutual release.

Variation (which may amount to partial discharge) can generally take *any form*, except that contracts unenforceable unless evidenced in writing can be varied only in writing — *see Morris* v. *Baron* (1918). (*Total rescission* can *always* be made in any form, e.g. a specialty contract can be rescinded orally — *see Berry* v. *Berry* (1929).)

(c) *Novation* A contract can also be discharged by the parties making a fresh contract in substitution for the old. But this method is available only where the contract is not yet wholly performed on either side, i.e. is still partly executory on both sides. A new contract substituted for an earlier in this way is called a *novation*.

Discharge by operation of law

6.   Operation of law
     This can occur in one of the following ways:

(a) *estoppel by record* — a person is estoppel from raising facts disposed of by a judgment in earlier litigation;

(b) *set off and counterclaim* — if the defendant is owed money by the plaintiff he may set it off, as a defence to the plaintiff's claim on the contract, or counterclaim for it;

(c) *merger* — a contract is discharged if it is merged in a higher obligation, e.g. a deed swallows or merges into itself a simple contract on the same terms and between the same parties;

(d) *unauthorised material alteration* — if one party makes a material alteration to a contract without the consent of the other, the contract is automatically discharged — a material alteration being one that alters the effect of the contract, e.g. altering the crossing or the amount payable on a cheque;

(e) *contracts for personal services* — these are automatically discharged by death in most cases, while other contracts enure for the benefit of the estate of the deceased;

(f) *discharge in bankruptcy* — where a bankrupt obtains his discharge or reaches a composition with his creditors (*see* 24: **26**) the order for discharge or composition automatically cancels liability on all exisiting debts as at that date (with certain exceptions: *see* 24: **27**).

Discharge by frustration

7. The doctrine of frustration

Where, at the outset, it is clearly impossible to perform a contract, the contract lacks an essential element for validity and so is void, e.g. a contract to walk across the Atlantic.

Sometimes, however, a contract, though possible when made, subsequently becomes impossible to perform, e.g. a lawful contract involving trade between Britain and Russia became impossible when the Crimean War broke out between the two countries — *see Avery* v. *Bowden* (1856).

'The doctrine of frustration operates as a rule which the court will apply in certain limited circumstances for the purpose of deciding that contractual obligations, ex facie binding, are no longer enforceable against the parties', said Lord Radcliffe in *Davis Contractors Ltd* v. *Fareham UDC* (1956). More recently, Lord Simon said in *National Carriers Ltd* v. *Panalpina Ltd.* (1981) HL, that 'Frustration takes place where there supervenes an event (without default of either party and for which the contract makes no sufficient provision) which so significantly changes the nature (not merely the expense or onerousness) of the outstanding contractual rights and/or obligations from what the parties could reasonably have contemplated [when the contract was made] that it would be unjust to hold them to the literal sense of its stipulations' (but consider *Amalgamated Investment* v. *John Walker & Sons* (1976)).

The limited circumstances in which frustration occurs include:

(a) *Basis destroyed* If the contract depends on the continued existence of some thing and that thing is destroyed. For example, the hire of a theatre was frustrated by the theatre being burned down — *see Taylor* v. *Caldwell* (1863).

(b) *Non-occurrence of an event* If the contract depends on the occurrence of an event that does not, in fact, happen; compare the following cases:

  (*i*) To watch the coronation procession of Edward VII, A hired a room from B. The procession was cancelled because of the illness of the King. It was held that the contract was frustrated (*Krell* v. *Henry* (1903)).

  (*ii*) A hired a boat from B to watch the coronation review of the fleet by Edward VII. The fleet assembled, but the King was unable to be present because of illness. It was held that the contract was not frustrated, as A could have used the boat to see at least a major part of what he wanted (*Herne Bay Steamboat Co.* v. *Hutton* (1903)).

(c) *Death or illness, etc.* A contract for personal services may be frustrated by the death or unduly prolonged illness of the employee — *see Robinson* v. *Davison* (1871). In a modern case an apprentice's training agreement was frustrated by his detention for a crime — *see Shepherd & Co. Ltd* v. *Jerrom* (1986) CA (and consider *Condor* v. *Barron Knights* (1966)).

(d) *Government interference* Where the government prohibits performance for such a period that it would be unreasonable to expect performance after the prohibition ceases — *see Metropolitan Water Board* v. *Dick, Kerr & Co. Ltd* (1918).

(e) *Change in law* Where a contract is legal when made, but subsequently becomes illegal through a change in the law — *see Avery* v. *Bowden* (1856).

(f) *Method of performance impossible.* If a particular manner of performance is essential and, when the time comes for performance this particular method has become impossible.

(g) Certain cases involving leases of land — *see National Carriers Ltd* v. *Panalpina Ltd* (1981).

Frustration only applies in exceptional cases. It will not, for example, apply in the following cases:

(a) *Express terms may cover the contingency* complained of. The court will refuse to treat the contract as frustrated where to do so would be contrary to such express terms — *see British Movietonews Ltd* v. *London etc. Cinemas Ltd* (1951).

(b) *Self-induced frustration* cannot be pleaded, as it may amount to breach of contract — *see The Eugenia* (1964).

(c) *Sales of land* are probably not subject to frustration — *see Paradine* v. *Jayne* (1647).

(d) *The event is not vital to the contract* In *Davis Contractors Ltd* v. *Fareham UDC* (1956), A contracted to build 78 houses for B in eight months for £92,000. It was impossible to meet the contract date and rises in costs added £17,000 to A's bill. There was no clause in the contract to cover this eventuality. The time ultimately taken by A was 22 months. A claimed that the original contract was frustrated by impossibility and sued for £109,000 on *quantum meruit*. It was held that the contract was not frustrated and, therefore, A had no *quantum meruit* claim. He should have foreseen his troubles and written a clause into the contract to cover them.

8. Effects of frustration

The contract is discharged for the future, but is not void *ab initio*. Therefore it may be important to ascertain who should bear losses and who should pay for services already rendered.

(a) Before 1943, at common law the loss lay where it fell, i.e. *money payable before* frustration remained payable, and money *paid before* frustration could not be recovered, and money that did not become payable till after frustration ceased to be payable — *see Chandler* v. *Webster* (1904). This harsh rule was later modified to allow distribution of loss where there had been total failure of consideration — *see Fibrosa Case* (1943) HL.

(b) The Law Reform (Frustrated Contracts) Act 1943 reformed the above position by providing:

   (*i*) money paid before frustration is prima-facie recoverable;
   (*ii*) money payable before frustration prima-facie ceases to be payable;
   (*iii*) benefits received before frustration must be paid for, and a party who has undergone expenses is entitled to compensation — *see BP* v. *Hunt (No. 2)* (1979).

NOTE: The Act can be excluded by express agreement (but *see BP Exploration* v. *Hunt (No. 2)* (1983)). In any case, it does not apply to charterparties, carriage of goods by sea, sales of specific goods and insurance contracts.

Discharge by breach

9. Effect of breach

Breach occurs where one party:

(a) *repudiates* his obligation;
(b) *disables* himself from performing his part of the contract;
(c) *fails to perform* his part of the contract on the date agreed.

In **(a)** and **(b)** the breach may, of course, occur before the date fixed for performance and is then called an *anticipatory breach*.

Example _____

In *Hochster* v. *De la Tour* (1853), A hired B to act as a courier commencing employment 1 June, but wrote to B in May repudiating the agreement. It was held that B was entitled in May to sue for breach of contract and need not wait until June.

The effect depends largely on whether the breach is of a condition or of a warranty, using the traditional categories (*see* 7: **1**):

(a) *breach of warranty* — the injured party can only sue for damages and must go on with the contract, i.e. the breach does not operate to discharge the contract;

(b) *breach of condition* — the injured party can choose whether:

- (*i*) to treat the breach as a breach of *ex post facto* warranty (and sue for damages while going on with the contract); or
- (*ii*) to treat the breach of condition as automatically discharging the contract.

NOTE: If he chooses alternative (ii) he cannot also sue for damages for breach, as he has indicated a willingness to regard the contract as dead and has therefore waived his right of action for damages (but if he has incurred expense under the contract he can bring a quasi-contractual *quantum meruit* action for compensation).

If he chooses alternative (i) he keeps the contract alive and should immediately commence action to enforce it, i.e. should sue for damages or specific performance. If he delays suing, he takes the risk that some unforeseen event may occur to discharge the contract by frustration, thus depriving him of his right of action.

Example _____

In *Avery* v. *Bowden* (1856), A hired B's ship to carry a cargo from Russia. Later B repudiated the contract, thus entitling A either to treat the contract as discharged or to sue for damages. A delayed a decision hoping B would change his mind before the performance date. War broke out between Russia and Britain before the performance date, frustrating the contract. It was held that A had lost his right to sue for damages by his delay. (Consider though, *White and Carter* v. *McGregor* (1961).) Further, if he chooses alternative (i) a supervening event could entitle the other party to cancel the contract under one of its express terms — *see The Simona* (1988).

Proper law

10. Proper law

The proper law of a contract is the law that governs it. Often the parties state in an express clause that the law of a particular country is to apply. In the absence of such a term the courts look at where the contract is made and where it is to be performed, in order to see with which country the contract has its closest and most real connection.

Limitation

11. Limitation

The Limitation Act 1980 lays down that actions for breach of contract must be commenced within a certain time of any breach, otherwise the right lapses and it cannot be enforced by action. The periods are:

(a) for simple contracts, 6 years (s. 5);
(b) for contracts by deed, 12 years (s. 8).

The limitation period is generally calculated from the moment the breach occurs, subject to the two following major exceptions:
(a) if the plaintiff was under a legal disability at the date of the breach, e.g. minority or mental incapacity, time begins to run from the date when the disability ceases or the plaintiff dies while still disabled (s. 28);
(b) if the action is based on fraud, concealment or mistake, time begins to run from the date when the fraud or mistake is discovered (or might reasonably have been discovered) and not from the date when the cause of action arose (s. 32).

Where there is an acknowledgement or part payment, it starts time running again, i.e. the plaintiff has a further 6 years (or 12 if a deed is involved) in which to commence the action (s. 29(5)). Payments of *interest* do not extend time, and are treated as payments of the principal money due (s. 29(6)). Acknowledgment of the *existence* of a debt is sufficient, even if it does not state the amount — *see Dungate* v. *Dungate* (1965).

Despite the possibility of the period of limitation being extended by acknowledgments or part payments, once the right of action is barred it cannot be revived by later acknowledgment or part payment (s. 29(7)).

There are special rules governing loans that do not provide a date for the repayment of the debt or do not effectively make the debt repayable on demand (s. 6).

Remedies

12. Remedies

The basic common law remedy for breach of contract is damages (*see* 9: **13, 14**).

Where a quasi-contract has arisen, the injured party can sue on a *quantum meruit* (*see* 10: **7**).

In appropriate circumstances, an equitable remedy will be available. The following are the principal ones:

(a) specific performance (*see* 23: **6**);
(b) injunction (*see* 23: **7**);
(c) rescission (*see* 23: **5**);
(d) rectification (*see* 23: **5**).

13. Damages recoverable

The plaintiff can recover financial *compensation for his actual loss*, provided it is not too remote.

Under the rule in *Hadley* v. *Baxendale* (1854), damage is not too remote if the following hold:

(a) If the damage is the natural consequence of the breach. For example, in *Hadley* v. *Baxendale* (1854), B unduly delayed delivery of a mill shaft to A's mill and so the mill was out of action for a considerable time. A had not informed B that lack of the shaft would necessitate closing the mill. It was held that A could recover damages for the delay in delivery, but not for loss of profits occasioned by closure of the mill, as there was no way B could have foreseen that his delay would mean closure of the mill.
(b) Although not arising naturally from the breach, the damage is something that should have been foreseen by the defendant when making the contract.

Examples

(1) In *Hadley* v. *Baxendale* the mill-owner could have recovered damages for loss of profits if he had informed B that this was a likely result of delayed delivery.

Similarly, in *Victoria Laundry* v. *Newman Industries* (1949) where A was to supply a boiler to B's laundry and delivery was delayed five months, it was held that: (*i*) B could recover damages for loss of ordinary profits occasioned by the delay (as A knew the laundry would lose profits by his delay); (*ii*) but not special profits lost under a very valuable contract of which A did not know and which he could not reasonably have foreseen.

(2) The loss of resale value resulting from breach of contract (a ship charter) can be recovered. In *Koufos* v. *Czarnikow Ltd*, *The Heron II* (1976) HL, A commissioned B to carry goods by ship for delivery at port by a certain date, and A resold the goods in the port of delivery. B unduly delayed delivery,

and the resale value of the goods dropped materially. It was held that A could recover damages: (*i*) for delay in delivery and (*ii*) for loss of resale value.

(3) Foreseeable loss may now include 'disappointment, distress, upset and frustration caused by the breach'— *see Jarvis* v. *Swan Tours* (1973).

14. The measure of damages

Damages for breach of contract are intended to compensate the plaintiff, not to punish the defendant.

The injured party must minimise, or mitigate, the damage he sustains as far as he reasonably can; he cannot recover additional damages occasioned by his failure to mitigate.

Interest on any sum claimed is not allowed unless:

(a) the parties have previously so agreed; or
(b) the claim is on a bill of exchange or promissory note; or
(c) the court exercises its statutory discretion to award interest (under the Supreme Court Act 1981, s. 35a, or the County Courts Act 1984, s. 69).

Where the amount of compensation claimed is left to be assessed by the court, damages are called *unliquidated*.

Sometimes the parties agree in advance the amounts payable in the event of breach. Such an amount is called *liquidated damages*, and in any action for breach of the contract the court will award the pre-assessed sum unless it has been fixed in such a way as to break the rules against penalties.

Liquidated damages are a genuine pre-estimate of the measure of loss that a breach would occasion. A penalty, on the other hand, is a sum fixed at random to frighten a party into performing his contract — *see Dunlop Pneumatic Tyre Co.* v. *New Garage Ltd* (1915).

Consequently, a sum is a penalty:

(a) if it is extravagant having regard to the maximum possible loss that could result from the breach; or
(b) if failure to pay a sum of money results in liability to pay a larger; or
(c) if a single sum is payable upon the occurrence of any of several events of differing importance — *see Kemble* v. *Farren* (1829).

If a sum is a penalty, the court will not award it but will make its own assessment of damages. The fact that the *parties* describe a sum as a penalty or a clause as a 'penalty clause' is not decisive. The court will apply the above tests and, if satisfied that the sum is, in fact, a genuine pre-estimate of loss, will treat it as liquidated damages and award it to the plaintiff.

Progress test 9

1.   When, if ever, will partial performance suffice to discharge a contract?   (2)

2.   How far is it true to say that delay in performance is not vital in a contract?   (3)

3.   Summarise the rules governing the appropriation of payments. (4)

4.   How may an executed contract be discharged by agreement? (5)

5.   Explain briefly the effect of the Limitation Act (1980) on the discharge of contracts.   (11)

6.   A borrowed various sums of money from B in 1978. A then went to live in Australia and in 1988 returned on holiday to England, having in the meantime become a millionaire. B wrote reminding him of the loans in 1978. A wrote replying, 'I do remember borrowing some money from you some time, but I can't remember when or how much and I do not propose to bother with trivialities like this now. In any case the debt would be barred by the Limitations Acts'. Advise B.   (11)

7.   What exceptions are there to the general rule that supervening impossibility of performance will not discharge a contract?   (7)

8.   Summarise the main provisions of the Law Reform (Frustrated Contracts) Act 1943. Are there any contracts not covered by the Act? (8)

9.   Explain how a breach of contract may occur and state what is meant by an anticipatory breach of contract.   (9)

10.   What are the effects of breach of: (a) a condition; and (b) a warranty?   (9)

11. What is the rule in *Hadley* v. *Baxendale*? Give examples of the rule in operation.   **(13)**

12. When, if ever, may a plaintiff claim interest on a sum claimed against a defendant in an action for breach of contract?   **(14)**

13. What is meant by saying that a plaintiff must mitigate his loss? **(14)**

14. Define: (a) a penalty; and (b) liquidated damages.   **(14)**

10
Quasi-contract

The main features of quasi-contract

1. The doctrine of quasi-contract

The doctrine of quasi-contract is usually treated as an appendix to the law of contract and is sometimes (e.g. Lord Sumner in *Sinclair* v. *Brougham* (1914)) said to be based on an implied contract. The better view is that it is a quite separate doctrine that applies in four well-defined instances:

(a) money paid at the request of another (*see* 10: **2**);
(b) money had and received to the use of another (*see* 10: **3**);
(c) money voluntarily paid under a material mistake of fact (*see* 10: **4**);
(d) money paid upon a total failure of consideration or under a contract that is void for illegality or frustration (*see* 10: **5**).

In each of these cases, one party is unjustly enriched at the expense of another and the law allows that other to recover his money.

2. Money paid at the request of another

If A, at the express or implied request of B, pays to X a sum of money legally owed by B to X, the law implies a quasi-contract between A and B, under which B must pay compensation to A for the money paid by A on his behalf, e.g. where A pays rent owed by B, to avoid seizure of his own goods which are on B's premises — *see* *Edmunds* v. *Wallingford* (1885).

3. Money had and received to the use of another

If A wrongfully obtains money to which B is legally entitled, B can sue A for recovery of the money in a quasi-contractual action for money had and received, e.g. where a servant receives money on behalf of his master and refuses to pass it on to the master.

Example _____

In *Reading* v. *Attorney-General* (1951), B used the authority of his army uniform to assist in smuggling activities. It was held that the army, as his employer, was entitled to claim the profit he made by smuggling.

_____

In the case of torts such as conversion (*see* 15:**22**), trespass to goods (*see* 15:**20**) and to land (*see* 15:**10**) and deceit (*see* 16:**10**), the person who has suffered loss may 'waive the tort' and bring his action against the tortfeasor for money had and received.

4. Money paid voluntarily under a material mistake of fact

Where money is paid under a mistake of fact it is generally recoverable by the payer, e.g. where an employer overpays wages under a mistake as to the employee's entitlement — *see Larner* v. *LCC* (1949).

Money paid under mistake of law is generally irrecoverable, except in the following cases:

(a) where the payee knew of or induced the payer's mistake;
(b) where the money was paid to an officer of the court, e.g. a trustee in bankruptcy — *see Ex parte James* (1874);
(c) where money was paid under an unjustified threat of legal proceedings;
(d) where the payee was under a fiduciary duty to the payer, e.g. where paid by a beneficiary to his trustee;
(e) where the mistake of law is treated legally as one of fact, e.g.:

  (*i*) mistakes of foreign law;
  (*ii*) mistakes as to private rights, such as ownership of property.

5. Void contract

This occurs when there is:

(a) *Total failure of consideration* Where a valid contract has been made between A and B (supported by consideration) but subsequently B fails to render any of the promised consideration, there is said to be a total failure of consideration and A can sue for recovery of any money he has paid.

Contrast the case where the consideration has only partly failed, e.g. where A pays money for goods to B, who later delivers some but not all of the goods. Here A can sue only for breach of the contract, recovering damages by way of compensation but not the complete sum that he has paid.

(b) *Money paid on an illegal contract* Money paid or property transferred under an illegal contract may be recovered by the transferor, with the aid of the court, only in the following exceptional cases:

(*i*)   where the transferor repents of making the contract, before any part of the illegal purpose is carried out; or

(*ii*)   where:

(1)   he is not *in pari delicto* (equally guilty), e.g. where he was innocently induced to make the contract by the fraud of the defendant; or

(2)   the transferee was under a fiduciary duty to protect the plaintiff's interests, e.g. as his trustee or lawyer; or

(3)   the contract is made illegal by a statute intended to protect a class of which the plaintiff is a member.

6.   Accounts stated

Where there has been a series of transactions between A and B and they agree a balance, showing a sum payable by A to B, the agreed balance constitutes an 'account stated'.

If B now has occasion to sue A for the amount agreed, he does not need to prove the details of the transactions between them, but can rely entirely on the account stated as an admission of indebtedness.

7.   *Quantum meruit*

Where there is a breach of an essential condition in a contract, the injured party may either:

(a)   seek to enforce the contract and sue for damages (of an *ex post facto* warranty) by way of compensation; or

(b)   treat the contract as discharged, in which case he cannot sue for damages for its breach.

However, where he adopts course **(b)** above and treats the contract as discharged, he is entitled to bring a quasi-contractual action for compensation for work done or services rendered, etc. This is called a *quantum meruit* action (literally 'how much is it worth?') and it may be available even where there was no contract between the parties, but reasonable compensation is sought for work done.

Example

In *William Lacey Ltd* v. *Davis* (1957), L, a builder, did certain work for D on the understanding that D would give him a contract later for some major building work. D did not give L the expected contract, and L sued for: (*i*) damages for breach of contract; or (*ii*) *quantum meruit* relief. It was held that there was no contract between L and D and, therefore, L could not claim damages, but he was entitled to reasonable compensation on a quasi-contract.

A claim on a *quantum meruit* can arise in the four following cases:

(a) Where the defendant has abandoned or repudiated the contract, e.g. where, after commissioning a writer to do a series of articles, a magazine closes down before the series is completely written; here the writer can sue on a *quantum meruit* for the articles actually done — see *Planché* v. *Colburn* (1831), but note that in this case the writer could not sue for money due under the contract, as he had not completed his performance and so had not discharged his obligations.
(b) Where one party has done work under a void contract and the defendant has received the benefit of it — see *Craven-Ellis* v. *Canons Ltd* (1936). Here again the plaintiff could not have sued on the contract, since it is void.
(c) Where the parties have agreed to terminate a contract and the plaintiff has performed a substantial part of his obligations. Here again the plaintiff can sue on *quantum meruit*, but not upon the contract, as he has agreed to its termination — see *Dakin* v. *Lee* (1916).
(d) Where one party has obtained a benefit that he could not reasonably expect to get without paying for it, e.g. where a builder leaves the building materials on X's land and X uses the materials, the builder can sue on a *quantum meruit* — see *Sumpter* v. *Hedges* (1898).

Example

In *Gilbert & Partners* v. *Knight* (1968), A contracted to pay B £30 for supervising building work at A's house. Later A commissioned additional work, which B supervised without mentioning a fee. B subsequently claimed an extra £105 for the additional supervision involved. It was held that B failed, because he could not claim on *quantum meruit* while the original contract subsisted. He should at the outset have secured a fresh contract.

Progress test 10

1. What is a quasi-contract? When, if ever, can money paid by mistake be recovered? **(1, 4)**

2.   Explain what you understand by actions for: (a) money paid to the use of another and (b) money had and received.   **(2, 3)**

3.   What do you understand by the term 'account stated'?   **(6)**

4.   What is the meaning of *quantum meruit*? In what circumstances is such an action appropriate?   **(7)**

5.   A employed B as architect to supervise the building of a house for £5,000, agreeing to pay him scale fees amounting to 10 per cent of this sum. When the house was half-built, A changed his plans and spent a further £2,000 on making the house larger. B supervised the additional work and now claims to be entitled to a further £200 being 10 per cent of the additional £2,000 spent. Advise A.   **(7)**

11
Agency

Introduction

1. Definitions

An *agent* acts on behalf of another (the *principal*) in making contracts with a third party. *Agency* is the relationship between the agent, his principal and the third party. It has recently been confirmed that a promotion contract is not the same as an agency — *see Comet Group PLC* v. *British Sky Broadcasting* (1991).

There are two classes of agent, although the distinction is no longer one of great importance.

(a) A *special* agent is authorised to act on behalf of the principal for a purpose outside the normal course of the agent's business. In *Brady* v. *Todd* (1861), D's agent sold a horse to P, warranting that the horse was 'quiet in harness'. This was an unauthorised warranty, and it turned out to be false. As D's agent was not in the business of selling horses, he was a special agent; the warranty was therefore not binding on D.

(b) A *general* agent acts on behalf of the principal in the normal course of business. In *Howard* v. *Sheward* (1866), D and his agent were both horse dealers. D's agent sold P one of D's horses warranting that 'the horse is sound'. Again the warranty was unauthorised and false, but because the agent was a horse dealer himself, he was a general agent and the warranty was binding on D. 'It cannot be out of the scope of a horse-dealer's business to give a warranty, if a warranty may ordinarily form part of the transaction between buyer and seller' (Willes J). There many examples of general agents (*see* 11: **3**).

When an agent enters into a contract with a third party he may:

(a) *disclose* that he is acting for a principal and identify or *name* the principal (*see* 11: **16**);
(b) *disclose* that he is acting for a principal but leave the principal unidentified or *unnamed* (*see* 11: **17**).

2. Characteristics of principal and agent

A man may always act through an agent unless he is required by statute to act in person — *see Re Whitley Partners* (1886).

The use of an agent is not normally a way of avoiding incapacity (*see* 6: **8–10**). The principal must almost always have capacity to make the contract, although this is not necessarily true of the agent. No consideration is required to support an agency, although in practice, of course, agents are always paid. (The sole exception to the general rules just given is an enduring attorney appointed under the Enduring Powers of Attorney Act 1985, who acts on behalf of his principal but subject to the supervision of the Court of Protection and remains 'in office' despite any intervening incapacity of his principal.)

Agents' powers are very various.

(a) Many agents are *mercantile agents* within the definition in the Factors Act 1889, s. 1(1): one 'having in the course of his business as such agent authority either to sell goods or to consign goods for the purpose of sale, or to buy goods, or to raise money on the security of goods'.

(b) A *del credere* agent is an agent employed to sell goods and who promises to make sure that clients introduced by him to the principal will pay for the goods sold.

> NOTE: This is not a contract of guarantee and therefore does not require to be evidenced in writing.

(c) Some agents (e.g. stockbrokers) have power to make contracts for P but are under general fiduciary duties.

(d) Some agents (e.g. estate agents) have no power to make contracts for P — *see Sorrell* v. *Finch* (1977).

3. Examples of agency

Some examples are:

(a) *Factors* A factor is an agent employed to sell goods for a commission. A factor has *possession of the goods* (unlike a *broker*), and can therefore claim a *lien* over the goods for unpaid commission. He can also *pledge*, *insure* or *sell* the goods, even if he exceeds his actual authority by so doing, and receive payment (Factors Act 1889).

If a professional factor has possession of goods otherwise than for the purpose of sale he can nevertheless give a good title to an innocent purchaser of the goods, since the principal is estopped from denying that he was entrusted with sale (Factors Act 1889, s. 2).

(b) *Brokers* A broker is a mercantile agent employed to make commercial contracts between other parties for a commission usually called *brokerage*. (An agent employed to make a non-commercial contract, e.g. a contract to hire a singer for a concert, is therefore not a broker.)

Unlike factors, brokers *do not have possession* of goods for sale and cannot sell in their own name. They have no lien over goods and no power to pledge them. A broker is primarily an agent for the seller of goods, but on making a contract with a purchaser, becomes an agent for the purchaser also.

(c) *Bankers* The relationship between banker and customer is primarily that between debtor and creditor, but, in addition, the banker is employed to pay sums of money at the direction of the customer. A banker has a *general lien* over securities belonging to the customer and which have previously been deposited with him and can retain such securities pending settlements of debts owed by the customer to the bank. He must not disclose the state of a customer's account, except under compulsion of law. (For further details concerning banks, banking students *see* Appendix 1.)

(d) *Auctioneers* These are agents employed to sell goods by auction. An auctioneer is primarily an agent for the seller, but when he accepts a bid from a purchaser he becomes an agent for the purchaser also, e.g. he can sign a note or memorandum on behalf of the purchaser so as to satisfy the Law of Property Act 1925, s.40 (*see* 20: **12**).

He does not warrant the seller's right to sell property, but is liable to an action for damages by the purchaser if he fails to deliver property sold and is liable to the seller if he delivers before receiving payment. He has *possession* of goods and a *lien* over them for his commission. He must sell only for cash (unless otherwise authorised) and at the best price available. If the seller fixes a minimum, or, *reserve* price, the auctioneer is liable in damages to the seller if he sells the property for less than the reserve price. In such cases, however, the buyer obtains a good title to the goods, unless he knew of the auctioneer's breach of authority.

(e) *Estate agents* These are agents employed to sell land or houses as agents for the seller. The scope of their authority varies, e.g. where an estate agent receives a deposit from a buyer to confirm purchase, it is a question of fact in each case whether he does so:

    (*i*) as agent for the seller; or

    (*ii*) merely as an independent stakeholder.

Money received by an estate agent in the course of his work is held on trust for the person who is entitled to it or as stakeholder for the person who will in due course become entitled to it as given in Estate Agents Act 1979, s. 13.

Creation

4. Express creation

'The relationship of principal and agent can only be established by the consent of the principal and agent. The consent must have been given by each of them, either expressly or by implication from their words and conduct', said Lord Pearson in *Garnac Grain* v. *Faure & Fairclough* (1967).

Where the agent is employed to execute a deed on behalf of his principal, his appointment must also be by deed and the agency is called a power of attorney.

Where the agent is appointed to sign a lease for more than three years on behalf of his principal, the Law of Property Act 1925, s. 54, specifies that his appointment must be in writing.

In most other cases the agent's appointment can be in any form.

5. Implied agency

This occurs in the following situations:

(a) Members of families may, in the particular circumstances of individual cases, enjoy an implied agency to act for each other. There are no special rules governing the pledging of credit as between spouses or co-habitees, although it is generally thought that, within a domestic establishment, a wife has implied authority to pledge her husband's credit for household necessaries — see *Jewsbury* v. *Newbold* (1857). Of course, such authority can be expressly revoked — see *Jolly* v. *Rees* (1863).

(b) An agent expressly appointed for one purpose may have implied authority to perform acts reasonably and ordinarily incidental to that purpose. An estate agent appointed to negotiate the sale of a house therefore has implied authority to receive the deposit — see *Burt* v. *Claude Cousins & Sons Ltd* (1971). (*See also* 11: 3(*e*).)

(c) An agent appointed in a particular market has implied authority to do anything that is customary in that market. Authority is not implied if the custom is unreasonable and an agent is, in general, not allowed to perform unreasonable customary duties. In *North & South Trust Co.* v. *Berkeley* (1971), P employed A, who were Lloyd's brokers, to insure goods in transit. A placed the insurance with D, who were

Lloyd's underwriters. On arrival the goods proved short and P claimed on the insurance. A arranged for assessors to investigate the claim and, in accordance with the market custom, sent their report only to D. The question was whether by following this custom, A were acting in breach of their duty as agents of P. Donaldson, J, accepted that they were. The custom was unreasonable: 'Fully informed consent apart, an agent cannot lawfully place himself in a position in which he owes a duty to another which is inconsistent with his duty to his principal'.

(d) In an emergency, an agent may act beyond his authority. In *Great Northern Railway* v. *Swaffield* (1874), P were D's agents to transport his horse. On arrival, D did not collect the horse, and so P recovered the cost of its stabling and feed. This agency of necessity is rare and the courts are reluctant to extend it. It can exist only when three conditions are satisfied:

    (*i*)   there must be a pre-existing agency;

    (*ii*) there must be actual and definite commercial necessity;

    (*iii*) it must be impossible to communicate with the principal.

6. Agency by estoppel

Where A allows third parties to believe that B is acting as his agent, he will be estopped from denying the agency if such third parties rely on it to their detriment.

This role applies even where no agency was ever intended by the principal. Similarly, a husband, partner or employer who allows a wife, partner or employee to act as his agent cannot evade liability for the agent's contracts even after the agency is revoked, unless he has expressly notified third parties with whom the agent has habitually been dealing, of the revocation of the agency — *see Scarf* v. *Jardine* (1882).

7. Ratification

Ratification is where the principal adopts an unauthorised act of his agent as his own. If ratification is not possible, the agent remains personally liable. Ratification is effective if the following conditions are fulfilled.

(a) The agent must have purported to act on behalf of his principal: 'Civil obligations are not to be created by or founded upon undisclosed intentions' — Lord MacNaghten in *Keightley Maxted* v. *Durant* (1901).

(b) The principal must have been in existence at the time the contract was made. Under the Companies Act 1985, s. 36(4), a contract made on behalf of a company that is not yet in existence takes effect as a contract with the person purporting to act for the company.

(c) The principal must have been competent to make the contract himself at the time when the contract was made. A principal who was an enemy alien when the contract was made cannot later ratify it — *see Boston Deep Sea Co.* v. *Farnham* (1957).

(d) A purported contract that is void cannot be ratified. An *ultra vires* act performed by the director of a company cannot be ratified by the shareholders — *see Ashbury Railway Carriage Co.* v. *Riche* (1875) (but also *see* 4:**10**).

(e) The principal must have had full knowledge of the facts — *see Marsh* v. *Joseph* (1897).

(f) The principal must ratify within a reasonable time, and cannot ratify if the contract can no longer be made. A contract of fire insurance cannot be ratified after a fire — *see Groves* v. *Matthews* (1910).

Ratification operates to put all parties in the position they would have been if the agent's act had been authorised from the beginning. This was established in *Bolton* v. *Lambert* (1889). A contracted to buy a house from D on behalf of P. The contract was not authorised, and D repudiated it. P later ratified the contract and it was held that this was effective in spite of D's repudiation.

Termination

8.   By act of the parties
As agency is founded on consent (*see* 11: **4**) The agent's authority can be terminated by:

(a) express revocation by the principal; or
(b) express renunciation by the agent,
unless steps have been taken to make the agency irrevocable (*see* 11: **9**).

There are two situations to consider:

(a) *Where the principal and agent are subject to a binding contract*. In the absence of an express term, agency founded on a contract can be terminated on reasonable notice. In *Martin-Baker Aircraft* v. *Canadian*

Flight (1955), McNair, J, assessed reasonable notice at 12 months and this had been followed in subsequent cases.

(b) *Where there is no contract* An agency agreement may not impose immediate contractual obligations. An estate agent, for example, may be paid only on sale. If the agency is terminated before he negotiates a sale, he has no claim. It was established in *Luxor* v. *Cooper* (1941) that there was no implied term that the principal could not sell elsewhere. 'If B is under no obligation to do the work, why should A be under an implied obligation not to prevent him from doing it?' said Lord Romer.

9. Irrevocable authority

Revocation is not possible where:

(a) the authority is 'coupled with an interest', i.e. where the agent was appointed in order to enable him to secure some benefit already owed to him by the principal — *see Smart* v. *Saunders* (1848); or

(b) a power of attorney is expressed to be irrevocable and is given to secure:

   (*i*) a proprietary interest of the donee of the power; or

   (*ii*) the performance of an obligation owed to the donee

because while these conditions remain unaltered, the power remains irrevocable by the donor (except with the consent of the donee), even on the death or the incapacity or bankruptcy of the donor under the Powers of Attorney Act 1971, s. 4(1); or

(c) revocation would involve personal loss to the agent; the principal may be estopped from revoking without the consent of the agent — *see Seymour* v. *Bridge* (1885); or

(d) the principal cannot revoke so as to damage the interests of innocent third parties, e.g. by breaking contracts the agent has already made with them.

10. By operation of law

Like any other contract, an agency agreement will come to an end:

(a) in the event of supervening illegality (*see* 8: **14–17**) or frustration (*see* 9: **7, 8**);

(b) at the expiration of the term (if any) agreed in the contract; or

(c) when the terms of the contract have been fulfilled.

There are special rules concerning the following situations:

(a) *Death* The death, or, if a company, dissolution, of the principal terminates the agency. Except in the case of a power of attorney, the agent is then personally liable for his acts. The death of the agent also terminates the agency.

(b) *Bankruptcy* The bankruptcy of the principal terminates the agency. The bankruptcy of the agent terminates the agency if it renders him unfit to perform his duties. (For the general law of insolvency, *see* Chapter 24.)

(c) *Insanity.* In *Yonge* v. *Toynbee* (1910), X employed T as solicitor to sue Y. T commenced the action and brought the case to court. Unknown to T, X had gone insane in the meanwhile. It was held that T's agency was automatically terminated and he was therefore liable to Y for damages for breach of warranty of authority. This rule will not affect a person who has been appointed under the Enduring Powers of Attorney Act 1985 (*see* 11: 2).

Duties of principal and agent

11. Duties of agent

Apart from the obvious duty to obey the principal's instructions, these are as follows:

(a) *To exercise due care and diligence* on the principal's behalf, plus any special skill he professes to have — *see Keppel* v. *Wheeler* (1927). This applies also to gratuitous agents — *see Chaudhry* v. *Prabhakar* (1988).

(b) *To disclose* to the principal any material information he may receive in execution of his task.

(c) *Not to disclose confidential information* entrusted to him by his principal. There is a distinction between the information acquired and the experience gained by the agent in the course of his employment. The information remains the property of the principal and must not be divulged; the agent may, however, make use of his experience.

(d) *Not to delegate performance of his duties* (*delegatus non potest delegare*: a delegate cannot delegate), but this prohibition is not strictly applied and the agent may delegate performance where that is required by commercial necessity or ordinary usage.

(e) *Not to make any secret profit* If, beyond his commission, he receives any extra profit in the course of his duties, he must disclose this to the principal. If he fails so to disclose such additional profit:

　　(*i*)　the principal can sue him for the amount kept secret;

    (*ii*) the principal can refuse to pay the agent's commission, and can terminate the agency without notice;

    (*iii*) the principal can sue the agent and the third party for damages to compensate him for any loss he has sustained — see *Salford Corporation* v. *Lever* (1891).

(f) *To avoid any conflict of interests* 'No agent who has accepted an employment from one principal can in law accept an engagement inconsistent with his duty to the first principal from a second principal, unless he makes the fullest disclosure to each principal of his interest and obtains the consent of each principal to the double employment' said Scrutton, LJ, in *Fullwood* v. *Hurley* (1928). In practice, of course, commercial agents (*see* 11: **3**) have many principals at any one time.

12. Duties of principal
These are:

(a) *To pay any agreed commission* or remuneration and not to prevent or hinder the agent from earning this — see *Rhodes* v. *Forwood* (1876). The agent has a *lien* over goods belonging to the principal, enabling him to hold such goods until commission is paid.

When commission becomes payable depends on the contract between principal and agent, e.g. when the agent is employed to sell goods or land, his commission may become payable:

    (*i*) when he introduces a client (whether sale results or not); or

    (*ii*) on completion of the sale, and payment of the price. (The signing of an agreement 'subject to contract' does not amount to completion — see *Luxor* v. *Cooper* (1941).)

(b) *To indemnify the agent* against liabilities properly incurred in the discharge of his duties — see *Christoforides* v. *Terry* (1924).

    As against third parties, the principal is liable for torts and breaches of contract committed by his agent in the course of his employment if the agent is in the position of a servant. This liability is vicarious, i.e. indirect liability for the actions of another.

    The extent of the vicarious liability depends on whether the agent is a servant or an independent contractor, i.e. on whether he is under the control of his employer as to what and how to do his work, or merely, as in the case of an independent contractor, as to what he is to do. Most commercial agents fall into the latter category and the principal's vicarious liability is therefore restricted.

    Vicarious liability is primarily important in the law of torts and is dealt with more fully later (*see* 14: **14–17**).

The authority of the agent

13. The authority of the agent
The extent of the agent's authority depends:

(a) *on his contract* with his principal, or
(b) *on the law*, where this implies a particular authority for particular kinds of agency.

Thus, the law attributes special authority to auctioneers, factors (professional selling agents), brokers and bank managers (*see* 11: **3**). For example, in *Watteau* v. *Fenwick* (1983), the manager of a public house was forbidden to order tobaccos by his principal, but did so. It was held that the principal was liable to pay the seller, as a manager of a public house would usually have authority to make orders of this kind and the seller could therefore rely on the agent's ostensible authority in the absence of express knowledge of the limitation imposed by the principal. (But consider *The Ocean Frost* (1986)).

14. Breach of warranty of authority
Every person professing to act as agent for another impliedly warrants that he has authority to make binding contracts on behalf of his principal.

If, therefore, an agent lacks the authority he professes to have, he is liable to action for damages for breach of the implied warranty of authority, brought by the person with whom he has been dealing — *see Collen* v. *Wright* (1857).

The agent is still liable for damages, even if he was acting in good faith, genuinely believing he had the authority he claimed, e.g. where his authority has been terminated without his knowledge by his principal's death or insanity — *see Yonge* v. *Toynbee* (1910).

He is not liable, however, if his lack of authority was known to the third party at the time of making the contract or if the third party agreed to exclude the liability — *see Lilly* v. *Smales* (1892). (Where a dishonest agent deliberately claims authority he knows he does not possess, he is also liable to an action for *fraud* by the third party.)

15. Relations between principal and third parties
Generally, once he has made a contract on behalf of his principal, the agent drops out of the transaction and privity of contract exists between the principal and the third party (*see* 6: **6, 7**).

The results of an agent's contract, however, differ slightly depending on whether:

(a) he has disclosed the name of his principal and the fact of the agency (*see* 11: **16**); or
(b) he has concealed his principal's identity (and also perhaps the fact of the agency) (*see* 11: **17**).

16. Agent acting for named principal

Here the agent generally incurs neither rights nor liabilities under the contract, and drops out as soon as it is made — *see Gadd* v. *Houghton* (1876). There are exceptions, however:

(a) If the agent signs a deed he is personally liable on it and the principal incurs no liability *unless* the agent was himself appointed by deed (a *power of attorney*) — in which case the agent drops out and the principal is liable in the ordinary way.
(b) If he signs a bill of exchange in his own name, the agent is personally liable on it. To avoid this he should make it clear that he is signing merely as agent, e.g. by signing 'for and on behalf of' a named principal. A director signing a cheque on behalf of his company should always take this precaution.
(c) Where trade custom makes the agent personally liable, but such cases are rare.

17. Agent acting for unnamed principal

This covers cases where the agent conceals the identity of the principal, while admitting that he is acting merely as agent.

Here the agent drops out in the normal way, provided he makes it clear he is acting as agent. If he fails to do so he is personally liable on the contract. (The exceptions stated under 11: **16** apply here also.)

The doctrine of the undisclosed principal covers cases where the agent conceals both the identity of the principal and also the fact that he is merely acting as agent. In this situation the third party can enforce the contract against either the agent or against the principal, when he discovers his existence.

The third party thus has an option whether to regard the agent as primarily responsible on the contract or, as soon as he knows of his existence, to transfer liability to the principal.

NOTE:
(1) He cannot enforce the contract against both. If he sues one, he cannot later sue the other also.
(2) He may be estopped from suing the principal, if he allows the principal to think that he has settled matters satisfactorily with the agent,

e.g. by unreasonably delaying action against the principal after discovery of his existence — *see Heald* v. *Kenworthy* (1855).

Progress test 11

1.   Define agency and explain what sorts of agency can occur. **(1, 2)**

2.   Explain how a factor differs from a broker.   **(3)**

3.   In what ways can an agent be appointed?   **(4–7)**

4.   A, B and C are partners. A and B run the business and C is a 'sleeping partner' who plays no active part in the management of the firm. Ostensibly on behalf of the firm, C borrows a large sum of money from X and then absconds with the money. X now wishes to sue the firm for the return of the money. Advise A and B.   **(5, 13, 14)**

5.   In what circumstances may agency occur: (a) by ratification; and (b) by implication?   **(5, 7)**

6.   A (a minor) owns a car that he regularly allows his friend B (also a minor) to drive. While B is driving, a tyre bursts and B commissions C's garage to fit a new tyre. B now refuses to pay for the tyre. Can C claim damages against A?   **(5)**

7.   Explain how an agency may be terminated: (a) by act of the parties and (b) by operation of law.   **(8, 10)**

8.   What are the duties of an agent towards his principal?   **(11)**

9.   What are the duties of a principal towards his agent?   **(12)**

10.   What is meant by vicarious liability?   **(12)**

11.   What is the difference between actual and ostensible authority in agency?   **(13)**

12.   In what circumstances may a person acting as agent for

another be liable for breach of warranty of authority, and what does this mean? **(14)**

13. In what circumstances may an agent be personally liable on a contract that he has made on behalf of his principal? **(14, 16)**

14. Explain what is meant by the doctrine of the undisclosed principal. **(17)**

15. A employs B, the owner of a ship, to carry a small cargo of rice from Bombay to London. On the way the rice is damaged by water and expands, presenting a threat to the safety of the ship. B stops at Lagos and sells the rice for much less than could have been obtained in London. A wishes to sue B for loss of profit. Advise B. **(5, 11)**

12
Mercantile law

Assignment

1. Transfer of contracts

Rights and liabilities under a contract can be transferred in some cases. In this case — in accordance with the doctrine of privity — if, in a contract between A and B, B transfers his contract to X, B drops out and the contract now subsists between A and X; B generally has no further rights or obligations:

(a) *rights* can be transferred by assignment (*see* 12: **2, 3**);
(b) *liabilities* can only be transferred by agreement of the parties (for novation *see* 9: **5**) or where the contract expressly provides.

In a contract between A and B, if performance is not a personal matter, B can always delegate performance to some other person, e.g. his employee. This does not involve transfer of duties, and privity still exists between A and B.

2. Methods of assignment

A right or benefit arising under a contract is called a chose (or thing) in action, i.e. a personal right of property that can be enforced only by suing (by action) and not by taking physical possession — *see* *Torkington* v. *Magee* (1902).

Contrast a chose (thing) in possession, which is a piece of property capable of actual physical possession.

Choses in action can be assigned in two ways:

(a) *under the Law of Property Act* 1925, s. 136 (*see* 12: **3**);
(b) *equitable assignments*, which means any assignment that, though valid, fails to comply with the requirements of the Law of Property Act 1925, s. 136, e.g. an oral assignment.

In an equitable assignment, the assignee (X) cannot sue in his own name, but must join the assignor (B) as co-plaintiff in any action against the debtor or other obligee (A), or as co-defendant if he refuses. Thus the action will be either *X and B* v. *A*, or *X* v. *B and A*. The essential points are:

(a) intention to assign (no particular form is necessary);
(b) notice is necessary to the obligee to prevent him, for example, from paying the assignor — *see Dearle* v. *Hall* (1828);
(c) value is necessary only in assignments of future rights, e.g. the assignor's expectations under a will.

3. Statutory assignments
Assignment under the Law of Property Act 1925, s. 136, transfers:

(a) the full legal obligation;
(b) the right to enforce it; and
(c) powers to give a full discharge.

The requirements are:

(a) the assignment must be absolute, e.g. not by way of loan;
(b) it must be of the whole debt or other obligation;
(c) it must be in writing, signed by the assignor, but it need not be for value — *see Re Westerton* (1919);
(d) express notice in writing must be given by the assignee to the other party to the contract, i.e. the debtor or other obligee, to avoid him performing the contract in favour of the assignor, so, if A owes B £100, B can sell his rights to collect payment to X (in the form set out above) and this will entitle X to enforce the debt against A. However, X should notify A in writing of the transfer to prevent any possibility of A paying B.

The effects are:

(a) The assignee (X in the above example) can sue in his own name to enforce the chose, e.g. by suing A for debt;
(b) The assignee (X) takes subject to equities having priority over his assignment, e.g. if A has paid off part of his debt to B before receiving notice of the assignment, X cannot compel A to pay the full amount (but must try and recover the money from B).

Negotiable instruments

4. Negotiable instruments
Certain classes of chose in action (*see* 19: **9**), called negotiable

instruments, can be transferred or negotiated without the formalities and restrictions affecting most choses in action under the Law of Property Act 1925, s. 136 (*see* 11: **3**) or the rules of equity (*see* 11: **2**).

The characterisitics of negotiable instruments are:

(a) title passes by delivery (or by delivery + indorsement), whereas a legal assignment of an ordinary chose in action must be in writing under the Law of Property Act 1925, s. 136;

(b) no notice is necessary to the debtor or other obligee, whereas in assignments of ordinary choses, notice is necessary, either under the Law of Property Act 1925, s. 136 or the rule in *Dearle* v. *Hall*;

(c) the holder can sue in his own name, whereas an assignee of an ordinary chose in action cannot so do if the assignment is merely equitable;

(d) a bona-fide transferee for value takes free of any defects in the transferor's title, whereas an assignee of an ordinary chose gets no better title than his assignor;

(e) a transferee in due course (*see* 12: **7**) takes free of any defences that could have been raised by the debtor against the transferor, whereas any defence available against an assignor can be raised against the assignee of an ordinary chose in action.

A chose in action may become negotiable either by statute or by mercantile custom. Instruments negotiable by statute include bills of exchange and promissory notes. Instruments negotiable by custom include bank notes, share warrants, bearer debentures and exchequer bills.

Note that the following are *not* negotiable instruments: bills of lading, Post Office orders, share certificates, IOUs and receipts.

The most important class of negotiable instruments is bills of exchange (including cheques).

Note for BANKING STUDENTS: A special Appendix containing the Bills of Exchange Act 1882 is included at the end of this book for students doing examinations in banking, in which there are usually compulsory questions on bills and cheques. Other students should not need to consult Appendix 1 unless their examiners insist on a detailed knowledge of this subject.

5.　Bills of exchange

A bill of exchange as defined in the Bills of Exchange Act 1882, s. 3(1) is:

(a) an unconditional order in writing;

(b) signed by the drawer; and

(c) addressed to a drawee;

(d) ordering the drawee;

(e) to pay a fixed sum of money;

(f) on demand or at a fixed or determinable future time;

(g) to, or to the order of, a specified payee or to bearer.

> NOTE: (1) *Three parties* There are usually three parties to a bill at its outset — the drawer, drawee and payee. (A cheque is a bill of which the drawee is a bank.)
>
> (2) *Unconditional order*, e.g. not merely payable in certain circumstances such as 'provided the war is over'. However, a bill may validly indicate a particular fund out of which the money is to be paid, e.g. where a cheque stipulates a particular account.
>
> (3) *Fixed sum* The sum is regarded as sufficiently certain even if it is payable with interest or by instalments or is made subject to fluctuations of international rates of exchange.
>
> (4) *Date* An undated or wrongly dated bill is not necessarily invalid. If undated, a holder may himself fill in the date of issue or acceptance. Any date appearing on a bill is presumed to be the right one unless the contrary is proved. Antedating, post-dating, or Sunday dating do not affect the validity of a bill.

Bills of exchange require to be supported by consideration like other contracts, but note the following:

(a) consideration is presumed, i.e. the presumption is in favour of any holder seeking to enforce a bill (whereas in ordinary contracts it is for the plaintiff to prove that he has given consideration).

(b) past consideration will suffice, i.e. any antecedent debt or other obligation (Bills of Exchange Act 1882, s. 27).

6. Cheques
These are bills of exchange that are:

(a) drawn on a banker; and

(b) payable on demand.

The relationship of banker and customer is basically that of debtor and creditor and the rules laid down by the Bills of Exchange Act 1882 for ordinary bills apply to cheques unless they are incompatible.

The Cheques Act 1957 makes slight modifications in the law relating to cheques, mainly for the protection of bankers and the Cheques Act 1992 makes others, mainly for the protection of their customers.

7. Position of holders

Any holder can enforce a bill against the drawer or, once the drawee has accepted liability, against the drawee.

(a) A *holder for value* is a person who holds a bill for which valuable consideration has at some time been given, not necessarily by him. Thus, if A pays a debt to B by cheque and B gives the cheque to X as a present, X is a holder for value.

(b) A *holder in due course* is a person who has taken a bill:
- (*i*)   complete and regular on the face of it;
- (*ii*) before it was overdue;
- (*iii*) without notice of any previous dishonour;
- (*iv*) in good faith;
- (*v*)   for value;
- (*vi*) without notice of any defect in his transferor's title.

The law relating to negotiable instruments is largely designed to protect a holder in due course and the law presumes that every holder is in this category. Such a person can enforce the bill against the drawer (or against the acceptor, i.e. a drawee who has accepted liability) as though he had a perfect legal title, notwithstanding any defects in the transferor's title. Thus, if B fraudulently obtains a cheque for £100 from A and then negotiates it to X for value in the ordinary course of business, X, as a holder in due course, can insist on payment of the cheque by A.

Nemo dat quod non habet

8. The *nemo dat* rule

Nemo dat quod non habet means 'no one can give what he has not got'. It expresses a basic rule of law: a transferor of property (real or personal) cannot transfer a better right to that property than he himself has at the time of transfer.

A thief, therefore, cannot normally transfer to a purchaser the legal ownership of the thing stolen and a borrower of goods cannot normally transfer the legal ownership of the goods to a purchaser if he attempts to sell them in defraud of the lender.

In the following cases, the *nemo dat* rule does not apply and the transferor can give a better title than he himself possesses:

(a) *Negotiable instruments* A person who purchases a negotiable instrument that is complete and regular on the face of it, in good faith and in ordinary course of business, without notice of any defect in the instrument or in the transferor's title, is a holder in due course. Such a holder obtains a valid title even though the transferor's title was defective (Bills of Exchange Act 1882, s. 29).

(b) *Sale under court order*, e.g. where the court orders an official to sell a debtor's property to satisfy an unpaid creditor.

(c) *Sale by a factor* A factor in possession of goods can give a good title to a bona-fide purchaser, even though he is exceeding his authority in selling the goods: (Factors Act 1889, ss. 1 and 2).

(d) *Sales under the Sale of Goods Act 1979, s.25.* Under this Act, wherever a purchaser gains possession of goods without paying for them or a seller remains in possession after sale, he can give a valid title to a bona fide purchaser who is unaware of the previous sale.

(e) *Sales under voidable title* Where the seller has merely a voidable title to the property sold, he can nevertheless give a good title to a bona fide purchaser from him, provided his title has not already been avoided at the time, e.g. where X obtains goods by misrepresentation from P and sells them to B for value, B gets a good title — *see Phillips* v. *Brooks* (1919).

(f) *Owner is estopped from denying the seller's title* If the true owner of goods allows another to act as though he had a right to dispose of property, he cannot later object if that person sells the property to an innocent purchaser — *see Pickard* v. *Sears* (1837).

(g) *Under the Hire-Purchase Act 1964, s. 27*, a hirer who disposes of a hired motor vehicle to a private purchaser (i.e. not a motor dealer or finance company) may make a good title *provided* the purchaser takes it in good faith and without notice of the hire-purchase agreement. This provision of the Hire-Purchase Act 1964 has not been repealed (*see* 12: **23, 24**).

(h) *Sales in market overt (open market).* Where goods are sold in any well-established market overt the purchaser will gain a good title notwithstanding any defect in the seller's title, provided he had no notice of the defect (Sale of Goods Act 1979, s. 22 (1)).

NOTE: (1) *Market overt means* (a) any shop in the City of London, where such goods are normally sold, and (b) any open market elsewhere in England, but not in Wales or Scotland established by Royal charter, statute or ancient custom.

(2) *Time of sale* must be between the hours of sunrise and sunset on the appointed market day (or, in the City of London, on any day other than Sunday) — *see Reid* v. *Metropolitan Police Commissioner* (1973).

(3) *Place of sale* must be in the public part of any shop or stall, in view

of passers-by, and the market-dealer must be the seller not the purchaser.

(4) *Things sold* include any form of *personalty*, except horses.

Sale of goods

9. Sale of Goods Act 1979

The law relating to the sale of goods is now contained in the Sale of Goods Act 1979. This Act was a consolidation of the like-named Act of 1893, which was based on ancient rules of common law and the law merchant, as expanded and modernised by the judges. The 1893 Act was amended by, *inter alia,* the Supply of Goods (Implied Terms) Act 1973 and the Unfair Contract Terms Act 1977 and these Acts have also been re-enacted in the 1979 Act.

The term 'goods' includes all chattels and personal or other choses in possession, e.g. harvested crops, ships, goods in process of manufacture, etc. It does not cover sales of work and materials, e.g a sale in which the purchaser is buying materials worked upon by the vendor to produce a complete article, where the element of work outweighs the value of the actual materials. Therefore the purchase of a portrait from the painter otherwise than by a dealer is not covered by the Act — *see Robinson* v. *Graves* (1935). Transactions of this kind are now dealt with by the Supply of Goods and Services Act 1982 (*see* 12: **14**). Contracts for the sale of goods can be made in any form. If the purchaser desires definite proof of purchase he may ask for a receipt or, if he is not to take possession of the goods, a bill of sale (*see* 22: **15**).

10. Ascertained and unascertained goods

Specific or ascertained goods are identified and agreed upon at the time the contract is made. Unascertained goods are goods that exist when the contract is made, but are not specifically identified, e.g. are merely referred to by description, such as '500 tons of coal from your mine'. Future goods are goods not yet manufactured.

If specific goods perish *before* the contract is made the contract is automatically void. The same will apply if they perish *after* the contract is made, provided they perish without the fault of either party and before the legal property in them has passed to the purchaser.

In the case of specific goods, the ownership or legal property in them passes to the purchaser whenever the parties intend that it shall do so, e.g. in a sale to which no special conditions are attached, the legal property in the goods will pass as soon as the contract is made (even though delivery is not to take place until some later time) under the Sale of Goods Act 1979, s. 17.

In the case of unascertained goods, the property in them passes only when:

(a) they have become ascertained; and
(b) the buyer has been notified of this, s. 18.

If goods are damaged or destroyed after the contract has been made but before the property in them has passed to the purchaser, the seller bears the loss. However, after the property has passed to the purchaser, if the goods are destroyed (even though they are still in the possession of the seller), the risk falls on the purchaser, in the absence of contrary agreement.

The seller may let the buyer have goods on approval ('on sale or return'). Here the property in the goods passes to the purchaser when he signifies acceptance or adopts the goods as his own (e.g. by using them) or retains them for an unreasonably long time or at such other time as the contract may provide.

11. Implied conditions and warranties

The Sale of Goods Act 1979 provides for the following terms to be implied into any contract for the sale of goods.

(a) *Implied undertakings as to title — s. 12*
  (*i*) a condition that the seller has the legal right to sell the goods or will have at the time the property is to pass;
  (*ii*) a warranty that the goods are free from any charge or encumbrance not disclosed or known to the buyer and that they will remain free until the time when the property is to pass;
  (*iii*) a warranty that the buyer will enjoy quiet possession of the goods.

These terms cannot be excluded from any contract for the sale of goods.

(b) *Implied condition as to description — s. 13* A condition that in a sale by description, where the buyer merely describes the type of goods he wants and leaves it to the seller to provide them, the goods will correspond with the description, but see *Harlington and Leinster Enterprises* v. *Christopher Hull Fine Art* (1990).

(c) *Implied undertaking as to quality and fitness — s. 14* (*i*)   a condition that goods sold in the course of a business are of merchantable quality (goods are of merchantable quality if they are as fit for the purpose for which goods of that kind are commonly bought as it is reasonable to expect having regard to any description applied to them, the price, and all other relevant circumstances);

(*ii*) a condition that goods supplied for a particular purpose are reasonably fit for that purpose;

(*iii*) an implied warranty or condition may be incorporated by the custom of a particular trade.

(d) A condition, in sales by sample, that the bulk will correspond with the sample(s) on which the order was based and that the buyer will have a reasonable opportunity to compare the bulk with sample and that the goods will be reasonably free of any defect not likely to be apparent on such examination (*see* the Sale of Goods Act 1979, s. 15(2)).

NOTE: The terms implied in paragraphs **(b)**, **(c)** and **(d)** cannot be excluded from a consumer sale and can be excluded from a non-consumer sale only so far as is fair and reasonable. A consumer sale means a sale of goods, other than by auction or by competitive tender, by a seller in the course of a business where the goods:

(a)   are of a type ordinarily bought for private use or consumption; and

(b)   are sold to a person who does not buy or hold himself out as buying them in the course of a business (Unfair Contract Terms Act 1977).

12. Rights of the seller
These include the following:

(a) *Seller's lien* A seller is entitled to retain possession of the goods until payment has been made or tendered, unless the contract excludes the lien. This lien is merely a right to retain possession and the seller can re-sell the goods to recover his money only in certain exceptional circumstances.

(b) *Stoppage in transit* The seller may order the stoppage of goods in their transit to the buyer if the buyer becomes insolvent before the goods are delivered to him (or his agent) and before he has paid for them (Sale of Goods Act 1979, s. 44).

(c) *Retention of title* A seller may include in his terms of sale a clause that preserves his legal rights of ownership until he has been paid; this is commonly called a 'Romalpa' clause, after the name of the main case in which it was considered (and held to be a valid term) — *see*

Aluminium Industrie BV v. *Romalpa Aluminium Ltd* (1976). This has close links with the general rule about the passing of property in goods (*see* 12: **10**).

13. *Ex post facto* warranties

The buyer may treat any breach of condition by the seller as grounds for repudiating the contract or he may elect to treat it as merely a breach of warranty, go on with the contract and sue for damages, e.g. may treat it as a breach of an *ex post facto* warranty (*see* 7: **4** and 9: **9**).

He must treat a breach of condition in this way wherever he has accepted a substantial part of the goods and it is impossible to separate those that are accepted from those that are rejected (Sale of Goods Act 1979, s. 11, and *see Bernstein* v. *Pamsons Motors* (1987), but note *Rogers* v. *Parish* (1987)).

Supply of goods and services

14. The Supply of Goods and Services Act 1982

The successful operation of the Sale of Goods Acts 1893 and 1979, combined with the consumer movement of the 1960s and 1970s, led to the introduction of similar legislation for comparable contracts that were not covered by the basic sale of goods provisions. This was the Supply of Goods and Services Act 1982, which deals with the following three classes of case:

(a) *Contracts for the transfer of property in goods* These include such transactions as barter (where goods are exchanged for other goods or for coupons) and contracts for work and materials (e.g. roofing a house); the Act does not deal with contracts already within the Sale of Goods Act 1979, hire-purchase agreements, deals involving trading stamps, transactions made by deed when there is no consideration, contracts operating by way of mortgage, pledge, charge or other security (s. 1). In the contracts covered by the 1982 Act there are now (ss. 2–5):

> (*i*) an implied term that the transferor has (or will have) the right to transfer the property;
>
> (*ii*) in transfers by description, an implied term that the goods will correspond with the description;
>
> (*iii*) an implied term that the goods will be of merchantable quality, with the exception of any defects specifically drawn

to the transferee's attention or reasonably discoverable by examination;

(*iv*) in transfers by sample, an implied condition of correspondence with the sample.

(b) *Contracts for the hire of goods* The contracts covered exclude hire-purchase agreements and trading stamp agreements. In contracts covered by the Act there are now (ss. 7–10):

(*i*)   an implied warranty that the hirer has (or will have) the right to transfer possession of the goods;

(*ii*) in hirings by description, an implied condition that the goods will correspond with the description;

(*iii*) an implied condition that the goods are of merchantable quality, with the exception of any defects specifically drawn to the hirer's attention or reasonably discoverable by examination; and

(*iv*) in hirings by reference to a sample, an implied condition of correspondence with the sample.

(c) *Supply of services* If a contract for the supply of services is made *in the course of a business*, there is an implied term that the supplier will carry out the work with reasonable care and skill (s. 13). There is also an implied term that the work will be done within a reasonable time (if the contract does not specify the precise time) (s. 14). If the consideration (price) for the work is not fixed, there is an implied term that the party who contracts with the supplier will pay a reasonable charge (s. 15).

The similarity of these new terms with those implied under the Sale of Goods Act 1979 (*see* 12: **11**) means that cases under the 1979 Act may be used as 'guidelines' in interpreting the 1982 provisions.

Gifts

15. Gifts

A gift is a transfer of property from one person to another without consideration. Gifts may be made as follows:

(a) *by will* (*see* Chapter 24);

(b) *donatio mortis causa* (*see* 12: **16**);

(c) *inter vivos* it is generally sufficient if the donor hands the present to the donee, but where a special form of transfer is legally required for the particular type of property (e.g. shares or land), this form of transfer must be used, e.g. a deed.

A promise to make a gift cannot be sued upon (unless it is made under seal), as it is not supported by consideration. Even if made under seal, the court will not order specific performance of such a promise because of the absence of mutuality (*see* 23: **6**).

Gifts may be made subject to a condition precedent or subsequent. Thus, giving an engagement ring to one's fiancée is subject to an implied condition subsequent that the parties shall marry; if the marriage does not take place, the ring is normally returned.

16. *Donatio mortis causa*

This is a gift by delivery of property in contemplation of the donor's imminent death, upon a condition (express or implied) that the gift is not to take effect unless the donor dies.

Requisites of a valid *donatio mortis causa* are as follows:

(a) *contemplation of death* — the donor must be *in extremis*, i.e. in imminent peril of death, either by illness or otherwise, indeed, it would be enough if a donor knew he had cancer, even if he actually died of some other cause — *see Wilkes* v. *Allington* (1931);

(b) *conditional upon death* — it is a present gift, but it ceases to be effective if the donor, in fact, recovers and does not die because it takes effect immediately, it pre-dates any gift by will (which does not become effective until death) and, therefore, if jewels are given to A by will made a year before death and to B by *donatio* a week before death, the gift by will lapses;

(c) *delivery essential* — words of *intention* to make a gift are insufficient, without delivery, actual or constructive, e.g. by handing the donee the keys to a safe where the property is kept so mere delivery for safekeeping is not enough, there must be an actual intention to transfer ownership — *see Trimmer* v. *Danby* (1856) — and delivery must be to the donee or someone on his behalf;

(d) *property that can pass* — all pure personalty can be made the subject of a *donatio*, e.g. promissory notes, cheques drawn in favour of the donor by a third party, bonds, saving certificates, but cheques drawn by the donor himself are automatically revoked by death and therefore cannot be the subject of a valid *donatio*.

Further, there can be no *donatio* of realty or leaseholds. If a chose in action is given, the gift will be ineffective *unless* the proper method of transfer is used.

17. Imperfect gifts

If the donor retains the property given, but states before witnesses or in writing that he will hold the property in trust for the donee, an enforceable trust may arise (*see* 23: **19, 7**). The normal rule is that an imperfect gift will not be enforced.

In the following exceptional cases an imperfect gift will nevertheless be enforced:

(a) where the donee is subsequently appointed personal representative of the donor, he may assert a valid claim after the donor's death — *see Strong* v. *Bird* (1874);

(b) where any conveyance of land is made to a minor, it automatically operates as though it were an agreement for valuable consideration for the grantor to hold the land as trustee for the minor until he reaches the age of 18 (Settled Land Act 1925, s. 27).

Bailment

18. Bailment

A bailment is a delivery of goods by one person to another for some limited purpose, on condition that when the purpose has been accomplished the goods are to be returned.

The consideration in a contract of bailment is the bailor's parting with possession of his goods. Consequently, a bailment is an enforceable simple contract, even if no money changes hands.

There are various types of bailment.

(a) *Deposit* This means goods are deposited for safe custody, e.g. in a cloakroom. The bailee cannot use the goods and must (subject to the contract) take reasonable care of the goods while in his possession. He must return them to the bailor and no exclusionary clauses guarding him against consequences of negligence will protect him if he returns the goods to some person other than the bailor or the bailor's agent — *see Alexander* v. *Railway Executive* (1951).

(b) *Loan for use* The bailee is entitled to use the goods loaned and is not liable for fair wear and tear, unless he deviates from the conditions of the loan.

(c) *Hire* Here the bailor impliedly warrants the fitness of the goods for the purpose hired. The bailee must take reasonable care of the goods and use them in accordance with the terms of the contract. He is not liable for loss by robbery or accidental fire occasioned without negligence.

Hiring is automatically determined if the hirer attempts to sell the goods — *see Helby* v. *Mathews* (1895).

(d) *Innkeepers* They are responsible for the safety of their guests' belongings in certain cases (*see* 12: **22**).

(e) *Pawn or pledge* of chattels as security for a loan (*see* Chapter 22).

19. Duties of bailee

These are:

(a) *To take reasonable care* of the goods bailed to him. What is reasonable depends on the type of bailment. If the bailee has been paid to provide safekeeping for goods his duty is higher than if he received no payment.

Contracts of bailment frequently contain clauses restricting the duty of care or excluding it, but if the bailee returns the goods to the wrong person he has no protection from such a clause — *see Alexander* v. *Railway Executive* (1951).

(b) *To return the goods* in accordance with the contract. If he fails to do so he is liable for loss or damage, notwithstanding the exercise of reasonable care — *see Shaw* v. *Symmons* (1917).

> NOTE: By the Unsolicited Goods and Services Act 1971, where a person becomes an 'involuntary bailee' (e.g. has unsolicited goods delivered to him by post, so that he cannot easily refuse to take delivery) the following rules apply.
>
> (1) The goods become the property of the recipient (a) after 30 days, if notice has been given to the sender with a demand for their removal, or (b) after 6 months if no notice has been given to the sender.
>
> (2) These rules apply if the goods were sent (a) without prior request; (b) without an agreement to acquire or return them; or (c) without cause to believe they were sent with a view to their being acquired for the purposes of a trade or business.

20. Duty of bailor

If the goods are bailed for a particular purpose of which the bailor knows (e.g. hire of a car), he is under a duty to disclose any defect rendering the goods unsuitable for that purpose. He impliedly warrants the fitness of any goods hired in this way, and owes a duty of reasonable care in this respect (*see* 12: **14**).

In other bailments the bailor generally owes no duty of care, save to warn the bailee if goods are dangerous, e.g. where explosives are deposited in a cloakroom.

21. Innkeeper and guests

A hotelier or innkeeper is one who holds himself out as ready to receive all travellers who:

(a) are willing to pay a reasonable price for the accommodation offered; and

(b) come in a condition fit to be received (Hotel Proprietors Act 1956, s. 1).

An innkeeper must accept all travellers provided he has enough room and they are willing to pay and in a fit condition to be received. Failure to accept reasonable travellers renders him liable to damages — *see Browne* v. *Brandt* (1902).

Any person is a traveller who calls for a meal or a drink — *see Williams* v. *Linnett* (1951), but he is entitled to protection of his luggage only if he stays the night. The innkeeper has a right to retain all a guest's luggage for non-payment of his charges. This lien (*see* 12: **28**) does not extend to things over which the innkeeper owes no duty of care, e.g. the guest's car or pet animal.

By the Innkeepers Liability Act 1878, the hotelier is given a statutory right to sell such goods as are subject to his lien and reimburse himself for his charges out of the proceeds of sale. The right to sell becomes exercisable when the goods have been retained for six weeks; and one month's notice of the sale must be given to the guest to give him a final chance of paying his bill.

22. Innkeeper's liability

The innkeeper is responsible for his guests' luggage (but not their pet animals, cars, etc.) and can evade liability only on the grounds that damage or loss was caused by:

(a) Act of God;
(b) the Queen's enemies;
(c) the guest's own negligence;
(d) inherent vice in the goods.

By the Hotel Proprietors Act 1956, the innkeeper's liability is restricted to £50 for any one article or £100 in respect of any one guest, unless:

(a) the loss or damage was caused by the wilful default or negligence of the innkeeper or his servants; or

(b) the goods were deposited with the innkeeper for safe custody in some place specially provided, e.g. the hotel safe.

A notice of these restrictions on liability must be given to the guest before or at the time of registering (when the contract is made), and a notice placed in the room is therefore inadequate — *see Olley* v. *Marlborough Court Hotel* (1949).

Hire purchase

23. The Consumer Credit Act 1974

The law on hire purchase has been extended to other credit transactions by the Consumer Credit Act 1974, which replaces several earlier Acts on related matters.

The new Act regulates all consumer credit agreements under which:

(a) the creditor provides the debtor with credit not exceeding £15,000; and

(b) the debtor is an individual.

'Credit' includes a cash loan or the credit for a hire-purchase agreement. Advertisements to provide credit are also subject to regulation by the Act.

Part III of the Act (ss. 21–42) deals with the licensing of credit businesses. A licence is required to carry on a consumer credit business. The licensing system is administered by the Director General of Fair Trading, whose job it is to superintend the working and enforcement of the Act.

24. Hire purchase

There are three different types of instalment agreements:

(a) *Hire purchase*, where a person hires goods for a specified period (by monthly or weekly instalments) and has an option to purchase the goods hired at the expiry of the period of hire (usually with the last scheduled payment). During the period of hire, he is a mere bailee of the goods.

(b) *Credit-sale*, where goods are sold to a purchaser (who obtains both possession and title) by instalments.

(c) *Conditional sale*, where a person agrees to buy goods and obtains immediate possession, but the transfer of title is postponed until the fulfilment of a condition, e.g. the completion of stated instalments of purchase price.

25. The agreement

Parts V and VI (ss. 55–86) of the Consumer Credit Act 1974 deal with the agreement. Under s. 61 a consumer credit agreement is not properly executed unless:

(a) a document in the form prescribed by regulations is signed by both creditor and debtor;

(b) the document embodies all the terms of the agreement other than the implied terms;

(c) the document, when presented to the debtor for signature, is legible and complete. A copy of the document must be supplied to the debtor.

An agreement that is the result of oral representations made to the debtor away from trade premises can be cancelled by the debtor within a cooling-off period of five days.

The agreement contains implied terms similar to those implied into a contract for the sale of goods (*see* 12: **11**).

26. Dealer as agent

In many hire-purchase transactions there are, in fact, three parties involved. Thus A wishes to obtain a car and arranges to take one stocked by B, a dealer, who arranges hire purchase through C, a finance company. The resulting hire-purchase contract will be between A (the hirer) and C (the owner, who will have purchased the car for cash from B).

Under s. 56 of the Consumer Credit Act 1974, representations made by a dealer will be deemed to have been made by him as agent for the owner (C). Therefore, if B has misunderstood the age or condition of the car in the above example, A may be able to sue C for misrepresentation.

27. Right to end the agreement

Under the Consumer Credit Act 1974, ss. 99 and 100, the debtor can terminate the agreement by giving notice to the creditor and, as well as returning the goods, paying:

(a) all instalments due before termination;

(b) any damages for failure to take reasonable care of the goods;

(c) a minimum payment up to one half of the hire-purchase price.

If the hirer paid less than half at the date of termination, he can be compelled to make up the difference; if he has paid more than a half, he cannot recover any of the money he has paid.

If he has paid more than a third then, generally, the goods, cannot be taken from him ('snatched back') without a court order (s. 90).

Liens

28. Liens
A lien is a right over the chattels of another, arising by operation of law (independently of any contract) and giving the lienor a right to retain the goods until the owner has settled some debt connected with the chattels or, in the case of some liens, unconnected with the chattels.

(A lien should be distinguished from the deposit of chattels by way of security for a loan, where the lender's right of retention depends on contract, i.e. a pawn or pledge (*see* 22: **14–19**).)

Liens are of three kinds:

(a) common law or possessory (*see* 12: **29**);
(b) maritime (*see* 12: **30**);
(c) equitable (*see* 12: **31**).

29. Common law or possessory liens
These arise where the creditor has actual possession of some of the debtor's property, and has a right to retain such chattels until an outstanding debt is paid.

NOTE:
(1) A common law lien cannot arise independently of possession, i.e. the creditor is not entitled to obtain possession solely for the purpose of claiming such a lien (compare this with equitable liens — 12:**31**).

(2) A common law lien is exercisable only by detaining the goods until the debt is paid, i.e. there is no right of sale, save in exceptional cases where such a right is given by statute.

(3) A statutory right of sale is given to innkeepers (Innkeepers Liability Act 1878), unpaid sellers of goods who have remained in possession (Sale of Goods Act 1979) and repairers (Torts (Interference with Goods) Act 1977); *see* 15: **19**).

(4) A common law lien is extinguished by: (a) agreement, express or implied, (b) payment of the debt; (c) loss of possession; (d) taking security for the debt, etc.

A common law lien may be general or particular:

(a) *a general lien* is available against the owner of the goods in respect of any charges owing to the creditor, who may retain for this purpose any goods of the debtor coming into his possession at the time the lien arises, e.g. factors' liens;

(b) *a particular lien* is available only against the particular goods in connection with which charges have been incurred, e.g. a carrier's lien for his freight charges.

30. Maritime liens

A maritime lien is a line attaching to a ship in favour of the shipmaster (for disbursements), seamen (for their wages), salvors (for charges in connection with salvage), etc.

The lien is exercised against the ship, not against the owners. If owners sell a ship subjected to a lien, the purchasers will take the ship with the lien attached. The method of exercise is generally to attach a notice of lien to the mast of the ship; port authorities may then refuse to let the ship sail until the debt is paid.

31. Equitable liens

Unlike common law liens, these are not founded on possession and can be exercised by obtaining a court order for sale, but, like all equitable rights, they are extinguishable by sale of the property to a bona-fide purchaser for value without notice of the lien.

They arise mainly in connection with the sale of land, e.g. a vendor of a house who has given up possession to the purchaser has a lien over the house and land for any unpaid purchase money. Similarly, a purchaser of land who has paid a deposit has a lien over the land for the amount of his purchase money.

Progress test 12

1. Define a chose in action and explain how it can be assigned. **(1–3)**

2. What is meant by 'negotiability'? What are the characteristics of a negotiable instrument? **(4)**

3. Define a bill of exchange. How does an ordinary bill of exchange differ from a cheque? **(5, 6)**

4. Explain what is meant by (a) a holder for value and (b) a holder in due course of a bill of exchange **(7)**

5. Explain what is meant by *nemo dat quod non habet*, and summarise the exceptions to this rule.   **(8)**

6. Distinguish between ascertained and unascertained goods, and explain when the property in unascertained goods will pass to the purchaser under a contract for sale of goods.   **(10)**

7. Summarise the conditions and warranties implied by the Sale of Goods Act 1979.   **(11)**

8. Write explanatory notes on the following: (a) sale or return; (b) seller's lien; (c) stoppage in transit; (d) *ex post facto* warranty. **(10, 12, 13)**

9. Summarise (a) the contracts affected by and (b) the terms introduced by the Supply of Goods and Services Act 1982.   **(14)**

10. Explain the distinction between gifts *inter vivos* and *donationes mortis causa*.   **(15, 16)**

11. A nursed B during B's last illness. On his death-bed B gave A his bank deposit book, a cheque signed by C in favour of B (and endorsed by B to A) and the lease of his flat. After B's death, can A enforce these gifts?   **(16)**

12. Define bailment and explain the duties of bailor and bailee in a contract of bailment.   **(18–20)**

13. Define a lien and explain the extent of an innkeeper's lien. **(21–28)**

14. What is hire purchase and how does it differ from (a) conditional sale and (b) credit sale?   **(24)**

15. A door-to-door salesman persuaded Mrs A to sign a hire-purchase agreement for a suite of furniture she could not afford. For some days she was afraid to tell her husband about the contract but has now done so and Mr A and Mrs A wish to avoid the contract. Discuss.   **(25, 27)**

16. Distinguish between possessory and equitable liens and explain the difference between general and particular liens.   **(29–31)**

Part three

The law of torts

Part three

The law of torts

13
Nature of tortious liability

1. Meaning of tort

The Norman-French word *tort* means simply 'a wrong'. In English law, it is used to denote a wrong that is actionable at the suit of the party injured (though, as shall be seen, the 'injury' may be merely notional). Such wrongs are redressible by an award of damages to the injured person – we speak, therefore in relation to torts, of civil wrongs, to distinguish them from criminal wrongs. Initially, no such distinction was made.

2. Historical background

Early English law made no distinction between crimes and civil wrongs. Generally speaking, a wrong committed by X upon Y would only come to the attention of the early courts if the peace of the community was threatened. As the Norman and Plantagenet kings developed strong central governments, so the punishment of those wrongs that threatened the peace of the realm fell to Royal courts. Such wrongs formed the basis of our crimes and were known generally as felonies. Those lesser wrongs that, although involving a breach of the peace, nevertheless did not ostensibly threaten law and order, but only affected the party complaining of the wrong, formed the basis of torts and were known generally as trespasses.

By the thirteenth century, such wrongs were actionable in the Royal courts, but only at the suit of the injured party upon the issue of a writ purchased by him from the Chancery (*see* 1: **13**).

The fourteenth century saw a new development in the form of the action on the case, related to trespass, but differing from it in one important respect; whereas trespass was concerned with direct, forcible injuries (a vestigial form of breach of the peace), the action on the case covered consequential injuries (i.e. those which did *not* involve a direct application of force).

These two 'branches' were important, because it was necessary for a plaintiff to 'fit' his claim into one or another of these categories, known as 'forms of action'.

The forms of action, of which there were many, apart from trespass and case as it is commonly known, defined and regulated the availability of litigation in the common law courts in respect to most branches of the law. The Common Law Procedure Act 1852 effectively abolished the forms of action, thus enabling the courts to admit of actions in a much wider variety of circumstances. The case of *Rylands* v. *Fletcher* (1868), for example, was an innovation of this kind. On the other hand, the stranglehold that the forms of action had can be seen in the persistence of the categorisation of torts, in the old style, into trespass, nuisance, negligence, etc.

Tortious liability

3. Torts distinguished from other wrongs

No one would disagree that torts differ from other legal wrongs — crimes, breaches of contract, etc. However, there is considerable disagreement as to how, if at all, the notion of a *tort* should be defined.

It is considered appropriate to deal with the two problems together, because one definition — that of Sir John Salmond — seeks to define tort by reference to the differences between a tort and other wrongs, namely, 'a tort is a civil wrong for which the remedy is a common law action for unliquidated damages, and which is not exclusively the breach of a contract, or the breach of a trust or other merely equitable obligation'.

These differences can be briefly summarised as follows:

(a) *Tort and crime distinguished*
    (*i*) Crimes are offences — they are prosecuted and punished by the state and the action takes place in a criminal court (before a magistrate, or judge and jury).
    (*ii*) Torts are not punished at all; the party injured sues the guilty party (called a tortfeasor) in a civil court (usually a judge, but seldom with a jury).

(b) *Tort and breach of contract distinguished*
    (*i*) The right to sue in contract depends not on the plaintiff being injured, but on the existence of a contract between himself and the defendant.
    (*ii*) Such rights and duties as are involved (*see* Chapter 5) are

primarily devised by the parties making the contract and are not, as in the case of tort, fixed by the law.

(*iii*) A person who is not a party to contract cannot sue for breach of it, even if he suffers injury as a direct result.

If breach of a *duty fixed by law* (i.e. a duty in tort) causes injury to anyone, that person will have a right to sue. This can be seen in the important case of *Donoghue* v. *Stephenson* (1932), where A bought a bottle of ginger beer from B and gave it to C to drink. Somehow, a snail had been allowed to get inside the bottle, contaminating its contents and C suffered food poisoning as a result. Notwithstanding the fact that C was a party to no contract, either with B or with the manufacturers of the ginger beer, she successfully sued the latter in tort, in what has come to be a momentous decision (*see* 16:4).

On the other hand, a situation may give rise to liability in both contract and tort. Thus, if A privately hires Doctor X to attend Mrs A, and X negligently causes harm to Mrs A:

(1) A may sue X for breach of contractual duty; and

(2) Mrs A may sue X for the tort of negligence

(c) *Tort and breach of trust distinguished.*

(*i*) As with contracts, the duties arising under a trust are the creations of the trust itself – in tort, they are fixed by the law.

(*ii*) Trusts are governed by that branch of the law known as equity (*see* Chapter 23) whereas torts are common law wrongs.

The other definition of the field of the law of tort is that of Sir Percy Winfield. While Winfield's definition has regard to the distinctions between torts and other wrongs (above), he seeks not to define 'a tort', but rather, 'tortious liability', namely, 'tortious liability arises from the breach of a duty primarily fixed by law: such duty is towards persons generally, and its breach is redressible by an action for unliquidated damages'.

The fact that torts are different from breaches of contract, crimes, etc., is implicit in this definition (e.g. duty *primarily fixed by law* and *not by the parties* etc.), as is the fact that 'breach is redressible by. . . damages'.

Where Winfield's definition differs substantially from Salmond's is in his refusal to define a *tort* as such. His definition, therefore, is at the heart of the theory that we have a law of *tort*, based on some general principle of liability and dealing with all instances (including any that may not, as yet, have been brought to the courts' attention) of unjustifiable harm.

Salmond on the other hand, lends his definition to the theory that we have a law of *torts*, concerned with a series of limited and separate wrongs.

It is fair to say that the historical development of the law tends to lend support to Salmond's view; Winfield's, however, is possibly currently favoured, at least among some academics. Whichever definition is accepted, the student will have to accommodate several difficult concepts; these will not invariably serve to support his chosen view of the subject as a whole. Furthermore, as Street pointed out 'much ink has been spilt in unsuccessful attempts to define a tort'.

4.   *Damnum sine injuria* (harm without legal injury)

Despite the objections of Winfield's supporters, it is well settled that not all unjustifiable harm is actionable. The injury, of itself, is not enough. In order to succeed in an action for tort, the plaintiff must show:

(a) that he has suffered harm; and
(b) that the defendant has violated a legal right of the plaintiff.

Where there is harm without violation of a legal right, i.e. *damnum* without *injuria*, the plaintiff has no redress.

Thus, if a trader is ruined by the legitimate competition of his rivals he has no redress in tort — *see Mogul Steamship Co. Case* (1892) HL. Similarly, if the owner of land legitimately digs wells on his own land, with the result that water, percolating under the land, is diverted from the reservoir owned by a neighbouring town, the town has no remedy — *see Mayor of Bradford* v. *Pickles* (1895) HL. This is so *even if* the defendant maliciously dug the wells for the express purpose of interrupting the flow of water to the reservoirs, as he was only doing what he was legally entitled to do (*see* 13: **7** and Chapter 25).

Example

In *Electrochrome Ltd* v. *Welsh Plastics Ltd* (1968), A's lorry, negligently driven, damaged B's fire hydrant near C's factory and, as a result, the water supply was cut off and C's factory lost a day's work. C sued A for negligence. It was held that C had suffered *damnum*, but the *injuria* was B's. Therefore C had no claim.

Such 'economic' loss as this generally falls outside the law of tort (*see* 16: **9**). 'There is a long line of authority for a principle of law that, in order to enable a person to claim in negligence for loss caused to him by reason of loss of or damage to property, he must have had either the legal ownership of or a possessory title to the property concerned at the time when the loss or damage occurred', said Lord Brandon in *The Aliakmon* (1986).

5. *Injuria sine damno*

By contrast, a plaintiff may be able to sue for an infringement upon his rights even though he has suffered no harm at all. Here there is *injuria* (legal injury) irrespective of *damnum* (actual harm).

Such instances constitute a number of particular torts that are said to be actionable *per se*, i.e. without proof of harm or damage. Trespass and libel are examples of such torts. The reasons for their being actionable *per se* are historical (*see* 13:2) as trespass involved a direct and forcible interference with the plaintiff, harm could be presumed.

6. Protection of rights or redress for wrongs?

In the light of **4** and **5**, it may seem impossible to answer this question in relation to torts. Certainly, a tortious claim is based upon the commission of a wrong, actual or alleged. On the other hand, there is much to be said for the view that the law of tort seeks to uphold rights, equally.

Thus, it could be said that one's right to a good name is protected by the defamation laws. A defendant who has attacked the plaintiff's reputation will be required to justify his attack and, if he can do so, then the court will uphold *his* right to comment on the subject of the plaintiff, even if it is embarrassing or damaging to the latter. Thus to speak of, say, libel as a 'wrong' pure and simple, is to risk over-simplification, given the various 'rights' that the court must consider and the complex issues involved (*see* Chapter 28).

7. Motive, malice and intention in tort

In general, the law is not concerned with the motive with which an act is done in determining whether an act is tortious or not. Thus, a good motive will not excuse a wrongful act. As a corollary, a bad motive (i.e. malice) will not make an otherwise lawful act unlawful — *see Mayor of Bradford* v. *Pickles* (1895) HL (*see* Chapter 25).

In some cases, however, malice is an essential ingredient; these are:

(a) malicious prosecution;
(b) injurious (or malicious) falsehood;
(c) conspiracy (sometimes).

Malice serves a notional function in other torts (e.g. publication of defamatory material must be malicious in the sense of being not innocent (*see* 28: **6**)) and may also defeat the defences of fair comment and of qualified privilege in actions for libel (*see* 28: **12**).

Intention is not normally a necessary ingredient, in the sense that it is not strictly necessary to prove that the defendant intended the consequences of his act, though proof that he did will obviously be cogent evidence of fault (*see* 13: **8**).

On the other hand, it must be shown that the defendant's conduct was volitional. Thus, if X seizes Y's arm and with it strikes Z, Y is guilty of no tort. Inevitable accident or, occasionally, Act of God, may also be good defences to actions in tort (*see* 27: **7**).

8. Fault, negligence and strict liability

We have seen (*see* 13: **7**) that while it is not normally necessary to prove that the defendant intended the consequences of his act, if intention can be proved, then fault can be attributed to the defendant. It is, then, generally necessary to prove that the defendant is at fault. In the absence of intention, proof of negligence will suffice — *see* e.g. *Stanley* v. *Powell* (1891).

> NOTE: Negligence is also the name of an important, but complex tort (*see* Chapter 16). Here, however, it is used in the relatively straightforward sense of indicating a want of care on the defendant's part – a failure to take reasonable steps to avoid causing harm.

There are, however, certain areas where proof of fault in the sense of intention or negligence is not necessary. Such instances, which result from historical accident, requirements of policy, or a combination of these, are known as cases of strict liability.

Examples of the doctrine of strict liability are:

(a) breaches of certain strict duties (*see* Chapter 27);
(b) the principle that makes an employer liable for the torts of his employee (vicarious liability; *see* 14: **15**);
(c) liability for the harm done by dangerous animals (Animals Act 1971);
(d) the rule in *Rylands* v. *Fletcher* (1868) HL, which says that the occupier of land who, for his own purposes brings on to his land anything that is not naturally there and which is likely to do mischief if it escapes, must keep it at his peril. If he fails to do so, he is liable for all the direct consequences of its escape.

Liability is said to be *strict*, however, and not *absolute*. Thus, Act of God is a good defence to an action in the rule in *Rylands* v. *Fletcher*; a person injured by a dangerous animal has no cause of action if he consents to the risk of injury — *see Cummings* v. *Grainger* (1977) (*see* 17: **12**).

9. Liability for omissions

So far, liability for the defendant's *conduct* has mainly been discussed. Mention has been made however, of the failure to take reasonable care. While this may be evidence of *fault*, this is not what is meant by an omission as such. In general, one will only be liable for failing to act (i.e. an omission) where one is under a positive duty to act (e.g. a man, who is an excellent swimmer, fails to prevent his young child from drowning), or where the defendant has failed to remedy a dangerous state of affairs for which he is, for one reason or another, legally responsible — *see Goldman* v. *Hargrave* (1967) PC, and *Leakey* v. *National Trust* (1980).

10. Causation

Clearly, a defendant should not be (and is not) liable for harm to the plaintiff of which his act or omission is not the cause. In practice, however, situations are not always so simple as to admit of only one cause; the court will seek to establish therefore, whether the defendant's act is a sufficiently proximate cause as to incur responsibility (the terms operative or effective are sometimes used rather than proximate).

If the term proximate cause is adopted, however, it should be remembered that this does not necessarily refer to the 'last event' before the injury is suffered in a situation where more than one act or omission is involved.

11. Concurrent causes

Where two or more events can be seen to be causative in relation to the plaintiff's injuries both may be found to be operative or proximate — *see Baker* v. *Willoughby* (1970) HL. In that case, the House held that the two causes involved had led to *separate* injuries. On the other hand, concurrent causes may be found to contribute equally to the *same* injury — *see Rouse* v. *Squires* (1973).

12. Independent causes

Sometimes an event other than the defendant's act can be said to 'reduce the defendant's act to mere history'. Such an event is referred to as a *novus actus interveniens* (new intervening act) and has the effect of 'breaking the chain' of causation that might otherwise place responsibility at the defendant's doorstep.

Such an act may be committed:

(a) by a third party (in which case it must normally be shown that the third party could foresee the consequences of his act) — *see Philco* v. *Spurling* (1949);

(b) by the plaintiff himself — *see McKew* v. *Holland, Hannen & Cubitts* (1969) HL, where the plaintiff's act, though foreseeable, was unreasonable in the circumstances; or

(c) by a natural event — *see The Carslogie* (1952) HL.

The danger of seeing the principle of *novus actus interveniens* in a rigid way, involving a strict time-sequence of:

(a) an act by D; followed by

(b) an independent cause (*novus actus interveniens*); then

(c) harm to the plaintiff,

is shown by the case of *Liesbosch Dredger* v. *Edison* (1933) where a *predisposing* cause was sufficient to break the chain of causation.

On the other hand, a long series of events does not, of itself, weaken the link between what the defendant did and what the plaintiff suffered — *see Scott* v. *Shepherd* (1773).

13. Remoteness of damage: 1

This problem differs from that of causation in that it assumes that the defendant's act has caused the plaintiff's injuries and that, in every other respect, the defendant is guilty of a wrong (i.e. he has committed a tort); the question of remoteness looks at the extent of the defendant's liability. It can be said, then, that the rules relating to remoteness of damage are rules that limit the damages which the plaintiff will eventually recover.

14. Remoteness of damage: 2

The principle, generally, is that the defendant to an action in tort is not liable for all the consequences of his actions, but only for those consequences that the law regards as sufficiently proximate.

Two main tests have been devised to meet the problem.

(a) *Direct consequences* The leading case is *Re Polemis* (1921) (CA). The facts were that a stevedore employed by the charterers of a ship dropped a plank into the hold of a vessel, where it caused a spark, igniting gas that had leaked from cargo, and vaporised in the hold.

It was held that the fire was the direct consequence of the charterers' employee's negligence and that the charterers (defendants) should be liable for all such consequences as flowed directly from this negligent act (though it was agreed that foresight was a factor in determining the innocence or otherwise of their acts).

(b) *Reasonable foresight* The main test is the *Wagon Mound* test — *see Overseas Tankship (UK)* v. *Morts Dock (The Wagon Mound No. 1)* (1961) PC (an appeal from the Australian High Court). A allowed oil to escape from their ship the *Wagon Mound*, where it was anchored. The oil floated across the water to B's wharf, where it was ignited by a spark. The wharf was destroyed in the ensuing fire. It was found that the destruction of the wharf by fire was not reasonably foreseeable and, accordingly, A was not liable as a defendant should be liable only for those consequences of his act that can be said to be reasonably foreseeable. The court (The Judicial Committee of the Privy Council) in utilising this test, rejected the older rule in *Re Polemis*.

The reasonable foresight test has been followed in United Kingdom cases such as *Hughes* v. *Lord Advocate* (1963) in the House of Lords, and by the Court of Appeal in *Doughty* v. *Turner* (1964).

15. Scope of the rules relating to remoteness
In *The Wagon Mound (No. 2)* (1967) PC, a different plaintiff (this time the owner of a ship; in *Wagon Mound (No. 1)* it was the owners of the wharf) brought an action in nuisance arising out of the same situation as the earlier case. It was held that the same test (reasonable foresight) applied. Thus, the test as to remoteness of damage in relation to the torts of negligence and nuisance can be stated as being that of reasonable foresight.

On the other hand, the Court of Appeal has ruled that the *Polemis* test (direct consequences) applies in cases of the tort of deceit.

No strict rule has as yet been formulated, though it could be argued that the trend is to use the *Wagon Mound* test in those torts that, invariably, or, in the event, involve negligence and the *Polemis* test in those torts where negligence is not an issue.

No problem as to remoteness of damage exists in relation to cases where harm is intended – the defendant will be liable for all such harm as results; consider, for example, the so-called 'thin skull' cases — *see Smith* v. *Leech Brain* (1961), and *Robinson* v. *Post Office* (1974).

NOTE: Some textbooks deal with both causation and remoteness of damage in the context of the tort of negligence. While the vast majority of cases doubtless involve that tort, they are important issues in relation to tortious liability generally. Students are therefore advised, in reading such books, to be prepared to look for discussion in these topics within the chapters on negligence.

Progress test 13

1. Outline the history of the law of tort(s)   **(1, 2)**

2. How would you seek to define 'a tort'? Distinguish torts from
(a) crimes;
(b) breaches of contract.   **(3)**

3. Explain what is meant by *damnum sine injuria* and *injuria sine da*mno.   **(4, 5)**

4. Of what relevance is motive in the law of tort?   **(7)**

5. Explain 'fault' in relation to liability in tort. When may a person be so liable without any fault on his part?   **(8)**

6. Explain the terms (a) proximate cause, (b) concurrent causes and (c) 'break the chain of causation'.   **(10, 11, 12)**

7. What is a *novus actus interveniens*?   **(12)**

8. Outline the rules relating to remoteness of damage in tort.   **(13, 14)**

9. A negligently spills gasoline into the drain. Two blocks away, some workmen are repairing a gas main. One of them takes a cigarette from his pocket and asks a passer-by for a light. The match ignites gas that has accumulated due to vaporisation of the gasoline in the drain, which has been carried along underground. The ensuing fire causes the gas main to explode. X and Y are injured. Discuss the problems as to causation and remoteness of damage that may apply in their cases.   **(10, 11, 12, 13, 14)**

14

Capacity and defences in tort

Capacity in tort

1. Capacity

This refers to the question 'Who may sue in tort?'. Also (and perhaps more usually) it refers to the question 'Who may be liable?' (Or, more specifically, whether a given party, where a tort has been committed, can be said to be responsible in law for the tort). Accordingly, the general question, 'who may sue?' is dealt with first, then specific instances; the question of liability is dealt with in the context of each of these instances.

The general rule is that anyone may sue in tort. This includes minors (though procedure requires that an adult represent them as 'next friend'), aliens (so long as they are not enemies) and even convicted criminals. Since the Law Reform (Husband and Wife) Act 1962, husband and wife may sue each other (*see* 14: **9**(*a*)).

Locus standi (the right to bring an action) in certain torts depends on particular qualifications. For example, to bring an action in the tort of nuisance, a person must normally have some title to the land affected (*see* 15: **28**).

While it is not quite the same, one might well consider, in dealing with particular situations, whom the law seeks to protect in permitting an action in a particular case. For example, the Congenital Disabilities (Civil Liability) Act 1976 permits an action against a person whose breach of duty owed to a parent results in a child being born disabled. The passing of this Act, however, along with settlement out of court of many cases arising out of the thalidomide affair, meant that the courts did not pronounce definitely whether or not a duty could be said to be owed to an unborn child directly (consider here *McKay* v. *Essex Area Health Authority* (1982)).

Capacity – specific instances

2.   The Crown
At common law, the maxim 'the Crown can do no wrong' prevented actions against the Crown or its servants. This maxim now applies only to the Queen in her personal capacity. Under the Crown Proceedings Act 1947, the Crown, in the sense of 'the state' (but not the Queen herself) can be made liable in tort as if it were a person of full age and capacity in most cases (*see* 4: **51**).

3.   Foreign sovereigns and diplomats
They can always sue for tort, but they cannot be sued unless they waive their diplomatic immunity either by entering an appearance to defend an action against them or by commencing proceedings themselves (in which case the defendant can raise any appropriate counterclaim against the diplomat). General provisions on these matters are contained in the Diplomatic Privileges Act 1964 and the State Immunity Act 1978 (and consider here *R* v. *Secretary of State for Foreign and Commonwealth Affairs, ex parte Trawnik* (1986)).

4.   Corporations
They can sue and be sued in their own names; but as they can act only through human agents, their liability in tort is necessarily vicarious (*see* 14: **15**).

5.   Trade Unions
Trade unions can be liable in tort. The Trade Disputes Act 1906 made them immune. That was reversed in 1971 by the Industrial Relations Act. It was restored, with important exceptions, in 1974 by the Trade Union and Labour Relations Act. The immunity was abolished again in 1982 by the Employment Act, except that a trade union will only face liability for acts such as inducing breach of contract, intimidation or conspiracy if the action was authorised by a senior person in the union, so a limited immunity survives. Also, there are financial limits upon some tortious liability, but even this immunity is made subject to ballots by the Trade Union Act 1984 and individual members' rights of challenge under the Employment Act 1988. Further modifications were made by the Employment Act 1990 (*see* 4: **13**).

6.   Minors
They are fully liable for their torts, providing they are old enough

to possess any necessary element of intent, though in practice, actions are seldom brought against minors.

Where the tort directly arises from a breach of contract, the minor cannot be sued for tort if this would involve indirect enforcement of the contract, e.g. a minor fraudulently misrepresenting his age to induce a void contract of loan cannot be sued for the tort of fraud — *see Leslie* v. *Sheill* (1914). However, where the tort arises independently of the contract, he is fully liable, e.g. where a minor obtains a radio on a void hire-purchase contract and subsequently sells it, thus committing conversion by a bailee, he is fully liable — *see Ballett* v. *Mingay* (1943). Where negligence is an ingredient of the tort, then the minor will be judged, in all probability, according to the standards that can reasonably be expected of a child of the age of the child in question. Certainly, where contributory negligence is concerned, this is the standard used — *see Gough* v. *Thorne* (1966).

7. Parent

A parent is not liable for the torts of his children except where:

(a) he is vicariously liable, by having commissioned the tort; or
(b) he is personally liable for the tort of negligence by reason of allowing his child unreasonable opportunity of doing mischief, e.g by giving a very young child a loaded gun — *see Bebee* v. *Sales* (1916).

8. Mentally disordered and drunken persons

They are generally fully liable, save where intent is a necessary element and their condition is such as to negative the intent — *see Morriss* v. *Marsden* (1952).

9. Husband and wife

Liability in this relationship is as follows:

(a) *They can now sue each other* for torts, even though these were committed after the marriage (Law Reform (Husband and Wife) Act 1962). The court may stay the action, however, if it appears that no substantial benefit will accrue to either party or that the issue is one that could more conveniently be dealt with summarily in accordance with the Married Women's Property Act 1882, s. 17 (which provides for disposal of matrimonial property).
(b) *Liability of married women to third persons* A married woman is now fully liable for her own torts under the Law Reform (Married Women and Tortfeasors) Act 1935.

10. Executors and administrators

At common law, the general rule was that tortious rights and liability were extinguished by death (*actio personalis moritur cum persona*).

The Law Reform (Miscellaneous Provisions) Act 1934 abolished the common law rule, however, and provided that all causes of action subsisting against a (deceased) person or vesting in him shall survive. Thus actions by or against a deceased person subsist for or against his estate under the Act (with the notable exception of actions for defamation, which die with the party).

In the event that the action concerned results from a tort that is itself the cause of death, a cause of action is said to vest in the deceased at the instant of death — see *Rose* v. *Ford* (1937). Thus, his estate can recover to the extent that the deceased can be said to have suffered loss.

As well as the rule *actio personalis moritur cum persona*, however, there was another rule at common law, to the effect that 'the death of a human being could not be complained of as an injury' — see *Baker* v. *Bolton* (1808) (i.e. the death of A, in itself, is not a form of harm to B that the law recognises as actionable). This harsh rule was mitigated firstly by the Fatal Accidents Act 1846, and later by the Fatal Accidents Act 1976 and the Administration of Justice Act 1982. These statutes have created a new category of persons with capacity to sue (*see* 14: **11**).

11. Dependants

The 1846 Act (*see* 14: **10**) allowed actions by dependants of a person who was killed by another's tort. This was the major exception to the general rule (*see* 14: **10**). The 1976 Act (as amended) provides that the executors or administrators may bring an action on behalf of the deceased's dependants. These are defined as:

(a) *wife or husband of the deceased*;
(b) any person who is a *parent or grandparent* of the deceased;
(c) *children or grandchildren*; and
(d) *brother, sister, uncle or aunt* of the deceased (Fatal Accidents Act 1976, s. 1(3)). Such persons may sue in circumstances 'where death is caused . . . such as would (if death had not ensued) have entitled the person injured to maintain an action' (Fatal Accidents Act 1976, s. 1(1)).

12. Joint tortfeasors

These are wrongdoers who concert a common action, i.e. 'a joint act done in pursuance of a concerted purpose' — *see Brooke* v. *Bool* (1908). Their liability is *joint and several*, i.e. the person injured may sue any one of them for the whole amount of the damages or may sue them jointly in one action and, among themselves, they are bound to contribute fair shares of damages payable, even if one of their number has been compelled to pay all. Joint tortfeasors are persons who:

(a) commit the same wrongful act; and
(b) cause the same harm, e.g. where A and B together assault C.

However, where there are two distinct torts causing the same damage the doers are not joint tortfeasors, e.g. where A and B independently driving separate cars both negligently hit and injure C.

The Civil Liability (Contribution) Act 1978 provides that any person liable in respect of damage suffered by another person may recover contribution from any other person liable in respect of the same damage, whether that other person's liability arises by tort, breach of contract, breach of trust or otherwise. (This Act completely replaces earlier provisions on this topic contained in the Law Reform (Married Women and Tortfeasors) Act 1935, s. 6, which were repealed by the 1978 Act.)

13. Employers

An employer may be liable in tort:

(a) *at common law* (in negligence) for breach of his duty to provide:
   (*i*) a safe system of work — *see Cook* v. *Square D Ltd* (1991);
   (*ii*) a competent staff;
   (*iii*) adequate plant, machinery, etc — *see Wilsons & Clyde Coal Co.* v. *English* (1938);
(b) for breach of a specific statutory duty, e.g. under the Factories Act 1961. Some such duties are said to be *strict* in the sense that liability follows automatically from a breach of duty, irrespective of negligence — *see Groves* v. *Wimborne* (1898) (on the Factory Acts) and sometimes, a statutory duty may overlap with a common law duty such as is the case in the Health and Safety at Work, etc., Act 1974, which relates to dangerous machinery — *see* 14: **13** (*a*) (*i*);
(c) vicariously (*see* 14: **14–17**).

Vicarious liability

14. The rule

'He who acts through another, acts for himself' (*qui facit per alium facit per se*). Thus, a person who authorises the commission of a tort, expressly or impliedly, by another, is liable in damages just as if he himself had committed that tort. Liability so arising is called *vicarious liability*: it is indirect.

Vicarious liability is, said Sir Percy Winfield, to consist of 'the liability A may incur towards C for the negligence or other tort of B where a *special relationship* exists between A and B, and B's tort is *referable to that relationship*'.

15. Special relationship

In practice, the most common relationship that gives rise to vicarious liability is that of master (employer) and servant (employee). Whether this relationship exists or not is a question that is decided by reference to the following tests:

(a) is the alleged servant employed under a *contract of service* (or is it one *for services*, in which case he will probably be an independent contractor, for which *see* 14: 17)?;

(b) is he *under the control* of another in the sense not only of what he must do, but also how he should do it (the *control* test) — *see Mersey Docks* v. *Coggins & Griffiths* (1947)?;

(c) is he an *integral part* of the other's business (this is a useful test in cases involving experts, such as surgeons, who cannot be said to be 'controlled' — *see Cassidy* v. *Minister of Health* (1951).)?

(d) is there provision for *another* to arrange for payment of national insurance contributions, wages, income tax, etc., and what is the extent of the power of dismissal — *see Ready Mixed Concrete* v. *Minister of Pensions* (1968)?

Not *all* these tests are necessarily applied in a given case. The first one is the *basic* test; the rest are guidelines that have been used in the cases cited and elsewhere.

As well as in the master-servant relationship, vicarious liability arises in the case of *partner and co-partner* and *principal and agent*. However, there is not normally vicarious liability in cases of casual delegation. An example is given by *Morgans* v. *Launchbury* (1972). Here, A regularly used his wife's car to drive to and from work, frequently arriving home intoxicated. He agreed that in future he would get a friend to drive should he get drunk again. One night A asked B to drive the car to A's home, but an accident occurred while B was driving towards a restaurant. It was held that Mrs A (the car-owner) was not liable for B's negligence, as B was not acting on her instructions (B was not her agent).

If there is delegation of a *particular task*, however, even without reward, the person committing the tort will be treated as the other's agent and vicarious liability will be incurred by that other — *see Ormrod* v. *Crosville Motor Services* (1953).

16. Referability

This generally equates with the question: 'Was the tort committed by the servant (or agent) *in the course of his employment*?' (i.e., was the servant doing improperly what he was employed to do). There is no universal rule applicable in every case. While, obviously, no servant is legitimately employed to commit crimes, a fraud *has* been held to have been perpetrated in the course of a clerk's employment — *see Lloyd* v. *Grace Smith* (1912). Perhaps the closest to a rule we can get is: Is the servant (employee/agent) at the material time engaged in the furtherance of his master's business, or is he on a 'frolic of his own'? *Joel* v. *Morrison* (1834). With this in mind it can be seen that:

(a) it is irrelevant whether the servant is doing something for his own convenience, while engaged at his job;

Example

A's employee, B, was delivering petrol to a garage. While the petrol was flowing from the lorry to a tank B lit a cigarette and negligently caused an explosion by throwing away the match. It was held that A was vicariously liable, as at the time of disposing of the match, B was in the course of his employment — *see Century Insurance* v. *Northern Ireland Road Transport Board* (1942).

(b) it *may* even be irrelevant if the servant is expressly *forbidden* from doing something — *see Limpus* v. *London General Omnibus Company* (1862).

Whether or not it is relevant will depend upon whether the prohibition is such as *in itself and by itself delimits the scope of the servant's employment* or not — *see Rose* v. *Plenty* (1976).

For example, an instruction that 'bus conductors must not drive buses' *delimits* the job of conductor; he is thereby confined to conducting and, any torts committed in the course of driving will *not* be in the course of his employment — *see Beard* v. *London General Omnibus Company* (1900) and compare *Ricketts* v. *Tilling* (1915). On the other hand, a prohibition may be such that, if a servant disregards it, he is deemed merely to be *doing improperly what he is employed to do*; i.e. he *is* in the course of his employment — *see Rose* v. *Plenty* (1976).

17. Independent contractors

Generally, an employer is not liable for the torts of his independent contractors. There are, however, several exceptions, including the following:

(a) where the wrong committed by the contractor amounts to a tort of strict liability — *see Rylands* v. *Fletcher* (1868);

(b) where work is done over or on a highway — *see Tarry* v. *Ashton* (1876), or involves fire — *see Balfour* v. *Barty-King* (1957), or involves 'extra-hazardous' activities — *see Honeywill* & *Stein* v. *Larkin* (1934);

(c) where the employer is a carrier or bailee for reward and injury is suffered by charges or goods in his safekeeping.

These are examples of *non-delegable* duties – in other words, it could be said that the employer is *personally*, rather than vicariously liable. An employer of independent contractors will be liable in any case if he himself is guilty of a breach of duty – as by hiring a contractor to commit trespass.

General defences in tort

18. *Volenti non fit injuria* (consent negates legal injury)

To be effective as a defence, the *consent* must be to the full risk of the injury – mere knowledge (*sciens*) of that risk is not enough — *see Dann* v. *Hamilton* (1939).

(a) However, such consent as *is* offered *need not be express* – indeed, it is sometimes said that consent *as such* is not necessary and that the defence consists of the *voluntary assumption of the risk* (on the part of a plaintiff) of the injury of which he complains.

Example

A and B were professional shotfirers, who chose to disregard certain instructions as to the use of explosives. Both were injured in the process of blasting. It was held that the defence of *volenti* applied — *see ICI* v. *Shatwell* (1965).

Similarly, it can be inferred that spectators of dangerous sports are *volens* with regard to the risk of accidents — *see Hall* v. *Brooklands Auto-Racing Club* (1933) and *Murray* v. *Harringay Arena* (1951); though probably not to unusual risks, not normally incidental to the sport in question — *see Payne* v. *Maple Leaf Gardens Ltd* (1949) (a Canadian case); participants in sports, too, are taken to have assumed the risks involved in participation — *see Simms* v. *Leigh RFC* (1969), but only up to a point — *see Condon* v. *Basi* (1985).

(b) Consent (or assumption of risk) *must be real and freely given* and the plaintiff must have a real choice — *see Burnett* v. *BWB* (1972) — consent must not be induced by 'threats or the pressure of duty'.

Example

A policeman was injured in stopping a runaway horse in pursuance of his duty. It was held that he had not consented to injury — *see Haynes* v. *Harwood* (1935) and also *Baker* v. *Hopkins* (1959), and *Chadwick* v. *British Transport Commission* (1967).

However, where an ordinary citizen, under no duty, was injured in stopping a horse, he was *volens* (i.e. had consented) to his injuries — *see Cutler* v. *United Dairies* (1933).

> NOTE: These cases can be distinguished by virtue of the fact that in the former, some children were nearby and there was therefore a strong likelihood of injury to someone had the horse not been stopped. It is arguable that, had the facts been similar in the *Cutler* Case, the plaintiff could have been said to have been under a *moral duty* to assist — the law is generally unwilling to allow the defence of *volenti non fit injuria* against a rescuer — *see Baker* v. *Hopkins* (1959). It is regarded as important not to discourage such actions.

(c) *Employer's liability* It is often said that *volenti* is not a defence in cases of breaches of employers' duties to their employees — *see Smith* v. *Baker* (1891). It is submitted, however, that in so far as this is true, it is by virtue of the fact that an employee will normally have *no choice* in the matter (except, of course, to risk the loss of his job) — *see Burnett* v. *BWB* (1973). If a *free choice* clearly exists and an employee submits himself to injury, there seems to be no good reason why the defence of *volenti non fit injuria* should not apply (compare *ICI* v. *Shatwell*).

(d) A related topic is that of *exclusion of liability*. Prior to the Motor Vehicles (Compulsory Insurance) Act 1971, a notice repudiating liability for accidents to passengers caused by the negligent driving of an uninsured driver was held to amount, on the part of the passenger to *volenti non fit injuria* — *see Buckpitt* v. *Oates* (1968). The

1971 Act, however, made any 'antecedent understanding between driver and passenger . . .' of no effect. This provision has now been repealed and this point has been replaced by the Road Traffic Act 1988, s. 149. It is a nice question whether or not in such cases the injured passenger can still be said to consent to the *injury*; but certainly, he can no longer be said to have *waived his right to sue* by agreement — *see Pitts* v. *Hunt* (1990).

In similar, but broader vein, is the Unfair Contract Terms Act 1977, s. 2, which provides:

'(i) A person cannot by reference to any contract term or to a notice given to persons generally or to particular persons exclude or restrict his liability for death or personal injury resulting from negligence' (the section goes on to restrict exclusions for other loss or damage to reasonable exclusions).

Section 1 (3) provides 'where a contract term or notice purports to exclude or restrict liability for negligence, a person's agreement to or awareness of it is *not* of itself to be taken as indicating his *voluntary acceptance of any risk*'.

These provisions only apply, however, where the party seeking to exclude liability does so in connection with business. Outside cases of business liability, the possibility of excluding liability by means of contract terms or notices remains. Thus, even if *volenti* cannot be shown, P's claim may still fail in such cases — *see White* v. *Blackmore* (1972). Furthermore, the Occupiers Liability Act 1984 permits exclusion in circumstances unconnected with the occupier's business purposes. Farmers can now exclude liability towards ramblers, potholers and students on field trips.

19. Mistake

Generally, mistake is no defence in tort, whether it is a mistake of fact or of law, except in the following torts.

(a) malicious prosecution;
(b) false imprisonment;
(c) torts requiring malice as a constituent element, e.g. injurious falsehood;
(d) deceit.

20. Accident

This can *only* be a defence where the *accident is inevitable*, i.e. where the consequences of an act are not foreseen and are not intended and could not have been avoided by any reasonable care by the defendant. (Contrast mistake, where the consequences are foreseen, but the defendant wrongly imagines that his act is still justified.)

'*Act of God*' is a special form of inevitable accident and arises where damage is caused by the operation of natural causes without human intervention which are *so unforeseeable that a reasonable man could not be expected to foresee or guard against them.*

The element of unforeseeability characterises both the defences of inevitable accident and Act of God and makes them a rare application.

Examples

(1) In the case of *Stanley* v. *Powell* (1891), X, while out shooting, fired at a bird, but his shots ricocheted off a tree and injured the plaintiff. It was held that this was an inevitable accident and not actionable.

(2) In *Nichols* v. *Marsland* (1875), unprecedented rainfall caused artificial pools on X's land to overflow and flood the plaintiff's land. It was held that this was an Act of God, as it was wholly unforeseeable because of the unprecedented rainfall (but compare *Greenock Corporation* v. *Caledonian Railway* (1917)).

Act of God is a defence to torts of strict liability, such as *Rylands* v. *Fletcher*, whereas an inevitable accident, such as was involved in *Stanley* v. *Powell* probably is not.

21. Necessity

This arises where the commission of a tort is admitted by the defendant, but it is argued that the act was done in order to avoid much more serious harm.

Examples

(1) *Cope* v. *Sharp* (1912), where property was damaged to make a firebreak (which turned out to be unnecessary).

(2) *Esso Petroleum* v. *Southport Corporation* (1955), where oil was discharged by a ship's captain at sea to save the lives of the crew.

(3) *Rigby* v. *Chief Constable of Northamptonshire* (1985), where damage by fire followed a CS gas cylinder being fired into a gun shop where a dangerous man was hiding. The police successfully raised necessity to all claims except negligence. They had allowed the fire brigade to leave the scene before firing the cylinder.

---

22. Statutory authority

This consists of an assertion that the activity complained of was authorised by legislation. There are two aspects:

(a) *Absolute authority* Acts done in pursuance of an express command of Parliament are not torts and harm caused thereby is not actionable, unless it is caused by negligence. Thus, where the building of a railway under authority of statute causes harm to neighbouring landowners, they have no remedy, but, if the harm to them were caused by *negligence* of the railway company, e.g. by allowing sparks to escape and cause fires, liability would arise — *see Smith* v. *L & SW Rail Co*. (1870).

(b) *Statutory permission* Where the legislature gives *mere permission* to do something, it must be done in as harmless a manner as possible. Thus, where permission was given to erect a smallpox hospital, it was held that nuisance caused by the hospital was actionable — *see Metropolitan Asylum District* v. *Hill* (1881).

23. Limitation of actions

Not 'a defence' as such but the rules limiting the period during which an action may be brought may serve to prevent a successful action from being brought, as much as the general defences proper.

The standard limitation periods are three years in cases involving death or personal injuries and six years in other cases. There are several exceptions to these limits. This is a very complex area. An action begins when the writ is issued, not when the case is tried. The reasons for the limitation of actions are clear. Evidence can become stale. Defendants must be allowed to carry on with their lives. On the other hand, plaintiffs must be given sufficient time to assemble their cases. Generally, the time begins to run when the damage is suffered.

This used to be a problem with personal injuries that did not become apparent for a long time, such as certain industrial diseases. The Limitation Act 1980 provides that the time begins when the plaintiff either knows or ought to know that his condition is attributable to the defendant's acts. Where the damage does not involve personal injuries, the Latent Damage Act 1986 provides that a time limit of three years begins to run when the damage, perhaps following negligent building work, was discovered (or ought reasonably to have been discovered). There is an overall limit of 15 years from the completion of the building.

Where the injury is, in fact, death, the limitation period is fixed by the Fatal Accidents Act 1976 (as amended) and is three years from death, or from the date of knowledge of the person on whose behalf the action is brought (*see* 14: **10, 11**).

Progress test 14

1.   Explain the tortious liability of (a) a foreign sovereign or representatives and (b) the British Crown   **(2, 3)**

2.   Outline the capacity (in tort) of (a) minors and (b) their parents.   **(6, 7)**

3.   A, who is 20 years of age, gives his three-year-old son the use of his air-pistol. The child accidentally shoots B, an adult, and B wishes to sue A. Advise B.   **(6, 7, 14, 15, 20)**

4.   What are joint tortfeasors? What is their capacity in tort?   **(12)**

5.   Explain (a) vicarious liability, (b) a contract of service and (c) an independent contractor.   **(14, 15)**

6.   In what circumstances will an employer be liable for torts committed by (a) independent contractors and (b) agents or servants?   **(16, 17)**

7.   A takes his car to B's garage. B hands the car over to C, his employee, and tells him to effect the repairs. Having done the repairs, C takes the car out to test it, but, while out, decides to go joy-riding. In the course of his joy-ride he collides with D's car. Advise A and D as to whether they can bring actions vicariously against B.   **(16)**

8.   Explain what is meant by *volenti non fit injuria*. When is this defence available in tort?   **(18)**

9.   Distinguish *volenti non fit injuria* from a situation where a defendant purports to exclude his liability. What legal effect do such exclusions have?   **(18)**

10.   When, if ever, can (a) accident and (b) necessity, be a defence to an action in tort?   **(20, 21)**

11.   Summarise the statutory rules relating to the limitation of actions in tort.   **(23)**

15
Trespass and nuisance

General

1. Trespass

This is probably the oldest form of tortious liability. The ancient writ of trespass dates back to a time when criminal and civil liability had not yet been recognised as separate. Consequently, some forms of trespass are still both crimes and torts, e.g. assault and battery. Trespass means direct interference with the person, goods or land of another. Trespass is actionable *per se*, i.e. without proof of actual damage suffered on the part of the plaintiff. Nor does it require intention on the part of the defendant; volition is, however, necessary (*see* 13: 7).

2. Early developments

The early writ of trespass was confined to actions whereby a 'breach of the King's Peace' was occasioned (*vi et armis et contra pacem regis*: with force of arms and against the King's Peace).

From the time of Edward I (1272–1307), however, two other varieties of trespass existed:

(a) trespass *quare clausum fregit* (i.e. trespass to land); and
(b) trespass *de bonis asportatis* (i.e. the unlawful taking of chattels).

During the thirteenth century, the scope of the action of trespass was further extended, as was the scope of other forms of action; in part at least by virtue of the statute *In Consimili Casu* 1285. Thus the extension of common law writs by analogy became possible and the restrictions that had been imposed by the Provisions of Oxford 1258 were overcome.

The writ of trespass proved, as F. W. Maitland (1850–1906) phrased it, the most 'fertile mother of actions'. Medieval lawyers, without creating entirely new writs, managed to extend trespass to cover indirect injuries to property and person. Such analogous claims were called 'actions of trespass on the case'. They differed from ordinary trespass in that:

(a) the plaintiff had to prove that he had suffered actual damage; but
(b) that it did not involve the direct application of force.

3. Actions on the case
These lay for 'consequential' (indirect) injuries not amounting to trespass and included the following.

(a) *nuisance* — indirect interference with property of another, i.e. interference with his enjoyment of his property;
(b) *negligence* — injury of another's person or property unintentionally by carelessness amounting to breach of a legal duty to take care;
(c) *assumpsit* — this action lay where one person had voluntarily undertaken a duty to another not previously imposed on him by law, and committed a breach of this duty (this action on the case is the ancestor of the law of contract).

Trespass to the person

4. Scope of tort
This tort really comprises three separate heads:

(a) assault (*see* 15: **5**);
(b) battery (*see* 15: **6**);
(c) false imprisonment (*see* 15: **7**).

5. Assault
An attempt or threat to apply force to another whereby that other is reasonably put in present fear of violence, e.g. shaking your fist at someone or pointing at him a gun that he reasonably believes to be loaded and thinks you may fire — *see R.* v. *St George* (1840).
Thus the following points are important:

(a) mere threats are sufficient, but if actual force is applied then the tort of battery is committed;
(b) the essence of the tort is fear, so mere abuse is not enough, but a false alarm could amount to assault if it causes fright;
(c) a threatening act may be so qualified as to negate reasonable grounds for fear, e.g. in *Turberville* v. *Savage* (1669), where X put his

hand on his sword and said, 'If it were not assize time' he would resort to violence. It was held that there had been no assault;

(d) assault is also a crime and a certificate of acquittal or proof of punishment is a bar to later civil proceedings for tort (Offences against the Person Act 1861, s. 45).

6. Battery

This means the intentional application of force upon the person of the plaintiff, against his will; this force, in practice need only be nominal: 'The least touching of another in anger is a battery' — Holt, CJ, in *Cole* v. *Turner* (1704), and the touching must be 'hostile' — *see Wilson* v. *Pringle* (1986).

Battery is often combined with assault in civil actions. It is a crime, as well as a tort; the following points should be noted.

(a) the touching must be voluntary, accident will be a defence to an action for battery — *see Stanley* v. *Powell* (1891).

(b) it must also be intentional, and whereas, formerly, a 'negligent' battery was actionable, such unintentional touchings, where they cause injuries, are now actionable in the tort of negligence — *see Letang* v. *Cooper* (1964) (an unintentional touching, such as that which may occur in a crowd jostling to get on to a bus, will not give rise to liability where no injury is caused and is regarded as accidental).

7. False imprisonment

The total deprivation of the freedom of another for any period, however short, without lawful justification.

(a) restraint may be 'physical' (e.g. a locked room) or 'practical' (e.g. where P is surrounded by threatening persons);

(b) restraint must be total, because so long as the plaintiff has a means of egress, no imprisonment has taken place (even if he is inconvenienced) — *see Bird* v. *Jones* (1845);

(c) the imprisonment must be occasioned by an act of the defendant — it is no tort that he failed to free the plaintiff (unless he is under a duty to that person (*see* 13: 9) — *see Herd* v. *Weardale Steel Co.* (1915);

(d) it is still false imprisonment even if the plaintiff is not aware of the fact that he is not free to go as he pleases — *see Meering* v. *Grahame-White Aviation Co.* (1919).

8. Defences to trespass to the person
These include:

(a) *self defence (in assault or battery)* This is a valid defence where it is used to protect one's person or property, but force used must be reasonable in the circumstances, e.g. you may not stab a man who merely slaps your face — *see Cook* v. *Beal* (1697). Reasonable force may also be used to eject a trespasser from land, and will not then constitute battery — *see Collins* v. *Renison* (1754).

(b) *exercise of parental authority* This may be delegated to a schoolteacher or anyone else *in loco parentis* — *see Cleary* v. *Booth* (1893). Any force used must be reasonable. However, the Education (No. 2) Act 1986 has removed the right of a 'member of staff' of a school within the definition in the Act (broadly, one which receives public funding) to administer corporal punishment. A husband no longer has a legal right to chastise his wife by force or imprisonment — *see R.* v. *Jackson* (1891).

(c) *judicial authority* Arrest or imprisonment is obviously justifiable if under judicial authority, providing the authority is properly given, e.g. arrest under a justices' warrant.

(d) *arrest of criminals* Powers of arrest are governed by the Police and Criminal Evidence Act 1984, s. 24 (*see* 25: **8**)

(e) *Consent and inevitable accident* (*see* 14: **18, 20**).

9. Criminal proceedings

Assault and battery constitute crimes as well as torts and so, in some circumstances, may trespass to chattels (goods).

Generally, if D has been tried summarily, for assault, and has been convicted and punished or the case against him dismissed, then no further proceedings, either criminal or civil, may be brought against him in respect of the same act (Offences Against the Person Act 1861, s. 45).

Trespass to land

10. Trespass

This means entering or remaining on land in the possession of the plaintiff or depositing material thereon without lawful justification. Trespass therefore consists in interference with possession (as distinct from nuisance, which is interference with enjoyment of occupation). Consequently, the plaintiff must be the possessor of the land, not necessarily the owner; in fact, the possessor may have an action for trespass against the owner, if his lawful possession is interfered with by the owner.

Like other forms of trespass, trespass to land is theoretically actionable *per se*. It may be committed by entering on land, sitting on a fence, dumping rubbish, allowing cattle to stray, etc. The tort is technically called trespass *quare clasum fregit*, since the ancient writ of trespass began with these words, whereas he has broken the 'close' or boundary (*see* 15: 2).

11. Notes on trespass to land

Some things to note are:

(a) *it is a tort, not a crime* Notices saying 'Trespassers will be prosecuted' are therefore incorrect; a trespasser cannot be prosecuted, as it is not a crime.

(b) *it may be committed unawares*, e.g. by walking across land which is private, in the mistaken belief that there is a public right of way across it.

(c) *unauthorised use* A person on land with permission of the occupier may commit trespass if he exceeds the scope of his permission, e.g. where a person used a public footpath across land for the purpose of spying on the owner's race-horses in training — *see Hickman* v. *Maisey* (1900).

(d) *it may be perpetrated through a non-human agency*, e.g. cattle, rubbish, missiles, roots of trees, etc. Thus, where A's horse kicked B's mare through the fence separating A's land from B's, A was held liable for trespass — *see Ellis* v. *Loftus Iron Co.* (1874).

(e) *the tort is not confined to trespasses to 'land' in the sense of the land's surface* Thus, trespass to land may be committed by interfering with the airspace above P's land, as with a sign — *see Kelsen* v. *Imperial Tobacco Co.* (1957) — or by burrowing underneath it. The Civil Aviation Act 1982 provides a defence to such trespasses as may technically be committed whenever aeroplanes fly over P's land, though it also provides that if anything should fall out of the plane, or any damage caused by the aircraft in some other way, then liability will be strict.

12. Trespass *ab initio*

A person entering the plaintiff's land with permission may become a trespasser if the permission is withdrawn, or if he exceeds the scope of permission, e.g. by doing an unlawful act — *see Hickman* v. *Maisey* (1900).

A distinction is drawn between private permission and public licence:

(a) *private permission* from the occupier. If the permission is revoked, e.g. because of unruly conduct, the defendant becomes a trespasser from the moment of revocation (and must be given a reasonable time to leave, before force can be used to eject him);

(b) *public licence*, e.g. where the law gives to the public a right of entry, such as the right of travellers to enter inns, but, if a person entering the plaintiff's land or premises under such a public right abuses his right, he becomes a trespasser;

    (*i*) if the abuse consists of non-feasance, i.e. not doing something he should do, he becomes a trespasser from that moment. Thus, where customers at an inn became rowdy and refused to pay for drinks, their licence to remain was revoked and they became trespassers at that time — *see Six Carpenters' Case* (1610);

    (*ii*) if the abuse consists of a misfeasance, i.e. doing something wrongful, he becomes a trespasser from the moment of entry (i.e. *ab initio*), so, a hotel guest who after a week at a hotel does something positively tortious, loses his licence to be there and can be sued for seven days' trespass, as though he had never had such a licence.

NOTE: The doctrine of trespass *ab initio* has recently been doubted by the CA as largely inapplicable to modern circumstances and doubt has been thrown on the validity of the decision in the *Six Carpenters' Case* (above) — for instance in *Chic Fashions (West Wales)* v. *Jones* (1968), although the same judge (Lord Denning) applied the doctrine and referred to the *Six Carpenters' Case* without criticism in *Cinnamond* v. *British Airports Authority* (1980). The doctrine will certainly not apply so as to make someone a trespasser for the purpose of the law of burglary (*see* 28: **6**).

13. Trespass by relation back

A person's possession of land dates back in law to the time when he became entitled to possession, even though he did not actually take possession until some time later. He can therefore sue for trespass committed any time after he became entitled to possession, e.g. where the heir to land returns from abroad to discover that a trespasser has been occupying the land since the death of the owner some years before. This is called 'trespass by relation back' to the date of entitlement to possession.

14. Trespass by severance

Trespass can also be committed by severance, i.e. by detaching something attached to the land, such as fruit, crops, flowers or timber.

In such cases the plaintiff may sue for the value of the thing severed, or for compensation for the diminution in the value of the land by reason of the severance.

15. Trespass and incorporeal rights

A person who, while not the possessor of the land as such, nevertheless is the owner of something attached to the land (such as in 15: **14**) may sue in respect of this thing. Interference with servitudes, such as rights to light or to the use of land, are protected not by the tort of trespass, but that of nuisance.

16. Who can sue?

Notice that trespass is a tort against possession, not against ownership. Therefore any person in possession of land can sue for trespass.

It is no defence to show that the plaintiff's right of possession is defeasible by a third person, e.g. where the trespasser proves that the plaintiff holds the land under a lease that is void for some reason. This principle is technically expressed by saying that *jus tertii* (the right of a third party) is no defence.

17. Remedies for trespass

These are:

(a) *damages* This is usually the amount necessary to compensate the plaintiff for any diminution in the value of the land or for any loss caused to him by interrupted possession.

(b) *injunction* This forbids continuation or repetition of the trespass.

(c) *animals* The Animals Act 1971, s. 1, entitles the occupier of property to detain livestock that strays on to his land, subject to compensation being paid for any damage caused thereby. He must, however, take reasonable care of detained animals, and must report their detention to the police within 48 hours.

(d) *re-entry and ejection* Under the Statute of Forcible Entries 1381, it was an offence to use force to enter property, even if the person using such force was an occupier who had been dispossessed by a trespass (e.g. a holidaymaker whose house is 'squatted' in during his absence). If the occupier could re-enter peaceably, he could use reasonable force to eject the trespasser — as, indeed he could where he had not been dispossessed at all — *see Hemmings* v. *Stoke Poges Golf Club* (1920).

The Criminal Law Act 1977, however, repealed the Statute of Forcible Entries 1381 and substituted two offences:

(*i*) 'using or threatening violence for the purpose of securing entry into any premises . . . without lawful authority . . . provided there is someone present . . . on the premises who is opposed to the entry' (s. 6); and

(*ii*) by s. 7, 'failing to leave premises, having entered as a trespasser on being required to do so' by a 'displaced residential occupier'.

While the offence under s. 6 may still, prima facie, be committed by the occupier himself (as in the example given above), s. 6(3) provides for the defence that he is a 'displaced residential occupier'. Thus the owner of a dwelling house may now re-enter his premises, by force if necessary, and eject trespassers therein, the common-law remedy of ejectment being unchanged.

The Public Order Act 1986, s. 39, was intended to provide a remedy against the so-called 'peace convoys' and 'travellers' that invade farmland, particularly in the summertime. Where damage has been caused or threatening abusive or insulting words or behaviour used or 12 or more vehicles have been brought onto land and a direction to leave, given by a senior police officer, has not been followed, then an offence has been committed (*see* also 29: **15**).

18. Defences
The general defence is justification of entry, e.g. by showing that it was made with the consent of the possessor or under process of law, e.g. by court order, as where a bailiff enters to seize the occupier's property in pursuance of a court order. Necessity may also be a defence in some cases (*see* 26: **10**).

Wrongful interference with goods

19. Wrongful interference with goods
This is a general term, given to a number of possible varieties of torts, by the Torts (Interference with Goods) Act 1977. Section 1 of this Act defines 'wrongful interference with goods' as involving any of the following:

(a) conversion of goods (known formerly as trover);
(b) trespass to goods (trespass *de bonis asportatis* (*see* 15: **2**));
(c) negligence, in so far as it results in damage to goods; and
(d) any other tort, in so far as it results in damage to goods.

Then s. 2 abolishes the tort of detinue (unlawful detention of goods). Negligence and 'any other torts' are dealt with elsewhere; this leaves trespass and conversion to be considered.

20. Trespass to goods

Trespass *de bonis asportatis* lay originally, like trespass to the person, for direct interferences — this time, though, to goods rather that to the person. This may include causing direct injury to the goods (such as throwing acid on to P's clothing, burning it); or it may involve the removal of the goods from P's possession. The following features can be stated.

(a) the action is founded on possession, not ownership, so the plaintiff need only be the borrower of goods or bailee — *see The Winkfield* (1902);

(b) like trespass generally, trespass to goods is actionable *per se* (without any need for actual damage);

(c) the interference (or touching) must be intentional or negligent;

(d) A finder of lost chattels (goods) does not commit trespass, unless the owner is known, or could be easily ascertained, and he keeps them nevertheless — in fact, the finder of goods has a title to sue anyone other than the owner himself (as the action is based on possession) — *see Armory* v. *Delamirie* (1722).

21. Trespass and detinue

The tort of detinue has now been abolished. Detinue derived, in fact, from the old action of debt. It differed from that action in that it referred, not to a sum of money owed by D, but to chattels owned by P, which were in D's possession and which D wrongfully detained. Thus, D may have acquired the chattel (goods) quite innocently (e.g. by a loan), and was not, therefore, guilty of any trespass, but may still be liable for their retention.

The Torts (Interference with Goods) Act 1977, s. 2, has extended the definition of conversion so as to include the wrongful detention of goods as well as other dealings with goods that are inconsistent with the plaintiff's title (*see* 15: **22**).

22. Conversion

This action was once known as 'trover' as it relied on a fictitious 'finding' of the goods (trover = to find).

It may nowadays be defined as any dealing with goods that is adverse to the plaintiff's right to them. Thus, the taking of goods may amount to conversion; so, however, might the destruction of goods that are lawfully in the defendant's possession as bailee, and their unauthorised sale by the defendant — *see Consolidated Co.* v. *Curtis* (1892). The following main points therefore emerge.

(a) Like trespass, conversion is based on possession. There is also sufficient *locus standi* (title to sue) if the plaintiff has immediate right to possession.

(b) Whereas formerly loss or destruction of goods, to constitute conversion, had to be intentional, the Torts (Interference with Goods) Act 1977, s. 2, provides that an action will lie in conversion for loss or destruction of goods that a bailee has *allowed to happen* in breach of his duty to his bailor. In allowing an action for unintended loss or destruction the Act has filled a gap which would otherwise have resulted.

(c) 'Innocent' interference is no defence. Thus, so long as D acts intentionally, ignorance as to the owner's rights will not excuse him — *see Hollins* v. *Fowler* (1875). So a woman was guilty of conversion even where she moved another's goods, as she said, because she feared a burglary — *see Kirk* v. *Gregory* (1876) (*see* Chapter 23).

(d) Defences are, essentially:
  (*i*) that the defendant is the owner, or has the owner's authority to detain the goods;
  (*ii*) that the defendant had the consent of the possessor of the goods.

23. Trespass and conversion: remedies

Generally, the remedies for trespass and for conversion were (and remain) the same. They include the following:

(a) *damages*, assessed as the value at the time of the interference with the goods;

(b) *recaption and replevin* where goods are not damaged or destroyed, the plaintiff may retake them, by reasonable force if necessary;

(c) *injunction*, which is appropriate to prevent further use by D in a manner that is inconsistent with P's rights — the Torts (Interference with Goods) Act 1977, s. 3, has retained the possibility that the return of goods to the plaintiff may be ordered by the court instead of, or as well as, damages and has also removed the old anomaly whereby, as both the actual possessor and anyone who had a right to immediate possession (e.g. an owner of goods who has bailed them to P) could sue, a defendant may be liable twice in respect of the same goods; s. 7

provides that, if a converter of goods pays damages to the possessor, and then to the owner, then the possessor is accountable to the owner, who, in turn, should reimburse the converter.

Nuisance

24. Nature of nuisance

Nuisance is an action on the case. It consists of the unlawful interference with the use or enjoyment of another's land. Unlike trespass, it is not actionable *per se*, but, because of its nature, does not normally require physical injuries such as may be involved in cases of negligence — *see Fay* v. *Prentice* (1845). In this case the corner of the defendant's house projected over the plaintiff's land. It was held that to establish nuisance it was *not* necessary to show that rain fell from the overhang, so damaging the plaintiff's land. Thus, dumping rubbish on your neighbour's land, being direct, is trespass. Dumping rubbish on your own land, causing a smell, inconveniencing your neighbour, is indirect and, therefore, a nuisance. It is not necessary (in order for it to be a nuisance) that your neighbour should become ill as a consequence.

25. Varieties of nuisance

These are:

(a) *Public nuisance* The definition of nuisance given above refers primarily to private nuisance. A public nuisance may be said to have occurred where the interference is with the enjoyment of property whose use is shared by the public or a large number of public and is therefore defined as a nuisance that 'materially affects the reasonable comfort and convenience of life of a class of Her Majesty's subjects who come within the sphere of its operation' (Winfield). Thus, obstruction of the highway or of a waterway used by the public is a public nuisance — *see Rose* v. *Miles* (1815). In *Gillingham Borough Council* v. *Medway (Chatham) Dock Ltd* (1991), it was held that having been given planning permission to operate a port permits activity that annoys those living in the neighbourhood without incurring liability for public nuisance.

(b) *Private nuisance* As defined above, consists generally of an unlawful interference with the use or enjoyment of another's land. Such an interference may be:

   (*i*)   an interference with a corporeal hereditament (i.e. the land itself or use thereof) such as pollution; or (*ii*) an interference with an incorporeal hereditament or servitude (i.e. particular rights attaching to the land).

This last variety is an ancient form of wrong, as the particular right concerned is proprietary in nature, and may be 'natural' (e.g. the right to use of a stream — *see Young* v. *Bankier Distillery Co.* (1893)); or may be 'acquired' (e.g. the right to light — *see Colls* v. *Home and Colonial Stores* (1904)).

26. Public nuisance

This is a crime as well as a tort, since its effects are such as to go beyond a single person's interests. A person committing a public nuisance can therefore be prosecuted in the criminal courts, or sued, by the Attorney-General, acting on behalf of the public, to secure an injunction to prevent continuance of the nuisance.

A private individual may sue on his own behalf, but only if he suffers some special damage; that is, some loss or harm *over and above* that suffered by the public at large. (For example, where the defendant obstructed a waterway and, whereas the public were thereby inconvenienced, the plaintiff, who was dependent on the access provided by the waterway in order to deliver goods by barge, suffered considerable additional expense in having his goods carried overland — *see Rose* v. *Miles* (1815) and also *Castle* v. *St Augustine's Links* (1922)).

27. Private nuisance

This has the following features:

(a) The interference must be 'unlawful'. Thus a landowner was not liable when he abstracted percolating water from underneath his own property, and subsidence was caused in his neighbour's, even though he acted maliciously. It was held that, as he had a legal right to abstract the water, no action could lie — *see Bradford* v. *Pickles* (1895) HL.
(b) Where actual damage to the property or things on the property is suffered, the defendant will not be able to claim his own use of land was reasonable — *see St Helen's Smelting Co.* v. *Tipping* (1865); but,
(c) though it is not normally necessary for the plaintiff to show that the defendant's conduct is unreasonable, the defendant may not be liable if he can show he acted reasonably, having regard to all the circumstances, including the following:
   (i) *the locality* 'that may be a nuisance in Grosvenor Square which would be none in Smithfield Market': said Pollock,

C.B., in *Bamford* v. *Turnley* (1862) and *see also*: *Adams* v. *Ursell* (1913);

(ii) *sensitivity of plaintiff* if the alleged interference is only such as would affect a sensitive use of land, and not normally reasonable use, no nuisance is committed — *see Robinson* v. *Kilvert* (1889).

(iii) *defendant's intention* where D created a noise purely to annoy his neighbours, whose music-making he disliked, he was liable — *see Christie* v. *Davey* (1893). Had he merely been making 'reasonable noise' such as turning up his television set purely in order to hear it above the noise from next door, doubtless he would not have been liable.

NOTE: This situation should be carefully distinguished from that in *Bradford* v. *Pickles* (above); there D had a legal right to abstract water: here, we cannot speak of a 'legal right' to make a noise.

28. Parties to an action in private nuisance
Ask:

(a) *Who can sue?* Generally, the plaintiff must have a proprietary interest — he must be the occupier of the land affected. Thus, when C's wife was injured by broken glass falling from his kitchen ceiling, which had been broken by D's gutter collapsing, the wife had no remedy in nuisance — *see Cunard* v. *Antifyre* (1933). (This case is also cited to support the proposition that private nuisance cannot be brought for personal injuries unless negligence can be proved.)

(b) *Who can be sued?*

(i) The creator of a nuisance — even if he is no longer in occupation of the land from where the nuisance emanates — *see Roswell* v. *Prior* (1701).

(ii) The occupier of the land from whence the nuisance emanates. This is so even if he is not the creator of the nuisance, so long as he has 'adopted' or 'continued' the nuisance — *see Sedleigh- Denfield* v. *O'Callaghan* (1940) (either knowingly or negligently — *see Barker* v. *Herbert* (1911)).

(iii) A landlord who retains the power to inspect premises let by him — *see Wilchick* v. *Marks* (1934).

29. Strict liability
Where the nuisance involves premises adjacent to a highway and which fall into disrepair, then the occupier is strictly liable for all consequences, including personal injuries, not only to passers-by —

see Tarry v. *Ashton* (1876) — but also to adjoining occupiers — *see Wringe* v. *Cohen* (1940).

30. Defences to nuisance actions

Apart from the general defences of consent and statutory authority, several defences exist to an action in nuisance.

(a) where D's act is lawful and reasonable (*see* 15: **27**(*c*)).

(b) prescription where P has 'suffered' the nuisance for 20 years without complaint. It is no defence that D has conducted himself in the same way for 20 years if P has not, in fact, felt the effects and condoned them — *see Sturges* v. *Bridgeman* (1879), and *Miller* v. *Jackson* (1977), but compare *Kennaway* v. *Thompson* (1980);

(c) generally, a lack of intention or negligence to do the act which causes the nuisance: thus, if a tree collapses on to P's car due to rot, undiscoverable by reasonable inspection, or where a 'latent defect' in building materials causes the collapse of a wall, D will not be liable — *see Noble* v. *Harrison* (1926).

> NOTE: Such instances are sometimes called 'secret unobservable processes of nature'. Act of God, similarly, will be a defence for the same reasons.

(d) though not strictly a defence, D may show that the harm suffered by P was the result not of a continuous state of affairs, but an isolated event. This is not a nuisance, though of course, it is open to P to attempt to prove negligence on someone's part — *see Salisbury* v. *Woodland* (1970), but compare *British Celanese* v. *Hunt* (1969).

31. Remedies for nuisance

In addition to the normal remedies of damages and injunctions, the plaintiff has the self-help remedy of abatement.

Abatement consists in the plaintiff terminating the nuisance himself, without going to court, e.g. by cutting off overhanging branches of his neighbour's trees that are impinging on the air-space above the plaintiff's own ground. If life or property are endangered, or the nuisance can be abated without entering the defendant's land, the plaintiff can exercise his right of abatement without prior notice to the defendant — *see Lemmon* v. *Webb* (1894). If, however, he will need to enter the defendant's land to abate the nuisance, he must give notice of his intention to do so and, if then refused permission to enter, he must sue in the normal way.

Progress test 15

1. Define trespass and explain its origins.   **(1–3)**

2. Define assault and battery. How would you distinguish them? **(5–6)**

3. What is meant by false imprisonment? Can such a tort be done negligently, e.g. by omitting to act? In what circumstances may such imprisonment be justified?   **(7, 8)**

4. Define trespass to land. What is meant by trespass by relation back? In what circumstances may the occupier of land use force to prevent trespass?   **(10–17)**

5. A was motoring correspondent for a newspaper and was interested in a new 'secret' racing car being developed by B. Having been given permission by B to look at standard models in production at B's factory, he took the opportunity to sneak into B's 'secret' workshop and take photo- graphs of the new racing car. B has applied for an injunction to prevent A publishing the photo- graphs on the grounds that A was a trespasser. Discuss.   **(10–18)**

6. Summarise the remedies and defences appropriate in an action for trespass to land.   **(17, 18)**

7. Define (a) trespass to goods and (b) wrongful interference with goods, giving examples of both, including examples of how they developed.   **(19–20)**

8. Outline the remedies available in cases of wrongful interference with goods.   **(23)**

9. Distinguish public and private nuisance.   **(25)**

10. Distinguish trespass to land from nuisance. Who is liable in cases of the latter?   **(24, 28, 29)**

11. A has a clothes-line, supported by a tall post in his garden. One night, a boy climbs the post to steal apples from A's nearby tree. The next morning the post collapses, flattening B's greenhouse next door and injuring B's visitor C. Advise B and C.   **(28–30)**

16
Negligence

The tort of negligence

1. The meaning of negligence
The word negligence has two meanings in the law of torts:

(a) a 'state of mind', which may be such as to form the basis of liability in several torts, e.g. nuisance, trespass (*see* 13: **8**);
(b) a separate tort consisting of the breach of a specific duty, recognised by the law, and owed to the plaintiff.

The separate tort of negligence is a comparatively recent development, while the failure to take care in relation to others was recognised in 1676 (*Mitchil* v. *Alestree*), the tort itself was only formulated in the nineteenth century (*Blyth* v. *Birmingham Waterworks Co.* (1856)), where the notion of the 'reasonable man' first appears. The tort derives from trespass by way of the action on the case. Therefore, like all actions on the case, it is actionable only on proof of actual damage (i.e. is not actionable *per se*). It also lies for 'consequential' or 'indirect injuries' (*see* 16: **9**).

2. The tort of negligence
As a separate tort negligence has been defined as 'something more than heedless or careless conduct, whether in omission or commission: it properly connotes the complex concept of duty, breach and damage thereby suffered by the person to whom the duty was owing'— Lord Wright in *Lochgelly Iron & Coal Co.* v. *M'Mullan* (1934).

The necessary ingredients of actionable negligence therefore are:

(a) a legal duty of care owed to the plaintiff;
(b) breach of that duty; and
(c) consequent damage.

3. Legal duty of care

A general definition of the legal duty of care is difficult to state: there is no general duty to take care. Indeed, I may be as careless as I wish, so long as I do not cause anyone else harm; and even then may not be liable, if the harm caused is not a foreseeable consequence of my carelessness (*see* 13: **14**).

On the other hand, the law certainly requires a reasonable degree of care of us in our dealings with others and that degree of care, and the extent to which we are required to exercise it, will, in fact, vary from case to case. Thus, where a sick person seeks the aid of a doctor, more is expected of him than the passer-by who just happens to find someone injured on the road. The 'notional' duty of care may be expressed as a duty to take such care *as is reasonable* to avoid acts or omissions that it can *reasonably be foreseen* are likely to *cause injury* to someone.

4. The duty in fact

While a 'notional' duty may be elusive, whether or not a duty exists in a given case can be established more or less as a fact.

The means whereby this may be established is nowadays by an application of the 'neighbour test' formulated by Lord Atkin in *Donoghue* v. *Stevenson* (1932) HL:

> You must take reasonable care to avoid acts or omissions which you can reasonably foresee would be likely to injure your neighbour. Who, then is my neighbour? The answer seems to be — those persons who are so closely and directly affected by my act that I ought reasonably to have them in contemplation as being so affected.

The question, whenever a person suffers injury, then, is whether this can be said to have been reasonably foreseeable on the part of the person whose act (or omission) has, prima facie, caused the injury. Thus, where a pregnant woman hearing the noise of a road accident some distance away, sustained nervous shock, inducing a miscarriage, it was held that she was outside the scope of D's duty and so could not recover damages — *see Bourhill* v. *Young* (1943) HL. (To be actionable at all, 'nervous shock' must be more than mere upset — *see* 16: **14**.)

5. The standard of care

Even given the fact that D could have reasonably foreseen that P may suffer as a consequence of his act or omission, he may not be liable if his conduct was reasonable in the circumstances. Thus, the law 'exacts a degree of care commensurate with the risk created', said Lord Macmillan in *Read* v. *Lyons* (1947). The test, therefore, is whether a reasonable man would have foreseen the risk to the plaintiff in the circumstances of the case and, if so, whether he would have done (or desisted from doing) anything other than that which the defendant in fact did to avert the danger.

Thus, where P was injured when a cricket ball was struck out of D's ground during the course of a match, it was held that, although this was foreseeable, the risk of injury was so small that a reasonable man would have taken no further measures to prevent such an occurrence — *see Bolton* v. *Stone* (1951).

NOTE: The ground was, in fact, fenced off from the surrounding area and the spot where the ball was struck was a considerable distance from the spot where the plaintiff was struck.

On the other hand, where an employer endangered the sight of a one-eyed employee by failing to provide him with safety goggles, he was liable when the man was blinded, as he was aware of the great risk involved and could, quite reasonably, have provided the goggles — *see Paris* v. *Stepney Borough Council* (1951).

6. Normal practice

One rule of thumb that the courts have adopted, in order to determine the standard of care required of a defendant, is what practice is normal in such circumstances. Thus, the do-it-yourself householder is required, when fixing a handle to a door, to use the same screws as would be used by a competent carpenter, in order to avoid liability if his visitor is injured by the handle coming off — *see Wells* v. *Cooper* (1958). This is not a binding rule, however, and the courts have been known to find D liable even where he can show that he behaved 'perfectly in accord with normal practice' — *see Cavanagh* v. *Ulster Weaving Co.* (1960). The implication is that 'normal practice' in a particular trade or practice simply may not be good enough in the event that injury is caused!

7. Unforeseen dangers

Following from sections 5 and 6, it is obvious that, where the injury incurred by P results from a danger of which D could not reasonably be expected to be aware, then D should not be liable.

Example _____

P was paralysed as a consequence of being injected with a contaminated chemical. This had been stored in phials in a bath of phenol. The contamination had been caused by phenol penetrating hair-line cracks in the phials and going into solution in the chemical. It was held that D was not liable, as this was not a risk that was known to the medical profession at the time — *see Roe* v. *Minister of Health* (1954).

Perhaps it is fair to say, however, that, once such a case occurs, the risk can no longer be said to be unknown. Thus, if the same thing were to recur, the defendant in a case of this kind would probably be liable.

8. Specific duties

Certain duties are sufficiently well established as to amount to what are virtually separate torts: for example, the duty owed by an occupier of premises; the duty owed by a bailee of goods.

Two specific duties that have developed recently and have become of considerable importance are:

(a) the duty to prevent economic loss to the plaintiff; and
(b) the duty to avoid negligent statements.

9. Economic loss

The traditional view is that the tort of negligence arises in the event of personal injuries or damage to property only. Thus, injuries 'to the plaintiff's pocket' fell outside its scope. From the nineteenth century at least, the courts were willing to award damages in respect of economic loss so long as that loss was 'immediately consequential upon injury to the plaintiff's person or property' — *see Cattle* v. *Stockton Waterworks* (1875). Thus, if D's negligence causes damage to A's property, but, for some reason, P suffers financially, P cannot recover damages — *see Weller* v. *Foot and Mouth Institute* (1966).

On the other hand, when, due to D's negligence, power was cut off to P's factory, wherein molten metal had to be discarded lest it solidified as the temperature dropped, it was held that:

(a) P could recover not only the value of the molten metal, but also such economic loss as was consequential upon its loss (i.e. the profit he could have made on the finished product); but
(b) P could not recover the loss of profit occasioned by the lack of power, as this was not consequential upon any damage to his property — *see Spartan Steel* v. *Martin* (1973) and *see also Leigh and Sullivan v. Aliakmon Shipping, The Aliakmon* (1986) (*see* 16: **11**).

10. Negligent statements

Until 1963, the courts were only willing to allow liability in tort in respect of statements where:

(a) the statement was made fraudulently (in which case the tort of *deceit* was committed) — *see Derry* v. *Peek* (1889); or
(b) if made negligently, the consequences of the statement were physical injuries (i.e. to the person or to property) — *see Clayton* v. *Woodman* (1962).

In *Hedley Byrne & Co.* v. *Heller & Partners Ltd* (1964), it was held by the HL that liability would attach for negligent false statements, resulting in pecuniary (financial) loss to the plaintiff, so long as certain conditions applied. These conditions were:

(a) P must rely on the advice sought by him, and given by D;
(b) D must know, or be in a position such that he ought to know of P's reliance;
(c) the circumstances must be such that P's reliance is reasonable.

These three conditions, if fulfilled, constitute a 'special relationship' between P and D, that is the basis of liability. Over and above these, however, it is necessary that:

(a) D should not have disclaimed responsibility (though such disclaimers are now only valid if they satisfy the requirements of 'reasonableness' of the Unfair Contract Terms Act 1977, s.2) (*see Smith* v. *Bush* and *Harris* v. *Wyre Forest DC* (1989);
(b) the defendant should not enjoy any special immunity.

Examples _____

(1) R was defended by W, a barrister, on a criminal charge. R was convicted, but claimed that this was due to W's negligence. It was held that counsel enjoy an immunity from liability in negligence as public policy requires that persons involved with the administration of justice should enjoy freedom of action — *see Rondel* v. *Worsley* (1967). This decision was followed in *Arenson* v. *Arenson* (1972), where an arbitrator enjoyed a similar immunity. Clearly, this is desirable, as if a convicted criminal could bring such an action, it would, in effect, involve a complete retrial of the criminal action in circumstances where no grounds for a normal appeal exist. This immunity is not a complete one; it is confined to such work done by counsel as is intimately connected with the conduct of the case in court — *see Saif Ali* v. *Sydney Mitchell* (1978) (*see* 3: **55**).
(2) P took on the franchise of a petrol station owned by D. D told him that the station was assured of a particular turnover but the rerouting of a highway meant that motorists seldom used the station, in fact. It was held

that D was liable, as being in the petrol station sector, it was his business to know of highway plans such as these, which were bound to affect sales, and therefore he was negligent in making representations to P that failed to take account of such plans — *see Esso Petroleum Ltd* v. *Mardon* (1976).

(3) In reliance upon the audited accounts of a company, shares were bought and the company taken over. It appeared later that the accounts had not been carefully prepared. The case was brought, claiming for consequential loss. The House of Lords limited the extent of the duty of care owed by those preparing the accounts to the company members, to enable them to exercise proper control over the company. Those contemplating takeovers should make their own enquiries — a kind of 'buyer beware' for financial advice — *see Caparo Industries PLC* v. *Dickman* (1990). *See* also, *Morgan Crucible PLC* v. *Hill Samuel* (1991) and *James McNaughten Paper Group* v. *Hicks Anderson & Co.* (1991).

11. Negligence and public policy

There is no doubt that negligence is the most important of the actions in tort. In recent years the courts have been developing its principles swiftly and inconsistently. It is only possible to give the merest outline of this activity here.

In *Dutton* v. *Bognor Regis UDC* (1972) a local authority was held liable for the careless inspection of foundations while a house was being built. This case was approved in a broadly similar matter in *Anns* v. *London Borough of Merton* (1977). In this case, the House of Lords commented more generally on the scope of the duty of care in this tort. Lord Wilberforce, in particular, thought that the old practice of fitting new cases into old situations was wrong. These remarks had been closely scrutinised in *Yuen Kun Yeu* v. *A - G of Hong Kong* (1987), and *Curran* v. *Northern Ireland Co-ownership Housing Association* (1987). Then they were specifically overruled by a 7-judge House of Lords in *Murphy* v. *Brentwood District Council* (1990). Here it was held that a local authority is not liable in negligence to the owner or occupier of a building for the cost of a dangerous defects arising from careless-ness in assuring compliance with building regulations. Further to this, we have here a definite statement from the highest of courts to the effect that, unless a case falls within Hedley Byrne principles (*see* 16: **10**), there will be no duty owed in tort for economic loss.

Meanwhile, the House of Lords decided that liability in negligence could flow from faulty work rather than physical injury to the person or property — *see Junior Books* v. *Veitchi* (1982). However, the House seems to have gone smartly into reverse on this — *see Leigh and Sullivan* v. *Aliakmon Shipping* (1986) — and the Privy Council too — *see Candlewood Navigation Corporation* v. *Mistui OSK*

Lines (1985). In *Simaan General Contracting* v. *Pilkington Glass* (1988), Dillon, LJ, said that the *Junior Books* decision had been 'the subject of so much analysis and discussion that it cannot now be regarded as a useful pointer to any development of the law', and, in *D & F Estates* v. *Church Commissioners* (1988), the House of Lords has reverted to the original position regarding pure economic loss — that unless it is consequent upon physical damage, it is not recoverable in tort. This has now been applied in the *Department of the Environment* v. *Bates* (1989) case.

12. Proof of negligence: *res ipsa loquitur* (the facts speak for themselves)

Whereas, to establish a breach of duty, the plaintiff must normally prove a want of care on the part of the defendant, in some circumstances negligence can be presumed, on the grounds that:

(a) the defendant had sole control of the cause of mischief; and
(b) the accident that occurred was such as could not normally happen without negligence.

Thus, where P is injured while walking in the road by a barrel of flour falling from D's window, a presumption of negligence on D's part is raised — *see Byrne* v. *Boadle* (1863); or where P slips on yogurt on the floor of D's shop — *see Ward* v. *Tesco Stores* (1976).

The effect of this presumption is effectively to shift the burden of proof away from the plaintiff and on to the defendant (to try to prove that the incident was *not* caused by his negligence). Such explanations as he offers, therefore, must be consistent with the taking of reasonable care on his part. Thus, where a wall collapses onto P, the burden of rebutting the presumption of negligence falls on to D. If D can show that his work was carried out in accordance with stringent safety regulations, he will have discharged that burden — *see Walsh* v. *Holst* (1958).

On the other hand, the defendant's explanation, while perhaps revealing how the accident in fact occurred, may fail to satisfy the court that he was not negligent, after all.

Example

P was injured when the bus in which he was a passenger crashed. D (the bus company) showed that the accident was due not to negligent driving on the part of their driver, but to a fault in a tyre, which burst, causing the crash. It was held that they had nevertheless been negligent in failing to detect and remedy the fault — *see Barkway* v. *S. Wales Transport Co.* (1950).

13. Contributory negligence

At common law, a defendant could normally escape liability if he could show that, despite his negligence, the harm complained of would not have occurred if the plaintiff had not contributed to the accident by his own negligence — *see Butterfield* v. *Forrester* (1809).

The Law Reform (Contributory Negligence) Act 1945 has effectively abolished that rule and provides that, where a plaintiff suffers injury 'as the result partly of his own fault and partly of the fault of any other person . . .', then he can still recover damages, but the damages must be reduced 'to such extent as the court thinks just': Law Reform (Contributory Negligence) Act 1945, s. 1(1). The word 'fault' includes negligence, of course, but it is not necessary to show that the plaintiff is himself negligent, in the sense of being in breach of a duty of care, in order to establish contributory negligence. It is often said, then, that contributory negligence today consists of a failure on the part of the plaintiff to take reasonable care for his own safety. Thus, where P was riding on the tow-bar of a 'traxcavator' vehicle that was involved in a collision with another vehicle which was being negligently driven, he was guilty of contributory negligence, as the tow-bar was obviously a dangerous place to ride in the event of such a collision — *see Jones* v. *Livox Quarries* (1952).

It is also accepted now that a plaintiff may be found to have been contributorily negligent not only if his failure to take care regarding his own safety is actually, somehow, a contributory cause of the accident whereby he is injured, but also, where his conduct is such that, although in no way a factor that causes the accident, it nevertheless results in his injuries being greater than they would otherwise have been. Thus, P fails to wear a seatbelt and is injured when the driver of the car in which he is a passenger negligently collides with something and he is thrown through the windscreen — *see Froom* v. *Butcher* (1976). The court must, of course, be satisfied that, had he worn a belt, P would, in fact, have been spared at least some of his injuries.

14. Particular applications of negligence

There are several further areas where the tort of negligence has been utilised to meet particular requirements, which can be regarded separately.

(a) liability for nervous shock (*see* 16: **15**);
(b) liability for defective chattels (*see* 16: **16**);
(c) liability for premises (*see* 16: **17–25**).

15. Nervous shock

For a long time, nervous shock was not actionable at all, unless it stemmed from some actual injury, resulting from physical impact.

Where the shock was intentionally inflicted, however, the courts allowed the recovery of damages in *Wilkinson* v. *Downton* (1897). And later, the possibility of recovery for nervous shock in circumstances where the plaintiff was in genuine fear of physical injury was mooted — see *Dulieu* v. *White* (1901).

In *Hambrook* v. *Stokes* (1925), it was considered enough if the fear was that felt by a mother for the safety of her children and, after 1932, (*Donoghue* v. *Stephenson*) the courts tended to consider nervous shock in the same way they did physical injuries: i.e., is it reasonably foreseeable that the plaintiff will suffer nervous shock as a consequence of the defendant's acts?

Examples

(1) P suffered nervous shock as a result of witnessing the carnage, after a railway disaster caused by D's servants' negligence — see *Chadwick* v. *British Transport Commission* (1967).

(2) P was the mother of a family decimated in a car crash. She was not at the scene, but visited them later in hospital. Her nervous shock was held to be a foreseeable event producing an identifiable mental illness — *see McLoughlin* v. *O'Brien* (1981).

(3) P, on returning home, found her house on fire as a result of D's negligence. Her nervous shock was actionable too. It seems that the reaction may be either to physical or property injury — see *Attia* v. *British Gas PLC* (1987).

(4) The dreadful incidents at the Hillsborough football stadium in Sheffield in 1989, where 95 people died and 400 more were hospitalised, led to nearly 200 claims for compensation for nervous shock from those at the ground and others who saw the events on television — see *Jones* v. *Wright* (1991), at first instance and on appeal, and *Alcock & Others* v. *Chief Constable of the South Yorkshire Police* (1991), where 10 of the plaintiffs took the matter to the House of Lords. The House held that, for there to be a duty of care in nervous shock cases:

(a) there must be a sufficiently close relationship of love and affection with the victim to make nervous shock at that victim's plight reasonably foreseeable;

(b) there must be a sufficient proximity in time and space to the accident or its immediate aftermath;

(c) the plaintiff suffered nervous shock at the sight or sound of the accident or its immediate aftermath.

Those who suffered at seeing the events on television did not succeed in their claim.

16. Defective chattels

It was for a long time the case that liability would attach in respect of things that were dangerous *per se*. A person was also liable in respect of the dangerous condition of chattels, which was known to him, but of which he failed to warn their recipient — *see Farrant* v. *Barnes* (1862).

Donoghue v. *Stephenson* (1932) created the possibility of liability in respect of defects that were not known, but which ought to have been known by the supplier of the defective chattels. Thus the manufacturer of defective underwear was liable when their wearer got a rash from them — *see Grant* v. *Australian Knitting Mills* (1936). While it may have been thought that the liability thereby created was confined to 'consumer goods' (in *Donoghue* v. *Stephenson* it was a bottle of ginger beer) subsequent developments have shown that such liability goes further than this. Thus, when a dangerous chemical was mistakenly supplied to a school laboratory, resulting in an explosion, the suppliers were liable — *see Kubach* v. *Hollands* (1937). Furthermore, under the Consumer Protection Act 1987, Part I, there is strict liability for injuries caused by defective products.

17. Defective premises and land

In general, liability (if any) in respect of defective premises and land will be incurred by the occupier of the premises or land concerned. We speak, therefore, of occupier's liability. Non-occupiers may be liable in negligence if they render land dangerous without fault on the part of the occupier himself (*see* 16: **22 (c)**).

Occupiers' liability

18. Occupiers Liability Act 1957

This statute 'codified' the common law, and restated it adding little new material. In studying the subject, however, it is necessary to look at pre-Act cases for definitions, etc.

19. Who is an occupier?

Defined as the person who has overall control of the premises. Thus, he may be absent, leaving someone else on the premises. Such a situation may give rise to more than one occupier — *see Wheat* v. *Lacon* (1966). Indeed, the owner of premises, in employing independent contractors to work on the premises, may relinquish control to the contractors, so as to make them occupiers for the purposes of the Act — *see Bunker* v. *Brand* (1969).

20. What are the premises?

Liability may attach in respect of anything that is, in effect, capable of being occupied; thus a hole — *see Bunker* v. *Brand* (1969); a wall — *see Latham* v. *Johnson* (1913); and a lift — *see Haseldine* v. *Daw* (1941), have all been held to be premises. Thus, if A is injured while riding in B's car, liability would be in negligence if the injuries are due to B's negligent driving, but if the injuries are caused by, say, the seat collapsing and breaking A's leg, the liability might well lie under the Occupiers Liability Act.

21. To whom is the duty owed?

The Occupiers Liability Act is explicit on this. Section 2 (1) provides that an occupier owes the same duty, the 'common duty of care', to all his visitors. The term 'visitors' includes everyone who enters the premises with the express or implied invitation of the occupier, i.e. are not trespassers, who are not included in the provisions of the Act at all and must therefore be dealt with separately.

Where the visitor enters the premises in pursuance of a contract, the occupier may regulate his liability or even exclude it altogether, by the terms of the contract. If the situation amounts to one of 'business liability', then liability for death or personal injury cannot be excluded or restricted and liability for other loss or damage can only be excluded to the extent that such terms or notice, which purports to bring the exclusion clause to the plaintiff's attention, 'satisfies the requirements of reasonableness' (Unfair Contract Terms Act 1977, s. 2).

22. The common duty of care

This is defined (Occupiers Liability Act 1957, s. 2(2)) as a duty 'to take such care as in all the circumstances of the case is reasonable to see that the visitor will be reasonably safe in using the premises for the purposes for which he is invited or permitted by the occupier to be there':

(a) *'all the circumstances of the case'* These may include the vulnerability of the visitor, for example, if he is a child and whether the risk involved is one that is normally incidental to the visitor's trade or calling.

Example

A window-cleaner was injured when a window sash broke, and the window fell on his hand. It was held that the occupier was not liable as the cleaner should appreciate and guard against such dangers (though P's employers were liable for not providing a window-stop to protect him) — *see General Cleaning Contractors* v. *Christmas* (1952).

(b) *knowledge of danger on the part of the visitor* If the visitor knows of the danger and willingly accepts it, then the occupier will not be liable, but where the occupier attempts to bring the fact of a danger to the visitor's attention, his liability (or lack of it) will depend upon whether such a warning was 'enough to enable the visitor to be reasonably safe', so, when the attention of two sweeps was drawn to the fact that the flue they had been hired to clean was faulty, and should not be swept while the fire was alight, the occupiers were not liable for the sweep's death — *see Roles* v. *Nathan* (1963), but on the other hand, mere knowledge on the part of the visitor does not absolve the occupier from liability — *see Bunker* v. *Brand* (1969).

(c) *independent contractors* An occupier is not liable for damage caused to a visitor by a danger that results from the negligent work of an independent contract or, unless he is in some way negligent (e.g. in hiring a disreputable contractor, or failing to check the work where he may reasonably have done so).

Examples

(1) Where a piece of plaster fell from the ceiling of a store, injuring P, the store-owners were not liable, as the ceiling had been recently repaired by independent contractors — *see O'Connor* v. *Swan & Edgar* (1963).

(2) Where a cleaner negligently failed to clear ice from a doorstep, the occupier was liable when P slipped and was injured, as no more than a glance was required to ensure that the work had been properly done — *see Woodward* v. *Mayor of Hastings* (1945).

23. Defences

The occupier may raise any of the defences to torts generally (e.g. consent, statutory authority). In addition, the considerations dealt with above (warnings, independent contractors, etc.) may operate as defences, subject to the qualifications given.

24. Liability to trespassers

Trespassers are not covered by the Occupiers Liability Act at all: liability, if any, to trespassers exists at common law only.

Such duty as is owed by an occupier to trespassers was defined by the House of Lords in *British Railways Board* v. *Herrington* (1972) where it was decided that the occupier of premises owes to a trespasser a duty of 'common humanity'. The standard of care involved in this extraordinary duty was defined as being that standard which may reasonably be expected from the 'sensible and humane' man who finds himself in the situation of the defendant, having regard to the defendant's actual (subjective) 'knowledge, skill and resources'. The case, in fact, involved a child who was injured when he strayed on to D's live railway line through a hole in a fence, the existence of which was known to D.

The decision was followed in *Pannett* v. *McGuinness* (1973), but in *Penny* v. *Northampton Borough Council* (1974) the principle was applied so as to withhold recovery by a child trespasser. Here a boy was injured while playing on a rubbish tip occupied by the defendant council, when a friend threw an empty aerosol-spray can on to a bonfire, causing an explosion. It was held that the council could not be expected without a considerably larger budget than that available to them, to guard against such dangers, even if they were foreseeable. (*See also Ryan* v. *London Borough of Camden* (1982), *Simkiss* v. *Rhondda Borough Council* (1983).)

The duty owed to a trespasser is therefore partly, at least, subjective in the sense that it is not entirely dependent on an objective 'reasonable man' standard, but takes account of the subjective (actual) knowledge and available resources of the defendant. Although many of the cases to reach the superior courts involve child trespassers, the rule basically applies to adults, too, though presumably the factors that may create a duty towards children (e.g. whether something on the land is an 'allurement' to children) would not apply in respect of adults.

It has always been the case, and still is, that an occupier may not inflict intentional harm on trespassers — *see Bird* v. *Holbrook* (1828).

25. Occupiers Liability Act 1984

Under this statute it is possible for an occupier to exclude liability towards those whom he permits onto his land for purposes other than his normal business purposes, e.g. students on geology field trips. The 1984 Act has also restated the principles developed in *British Railways Board* v. *Herrington* (1972), and subsequent cases.

26. Defective Premises Act 1972

This Act provides that any person who undertakes work for (or in connection with) the provision of a dwelling owes a duty of care:

(a) to the person who commissions the work; and
(b) to any person who subsequently acquires an interest in the dwelling, e.g. a subsequent purchaser.

Progress test 16

1.   What is meant by the word 'negligence' in English law? What are the main ingredients of the tort of negligence?   (1, 2)

2.   Define, as nearly as possible the duty of care owed in negligence. What is meant by 'standard of care'?   (3–6)

3.   A visits B. On his way out of B's house, he pushes the gate open but the gate collapses. B has recently repaired the gate with 'superglu' adhesive. A suffers grazes and on his admission to hospital, he is injected with anti-tetanus serum. Unfortunately, owing to an allergy unknown to medicine, he suffers brain damage. Discuss.   (6, 7 and 18–25)

4.   What specific duties are owed in particular situations in the tort of negligence? What are the rules relating to (a) economic loss and (b) negligent mis-statement?   (8–11)

5.   What is meant by *res ipsa loquitur*?   (12)

6.   Outline the rules relating to (a) contributory negligence; (b) cases involving nervous shock; (c) liability for defective chattels. (13–16)

7.   What is meant by the common duty of care owed by an occupier of premises? What factors will effect this duty?   (22)

8.   X is a sewerage expert, who goes on to Y's land at Y's request to improve Y's drainage and sewerage system. While checking out a drain, X is overcome by noxious fumes, and becomes seriously ill. The fumes are the result of a blockage in Y's plumbing, which had recently been overhauled by Z, a well-known plumber. Discuss. (21, 22)

9.   What duty is owed by the occupier of premises to trespassers? (24, 25)

17
Strict liability

Meaning and scope of strict liability

1. The terms

The term 'strict liability' refers to those exceptional situations where a defendant is liable irrespective of fault on his part (*see* 13: 8). As a result, a plaintiff who suffers harm in certain circumstances can successfully sue without having to prove intention or negligence on D's part.

The term 'strict liability' is, however, preferred to 'absolute liability' as, generally, certain defences are available. Occasionally, statutes may create 'absolute' duties whereby liability will attach irrespective of how the breach of duty was brought about and these defences may not be available here. The main examples of strict liability are set out below.

The rule in *Rylands* v. *Fletcher*

2. The rule

Blackburn J in *Rylands* v. *Fletcher* (1868) said, 'The person who, for his own purposes, brings on his land and collects and keeps there anything likely to do mischief if it escapes, must keep it in at his peril, and if he does not do so, is prima facie answerable for all the damage which is the natural consequence of its escape'. In the House of Lords, Lord Cairns LC referred to the defendant's 'non-natural' use of the land as being essential to his liability. Liability under the rule will be limited by the following requirements by virtue of the formulation of the rule itself.

3. Dangerous objects

The defendant is liable only for things 'likely to do mischief'. A thing may fall within the rule because it is inherently dangerous (explosives, fire, etc.), or because it transpires in the particular circumstances to be dangerous.

Example

In *Crowhurst* v. *Amersham Burial Board* (1878), A's horse died when it ate the poisonous leaves of a tree that projected out of B's land into A's. B was liable under the rule in *Rylands* v. *Fletcher*.

4. It must be for D's 'own purpose'

It is enough, however, if he shares this purpose with a third party (though he will not be liable if the thing is for the benefit of both the defendant and the plaintiff) — *see Carstairs* v. *Taylor* (1871) (*see* 17: 8).

5. There must be an actual escape

Thus, in *Read* v. *Lyons* (1947), when R visited L's factory, and was injured by an explosion that occurred *within* the works there, the rule did not apply.

On the other hand, the rule is not confined to adjoining landowners. In *Miles* v. *Forest Rock Co.* (1918), the rule applied where escape was to a highway. What is necessary is that the escape should be 'to a place not subject to (the defendant's) control' said Viscount Simon.

6. Non-natural user/brought on to land

These are separate. That the user is 'natural' will negate liability — *see British Celanese* v. *Hunt* (1969).

The term 'natural' is nowadays taken to refer to 'normal', therefore artificial things may well not be non-natural, for example, domestic water supply — *see Rickards* v. *Lothian* (1913). In *Cambridge Water Company* v. *Eastern Counties Leather PLC* (1991), the storage of organochlorines in connection with a tanning business (which polluted a public water supply) was held not to be a non-natural use of land, thus (presumably!) amounting to a natural use.

Certainly the thing must be brought on to the defendant's land. Natural accumulations are outside the scope of the rule (even if they are dangerous) — *see Pontardawe RDC* v. *Moore-Gwyn* (1929).

7. Defendant is answerable for all damage

Rylands v. *Fletcher* is not actionable *per se* (i.e. proof of actual damage is necessary). Personal injuries have been held to fall within the rule — *see Shiffman* v. *Order of St. John* (1936).

8. Defences
These are:

(a) *plaintiff's default* if the plaintiff brought the injury on himself, he has no cause of action;

(b) *plaintiff's consent* where, for example, the plaintiff freely consented to the existence on the defendant's land of the source of the mischief, such as in *Peters* v. *Prince of Wales Theatre* (1943), where the idea of 'shared benefit' (between plaintiff and defendant (*see* 17: **4**)) was regarded as an element of this defence;

(c) *act of God* this is where the escape was caused by a completely unforeseeable natural catastrophe, of which 'human prudence is not bound to recognise the possibility' — *see Nichols* v. *Marsland* (1875);

(d) *uncontrollable act of a stranger* for this defence to apply the escape must be caused by the intervention of someone over whom the defendant has no control — *see Perry* v. *Kendricks* (1956) — and such an intervention must also be unforeseeable — *see Box* v. *Jubb* (1879);

(e) *statutory authority* where liability under the rule is expressly or impliedly excluded — *see Green* v. *Chelsea Waterworks Co.* (1894).

Liability for fire

While fires may be, naturally enough, the subject of the rule in *Rylands* v. *Fletcher*, liability may exist independently of that rule.

9. Fires intentionally started
A person who keeps a fire 'keeps it at his peril'. This is an ancient principle and we hear of liability for fires negligently allowed to spread as early as 1401 — *see Beaulieu* v. *Finglam*. If the fire is, in itself, dangerous, then liability will be strict under the rule in *Rylands* v. *Fletcher* — *see Balfour* v. *Barty-King* (1957). On the other hand, if the fire is merely a domestic one in a grate, negligence must be shown — *see Sochacki* v. *Sas* (1947).

10. Accidental fires
The Fires Prevention (Metropolis) Act 1774 provides that no action will lie against anyone on whose property a fire is accidentally begun (this is not confined to London). If the fire, once started, is negligently allowed to spread, the defendant will be liable (but not strictly) — *see Musgrove* v. *Pandelis* (1919). This applies even if the fire is started by a natural event or Act of God — *see Goldman* v. *Hargrave* (1967).

11. Combustibles

The rule in *Rylands* v. *Fletcher* will apply to situations where combustibles are stored in such a manner that they are likely to do mischief by igniting — *see Mason* v. *Levy* (1967).

Liability for animals

12. Ordinary liability in tort

A person may be liable in negligence for failing to control his animal — *see Mitchil* v. *Alestree* (1676); or in nuisance, where, for example, a stench is caused by animals — *see Aldred's Case* (1610). A man can assault another through the agency of his dog and he could even be liable in slander by teaching his parrot to recite defamatory words.

13. Dangerous animals

The law imposes a more specific liability on owners of animals in addition to the possibilities mentioned in 17: **12**. The law divides animals according to whether they belong to 'dangerous species': (Animals Act 1971, s. 1). There are now three main areas of concern:

(a) *Section 6* defines a 'dangerous species' as one
   (*i*)   that is not usually domesticated in the British Isles; and
   (*ii*) whose fully grown members have such characteristics that they are likely to cause severe damage unless restrained.

The keeper of such an animal is strictly liable for any damage it causes.

(b) On the other hand (apart from normal liability in tort: *see* 17: **11**) the keeper of a 'non-dangerous' species as defined in s. 2 is only liable, according to that section if:
   (*i*)   the damage is of a kind which the animal was likely to cause unless restrained; and
   (*ii*) the damage was the result of characteristics peculiar to the particular animal; and
   (*iii*) these characteristics were known, or ought to have been known, by the keeper.

The keeper of an animal is its owner or otherwise the head of the household where it is normally kept.

NOTE: Before the Animals Act a similar liability existed and was known as *scienter* (liability based on D's knowledge).

(c) *Defences.* The following are available under the Act:

(*i*) plaintiff's fault: s. 5(1);
(*ii*) *volenti* (consent): s. 5(2);

Example

Cummings v. *Grainger* (1977), where P was aware that a guard dog was in D's property, but nevertheless entered (as a trespasser) and was bitten. (See the Guard Dogs Act 1975, s. 1, however, which makes it an offence to permit the use of an unrestrained guard dog, unless it is secured; and requires a notice containing a warning to be exhibited.)

(*iii*) plaintiff is a trespasser: s. 5(3). This defence is only available if either the animal is not kept on the premises for protection of persons or property or, if it is, then where such keeping is reasonable — *see Cummings* v. *Grainger*;
(*iv*) contributory negligence: s. 10.

14. Liability for particular species
For cattle and dogs, liability is as follows:

(a) *Cattle trespass* At common law, whenever cattle strayed on to land possessed by someone other than their owner, liability was strict.

The Animals Act 1971, s. 4, provides that where damage is done by straying livestock to the land or to any property on it or if the landowner (or occupier) on to whose land the livestock stray reasonably incurs any expenses in keeping the livestock while it cannot be restored to its owner, the person to whom the livestock belongs is liable for the damage or expenses. 'Livestock' is defined in s. 11 as 'cattle, horses, asses, mules, hinnies, sheep, pigs, goats and poultry and also deer not in the wild state':

(*i*) the person to whom the livestock 'belongs' need not necessarily be the owner: s. 4(2);
(*ii*) damage must now be proved — the tort is not actionable *per se*;
(*iii*) the Animals Act 1971, s. 8, allows for liability in respect of any animals if they stray on to a highway and do damage there, where, for instance, the owner fails to fence the land (unless the area is one where fencing is not customary).

(b) *Dogs* The Animals Act 1971, s. 3, provides for strict liability on the part of the keeper of a dog that causes damage by killing or injuring livestock.

(c) *Dangerous dogs* Following several stories of ghastly injuries, the Dangerous Dogs Act 1991 prohibits people from having in their possession or custody dogs belonging to types bred for fighting and provides power to introduce controls over other dogs which present a serious danger to the public.

Statutory torts

15. Nature of liability

Where a statute imposes a duty on someone, the liability (if any) in tort that will result from a breach of this duty will depend on the exact wording of the statute. Thus certain duties imposed by statute are said to be absolute.

Example

Factory and Workshop Act 1878 — *see Groves* v. *Wimborne* (1898); Employers Liability (Defective Equipment) Act 1969 (which assumes negligence on the part of an employer whose employee is injured by defective equipment supplied (but not made) by him, where the defect is attributable to the fault 'of a third party').

In neither case is an injured person guaranteed a cause of action; he must prove:

(a) that there was, in fact, a breach of the statutory duty (whether absolute or qualified);

(b) that his damage was caused by the breach: in *McWilliams* v. *Sir William Arrol & Co.* (1962), the Factories Acts required provision of safety belts for 'spidermen' when climbing up scaffolding, but no belts were provided, though in an action on behalf of a man who had fallen to his death, it was found that he had not worn belts when they were available, so it was not his employer's breach of duty that caused his death, but his own practice of not wearing a belt;

(c) that he was a member of a class the statute was intended to protect — *see Groves* v. *Wimborne* (1898);

NOTE: The Guard Dogs Act 1975, s. 5 (*see* 17: **13**), provides 'the provisions of this Act shall not be construed as conferring a right of action in any civil proceedings'.

(d) that the injury complained of was one the statute was intended to prevent.

Example _____

A failed to keep sheep penned while in transit aboard his ship. Some of the sheep were washed overboard in rough weather. It was held that the purpose of the Order requiring pens (made under the Contagious Diseases (Animals) Act 1869) was to prevent the spread of disease among the animals, not to guard against animals being washed overboard. The sheepowner's claim failed — *see Gorris* v. *Scott* (1874).

_____

16. Defences

This will depend on whether the duty is absolute or qualified. If the duty is, indeed, absolute, then no defences will be available (even Act of God).

Most duties admit of some defences, however, and are to that extent at least, qualified. Thus, where the defendant properly delegated performance of the duty to the plaintiff himself, and the injury was caused by the plaintiff's own conduct, the defence of *volenti non fit injuria* applied — *see ICI* v. *Shatwell* (1965) (*see* 14: **18**). In other cases, normal defences may be available, including contributory negligence (*see* 16: **13**).

17. Other instances of strict liability

These occur particularly in specific cases of nuisance (*see* 15: **24–31**) as well as in relation to extra-hazardous activities other than those involving fire or *Rylands* v. *Fletcher* — *see Honeywill & Stein* v. *Larkin* (1934). Cases of vicarious liability may also be said to be 'strict' in the sense that, although negligence may have to be proved on the part of an employee, his employer may be liable without fault on his own part (*see* 14: **14–16**).

Progress test 17

1. Explain what is meant by strict liability.

2. Outline the rule in *Rylands* v. *Fletcher*. What are the limits to this rule? **(2–7)**

3. What defences are available in answer to a claim in *Rylands* v. *Fletcher*? **(8)**

4. In what circumstances will a person be liable for damage caused by fire? How does this differ from *Rylands* v. *Fletcher*? **(9–11)**

5. What practical difference results from distinguishing animals that are 'dangerous' from others in the law of torts?   **(12–14)**

6. A's bull escapes from his field. It rams B's car, denting it and, frightened by the noise, charges into C's china shop, damaging much of his stock. It finally gores D. Discuss the liability of A. Would it make any difference if the bull was one specially reared for bullfighting as opposed to stud?   **(12–14)**

7. What factors must be established to bring a successful action for breach of statutory duty?   **(15, 16)**

8. When will a statutory tort involve strict liability?   **(15, 16)**

18
Defamation

General requirements and definitions

1. Meaning of defamation

To defame someone is to attack their reputation (or, in other words, detract from their justified fame — *de*fame). A defamatory statement is one that involves an imputation against a living person (*see* 14: **10**) that is 'injurious to that person in his trade, or holds him up to hatred, ridicule or contempt': said Blackburn J, in *Capital & Counties Bank* v. *Henty* (1882)) or, as Lord Atkin said in *Sim* v. *Stretch* (1936), 'tends to lower the plaintiff in the estimation of right-thinking members of society generally.

2. Libel and slander

Such statements may be in permanent form, in which case they are referred to as libel or in transient form, in which case they are known as slander.

In fact, a 'statement' is not necessarily required – a picture or combination of words and pictures may constitute libel — *see Garbett* v. *Hazell, Watson* (1943). Indeed a wax effigy has been held to constitute a libel in certain circumstances — *see Monson* v. *Tussauds* (1894). No doubt gestures may constitute slander. On the other hand, radio and television are media for libel (Defamation Act 1952, s. 1), as are words spoken in plays (Theatres Act 1968, s. 4). Thus, 'statements in permanent form' must be liberally interpreted.

The main result of this distinction between libel and slander is a historical one. Libel is actionable *per se* (without proof of damage), while slander requires proof of special damage. (Special damage here means simply actual damage – more than the mere loss of face — *see Lynch* v. *Knight* (1861).)

To this general rule (that slander is not actionable *per se*), however, there are the following four exceptions:

(a) slander imputing a criminal offence punishable by imprisonment — *see Gray* v. *Jones* (1939);

(b) imputation of unchastity on the part of a woman under the Slander of Women Act 1891 — *see Kerr* v. *Kennedy* (1942);

(c) imputation that the plaintiff suffers from a contagious disease (such as would cause others to 'shun and avoid him');

(d) imputing professional incompetence against the plaintiff under the Defamation Act 1952, s. 2 (refers to words 'calculated to disparage the plaintiff in any office, profession, calling, trade or business').

3. The elements of defamation

To succeed in an action for libel or slander, a plaintiff must prove three things.

(a) that the statement complained of was defamatory (*see* 18: **4**);

(b) that it could reasonably be understood to refer to the plaintiff (*see* 18: **5**);

(c) that it was published to a third party (*see* 18: **6**).

These are dealt with below and the problems associated with these issues are discussed.

4. Defamatory statements and innuendos

A statement may, on the face of it, be defamatory in the sense outlined in (1) above. On the other hand, a statement may not be expressly defamatory but only by implication. Such a statement is said to consist of, or include an innuendo. There are two kinds of innuendos:

(a) *the true or legal innuendo* which is where words that are innocent in themselves derive a defamatory meaning from some extraneous facts.

Example

In *Cassidy* v. *Daily Mirror* (1929), a newspaper published a photograph of X with a woman, C, with a caption stating them to be engaged. It was held that Mrs X could recover damages from the newspaper. Although she was not even referred to, the suggestion that X was engaged might have led people who knew that she lived with X to believe that she was not, in fact, married to him.

(b) *the popular or false innuendo* which consists of an extension of the ordinary meaning of words — *see Allsop* v. *Church of England Newspapers* (1972) (reference to plaintiff as 'obsessed with the bent').

Whether a statement is claimed to be expressly defamatory or to depend upon an innuendo, is for the judge to decide as to whether the words are reasonably capable of bearing the defamatory meaning alleged by the plaintiff — *see Lewis* v. *Daily Telegraph* (1964). If the judge decides that they are so capable, it is for the jury (if any) to decide whether the statement is so understood by 'right thinking members of society' (*see* 18: **5**).

5. Reference to plaintiff

It is necessary that the statement:

(a) might reasonably be understood to refer to the plaintiff; this is a question for the judge; and
(b) is so understood by reasonable people; this is a question for the jury (*see* 18: **4**).

At common law it was irrelevant that the defendant did not intend to refer to the plaintiff but had someone else in mind — *see Newstead* v. *London Express Newspapers* (1940); or even a fictitious person — *see Hulton* v. *Jones* (1910).

It is not necessary for the plaintiff to be referred to by name (*see* 18: **4(a)**), but it is not enough if the defendant makes a statement that is so general that a particular plaintiff cannot be identified — *see Knupffer* v. *London Express* (1944).

The Defamation Act 1952, s. 4, however, provides for a defence in cases of unintentional defamation (applicable where the defendant publishes innocently in relation to the plaintiff, as in *Newstead* v. *London Express Newspapers* (1940)). For these provisions *see* 18: **13**.

6. Publication and repetition

This is the basis of liability: the defamatory statement must be published to a third person. The term 'third persons' does not include the defendant's spouse — *see Wenhak* v. *Morgan* (1888), but does include the plaintiff's spouse — *see Theaker* v. *Richardson* (1962).

Publication need not be intentional; it is enough if the circumstances are such that someone other than the plaintiff (or his spouse) is likely to read the statement — *see Huth* v. *Huth* (1915). Indeed the law presumes that statements made in the form of telegrams etc. are published to Post Office officials though, obviously, not intended for them to read.

Each publication of a defamatory statement gives rise to a separate cause of action and repetition of such a statement, even by someone who is not aware of its defamatory nature, constitutes a publication — *see Goldsmith* v. *Sperrings Ltd* (1977).

Innocent dissemination, however, does not amount to publication, Thus, while the newsagent, bookseller, etc., is prima facie liable when he sells a paper or book that is defamatory, it is a defence for him to show:

(a) he did not know, and;

(b) could not be reasonably expected to know (i.e. was not negligent in failing to know)

that the material circulated by him is defamatory. In *Vizetelly* v. *Mudies Select Library* (1900) a library was liable, as its failure to ascertain the defamatory nature of books was negligent.

Defences

7. Special defences

Defamation by its nature is subject to various special defences, apart from the defences available in torts generally (*see* 14: **18–21**).

8. Justification

This is a plea that the statement complained of is substantially true. To be defamatory, a statement must be false. 'Truth will out!' — *see M'Pherson* v. *Daniels* (1829).

Justification is a complete defence to the tort of defamation but is not a defence to an action in criminal libel (*see* 29: **17**).

Since the Defamation Act 1952, s. 5, was passed, it is possible, in cases where the statement complained of contains more than one charge (or imputation), for the defence to succeed, even if the truth of some of the imputations is not proved. What is necessary, however, is that 'the words not proved to be true do not materially injure the plaintiff's reputation having regard to the truth of the remaining charges'.

A price attaches to an unsuccessful plea of justification: the defendant may be liable to increased damages — *see Associated Leisure Ltd* v. *Associated Newspapers* (1970).

Formerly, a conviction in a criminal court was not sufficient evidence upon which to base a plea of justification — *see Hinds* v. *Sparks* (1964). Since the Civil Evidence Act 1968, s. 13, however, the conviction of P will now support the plea of justification.

The Rehabilitation of Offenders Act 1974 (which provides in s.

4(1) that, after a period of time, a criminal conviction is 'spent' and the convicted person is to be treated as if he never committed an offence) provides in s. 8(3) that even a 'spent' conviction may be relied upon to support a defence of justification, fair comment or privilege. However, this is only so if the defendant does not act maliciously.

9. Fair comment

This must be on a matter of public interest. Thus politicians, actors and other public figures must expect their conduct to be commented on. Provided such comments are fair, they have no cause for complaint. The term 'fair', however, here assumes a rather complex meaning. While generally the prime requirement is that such views as are expressed by the defendant are honestly held, the following factors are also relevant.

(a) The facts, upon which the comment is made, must themselves be substantially true — *see Broadway Approvals* v. *Odhams Press* (1965) — (though they do not necessarily have to be stated — *see Kemsley* v. *Foot* (1952)). On the other hand, if the facts are not stated, certain types of comment, particularly those that impute corruption or dishonesty to the plaintiff, will have to be proved substantially true (i.e. are the subject only of justification) — *see Campbell* v. *Spottiswoode* (1863).

(b) Malice defeats the defence. Implied malice, in the sense of a lack of honest belief in the statement, will suffice to defeat the defence; actual or express malice, in the sense of spite or 'ill will', will also render a comment 'unfair' — *see Thomas* v. *Bradbury, Agnew & Co.* (1906) and *Telnikoff* v. *Matusevitch* (1991).

(c) It is for the judge to decide whether the matter is one of 'public interest' and such matters need only be of interest to the public — they do not have to be in the public interest in the sense of 'for the public good' that the statement should be published — *see London Artists* v. *Littler* (1968).

(d) To support the defence, such facts as are relied upon as a basis for the comments must be true at the time the statement was made; it is not enough if these facts subsequently came to light — *see Cohen* v. *Daily Telegraph* (1968).

10. Privilege

Circumstances require that on certain occasions, the right to reputation should be subordinated to requirements of freedom of speech and/or comment. Such occasions are said to be privileged; statements made on such occasions are protected by law and proof that the statement was, in fact, made on such an occasion will found a defence to an action in defamation. There are two kinds of privilege: absolute (*see* 18: **11**) and qualified (*see* 18: **12**).

11. Absolute privilege

No action whatever can be brought in respect of statements made on occasions that are absolutely privileged, even if the statement is not only untrue but made maliciously. Such occasions are:

(a) statements made in Parliament (Bill of Rights 1689, Article 9);

(b) statements made in the course of judicial proceedings (e.g. by judge, juror, witness) — *see Addis* v. *Crocker* (1961);

(c) state communications (e.g. made by a Minister to the Crown or to another officer of State) — *see Chatterton* v. *Secretary of State for India* (1895);

(d) publications made by or addressed to the Parliamentary Commissioner (Parliamentary Commissioner Act 1967, s. 10);

(e) communications between a solicitor and his client, so long as they relate to the subject on which the solicitor has been retained — *see More* v. *Weaver* (1928).

12. Qualified privilege

This differs from absolute privilege in that it is destroyed if it can be shown that the defendant was actuated by express malice (such as spite or ill will, for which *see* 18: **9**) — *see Horrocks* v. *Lowe* (1974). Examples of occasions that are the subject of the defence are as follows:

(a) fair and accurate reports of Parliamentary proceedings;

(b) fair and accurate reports of judicial proceedings;

(c) fair and accurate reports of other public bodies, e.g. the United Nations, domestic tribunals, local authorities (the modern basis of these privileged occasions is found in the Defamation Act 1952, ss. 7–9 and Schedules);

(d) statements made in performance of a duty, but this is restricted, as stated by Lord Atkinson in *Adam* v. *Ward* (1917): 'where the person who makes a communication has an interest or a duty, legal, social, or moral to make it and the person to whom it is made has an interest to receive it. This reciprocity is essential'.

Example

In *Watt* v. *Longsdon* (1930), A wrote to A and B's employer and to Mrs B that B was misbehaving while abroad. It was held that publication to the employer was privileged as the relationship of employer/employee created the necessary reciprocity. No such reciprocity existed between A and Mrs B and so A was liable in respect of the publication.

On the other hand, an employer can give unfavourable references concerning an employee to a prospective employer — *see Jackson* v. *Hopperton* (1864);

(e) statements made in protection of an interest are also privileged, provided that reciprocity exists (*see* 18: **12**(*d*)).

> NOTE: While malice destroys the defence of qualified privilege, proof of malice on the part of one of several joint defendants does not deprive the others of their usual defences — *see Egger* v. *Chelmsford* (1965).

13. Apology and amends

These are not normally a defence except in the following circumstances:

(a) *Defamation Act 1952, s. 4* apology and offer of an amends is a necessary element of the defence for unintentional publication (*see* 18: **5**);

(b) *a newspaper* has a defence under the Libel Act 1843, if it can show:
- (*i*) a lack of malice or gross negligence in publishing;
- (*ii*) that a full apology has been made; and
- (*iii*) that a sum of money has been paid into court in lieu of damages (by way of amends).

14. Limitation

The Administration of Justice Act 1985, s. 57, has amended the Limitation Act 1980 by providing a special three-year limitation period (as opposed to the normal six) to cases of libel and slander. The High Court, however, can permit a claim to be brought after the three-year period, where facts relevant to his claim were not known to the plaintiff at the expiration of three years. In such cases, he may, at the Court's discretion, be allowed a further year in which to proceed (Limitation Act 1980, s.4(a)).

Progress test 18

1. What is meant by 'defamation'? Distinguish 'libel' and 'slander' (**1, 2**)

2.   What elements must be established to succeed in an action for defamation? Explain what is meant by an innuendo.   **(3–6)**

3.   Distinguish: (a) justification, (b) fair comment and (c) qualified privilege.   **(8–10, 12)**

4.   Where may the defence of absolute privilege be used to meet a case of defamation?   **(11)**

5.   X Co. ask Y Co. for a reference for Honest, who is presently employed by Y Co. and has applied for a senior post with them. The reference is made by Nasty, one of the directors of Y Co. In it, he falsely states that Honest has been involved in embezzlement. Copies of this reference are sent to X Co. and to Honest himself. The other directors of Y Co. are not aware that a reference has been given. Discuss.   **(6, 12)**

Part four

The law of property

19
Real and personal property

Introduction

1. Meaning of property

Property fundamentally means anything that belongs to a person, i.e. which is *proper* to that person — from the French word *propre*, which means one's own.

English law recognises *two kinds* of property:

(a) *real property*, i.e. freehold interest in land;

(b) *personal property*, i.e. any other kind of property, including leasehold interests in land.

2. Ownership and possession

The owner of property is the person who is entitled to *all legal rights* over that property, including the right to exclusive use and possession of it.

The owner may, however, part with possession, e.g. where the owner of a book lends it to another person. Here ownership remains vested in the lender, but the borrower now has possession of the book.

Ownership, therefore, is a legal concept, while *possession* is a matter of fact. Possession was recognised by the law before ownership. Thus, most of the older forms of action concerning property relate to wrongful dispossession, and in order to sue in such an action the plaintiff had merely to prove that he was *entitled* to possession of the property (and not that he was the owner). Even today, a plaintiff suing for trespass to land has merely to prove that he is entitled to possession of the land. In some cases the possessor of land may even maintain an action for trespass against the owner (*see* 15: **10** and **16**).

3. Importance of possession

Possession in law connotes two things:

(a) *control* over the property possessed (*corpus possessionis*); and

(b) *intention* to exert *exclusive* control (*animus possidendi*).

Control may be exercised by means of others, e.g. employees and agents. And a person who has effective control of property may not be the possessor if he has no intention to exert exclusive control, e.g. where he is merely the custodian of goods for another.

The maxim that 'possession is nine points of the law' means that the law protects the possessor of property, and presumes him to be the owner unless the contrary is proved. This protection may even be available against the true owner of the property.

4. Acquisition of ownership
Ownership may be acquired in the following ways.

(a) *originally*:
- (*i*) by asserting ownership and possession over something *not previously owned* by anyone else, e.g. catching fish at sea; or
- (*ii*) by asserting ownership over something abandoned by the previous owner;

(b) *derivatively*, i.e. acquiring ownership from a previous owner, either:
- (*i*) with his consent (sale, gift, etc.); or
- (*ii*) without consent, e.g. where the court orders the sale of a bankrupt person's property to pay his debts;

(c) *by succession*, i.e. by inheritance on the death of the former owner, either:
- (*i*) in accordance with the deceased's will; or
- (*ii*) upon intestacy where there is no will.

5. Legal and equitable interests
Rights of property protected by the common law were called legal rights and included possession and ownership.

However, where the owner of property was under a moral duty to hold it for the benefit of another (called a beneficiary), the common law would not protect the beneficiary's rights. In these cases equity intervened to enforce the claims of morality, and compelled the owner of the property to hold it as trustee for the beneficiary. (The right of the beneficiary was then called an equitable interest in the property.)

Since the Judicature Act 1873, both legal and equitable interests are enforced in all the courts, but they still exist separately. For example, T, by will, may leave property to A and B, directing them to hold it as trustees for the benefit of X. Here A and B will become the legal owners, and X will inherit merely an equitable interest in the property. (For a more detailed account of the law of trusts *see* Chapter 23.)

Kinds of property

6. Realty and personality

Real property means freehold interests in land and *personal property* means moveable property and leasehold interests in land.

These two kinds of property are so called because in the Middle Ages a person wrongfully dispossessed of property had a choice of two types of action.

(a) *a real action* (action *in rem*), i.e. an action for the recovery of the thing itself (Latin: *res* = thing) and such actions were available only in relation to what would now be called freehold land;

(b) *a personal action* (action *in personam*), i.e. an action for damages against the dispossessor personally, without any claim for the recovery of the property, this was originally the only type of action available where the property involved was something other than freehold land.

Eventually property recoverable by a real action came to be called realty, or, real property, i.e. freehold land. All other property was personalty.

7. Chattels real: leases

Although leasehold interests in land were originally classed as personalty for the reasons stated above, the courts from the fifteenth century onwards allowed a dispossessed tenant to bring a real action called an action for ejectment against a dispossessor. Leases therefore came to have some of the quality of real property and were called chattels real (i.e. personal property recoverable by a real action).

The Law of Property Act 1925 laid down that from 1 January 1926 leases were to be treated like freehold land, i.e. were to be treated as realty in all respects. Freehold and leasehold are now the only two legal estates allowed by the law (*see* 20: **10**).

8. Kinds of personalty

These are:

(a) *chattels real*, i.e. leases (now treated as realty (*see* 19: **7**));

(b) *chattels personal*, i.e. items of moveable property, such as furniture, clothes, cars, ships, books, paintings.

9. Choses in possession and in action

The word *chose* (French) means a 'thing' and all property, whether land or chattels, is classed as choses in possession or choses in action.

(a) *Choses in possession*, i.e. tangible things capable of physical possession, such as land, books, cars, pianos;

(b) *Choses in action*, i.e. intangible rights that can be enforced only by action in the courts and are not capable of physical possession, e.g. debts, patents, copyrights, cheques, shares in companies, but these can be sold like choses in possession, though the assignment must be in a certain form (*see* 12: 2). If A owns a car he has a chose in possession, but if he hires the car to B for 12 months, A now has only a chose in action, i.e. a right to sue B for recovery of the car at the end of the 12 months.

10. Methods of transfer *inter vivos*

The method required to transfer property *inter vivos*, i.e. during the life of the transferor, depends on the type of property:

(a) *real property*:
   (i) *transfer upon sale* is effected by a deed of conveyance; transfers not by deed may be void (Law of Property Act 1925, s. 52);
   (ii) *leases* must be granted under seal (if for more than three years);
   (iii) *gifts* of land must also be by deed;
(b) *personal property*:
   (i) *choses in possession* can normally be transferred by mere delivery, whether the delivery is actual (handing over the chose itself) or constructive (handing over the means to obtain it, e.g. a key to the place where it is kept);
   (ii) *choses in action* must be assigned as laid down by the Law of Property Act 1925, s. 136, the rules of equity or of some particular statute; negotiable instruments are transferable by mere delivery.

11. Kinds of proprietary rights

A person may have a right over their own property or over the property of another. A right over one's own things is called a *jus in re propria*. A right over property of another is called a *jus in re aliena*.

(a) *jura in re propria* include choses in possession such as land (immoveable property) and chattels (moveable property), and choses in action, such as debts, shares, patents.

(b) *jura in re aliena* include:

   (*i*) leases of land belonging to other people;

   (*ii*) rights of way, etc., across the land of another;

   (*iii*) rights over property of another by way of security, e.g. mortgages, pledges (*see* Chapter 22).

For more detailed rules on succession *see* 19: **12** and Chapter 24.

12. Succession upon death

When a person dies, his property remains to be disposed of by his personal representatives. The method of succession to the deceased's property will be governed:

(a) *by his will* (if any) and distribution will be arranged by his executors, i.e. personal representatives appointed by the will;

(b) *by the law of intestacy* (if there is no will) and distribution will be arranged by his administrators, i.e. personal representatives appointed by the court.

The method of transfer of property by personal representatives is essentially the same as in 19: **10**, save that the land is usually transferred by a document called a vesting assent, which need not necessarily be a deed.

For wills and intestacy, *see* Chapter 24.

13. Bankruptcy

Where a person is insolvent, he or his creditors may apply for his affairs to be administered under the supervision of the court and distributed among the creditors under a statutory scheme.

Administration by the court in this way is called bankruptcy and is usually effected by a trustee in bankruptcy appointed by the creditors and supervised by the court and/or the Department of Trade and Industry.

Insolvency means that a person is unable to pay his debts as they fall due or has insufficient funds to meet his liabilities. It does not always result in bankruptcy (*see* 24: **26**).

14. Securities

A lender of money may insist on being given some security for his loan, e.g. possession or the right to possession or sale, of some property belonging to the debtor. The lender's rights to the property in question are generally suspended so that they will become operative only if the borrower fails to repay the loan as agreed.

Security for loans may take the following forms:

(a) *mortgage* (of realty or personalty);
(b) *pawn or pledge* (of personalty);
(c) *conditional bills of sale* (for personalty);
(d) *assignment of a chose in action* (subject to a condition that the lender will assign it back to the borrower when the loan is repaid).

The law relating to securities is dealt with in Chapter 22.

The 1925 legislation

15. Need for reform

The English law of property is largely feudal in origin and, by the beginning of this century, it had developed from comparatively simple beginnings into a highly complex and comprehensive system containing many anachronisms.

The need for reform became apparent in the nineteenth century and several Acts were passed effecting piecemeal improvements, but it was not until 1925 that a full-scale overhaul was made of the law relating to both real and personal property.

Nineteenth-century reforms had included:

(a) the *Administration of Estates Act 1833*, which made land available for payment of a deceased's debts (previously only personalties could be claimed by ordinary creditors);
(b) the *Settled Land Act 1882*, which reformed the law relating to settlements (trusts) of land;
(c) the *Land Transfer Act 1897* and the *Conveyancing Act 1881* simplified methods of transferring land.

16. The 1925 legislation

After a preliminary Law of Property Act 1922, Parliament passed a series of Acts overhauling the law of real and personal property, its transfer, incidents and inheritance:

(a) *the Law of Property Act 1925* (the LPA) brought real and personal property into line in many respects and simplified land law;
(b) *the Settled Land Act 1925* (the SLA) codified the law relating to settlements and removed many restrictions on the powers of the tenant for life;

(c) *the Trustee Act 1925* (the TA) codified the rules relating to the appointment, retirement and duties of trustees;

(d) *the Land Charges Act 1925* (the LCA, now replaced by the Land Charges Act 1972 and the Local Land Charges Act 1975) and the *Land Registration Act 1925* (the LRA) provided for the registration of certain types of interest in land at a central land registry and made some such interests void unless so registered. The Land Registration Act 1988 opens the register to public inspection.

(e) *The Administration of Estates Act 1925* (the AEA) laid down the rules governing the payment of a deceased person's debts and the distribution of his property on intestacy.

17. Purposes of the Property Acts

These are the:

(a) *abolition of anachronisms* — Several ancient forms of feudal tenure, such as copyhold (*see* Chapter 20) were abolished and complicated rules of feudal law were also swept away, such as the old rule against double possibilities (called the rule in *Whitby* v. *Mitchell* (1890)) (*see also* 20:**23**);

(b) *assimilation of real and personal property* The law relating to realty and personalty was brought into line as far as possible, mainly by subjecting land to the rules that formerly had applied only to personalty.

(c) *simplification of conveyancing* The methods of transferring land were simplified, e.g. by providing for the registration of estates in land and transfer merely by changing the entry in the register. Registration on a compulsory basis has been substantially extended in recent years so that the overwhelming majority of domestic conveyancing is now done under the LRA — in 1984, the Solicitor General estimated that the programme of compulsory registration will be completed by 1994.

18. The Law of Property Act 1925

This, the most important of the Property Acts, provided for the following main matters.

(a) *legal estates were reduced to two,* namely freehold and leasehold (*see* 20: **10**);

(b) *legal interests were also reduced* — the most important ones are now easements, profits, rentcharges and mortgages (*see* 20: **18**);

(c) *equitable interests are overreached* on sale of the legal estate, i.e. when the legal owner of land sells it, the sale operates to cancel (overreach) any equitable rights attaching to the land, except in certain cases (*see* 20: **24**);

(d) *anachronistic feudal systems of tenure were abolished* (*see* 20: **2**);

(e) *feudal methods of transferring land were abolished*, and it was provided that transfer should be by *grant* only, i.e. by deed.

Progress test 19

1. Define property and explain the distinction between: (a) real and personal property, and (b) ownership and possession. **(1, 2)**

2. Summarise the ways in which ownership of property may be acquired. **(4)**

3. Explain the distinction between legal and equitable interests in property. **(5)**

4. A borrows a suitcase from B, to take on his holiday. He fills the suitcase with his (A's) clothes and, at the airport, hands the case to C, a porter. C loses the case. A and B wish to sue C for conversion. Advise A and B. **(3 and *see also* 15: 16)**

5. Explain the historical origins of the distinction between realty and personalty. **(6)**

6. Why are leases of land technically classed as personalty? **(7)**

7. Distinguish between choses in possession and choses in action and explain how each can be transferred. **(9, 10)**

8. Summarise the methods by which property can be transferred *inter vivos*. **(10)**

9. Distinguish between *jura in re propria* and *jura in re aliena* **(11)**

10. Summarise the forms of succession to property on death of the owner. **(12)**

11. What are the principal forms of security for loans of money? **(14)**

12. Summarise the chief reforms effected by legislation in English property law in the nineteenth century. **(15)**

13. List the principal property statutes enacted in 1925 and explain their purposes. **(16, 17)**

14. Summarise the main provisions of the Law of Property Act 1925. **(18)**

20
Estates and interest in land

Tenure and estates

1. Meaning of tenure

Under the old feudal system of law, all land in England belonged to the King and all landholders were, therefore, merely tenants (*see* 1:11). Tenancies were granted in return for services to be rendered as follows:

(a) *to the King*, if the King was the landlord (tenants holding directly under the King were called tenants *in capite*);

(b) *to a mesne landlord* by tenants to whom tenants *in capite* or other major landholders made sub-grants by the process of sub-infeudation ('mesne' is pronounced 'mean').

The relationship of the tenant to his immediate landlord was called tenure.

2. Kinds of tenure: freehold

These are:

(a) *chivalric tenures*, e.g. knight service, where the tenant was required to perform military duties for his mesne lord, such as the provision of armed retainers (military tenures of this kind were abolished in 1660);

(b) *socage tenure*, involving non-military services, such as fixed agricultural work (or, in the later Middle Ages, rent in lieu of labour);

(c) *spiritual tenure*, where the church held land, e.g. in return for saying masses for the landlord's soul after his death.

3. Villeinage and copyhold

Agricultural workers (called *villeins*) were allowed to live on a tenant's land in return for labour. Villeins originally had no rights in the land, could not marry without their lord's consent, could not leave the land and could be sold with the land.

Shortage of labour in the later Middle Ages enabled villeins to force an improvement in their status by:

(a) substituting money payments called rent for the services formerly required; and

(b) obtaining recognition as tenants of the land on which they lived.

These tenancies were evidenced by copies of the rolls or records of the landlord's manorial court and this type of tenancy came to be called copyhold.

4. Meaning of estate

Tenure means the relationship existing between a tenant and his lord, and *estate* means the nature of the tenant's rights in his land.

Essentially, estates are of *two types*:

(a) freehold; and

(b) leasehold.

5. Estates of freehold before 1925

These were of the following types:

(a) *fee simple* — a grant of land to a tenant and his heirs forever (or until sold or otherwise disposed of);

(b) *estate tail* — an estate entailed so as to descend to specified heirs of the tenant, e.g. a tail male ('to A and the heirs male of his body') or a tail female ('to A and his heirs female');

NOTE: **(a)** and **(b)** above were classed as *estates of inheritance (fees)*, i.e. were capable of passing at the tenant's death to his heirs, instead of ceasing automatically.

(c) *estate for life*, e.g. a grant 'to A for life';

(d) *estate pour autre vie* (for the life of another), e.g. a grant 'to A during the life of B'.

NOTE: **(c)** and **(d)** above were called *mere freeholds*, because they could not be inherited by the heirs of the tenant.

6. Interests in land

An interest in land is a right in or over the land of another, e.g. a right of way across a neighbour's land.

7. Equitable estates and interests

In addition to the legal estates and interests described above, parallel equitable estates and interests (originally recognised and enforced only in the equity Court of Chancery) might exist simultaneously in the same piece of land.

For example, where land was granted 'to A in fee simple on trust for B', A (the *trustee*) had the legal estate in fee simple, subject to an equitable fee simple vested in B (the beneficiary) (*see* Chapter 23).

Since 1873, equitable interests are recognised and enforced in all courts (*see* 1: **26**).

8. Future interests

These are rights to obtain land at some future date, e.g. when the present owner dies.

A future interest is *vested* if the person entitled to it is ascertained, and his interest will take effect immediately on determination of the previous interest, e.g. a grant 'to A for life, remainder to B' — a *vested* remainder.

A future interest is *contingent* if the person entitled is not yet known or the vesting of the interest is dependent on the happening of some future event that may not occur, e.g. a grant 'to A for life, *if* he shall attain 18 years of age'. Such a grant will become vested as soon as A reaches his eighteenth birthday, but, if he dies before that date, the grant will lapse and revert to the grantor.

9. Reversions and remainders

A *reversion* is a future interest arising by operation of law, e.g. where the land reverts to the landlord at the end of a lease. A person who grants a lease always has a reversionary interest in the land and the land will automatically revert to him in due course.

A *remainder* is an estate that is granted so as to commence after the termination of an earlier grant, e.g. 'to A for life, remainder to B'. In this case B will obtain the land when A dies. If the remainder is dependent on an uncertain future event, it is called a contingent remainder (*see* 20:8).

Legal estates in land

10. The Law of Property Act 1925, s. 1

Only two legal estates can now exist in land.

(a) *fee simple absolute in possession* (commonly called *freehold*);
(b) *term of years absolute* (commonly called *leasehold*).

The characteristic of freehold is that it may last for an indefinite time, possibly forever, while a lease is for a fixed period.

11. Fee simple absolute in possession

Fee is a technical word indicating an estate of inheritance, i.e. an estate capable of passing to the tenant's heirs at his death:

(a) *simple* means it can pass to the general heirs, i.e. it is not entailed to a particular class of heirs;

(b) *absolute* means that the grant is not qualified, e.g. by provision for a gift over to another person in certain circumstances;

(c) *in possession* means that the tenant is entitled to physical possession, though he may contract to part with possession in return for a rental, e.g. where he grants a lease of the land.

12. Creation of a fee simple

Contracts to sell or otherwise dispose of land or any interest in land are normally drawn up in writing; this is because the contract must be evidenced in writing if a court action is to be based on it (*see* 5: **7**).

Such a contract is performed by the grantor executing a deed of conveyance, which operates to transfer the fee simple to the purchaser.

No special words are needed to create a fee simple, whether the grant is *inter vivos* or by will. The grantee automatically receives full estate or interest that the grantor had power to convey, unless a contrary intention appears in the conveyance, under the Law of Property Act 1925, s. 60. If the grantor wishes to reserve for himself certain rights over the land, he must do so expressly in the conveyance.

13. Position of the fee simple owner

He is the virtual owner of the land (subject to the Crown's theoretical overlordship). He is entitled to everything above, below or on the land, e.g. the air above the land, minerals or water below it and buildings or crops upon it.

In theory 'an Englishman's home is his castle', i.e. he can do what he likes with his land — but in practice recent legislation has curtailed his rights considerably.

Examples _____

(1) *The Town and Country Planning Act 1990* — consent of local planning

authorities is required for all building, mining or engineering operations and for any material change in use of the land.

(2) *Ownership of minerals* — at common law, gold and silver found under land belong to the Crown and, by various Acts of Parliament coal, petroleum and natural gas belong to the state. On the other hand, minerals and other inorganic substances, such as china clay and gravel, comprise part of the realty.

NOTE: Water percolating under land in *undefined channels* belongs to the owner of the soil and he can take it all if he wishes, even though by so doing he deprives neighbours of their share — *see Bradford* v. *Pickles* (*see* 13:**4**). If the water flows through *defined channels* (whether above or below the land), he can take as much as he wants for *normal purposes*, such as farming, even though he exhausts the supply to the detriment of his neighbours, but if the water is to be used for *extraordinary purposes*, such as supplying a factory, he must usually replace what he has taken.

14. Term of years absolute

This description includes leases for any period, even though this may be for less than a year, provided the lease has a certain duration.

Tenancies for uncertain periods are not legal estates, but are equitable only, e.g. tenancies at will (*see* 21: **2**). (Leases are dealt with more fully in Chapter 21.)

Co-ownership

15. Co-ownership of land

Where land is granted to several people simultaneously, they are either tenants in common or joint tenants.

Tenancies in common can now only exist in equity. Therefore if land is granted to A and B as tenants in common, they will hold as joint tenants on trust for sale (*see* 20: **16**).

16. Tenancies in common

These arise wherever land is granted in such a way as to suggest that the grantor intends the tenants to have distinct shares, though the land remains physically undivided, e.g. a grant 'to A and B equally' or 'to A and B in undivided shares'. Words conveying such a suggestion are called 'words of severance'.

After 1925, a grant to tenants in common operates only in equity. The grantees will be regarded as legal joint tenants, but they will hold the land on trust for sale (with power to postpone indefinitely). When the statutory joint tenants then sell (or when the survivor sells), the proceeds will be divided between them (or between the last survivor and the heirs of the deceased tenants). Thus, if land is granted to A and B as tenants in common, they will hold as joint tenants on trust for sale. If B dies, A will become solely entitled (under the rules of survivorship (*see* 20: **17**)), but will have to sell the land at some date and share the proceeds of sale with B's heirs. This form of ownership is now rather uncommon.

17. Joint tenancies
Wherever land is conveyed to two or more persons without words of severance, they hold it as joint tenants and each is theoretically entitled to the whole land. Such a grant might take the form of: 'to A and B jointly' or simply 'to A and B'.

Note the following points.

(a) *joint tenants are all entitled to the whole land* — they cannot claim any section of the land as their own private shares and if there is a house, then, theoretically, each is fully entitled to the use of *all* parts of the house simultaneously with all the other joint tenants;

(b) *not more than four joint tenants* — there cannot be more than four legal owners of land simultaneously under the Trustee Act 1925, s. 34 and, if land is conveyed to more than four persons, the *first* four named will hold as joint tenants (trustees) on trust for sale for the benefit of themselves and the remaining grantees;

(c) *the right of survivorship applies* (the *jus accrescendi*) — on the death of one joint tenant, the survivors inherit his share, so, if land is granted to A, B and C jointly and B and C die, A will become sole owner and trustee for the heirs of B and C;

(d) *the statutory trust for sale* — after 1925, whenever land is conveyed to joint tenants beneficially or to 'tenants in common' (who are now treated as joint tenants), they will hold the land on trust for sale (with power to postpone sale indefinitely) and, after sale, they or the survivor of them must distribute the proceeds of sale equally among all the tenants and/or their heirs. (This form of ownership is quite commonly used when a husband and wife both own their home).

Legal interests

18. Legal interests after 1925
The only interests that can now be created as legal interests (as distinct from merely equitable) are the following:

(a) *easements and profits à prendre* (*see* 20: **19** *and* 21: **16–22**);
(b) *a charge by way of legal mortgage* (*see* Chapter 22);
(c) *land tax or other charge on land* imposed by law and not by agreement of the parties;
(d) *rights of entry* exercisable over or in respect of a legal rentcharge (*see* 20: **20**).

19. Easements and profits

An easement is a right or privilege that the owner or occupier of one piece of land (the dominant tenement) has over the land of another (called the servient tenement), e.g. a right of way, light or support.

A *profit à prendre* is a right to take something from the land of another, e.g. to fish in his river.

Easements and profits are examples of rights *in alieno solo*, i.e. over the land of another (*see* 21: **16–22**).

20. Rentcharges

A rentcharge is rent (money payable from land) that is payable out of the profits of land to a person who has no tenurial interest in the land, e.g. where a tenant charges his land with an annual payment to his widowed mother until her death. (Where the recipient has a tenurial interest, e.g. a right of occupation, such money is called rentservice, e.g. the rent payable under a lease.)

Rentcharges could formerly be created by deed, will or statute. They can be extinguished by deed of release executed by the person entitled or by lapse of 12 years' non-payment without objection from the person entitled.

The owner of the rentcharge can enforce payment by:

(a) suing for debt;
(b) distraining (if the money is 21 days in arrears or more), i.e. by entering the land and seizing the tenant's chattels;
(c) taking possession of the land until the charge is paid; or
(d) in certain cases, appointing a receiver to take possession on his behalf.

The Rentcharges Act 1977, s. 2, prohibits the creation of new rentcharges. Under s. 3, every rentcharge will be extinguished at the expiry of 60 years from:

(a) the passing of the Act; or
(b) the date on which the rentcharge first became payable; whichever is the later.

Equitable interests

21. How they arise
They arise in the following ways:

(a) *express creation* — where A grants property to B to hold on *trust* for C, B becomes the legal owner and C acquires merely an equitable interest in the land (*see* Chapter 23);

(b) *implied creation:*

    (*i*) *an informal grant* of a fee simple, lease, or any of the interests listed in 20: **18** operates to create an equitable estate or interest (which may be converted into legal estate or interest under the rule in *Walsh* v. *Lonsdale* (*see* 20: **22**)) and, while a formal grant is one made by deed, an informal grant is one made in any other way, e.g. by letter;

    (*ii*) *any grant*, whether formal or informal, of an estate or interest not mentioned in the Law of Property Act 1925, s. 1, operates to create an equitable interest only, e.g. grants of entails and remainders (*see* 20: **5**).

22. The rule in *Walsh* v. *Lonsdale* (1882)
Legal estates and interests can be created only by deed or by will and an informal grant will create merely an equitable interest.

In such cases, however, equity will compel the grantor to execute a proper deed and so convert the equitable interest or estate into a proper legal interest or estate. This is done by ordering specific performance against the grantor — *see Walsh* v. *Lonsdale*.

Specific performance will be ordered in such a case only if:

(a) there is a binding written consent between the parties; or
(b) the equitable doctrine of part performance is applicable (*see* 5: **7**).

Where such a situation arises, the rule in *Walsh* v. *Lonsdale* lays down that the parties are to be treated as if their relationship was already formalised by deed. A binding agreement to create a lease is therefore usually as effective as a formal lease, i.e. the same covenants will apply on both sides. However, as the relationship of the parties pending the order for specific performance is only equitable, the grantee's interest is capable of being overreached on sale of the legal estate by the grantor (*see* 20: **24**).

23. Entails and future interests

These can now only exist as equitable interests, even though created by deed, under the Law of Property Act 1925, s. 1.

Consequently, after 1925, where there is an express grant of an entailed interest or a vested or contingent remainder, the grantee will obtain only an equitable interest.

Under the perpetuity rule, a grant of a future interest was void if there was any possibility that it might fail to vest in the grantee within 21 years after the death of a living person or persons, e.g. a grant 'to A for life, remainder to such of his children as become priests'. Here the grant to the children was void as none of them may ever decide to become priests.

The Perpetuities and Accumulations Act 1964 introduced a 'wait and see' rule whereby a gift is void only if circumstances make it clear that it *can vest only* outside the perpetuity period. A period of up to 80 years may be used as the 'test period'. This alternative system may be used *only* if the grantor specifically provides for it.

Accumulations of income are subject to similar restrictions.

24. Overreaching of equitable interests

In order to simplify conveyancing, the Law of Property Act 1925 provides that, wherever he sells it, a legal owner of land can convey a good title notwithstanding the equitable claims of any other person attaching to the land. Such equitable claims are said to be *overreached* or extinguished.

Thus if A and B are trustees of land for the benefit of C, they can sell the land without the concurrence of C and, if they do, C's interest in the land is overreached. His only claim will then be against the trustees for breach of trust (*see* 23: **31**).

In such cases the equitable or beneficial owner can sue to recover the land from the purchaser *only* if it can be shown that the purchaser knew or should have known of the equitable interest of C at the time he purchased the land. If, however, he is a bona-fide purchaser for value of the legal estate, without notice of the equitable claim, his purchase will overreach all equitable interests attaching to the land.

Strict settlements and trusts for sale

25. Strict settlements and trusts for sale

These are:

(a) *Strict settlement*. This is a trust the purpose of which is to secure the enjoyment of property by successive generations of beneficiaries, e.g. where a man wishes to prevent his heirs selling family heirlooms. The trustees in such a settlement are instructed to *retain* the property, not to sell it. However, the Settled Land Act 1925 now enables the tenant for life of settled land, i.e. the principal beneficiary, to sell the property or otherwise dispose of it himself without the concurrence of the trustees.

(b) *Trust for sale*. These are trusts in which the trustees are placed under a positive duty to sell the trust property, though they are generally given power to retain it for as long as seems advisable. After sale they must usually distribute the proceeds among the beneficiaries or invest the proceeds for their benefit.

(c) *Other* types of trust. There are several intermediary types of trust between these two above extremes. The general rules stated in Chapter 23 apply to all trusts *except* where the trust instrument lays down special rules.

26. Creation of strict settlements

These are created in the following way:

(a) *Inter vivos*. Where the settlor creates a settlement during his lifetime, he must do two things:

    (*i*) vest the property by the appropriate form of legal transfer in the trustees as legal owners;

    (*ii*) inform the trustees of their duties and the purposes of the trust.

Where the trust affects land, however, two documents are required to achieve these objects:

(a) *A vesting deed*, conveying the legal estate to the trustees.

(b) *A trust instrument*, which sets out the conditions of the trust. A purchaser of land from the trustees is concerned only with the vesting deed and, as he need not peruse the trust instrument (and can be prevented from doing so), he is not fixed with notice of the trust, therefore the interests of the beneficiaries in land can be more easily overreached (*see* 23:**3**).

In trusts of personalty, a trust instrument is required but not a vesting deed (unless the personalty is of a kind that should be transferred by deed, e.g. shares in a ship). Chattels can be transferred by mere delivery and the vesting in this case can therefore be oral.

(c) *By will*. Here the will is treated as the trust instrument and the property is conveyed to the trustees by the executors of the will signing a written authorisation, called a *vesting assent*.

27. Creation of trusts for sale

These most commonly arise by means of the operation of law, rather than by express creation.

By statute, a trust for sale arises automatically:

(a) wherever land is held by joint tenants;

(b) where executors hold property undisposed of by will;

(c) in cases of intestacy (*see* 24: **20**).

Progress test 20

1. Explain what was meant by tenure in medieval law. **(1, 2)**

2. Distinguish between an estate and an interest in land. **(4, 6)**

3. How do equitable estates and interests differ from legal estates and interests? **(7)**

4. What are future interests? Define: (a) reversion and (b) remainder. **(8, 9)**

5. How may a fee simple be created and how far is it true to say that the fee simple owner is the absolute owner of everything above, below or on his ground? **(12, 13)**

6. What is a term of years absolute, and how does it differ from a fee simple? **(10, 11, 13, 14)**

7. Explain the meaning of the following terms: (a) words of severance; (b) undivided shares; (c) *jus accrescendi* and (d) joint tenants. **(15–17)**

8. Define (a) easement and (b) *profit à prendre*. How does an easement differ from a profit? **(19)**

9. What is a rentcharge? How can it be created and how can it be enforced? **(20)**

10. Explain how an equitable interest may arise. **(21)**

11. State the rule in *Walsh* v. *Lonsdale* and explain its significance. **(22)**

12. What is the perpetuity rule?   **(23)**

13. Explain how an equitable interest can be overreached.   **(24)**

21
Leases, covenants and servitudes

Leases

1. Definition

A term of years absolute or lease means a tenancy of land for a period of time having certain duration. A lease is one of the two legal estates recognised by modern law under the Law of Property Act 1925, s. 1.

2. Kinds of tenancy

These are:

(a) *tenancy for fixed term* — a tenancy that is:
- (*i*) created by express agreement; and
- (*ii*) having a definite commencement and duration;

(b) *periodic tenancies* The tenant takes possession for an indefinite period but agrees to pay rent calculated on a yearly, quarterly, monthly or weekly basis and the tenancy so created is either yearly, quarterly, monthly or weekly according to the period over which rent is calculated, thus a grant 'To A at £800 per year' would be a yearly tenancy.

> NOTE: The period of notice required to terminate such a periodic tenancy would normally be: (a) six months for a yearly periodic tenancy; (b) three months for a quarterly tenancy; (c) one month for a monthly tenancy; (d) one week for a weekly tenancy. (These periods are subject to variation by agreement.)

(c) *tenancy at sufferance* This can only arise by implication of law where a tenant under a lease stays in possession ('holds over') after the expiry of his lease and he can be compelled to pay rent for as long as he remains, but the landlord can eject him at any time.

(d) *tenancy at will* This may arise by express agreement (rare) or by implication and may be determined at any time by either party, expressly or impliedly, e.g. on the death of either. Such a tenancy arises where possession is granted (with or without payment of rent) for no fixed period (where rent is accepted, a tenancy at will often becomes a periodic tenancy, weekly, monthly or yearly, depending on how the rent is calculated).

3. Creation of leases
How this is done depends on the period of time it is for:

(a) *leases for more than three years* must be created by deed in order to become a legal estate under the Law of Property Act 1925, s. 52, but a merely written lease creates an equitable interest capable of being converted into a legal estate by an order for specific performance — *see Walsh* v. *Lonsdale* (1882) (*see* 20:**22**) — and, even if merely oral, it may be enforced by equity in the same way if the equitable doctrine of part performance applies (*see* 5:**7**);

(b) *leases for not more than three years* need not be by deed and if supported by written evidence, these are legally enforceable provided they:

    (*i*) take effect in possession; and

    (*ii*) are at the best rent obtainable.

4. Determination of leases
Leases are determined:

(a) *by effluxion of time* — lease for a fixed period terminates automatically on the last day of the term without any notice being necessary;

(b) *by notice* — periodic tenancy requires to be determined by notice by the landlord or the tenant to coincide with the last day of any period and the length of notice may be fixed by agreement; otherwise it is implied by law, i.e. six months for yearly tenancies, one month for monthly tenancies or one week for weekly tenancies;

(c) *by surrender* to the tenant's immediate landlord;

(d) *by merger* where the tenant himself obtains a transfer of his immediate landlord's interest;

(e) *by forfeiture*, but only where the lease contains an express proviso that if the tenant breaks any of the covenants in the lease it is to be forfeited (*see* 21: **5**).

NOTE: The Leasehold Reform Acts 1967 and 1979 provide that, where a dwelling having a rateable value of not more than £750 (£1,500 in Greater London) has been leased for more than 21 years and has been occupied by the leaseholder for five years or more, the leaseholder has the right: (a) to enfranchise (i.e. buy the freehold), or (b) to extend the lease for 50 years. Failing agreement between the parties, the price for the freehold or rent for the 50 years can be fixed by the Lands Tribunal.

5.   Protection against forfeiture
This works in the following ways:

(a) *breach of covenant to pay rent* — the court will grant relief provided that:
   (i)   the tenant pays all arrears of rent and costs; and
   (ii) it is just and equitable that relief should be granted; and
   (iii) the tenant applies for relief within six months of the landlord taking possession of the land;

(b) *breach of other covenants* The landlord cannot forfeit until he has given reasonable notice (usually three months) specifying the breach complained of and requiring the tenant to remedy the breach and/or pay compensation if appropriate (Law of Property Act 1925, s.146). The tenant may then apply for relief at any time before the landlord has taken possession; relief may be granted on such terms as the court thinks just.

Covenants in a lease

6.   Express or implied covenants
In any lease the landlord may require the tenant to sign certain express covenants, e.g. to insure against fire. Where no covenants are expressed, the following covenants are implied by the landlord and the tenant (*see* 21:7, 8).

7.   Implied covenants by the landlord
These are:

(a) *covenant for quiet enjoyment*, i.e. that the tenant's possession will not be directly interfered with by the landlord or persons claiming under him;

(b) *covenant not to derogate from the grant*, i.e. that the landlord will not interfere with the tenant's enjoyment indirectly (in ways not amounting to breach of (a) above), say, by using adjoining premises in a 'manner inconsistent with the purpose of the lease';

(c) *fitness for habitation* — this is only implied in:
   (i)   furnished lettings; or

(*ii*) unfurnished lettings at low rents.

8. Implied covenants by the tenant
These are:

(**a**) *to pay the rent*;
(**b**) *to pay rates and taxes*, except those which are legally the landlord's personal obligation;
(**c**) *not to commit waste*, i.e. not to damage the property or permit it to depreciate unreasonably by neglect;
(**d**) *to repair* This obligation is primarily the landlord's and a tenant impliedly covenants merely to let the landlord enter and view the property to see what repairs are necessary, but if the lease is agreed subject to 'the usual covenants', the obligation to repair is transferred to the tenant.

9. Express covenants
In a formal lease the above covenants are usually set out expressly, plus the following additional covenants by the tenant:

(**a**) *not to assign or underlet* without the landlord's consent (the consent must not be unreasonably withheld: Landlord and Tenant Act 1927, s. 19);
(**b**) *to repair:*
>   (*i*) *long leases* — the tenant usually covenants to repair outside and inside;
>   (*ii*) *short leases* — the landlord covenants to repair outside and tenant inside;
(**c**) *to insure against fire.*

10. Enforceability of covenants
The original landlord and tenant are contractually liable on the covenants in the lease. Where the tenant assigns his lease (or himself takes a sub-tenant) or the landlord assigns his reversion, the binding effect of the covenants will depend on the law relating to restrictive covenants (*see* 21:**11–15**).

Restrictive covenants

11. Definition
Restrictive covenants are promises restricting the use of land and

which may be enforceable not only between the original promisor and promisee, but also between their assigns.

The enforceability of such covenants differs slightly:

(a) at law; and
(b) in equity.

12. Enforceability at common law

The benefit and burden of a covenant are enforceable in different ways at common law:

(a) *the benefit of the covenant* would pass to an assignee and be enforceable by him if the covenant touched and concerned land and was for the benefit of the land (not of the original covenantee personally), and the legal estate in the land had been obtained by the assignee.

(b) *the burden of the covenant* usually did not pass to the assignee, thus an assignee of a lease would not be bound by the tenant's obligations in the original lease.

13. Enforceability in equity

In equity;

(a) the *benefit of the covenant* would pass to an assignee if it touched and concerned land and the assignee had obtained an interest in the land that the covenant was intended to benefit;

(b) the *burden of the covenant* would pass to an assignee under the rule in *Tulk* v. *Moxhay* (1848) if:

    (*i*)   the covenant is *negative* in nature; and
    (*ii*) the assignee owns land capable of being *benefited*; and
    (*iii*) the burden of the covenant was *attached to the land* against which the claim is made and not merely against the assignee personally.

Thus, equity followed the law in its attitudes to the benefit of covenants and applied the more progressive *Tulk* v. *Moxhay* rule where the dispute involved the enforcement of the burden of a covenant.

Example

In *Tulk* v. *Moxhay* (1848), a sold land to B, exacting a covenant that B would not build on the land (the covenant to be enforceable against any person to whom B sold the land). B sold the land to C, who sold it to D (who took the land with notice of the covenant). D decided to build on the land and A sued for an injunction to prevent building. D relied on the doctrine of privity of contract (*see* 6:**6, 7**) and claimed he was not bound by the covenant, as he was not a party to it. It was held that the injunction was granted as the covenant 'touched and concerned' the land and has more than contractual implications.

14. Position now

The modern rules (following *Tulk* v. *Moxhay*) relating to covenants and their enforceability can be summarised as follows.

(a) the covenant must be for the benefit of a dominant tenement, which must be identifiable;

(b) an assignee *of the whole* of the dominant or quasi-dominant tenement may enforce the covenant;

(c) an assignee *of part* of the quasi-dominant tenement may enforce the covenant if:

(*i*) the intention in the original covenant appears to be that it shall pass for the benefit of part tenants;

(*ii*) the original intention was to benefit only part of the land, and the person claiming to enforce is the tenant of that part.

15. Discharge of covenants

This happens:

(a) *by waiver*;

(b) *by order of the court*;

(c) *by the Lands Tribunal* on the grounds that:

(*i*) the covenant has become obsolete; or

(*ii*) the persons benefited agree to the discharge; or

(*iii*) that discharge will not injure the persons benefited (Law of Property Act 1925, s. 84).

Easements and profits

16. *Jura in re aliena* (rights in the property of another)

Servitudes or rights over another's land are primarily of two kinds:

(a) *easements* — privileges without profit, e.g. rights of way, light, air support, water.

(b) *profits à prendre* — privileges giving a right to take something from another's land, e.g. hunting, shooting, fishing, grazing rights.

17. Nature of easements

These are privileges for the benefit of land rather than for the benefit of the owner of land, i.e. they are always appurtenant to land:

(a) *easements cannot exist in gross* — they cannot exist independently of ownership of land, i.e. cannot be personal rights, they must be appurtenant to land, i.e. must benefit a piece of land (and consequently the owner or tenant);

(b) *there must be a dominant and a servient tenement,* i.e. a piece of land to be benefited (the dominant tenement) and a piece of land burdened (the servient tenement);

(c) *they must be capable of definition,* i.e. must be capable of forming the subject matter of a grant.

Examples

(1) In *Re Ellenborough Park* (1956), A, B and C bought new houses overlooking a park and the owners of the park (who had provided the land on which the houses were built) covenanted not to allow building on the park. The park was sold to X, who decided to build. A, B and C claimed an easement to view the unbuilt park and to walk over it. X claimed that the rights claimed were too vague to constitute easement. It was held that easement was established.

(2) In *Phipps* v. *Pears* (1964), two separate but adjoining houses, Nos. 14 and 16 Market Street, were owned by A and B. No. 14 was demolished, leaving the wall of No. 16 exposed to the weather. The wall was not weatherproof as it had adjoined the wall of No. 14 and was not designed to be weatherproof. No. 16 sustained damage, and B sued for infringement of an *easement of protection*. It was held that there was no such easement known.

18. Nature of profits

Profits:

(a) *may exist in gross,* i.e. independently of the ownership or occupation of land. (but note **(c)** and **(d)** below);

(b) *may be several or common,* i.e. belonging to one person (several) or shared by a group (common);

(c) *appurtenant* are those attached by agreement to land (and therefore similar to easement) and to be enjoyed only by the owner of a particular piece of land;

(d) *apendant* are those attached by law to a piece of land, i.e. a common or pasture, e.g. certain village greens.

19. Acquisition of easements and profits

This is achieved:

(a) *by Act of Parliament*, e.g. where a local authority is given a right to build roads across lands;

(b) *by express reservation or grant* (note that the Law of Property Act 1925, s. 62, provides that a grant of land carries with it all privileges and easements attaching to the land, whether the grant mentions them or not, unless a contrary intention appears);

(c) *by implied grant or reservation*, e.g. where an easement of necessity is implied in favour of a grantor who has retained a plot of land entirely surrounded by the land sold and therefore needs a right of way to enter and leave his land (the courts are reluctant to imply such reserved easements even in such exceptional circumstances, the maxim being, 'a grantor must not derogate from his grant') — easements will be readily implied in favour of a grantee wherever necessary for reasonable enjoyment of the land;

(d) *by prescription* (presumed grant) The court may presume an easement or profit in favour of any person who can show he has exercised the right claimed provided:

- (*i*) the enjoyment has been continuous for the period proved; and
- (*ii*) has been exercised '*as of right*' (i.e. without the consent of the owner of the land) *nec vi, nec clam, nec precario* (neither by force, nor secretly, nor merely by permission).

20. Methods of prescription
These are:

(a) *at common law* By proof of user from 'time immemorial', i.e. since 1189 and in practice, any long user will suffice to raise a presumption that the right has existed since 1189, but this presumption may be rebutted by proof that the right did not or could not have existed at some time since 1189 (*see* 2:5);

(b) *lost modern grant* Because of the difficulty of proving use since 1189, the courts will sometimes presume that a grant was made at some time since then but has since been lost, provided long use can be proved, e.g. 20 years — *see Bridle* v. *Ruby* (1988);

(c) *under the Prescription Act 1832* This Act aimed at making prescription easier than under **(a)** and **(b)**, though both those methods still exist.

21. Prescription Act 1832
This covers the following:

(a) *Profits* —

(*i*) if the claimant can show 30 years uninterrupted enjoyment, his claim cannot be defeated merely by showing that the user must have commenced since 1189;

(*ii*) on proof that the profit was enjoyed for 60 years continuously, the profit is indefeasible save by showing that it was enjoyed only under a written consent;

(b) *easements other than light* — the same principles apply here as they do to profits, but in the case of easements the periods are:

(*i*) 20 years; and

(*ii*) 40 years;

(c) *easements of light* If the right was actually enjoyed for 20 years it becomes absolute and can be defeated only by showing that it was derived from a written consent — the Rights of Light Act 1959 (as amended by the Local Land Charges Act 1975) making the period 27 years in some cases also enables the owner of land over which light passes to forestall prescription by registering with the local authority a notice that operates as an automatic infringement (a notional 'spite fence'). It seems that the courts are prepared to enter into discussions about the 'amount of light that is required in modern times' — *see Ough* v. *King* (1967) and *Allen* v. *Greenwood* (1979).

22. Extinguishment of easements and profits
This is brought about by:

(a) *Act of Parliament*;

(b) *release*, express or implied;

(c) *union of dominant and servient tenements in the ownership of one person.*

Progress test 21

1. Define a lease and explain the various forms a lease can take. (1, 2)

2. Distinguish (a) between a yearly and a monthly tenancy and (b) between a tenancy at sufferance and a tenancy at will. (2)

3. How may a lease (a) be created and (b) be determined? (3, 4)

4. What protection has a tenant against forfeiture of his lease? (5)

5. What covenants are generally implied in leases (a) by the lessor and (b) by the lessee? **(7, 8)**

6. What is meant by a restrictive covenant and how far is such a covenant enforceable today? **(11, 13, 14)**

7. State the rule in *Tulk* v. *Moxhay* (1848) and summarise the facts of the case. **(13)**

8. How may a restrictive covenant be discharged? **(15)**

9. Define easements and *profits à prendre*. Give examples of each. **(16–18)**

10. How do easements differ from profits? **(16–19)**

11. How may an easement be acquired and how may it be extinguished? **(19, 22)**

12. Explain the rules governing the prescription of easements and profits. **(19–21)**

22
Securities

Securities generally

1. Meaning of security

A security is some right or interest in property given to a creditor so that, in the event of the debtor failing to pay the debt as and when agreed, the creditor may reimburse himself for the amount of the debt out of the property charged.

Both real and personal property may be charged with repayment of a debt in this way.

2. Kinds of security

These are:

(a) *Mortgages* A mortgage is an assurance to the creditor of the legal or equitable interest in property as security for the discharge of a debt or other obligation, subject to a proviso that on repayment the mortgage shall become void. The word comes from Norman-French, *mort/gage*, meaning dead pledge.

The characteristic of this type of security today is that possession of the thing mortgaged remains vested in the mortgagor (until the debt is overdue).

(b) *Pledge or pawn* A pledge is a deposit of chattels with a lender as security for repayment of a loan. If the pledgee is a professional lender upon this type of security the pledge is called a pawn and the lender a pawnbroker. Such transactions are regulated by The Consumer Credit Act 1974 (*see* 22: **16, 17**).

A pledge thus differs from a mortgage in that the pledgee has possession of his security, while ownership remains vested in the borrower. In a mortgage, the mortgagee does not get possession but does obtain a legal or equitable interest in the property subjected to the mortgage, which he can enforce by selling the property, etc., if the debt is not paid.

(c) *Liens* A lien is a right that a creditor may acquire over property of a debtor, real or personal, either to retain the property until the debt is paid (a possessory lien) or to seek a court order for sale of the property if the debt is unpaid (an equitable lien) (*see* 12:**28**).

A lien differs from a mortgage or pledge in that it arises by operation of law, not from any agreement between the creditor and debtor.

3. Mortgages of real and personal property

Real property can be mortgaged and personalty can be mortgaged or pledged. Mortgages of land are dealt with in 22:**5–13**, and mortgages and pledges of personalty in 22:**14–19**.

4. Legal and equitable mortgages

As a mortgage consists of the transfer or assurance to the mortgagee of an interest in the property charged, it follows that the interest so conferred may be either legal or equitable.

A *legal mortgage* is one under which the creditor receives a legal interest in the property. A legal mortgage of land must therefore be created by deed, as a legal estate or interest in land can be created only in this way (Law of Property Act 1925, ss. 51 and 52).

An *equitable mortgage* is one under which the creditor receives only an equitable interest in the property, e.g. a mortgage of land made otherwise than by deed.

Mortgages of land

5. Legal mortgages before 1925

Mortgages of land were generally created by conveying to the mortgagee the entire estate of interest of the mortgagor in the land, subject to a promise by the mortgagee to reconvey the property on repayment of the loan on a certain date (normally six months from the date of the mortgage).

After the date for repayment (the legal date for redemption), the mortgagor lost his legal right to the land. From this time onwards, however, equity recognised him as possessing an equitable right to redeem and so to recover his land. The mortgagor's possession of both (a) a legal right to redeem on the contracted date, and (b) an equitable right to redeem later, was called his *equity of redemption* and was an equitable interest in land, that he could sell, mortgage, leave by will, etc.

As, after the expiry of the legal date for redemption, the

mortgagor would have only an equitable interest in the land, any second mortgage created by him could only be an equitable mortgage, even though created by deed.

6.   Legal mortgages since 1925

The mortgage by conveyance was abolished by the Law of Property Act 1925, which provided that legal mortgages can now take only the following forms:

(a)   *By lease to the mortgagee* for a long term of years, subject to a proviso for cesser on redemption, i.e. that the lease should cease automatically on repayment of the loan plus interest.

Mortgages of freehold are commonly effected by a lease for 3,000 years, and mortgages of leasehold by a lease for the maximum period possible, e.g. the period of the tenant's lease less 10 days. For example, if A has a lease for 99 years, of which 67 years remain unexpired, he may create a mortgage in favour of B by granting him a lease for 66 years plus 355 days.

(b)   *By charge by deed expressed to be by way of legal mortgage* (Law of Property Act 1925, s. 85) The mortgagee acquires the same rights and remedies in both types of mortgage. The legal charge is fundamentally an invention of the Act, is simpler than the mortgage by lease and is becoming increasingly popular.

> NOTE: Any attempt to create a mortgage by the old method of conveying the fee simple to the mortgagee operates as a grant of a mortgage lease for 3,000 years subject to cesser on redemption: LPA 1925, s. 85.

7.   Equitable mortgages

If the mortgagee receives merely an equitable interest in the land, his mortgage is said to be *equitable*. This may occur in the following ways:

(a)   *Any mortgage of an equitable interest*, whether by deed or otherwise. If the mortgagor himself has only an equitable interest in the property (e.g. as beneficiary under a trust), he can confer only a like interest on the mortgagee.

Such a mortgage may be by lease or charge (as in legal mortgages), which must be in writing (whether by deed or not) and signed by the mortgagor or his agent (LPA 1925, s. 53) or by mere deposit of title deeds.

(b)   *Any informal mortgage of a legal estate or interest.* Thus, an attempt to create a legal mortgage otherwise than by deed, operates to create an equitable mortgage. Similarly, a binding contract to grant a legal mortgage in the future immediately creates an equitable mortgage, which may be converted into a proper sealed legal mortgage by an order for specific performance under the rule in *Walsh* v. *Lonsdale* (*see* 20:**22**). In order for there to be a binding contract that can be enforced by court action if necessary, there must be:

   (*i*) written evidence of the contract; or

   (*ii*) sufficient part performance (*see* 5:**7**).

Such a mortgage can therefore be created by an informal lease or charge or by a binding contract to grant a legal mortgage or by mere deposit of the title deeds to the land (with the mortgagee) by way of security. Banks often accept equitable mortgages by deposit of title deeds as security for short-term loans.

8. Remedies of a legal mortgagee

The remedies are the same whether the mortgage is by lease or by charge (LPA 1925, s. 87). The remedies are available for non-payment of loan and/or interest as and when due or for breach of some other covenant in the mortgage.

(**a**) *To sue for debt* on the mortgagor's covenant to repay. This is the basic remedy and is open to all creditors (whether secured by mortgage or not).

(**b**) *To take possession of the land* A mortgagee who takes possession must account to the mortgagor for any loss to the property occasioned by his default, and because of this liability, the remedy of possession is rarely exercised — *see White* v. *City of London Brewery* (1889).

(**c**) *To foreclose*, i.e. to obtain a court order extinguishing the mortgagor's equitable right to redeem and vesting the full legal estate in the mortgagee. The courts are often reluctant to grant this remedy, and will first give the mortgagor a warning (called a foreclosure order nisi) allowing him a further six months in which to redeem. If he fails to redeem by the end of this period, the order is made absolute (LPA 1925, s. 88).

(**d**) *To sell the land*, under the power implied in all mortgages by deed (whether legal or equitable), unless a contrary intention is expressed (LPA 1925, s. 101).

> NOTE: The power of sale arises as soon as the legal date for redemption has passed, but it cannot be exercised until: (a) three months' notice has been served requiring repayment of the loan and the notice has expired or (b) interest on the loan is in arrear for two months or (c) there has

been a breach of some other covenant in the mortgage than the covenant to repay (LPA 1925, s. 103).

A mortgagee cannot buy the land for himself, but he is not bound to obtain the best price possible. After sale he is a trustee of any surplus monies (after deducting the amount of his loan + interest) and must pay them to the mortgagor (or any subsequent mortgagees: *see* below).

(e) *To appoint a receiver*, under the power implied in all mortgages by deed (whether legal or equitable), unless a contrary intention is expressed (LPA 1925, s. 101).
The receiver is appointed to collect all profits of the land and to use them in paying:

    (*i*)   rates, taxes, etc;
    (*ii*) his own charges;
    (*iii*) the mortgage under which he is appointed;
    (*iv*) any residue to the mortgagor.

Legally the receiver is treated as agent for the mortgagor, who is therefore responsible for his defaults (unless the mortgage provides to the contrary). Consequently, it is more beneficial to the mortgagee in most cases to appoint a receiver than to take possession himself.

The mortgagee's remedies are concurrent, so he can appoint a receiver and order sale at the same time.

9. Remedies of equitable mortgagees
These are:

(a) *to sue for debt*;
(b) *to sell*, if the mortgage is by deed (otherwise only if the mortgage contains an express power of sale);
(c) *to appoint a receiver*, if the mortgage is by deed (otherwise only if the mortgage contains an express power);
(d) *to foreclose* (but this remedy is not available if the mortgage is by charge and not by lease).

An equitable mortgagee cannot take possession unless an express power is given by the mortgage deed or contract.

10. Mortgagee's other rights
These are:

(a) *To consolidate*, i.e. to insist that several mortgages must be redeemed simultaneously or not at all. Today consolidation is allowed only where:

    (*i*) consolidation is expressly reserved in both or all the mortgages to be consolidated (LPA 1925, s. 93);

    (*ii*) the legal date for redemption has expired;

    (*iii*) the same mortgagor created all the mortgages;

    (*iv*) the same mortgagee has, at some time, acquired all the mortgages to be consolidated — *see Pledge* v. *White* (1896).

(b) *To tack on further advances.* If A borrows money from X on a first mortgage and from Y on a second mortgage, X is entitled to repayment in priority over Y. However, if X makes a further loan to A, Y is entitled to repayment of his mortgage *before* the further mortgage to X, unless X is entitled to tack his second mortgage on to his first, so gaining overall priority. Today tacking is allowed only (*see* the LPA 1925, s. 94) where:

    (*i*) any intervening mortgagee agrees; or

    (*ii*) an obligation to make further advances is imposed on X in the first mortgage, i.e. where, in effect, loans are to be made by instalments as part of the same mortgage; or

    (*iii*) no notice of the intervening mortgage is available to X when he makes his further advance (registration of the intervening mortgage constitutes notice for this purpose (*see* 22:**13**)).

(c) *Other rights of the mortgagee.* A first mortgagee is entitled to take possession of the title deeds to the property. Any mortgage created by deed (whether a first or later mortgage) gives the mortgagee power to insure the property against fire, up to two-thirds of its value (LPA 1925, s. 101).

11. Redemption of mortgages

At common law, the mortgagor was only entitled to redeem on the legal date fixed by the contract. After expiry of this date, his rights in the land were terminated and the mortgagee became absolutely entitled.

Equity, however, applied the maxim 'once a mortgage, always a mortgage' and gave the mortgagor a secondary, equitable right to redeem even after expiry of the legal date for redemption. The two rights of redemption together, legal and equitable, were called the *equity of redemption*.

The equity of redemption is an equitable interest in land and can be sold, mortgaged, devised by will, etc. Any person who obtains the equity of redemption in a piece of land can redeem the mortgage, e.g. where the mortgagor's heir inherits it by will or upon intestacy.

The equity of redemption is extinguished by:

(a) sale or foreclosure by the mortgagee;

(b) the mortgagor releasing it to the mortgagee; or

(c) lapse of time under the Limitation Act 1980, s. 17, i.e. by the lapse of 12 years from the date on which the mortgagee went into possession of the mortgaged land.

(Mortgages of personalty are governed by the Limitation Act 1980, s. 20, which provides that no action may be brought to recover the principal money secured on any property more than 12 years after the right to receive it accrued.)

12. Clogs on the equity of redemption

Any agreement that attempts to bar the mortgagor's right to redeem is void. Similarly, provisions in a mortgage that would mean that after redemption the mortgagor would not get back his property free of the mortgagee's claims are also void.

Such stipulations in a mortgage are called 'clogs on the equity', as they attempt to defeat the equity of redemption.

The general rule is that laid down by Lord Parker in *Kreglinger* v. *New Patagonia Meat Co.* (1914):

> There is now no rule in equity which precludes a mortgagee, whether the mortgage be made upon the occasion of a loan or otherwise, from stipulating for any collateral advantage, provided such collateral advantage is not either (1) unfair and unconscionable, or (2) in the nature of a penalty clogging the equity of redemption, or (3) inconsistent with or repugnant to the contractual and equitable right to redeem.

This point was emphasised by Browne Wilkinson, J, in *Multiservice Bookbinding* v. *Marden* (1978):

> . . . in order to be freed from the necessity to comply with all the terms of the mortgage, the plaintiffs must show that the bargain, or some of its terms, was unfair and unconscionable; it is not enough to show that, in the eyes of the court, it was unreasonable.

Many of the cases involve a type of solus agreement, which is a mortgage granted on an undertaking by, say, a garage owner to buy all his petrol or by a publican to buy all his beer from the mortgagee. The courts have decided the following:

(a) *A mortgage cannot be made irredeemable*, but it is legitimate for the mortgagee to insist that redemption shall be postponed for a reasonable period, e.g. that the mortgagor may not redeem within 20 years — *see Knightsbridge Estates Trust Ltd* v. *Byrne* (1939).

(b) *The mortgage must not be in restraint of trade.* A garage was mortgaged, the mortgage to be repaid in instalments over 21 years. The garage-owner also undertook to sell only the mortgagee's petrol for the same 21 year period. This period was too long and the agreement was in restraint of trade (*see* 8: **21**) — *see Esso* v. *Harper's Garage* (1968).

(c) *After redemption*, the mortgagor must get back his property unfettered, i.e. free of all claims by the mortgagee. Thus, where a mortgagor of an inn covenanted to buy all his beer from the mortgagee, even after redemption, the covenant was void — *see Noakes & Co. Ltd* v. *Rice* (1902).

(d) *Collateral advantages* given to the mortgagee in the mortgage must cease upon redemption. Thus, if, in addition to promising to repay the loan, a publican covenants to buy all his beer from the mortgagee until redemption, such a provision is valid — *see Biggs* v. *Hoddinott* (1898) — but the covenant must cease to be binding as soon as the loan is repaid.

13. Priority of mortgages

The mortgagor may create several mortgages on the same property. Where there are several mortgages, the value of the property (when sold) may not be sufficient to pay all the mortgagees. In this case it is necessary to ascertain which mortgagees have the first claim on the proceeds of sale. The equitable rules governing priorities are now augmented by the LPA 1925, s. 97, and the Land Charges Act 1972, s. 4, as follows:

(a) *legal or equitable mortgages* protected by deposit of title deeds rank for priority from the date of creation;

(b) *puisne mortgages* (i.e. legal mortgages not protected by deposit of title deeds) rank from the date of registration as Class C land charges and are void against a purchaser (including a mortgagee or chargee) unless so registered;

(c) *equitable mortgages* not protected by deposit of title deeds are called *general equitable charges* and like puisne mortgages, rank from date of registration and are void against a purchaser of the land unless so registered.

A first mortgagee will normally insist on receiving title deeds, and consequently registration is mainly necessary in the case of subsequent mortgages.

NOTE: where tacking on of further advances is allowed, this may alter the order of priorities, even among registered mortgages (*see* 22:**10**).

Sub-mortgages may be created by a mortgagee who wishes to borrow money on the security of a mortgage he holds himself. If his mortgage is by lease, he may create a sub-mortgage by sub-leasing to his creditor for a shorter term than he himself holds from the mortgagor. If the mortgage is by charge, he must assign his charge to his creditor subject to a proviso for reassignment on repayment of the loan.

Mortgages of personalty

14. Kinds of mortgage

A mortgage of personalty may be created by *assigning* to the mortgagee the legal interest in the personalty, on condition of re-assignment on repayment of the loan. The type of assignment will depend on the means required by the law for transferring title to the particular kind of personalty involved. Shares, copyrights, insurance policies, etc., therefore need a written assignment; chattels may be assigned by mere delivery, so no document is required to mortgage them.

This method, however, is too informal for most cases. The lender may require documentary proof of his rights (especially as the chattels may be left in the possession of the mortgagor), and if he parts with possession, the mortgagor may also require documentary proof.

The two principal methods of mortgaging chattels are:

(a) *by conditional bill of sale*, where the mortgagor is to remain in possession (*see* 22:**15**);

(b) *by pledge*, where the mortgagee obtains possession until redemption (lenders who make their business out of this sort of loan are called pawnbrokers and their transactions pawns (*see* 22:**16** and **17**).)

There are also special forms of company charges (*see* 22:**18**).

15. Conditional bills of sale

A bill of sale is 'a document given with respect to the transfer of chattels, and is used in cases where possession is not intended to be given', said Lord Esher, M.R., in *Johnson* v. *Diprose* (1893).

An *absolute* bill of sale is a documentary assignment of chattels, giving title without delivery. As most goods are sold by delivery, absolute bills of sale are rare — see *Koppel* v. *Koppel* (1966). They are appropriate, for example, where a ship is sold while at sea.

A *conditional* bill of sale is one used where chattels are given as security for a loan, i.e. it transfers ownership to the lender, but subject to a condition that the chattels shall be re-assigned to the borrower on repayment.

Conditional bills of sale must comply with the requirements of the Bills of Sale Acts 1878 and 1882, as follows:

(a) the bill must be *registered* at the Central Office of the Supreme Court within seven days of its creation and is void unless so registered;

(b) it must be *attested* by at least one witness, otherwise it is void;

(c) the *consideration* for the bill must be truly stated;

(d) the *interest* payable and the *date of repayment* must be stated, together with any additional conditions;

(e) *the chattels comprised* in the bill must be inventoried.

A conditional bill takes its priority from the date of registration.

The lender's remedy is seizure of the goods on grounds of failure to repay the loan as agreed, bankruptcy of the debtor or fraudulent dealing with the goods so as to remove them from the lender's power.

16. Pledges at common law

A pledge involves actual or constructive delivery of the chattels to the pledgee. Constructive delivery might be by giving the pledgee the key to a warehouse in which the goods are stored.

The pledgor remains the legal owner of the goods and the pledgee becomes a bailee who must return the goods on repayment as agreed. The pledgor is entitled to demand a receipt for deposit of the goods.

The pledgee owes a duty of care for the goods, and must make good any loss if they are damaged or stolen due to his negligence. (If, however, the goods were taken from him by robbery, i.e. theft with violence, he is excused from liability.) The pledgee generally has no right to use the goods deposited. Even if there is no written agreement, he still has a possessory lien over the goods until payment of his loan.

Plain common law pledges are comparatively uncommon, having been almost entirely replaced by pawns under the Consumer Credit Act 1974 (*see* 22:**17**).

17. Pledges under the Consumer Credit Act 1974

These are commonly called 'pawns' and the professional money-lenders 'pawnbrokers'; only the first of these is still used in the statutory provisions.

The 1974 Act, ss. 114–121 lay down the following rules:

(a) A pawn-ticket must be given for the pledge.

(b) Pawns are to be redeemable any time within six months or during the period agreed for the credit, whichever is longer; longer periods may be fixed by agreement between the parties.

(c) Pledges not redeemed within the redemption period:

    (*i*) if for less than £25, belong absolutely to the pawnbroker; and

    (*ii*) if more than £25 may be realised, but it is not necessary for them to be sold by public auction (as used to be the case).

Charges for keeping the pledge must not be increased on account of their non-redemption until after the period of credit and may be reviewed by the courts if excessive. (Surplus monies to go the pledgor.)

(d) Pledges are redeemable any time before sale.

(e) The pawnbroker must deliver up the goods on presentation of the pawn-ticket and repayment. (He is entitled to presume that the person presenting the ticket is lawfully justified in taking the goods.)

18. Company charges

Company charges are void against the liquidator and creditors unless registered with the Registrar of Companies. The types of company charges are listed in the Companies Act 1985, s. 396. They fall into two categories.

(a) *Fixed charges*. These are charges over a specific asset.

(b) *Floating charges*. 'A floating security is an equitable charge on the assets for the time being of a going concern. It attaches to the subject charged in the varying condition in which it happens to be from time to time. It is of the essence of such a charge that it remains dormant until the undertaking charged ceases to be a going concern, or until the person in whose favour the charge is created intervenes', said Lord MacNaghten in *Government Stock Co* v. *Manila Railway* (1897).

19. Suitability of pledges, etc.

Whether personalty is mortgaged by assignment or by pledge depends largely on the type of property (as well as upon who is to receive possession of the goods):

(a) *Choses in action,* such as shares and insurance policies, are generally mortgaged by assignment in due form, but they can also be pledged if so desired.

(b) *Small chattels* are generally pawned (or otherwise pledged), e.g. jewels, watches, clocks, clothing, musical instruments.

(c) *Large chattels,* or large quantities of chattels, will generally not be accepted by a pawnbroker or other pledgee because of difficulties of storage and, therefore, must generally be mortgaged by conditional bills of sale, e.g. collections of paintings, household furniture, grand pianos. Conditional bills of sale are unpopular because of the publicity involved in registration (*see* 22:**15**). A borrower will, therefore, usually try to pledge his chattels, if he can find a lender willing to accept them. Otherwise he will try to borrow without security.

Progress test 22

1. What kinds of security are recognised in English law? (**1, 2**)

2. Distinguish between a legal and an equitable mortgage. (**4**)

3. Explain the distinction between the legal date for redemption of mortgages of land and the equitable right to redeem. What is the equity of redemption? (**5, 11**)

4. What forms may be taken by legal mortgages after 1925? (**6**)

5. How may an equitable mortgage occur? (**7**)

6. Summarise the remedies open to a legal mortgagee where the mortgagor has failed to repay principal or interest. (**8**)

7. What remedies are available to equitable mortgagees? (**9**)

8. In what circumstances may a mortgagee today be able to apply the remedies of consolidation and tacking? (**10**)

9. How may the equity of redemption be extinguished and what is meant by a 'clog' on the equity? (**11, 12**)

10. Summarise the rules governing the priority of mortgages. **(13)**

11. How can chattels be mortgaged?   **(14)**

12. What is a bill of sale and how does an absolute bill differ from a conditional bill of sale?   **(15)**

13. Summarise the main provisions of the Consumer Credit Act 1974 that control the making of pawns.   **(17)**

14. What would be the most appropriate ways of using the following properties as security for a loan: (a) a grand piano; (b) a collection of valuable paintings; (c) an expectation under a will; (d) a leasehold house and (e) an interest under a trust fund?   **(19)**

Part five

Equity and trusts

23
Equity and trusts

Equity

1. Nature and scope of equity

Since the fusion of law and equity (*see* 1: **26**) all courts have been able to apply equitable rules and to award equitable remedies. Equity was never a complete system of law. It filled the gaps in the common law. Whereas the courts must apply the rules of common law and statute where appropriate, they have always had a discretion whether or not to apply an equitable rule or award an equitable remedy. In exercising this discretion, the courts have traditionally applied the maxims of equity (*see* 23: **2**), which are a set of principles of fairness. Where the rules of law and equity conflict, equity prevails.

The importance of equity today is in six areas of law:

(a) *equitable doctrines* (*see* 23: **4**)

(b) *equitable remedies* (*see* 23: **5–7**)

(c) *equitable protection* — equity has always protected persons at a disadvantage, such as women, infants or the victims of fraud and examples of such protection are the rules of estoppel (*see* 6:**5**) or rescission for fraud (*see* 8: **9**);

(d) *trusts* — the trust (*see* 23: **8–31**) is the great creation of equity;

(e) *securities* — the mortgage was a creation of the common law but its development has been by equity (*see* Chapter 22);

(f) *succession* — the rules governing administration of the assets of a deceased have also been developed by equity (*see* Chapter 24).

2. Maxims of equity

These maxims still express the spirit of equity, although they do not really cover all the technical rules now applicable:

(a) *equity will not suffer a wrong to be without a remedy* — an example is the enforcement of trusts, which were not recognised at common law;

(b) *equity follows the law*, which really means two things:

(*i*) equity will not interfere where a rule of law applies unless that rule is unconscionable;

(*ii*) equitable interests follow the model of legal ones; thus we have equitable mortgages or assignments as well as legal mortgages or assignments (*see* 12: **2** and 22: **4**);

(**c**) *he who seeks equity must do equity* Equitable relief will not be granted to a plaintiff who is not prepared to act equitably himself — this is the basis of estoppel (*see* 6: **5**) and applies to the present or future conduct of the plaintiff;

(**d**) *he who comes into equity must come with clean hands* This maxim differs from (**c**) in that it applies to the plaintiff's past conduct — *see Overton* v. *Bannister* (1844), in which a woman who was entitled to trust money when she came of age and fraudulently misrepresented to her trustees that she was of age and they paid the money — she could not obtain the money again when she really did come of age;

(**e**) *delay defeats equity or equity aids only the vigilant* — unreasonable delay in bringing a claim will defeat it, which is the equitable doctrine of *laches*;

(**f**) *equality is equity* — thus, in matrimonial cases, the basic inference may be that the parties should divide the property equally, but it has been said that, as Lord Pearson said in *Gissing* v. *Gissing* (1970), 'the decision of cases of this kind has been made more difficult by excessive application of the maxim "Equality is Equity" ' so the courts try to award a share proportionate to the parties' contributions;

(**g**) *equity looks to the intent rather than the form* — equity will, for example, treat a transaction as a mortgage, if that is its intention, even though it may describe itself as a conveyance;

(**h**) *equity acts in personam* The essence of equity is the enforcement of moral obligations owed by the defendant to the plaintiff personally, so, where T acquires property from G by promising to use it for the benefit of B, even if the promise is unsupported by consideration, equity will compel T to carry out his bargain, but B's right is a personal, moral right against T only. Therefore, if T sells the property to X, who has no notice of the trust, B cannot enforce the action against T for breach of trust (*see* 23: **31**) — equitable remedies operate against the defendant personally (*see* 23: **5–7**);

(**i**) *equity looks on that as done which ought to be done* — this is the basis of the rule in *Walsh* v. *Lonsdale* (1882) (*see* 20:**22**) and of the doctrine of conversion (*see* 23: **4(a)**);

(**j**) *equity imputes an intention to fulfil an obligation* — thus, where a man is under a duty and does something capable of being construed as performance of that duty — for example where A dies owing B £1,000 and in his will leaves a legacy of £1,000 to B — equity will not allow B both to take the legacy *and* to sue A's executors for the debt. 'Equity presumes that a man intends to be just before he would be generous', which is the basis of the doctrines of performance and satisfaction (*see* 23: **4(c)**, **(d)**));

(k) *where there is equal equity, the law shall prevail* — where plaintiff and defendant have equally sound moral claims, strict legal rules will decide between them;

(l) *where the equities are equal, the first in time shall prevail* — where two persons make equally sound competing claims to property, equity will usually decide in favour of the person whose claim arose first.

3. The limits of equitable protection

Where T acquires property from G by promising to use it for the benefit of B (*see* **2(h)**), both T and B have some interest in the property:

(a) T is the legal owner;
(b) B is equitable or beneficial owner.

Legal and equitable interests in property may thus exist side by side in the same property:

(a) the *legal owner* is in a stronger position;
  (*i*) he can sell the property so as to defeat, or, *overreach* any equitable interests attaching to it;
  (*ii*) he can recover the property from any person who wrongfully dispossesses him as his rights are *in rem*, fixed to the property itself;
(b) the *equitable owner* is in a weaker position:
  (*i*) his rights in the property itself (as opposed to the value of the property) can be destroyed or overreached by sale by the legal owner;
  (*ii*) his rights are enforceable only against persons who acquire legal ownership of the property with knowledge of his equitable interest.

Under the rule in *Pilcher* v. *Rawlins* (1872), such equitable interests are overreached by the *bona-fide purchaser of the legal estate for value without notice.*

Each of these four elements is important:

(a) *bona-fide* — the purchaser must act in good faith and make reasonable inquiries to see if any person has equitable claims upon the property;

(b) *purchaser . . . for value* — the purchaser must give valuable consideration (*see* 6:1) and not merely receive it as a gift or for illusory consideration;

(c) *of the legal estate*;

(d) *without notice* — if the purchaser has failed to make the reasonable inquiries that would give him actual notice of equitable interests he may be deemed to have constructive notice.

Equitable doctrines

4. Equitable doctrines

These consist of the following:

(a) *Conversion* Sewell, MR, in *Fletcher* v. *Ashburner* (1779) (*see Re Sweeting* (1988)) defined it in the following way:

> Money directed to be employed in the purchase of land, and land directed to be sold and turned into money, are to be considered as that species of property into which they are directed to be converted; and this in whatever manner the direction is given; whether by will, by way of contract, marriage articles, settlement or otherwise, and whether the money is actually deposited, or only covenanted to be paid, whether the land is actually conveyed or only agreed to be paid. The owner of the fund or the contracting parties may make land money or money land.

This is the principle behind the trust for sale (*see* 20: **25**).

(b) *Election* The doctrine of election was carefully discussed by Buckley, LJ, in *Re Gordon's Will Trusts* (1978). He distinguished two classes:

    (*i*) *Dual gifts* A by the same will confers beneficial interests on both B and C. The gift to B is valid; that to C is not as the property involved, in fact, belongs to B. B may then elect. Either he does not give effect to the will at all or he takes his own benefit and gives effect to A's gift to C.

    (*ii*) *Mutual settlements* Here A and B each make a settlement in favour of each other (or of C). B cannot both enforce the trust under which he benefits and repudiate the other.

(c) *Performance* Kenyon, MR, said in the case of *Sowden* v. *Sowden*

(1785), 'Where a man covenants to do an act, and he does an act which may be converted to a completion of this covenant, it shall be supposed that he meant to complete it'. The covenant may be of two kinds:

    (*i*) covenant to purchase and settle land;
    (*ii*) covenant to leave personalty by will or on intestacy.

(d) *Satisfaction* This doctrine differs from performance only in one way. The act done is different from the act agreed to be done. It will amount to satisfaction if such was the intention of the party acting.

(e) *Subrogation* This doctrine applies, for example, in a contract of insurance. After the insurer has met a claim, he acquires all the rights the claimant had against third parties. Many legal actions are brought by insurers in the name of an insured under the doctrine of subrogation.

Equitable remedies

5. Equitable remedies

One of the chief ways in which equity supplemented the law was by granting auxiliary or additional remedies where the common law remedy of damages proved inadequate. Equitable remedies have two characteristics:

(a) equity acts *in personam*;
(b) equitable remedies are discretionary — they are only awarded when the maxims of equity are met (*see* 23: **2**).

There are six remedies to consider:

(a) *specific performance* (*see* 23: **6**);
(b) *injunction* (*see* 23: **7**);
(c) *receivers* — a receiver may be appointed to collect and preserve all the profits of a property on behalf of a mortgagee, creditor, shareholder, or the beneficiary under a trust;
(d) *rescission* — rescission allows an innocent party to escape from his obligations under a contract on the ground of fraud or mistake (*see* 8: **2**, **9**) and, under the Misrepresentation Act 1967, s. 2(2), damages may sometimes be awarded instead of rescission (*see* 8: **8**);
(e) *rectification* — equity will rectify a document that wrongly records the intentions of the parties to it (*see* 7: **9**);
(f) *account* — a financial statement or account may be ordered where a fiduciary relationship exists and, thus, an agent may be required to

account to his principal, or a trustee to his beneficiary or one partner to another.

6. Specific performance

This is a remedy for breach of contract and consists of a court order compelling the defendant to perform his side of the contract. Specific performance is always discretionary and will only be awarded in the following circumstances.

(a) *where damages would be inadequate* — examples are as follows:
> (*i*) contracts for the sale or leasing of land, provided the requirements of writing or part performance are fulfilled (*see* 5: **7**);
> (*ii*) contracts to deliver specific or ascertained goods (Sale of Goods Act 1979, s. 52);
> (*iii*) contracts for the sale of valuable and unique chattels (*see Sky Petroleum* v. *VIP Petroleum* (1974)) and specific performance may be awarded in addition to or instead of damages;

(b) *where the enforcement of the order would not require constant supervision by the court* — specific performance will not be awarded to enforce a building contract or a contract of employment, but it may be awarded where the court can tell the defendant exactly what he must do and has been used to enforce a covenant to repair property under a lease — as Megarry, V-C, said in *Tito* v. *Waddell (No. 2)* (1977), 'The real question is whether there is a sufficient definition of what has to be done in order to comply with the order of the court';

(c) *where the contract is mutually enforceable* — a minor plaintiff cannot obtain specific performance of a contract that would not be binding on him (*see* 6:**10**), as it would be impossible for the adult defendant to claim specific performance against the infant;

(d) *where* the plaintiff has himself acted inequitably.

7. Injunction

An injunction is a court order. Usually it is *negative* or *prohibitory*, forbidding a person to do something. In rare circumstances it may be mandatory, and command a person to do something. Mandatory injunctions are rare because the courts will not make an order that requires supervision.

Injunctions may take different forms:

(a) a *quia timet* injunction may be awarded to prevent an apprehended injury before it has occurred, but only where there are strong grounds for supposing it to be imminent, and where the court can tell the defendant exactly what he must do: *Morris* v. *Redland Bricks* (1970);

(b) an *interim or interlocutory* injunction may be granted pending the decision of a case and two recently developed varieties of interim injunction are of particular interest:

(*i*) the Mareva injunction (from the case of *Mareva Companies Naviera SA* v. *International Bulk Carriers SA* (1975)), which prevents a debtor from transferring assets out of the jurisdiction of the court prior to final judgment;

(*ii*) the Anton Piller order (from *Anton Piller KG* v. *Manufacturing Processes Ltd* (1976)), which prevents a defendant from destroying or disposing of evidence in his possession before the trial;

(c) a *perpetual* injunction may be granted when a dispute has finally been settled and where damages are inadequate, while an interim injunction forbidding interference with a right of light is *made* perpetual when the right of light has been finally proved in court.

An injunction may be appropriate in a wide variety of cases:

(a) *contract* — whereas specific performance may enforce the performance of a contract (*see* 23:**6**), an injunction may restrain a breach. Sometimes an injunction can do in a negative manner what could not be done by specific performance: in *Warner Bros.* v. *Nelson* (1937), a film star under an exclusive contract was forbidden by injunction from making films with any other company;

(b) *tort* — an injunction may be granted to prohibit continuance of a nuisance or to forbid a trespass;

(c) *trusts* — an injunction may be granted to forbid a trustee from selling trust property to the detriment of beneficiaries.

An injunction will not be granted unless the party seeking it has sufficient interest in the matter. An injunction to enforce a public right can only be sought with the consent of the Attorney-General in a *relator* action (*see* 3: **7**). This was re-stated by the House of Lords in *Gouriet* v. *Union of Post Office Workers* (1977). The refusal of the Attorney-General to give his consent to a *relator* action is not subject to review by the courts.

Trusts

8. The nature of trusts

A trust is a relationship in which a person called a *trustee* is compelled, as legal owner, to hold real or personal property for the benefit of another person, called the *beneficiary* or *cestui que trust*. There may be several trustees in any trust and several beneficiaries. A trustee may himself be one of the beneficiaries. A trustee of property may be thought of as the legal owner, and the beneficiary as the beneficial or equitable owner.

There are four matters to consider:

(a) *classification* — trusts are of two kinds, as follows:
    (*i*) a *private trust* is for the benefit of a specified group of beneficiaries (*see* 23: **10–13**);
    (*ii*) a *charitable* or *public* trust is for a general charitable purpose, such as the advancement of education, which is for the benefit of a large and fluctuating group of people (*see* 23: **14–17**);

(b) *creation* — a person who creates a trust is called the *settlor* and trusts can arise in three ways:
    (*i*) a private or public trust can be created by *express* words of the settlor (*see* 23: **11**);
    (*ii*) a private trust may be presumed from the intentions of the settlor and it is then called an implied or *resulting* trust (*see* 23: **19**);
    (*iii*) a private trust may arise independently of express words or intention and it is then called a *constructive* trust (*see* 23: **20**, **21**);

(c) *variation of trusts* (*see* 23: **22**, **23**);

(d) *trustees*:
    (*i*) appointment (*see* 23: **24–26**);
    (*ii*) duties and powers (*see* 23: **27–31**).

9. Discretionary trusts and powers of appointment

There are three different situations to consider:

(a) the settlor S leaves property to the trustee T on trust for A, B and C, then T must divide the property equally between A, B and C — this is an *ordinary trust*;

(b) the settlor S leaves property to the trustee T on trust for such of A, B and C as T may decide — this is called a *discretionary trust*;

(c) the settlor S leaves property to such of his children A, B and C, as his widow W shall appoint with a gift over to D — this is called a *power of appointment*.

There is one great difference between a discretionary trust and a power of appointment. The trustee of a discretionary trust must

exercise his discretion. The property will go to such of A, B and C as
T may decide, but it must eventually go to at least one of them. If T
fails to decide, the court will intervene. As Lord Wilberforce said in
McPhail v. *Doulton* (the *Baden* case) (1970), 'the court, if called on to
execute the trust power, will do so in the manner best calculated to
give effect to the settlor's or testator's intentions. It may do so by
appointing new trustees, or by authorising or directing
representative persons of the classes of beneficiaries to prepare a
scheme of distribution, or even, should the proper basis appear, by
itself directing the trustees so to distribute.' (*See also Re Locker's
Settlement* (1977).) In the case of the power of appointment, however,
W may never exercise it at all. Then the property will eventually pass
to D and there is nothing A, B or C can do about it.

There was formerly a second great difference, that of the test for
certainty of objects. Since the decision in the *Baden* case, however,
the tests have been assimilated (*see* 23: **12**).

Express private trusts

10. Express creation

An express trust is one expressly created by a settlor, *inter vivos*
or by will, for the benefit of a particular person or group of persons
and not for some institution or public purpose. To create an express
private trust, the following conditions must be satisfied.

(a) *the three certainties* There must be the following:
  (i) *certainty of subject matter* — the trust property must be
      sufficiently identified, and the shares that the beneficiaries
      are to receive.
  (ii) *certainty of words* (*see* 23: **11**) — if there is no certainty of
      subject matter or words the trust fails and the grantee takes
      the property absolutely;
  (iii) *certainty of objects* (*see* 23: **12**) — if there is no certainty of
      objects, the particular trust will fail, but the grantee will be
      compelled to hold the property on trust for the settlor or his
      heirs;
(b) *proper constitution* (*see* 23: **13**);
(c) *perpetuity and inalienability* The trust must not infringe:
  (i) the rule against perpetuity (when the property *vests*); or
  (ii) the rule against inalienability (the *duration* of the trust) (these
      rules are considered elsewhere — *see* 20: **23**);

(d) *avoidance of voluntary settlements* Where a person conveys property to a trustee with intent to defraud his creditors, the settlement may, in certain circumstances, be avoided. Voluntary conveyances, for which no consideration has been given in return, and, indeed, those at a significant undervaluation, can be avoided and the property recovered from the trustees if the settlor goes bankrupt soon after making the settlement (Insolvency Act 1986, s. 339).

If all the terms have been completely defined by the settlor and the property has been conveyed to the trustees, the trust is executed. If some further document is necessary to convey the property to the trustees the trust is executory. A completely constituted trust (*see* 23: 13) will be enforced whether it is executed or executory. Revocation of the trust is impossible once it has been completely constituted, unless:

(a) the settlor expressly reserved the power to revoke; or
(b) the trust was procured by fraud; or
(c) the trust was created by mistake.

11. Certainty of words

The words of the grant must be clear and impose a definite duty on the trustee to carry out the trust. The test is the settlor's intention derived from the words used. No particular words need to be used, although the courts will more readily infer a trust where the word 'trust' has been used. A trust will not normally be inferred where the words are only precatory, that is merely requesting performance of the trust. A grant of property by will to the testator's widow 'in full confidence that she will do what is right as to the disposal thereof between my children', was found to be insufficiently commanding and the trust failed — *see Re Adams & Kensington Vestry* (1884). As Lopes, LJ, said in *Re Hamilton* (1895), 'The court will not allow a precatory trust to be raised unless on the consideration of all the words employed it comes to the conclusion that it was the intention of the testator to create a trust'. It has recently been said, however, that simple people are not expected to use 'stilted lawyers' language'. The court may even be satisfied with the repeated words, 'This money is as much yours as mine' — *see Paul* v. *Constance* (1977).

12. Certainty of objects

Certainty of objects means that the beneficiaries must be

sufficiently identified. In the case of powers of appointment (*see* 23: 9) the House of Lords decided in *Re Gulbenkian's Settlement Trusts* (1970) that a power was valid if it could be said with certainty whether any given individual was or was not a member of the class of objects of the power and that the power did not fail simply because it was impossible to ascertain every member of the class. In the *Baden* case (1970), a majority of the House of Lords decided that the same test was to be applied to ascertain the validity of a trust. The trust in that case was established to benefit the staff of a company. The trust deed authorised the trustees to make 'at their absolute discretion grants to or for the benefit of any of the officers and employees or ex-officers or ex-employees of the company or to any relatives or dependants of any such persons'. The House decided that this was capable of constituting a trust. Lord Wilberforce, delivering the majority speech, assimilated the tests of trust and power. 'The trust is valid if it can be said with certainty that any individual is or is not a member of the class.' Lord Wilberforce also mentioned the case where 'the meaning of the words used is clear but the definition of beneficiaries is so hopelessly wide as not to form "anything like a class" ' so that the trust is administratively unworkable or, in Lord Eldon, LC's, words, one that cannot be executed (*Morice* v. *Bishop of Durham* (1805)). I hesitate to give examples for they may prejudice future cases, but perhaps "all the residents of Greater London" will serve. I do not think that a discretionary trust for "relatives" even of a living person falls within this category'.

13. Completely and incompletely constituted trusts

A trust is not completely constituted until:

(a) the property has actually been *vested* in the trustees; or
(b) there is a *binding contract* so as to vest the property in them; or
(c) the settlor has made a binding *declaration of trust* to the effect that he will hold the property himself as trustee for some other person.

In creating the trust, any necessary formalities must be observed. Under the Law of Property Act 1925, s. 53(1)(b), (c), a declaration of trust respecting land must be proved by writing and the disposition of an equitable interest or trust subsisting at the time of the disposition must be in writing. A valid will, of course, must observe other formalities, (*see* 24: 1–3). If the settlor has failed to observe the necessary formalities a resulting trust will arise (*see* 23: 19(d)).

Express public trusts (charities)

14. Charities

The first attempt to define charities was in the preamble to the Charitable Uses Act 1601. That Act has now been repealed, but the Charities Act 1960 provides: 'Any reference in any enactment or document to a charity within the meaning, purview and interpretation of the Charitable Uses Act 1601, or of the preamble to it, shall be construed as a reference to a charity within the meaning which the word bears as a legal term according to the law of England and Wales'. It is not altogether clear what this means, but the definition of charities in current use is that of Lord Macnaghten in *Commissioners of Income Tax* v. *Pemsel* (1891): ' "Charity" in its legal sense comprises four principal divisions: trusts for the relief of poverty; trusts for the advancement of education; trusts for the advancement of religion; and trusts for other purposes beneficial to the community, not falling under any of the preceding heads'. In considering these four categories, it is necessary to remember two things. First, that changing social values render some of the old cases on education and religion unsafe. Second, in all cases it is necessary 'that the trust is one the administration of which the court itself could if necessary undertake and control' — Russell, J, in *Re Hummeltenberg* (1923).

(a) *Trusts for the relief of poverty* Poverty is a relative term. A gift for 'ladies of limited means' may be charitable whereas one to provide housing for 'the working classes' may not be. Trusts under this heading are an anomalous exception to the rule that a charitable trust must benefit the public or a section thereof—*see Re Scarisbrick* (1951).
(b) *Trusts for the advancement of education Re Hopkins' Will Trusts* (1965) raised the issue of whether a gift to the Francis Bacon Society for 'finding the Bacon–Shakespeare manuscripts' could be for the advancement of education. In deciding that it could be, Wilberforce, J, considered the meaning of 'education'. He thought that it 'must be used in a wide sense, certainly extending beyond teaching, and that the requirement is that, in order to be charitable, research must either be of educational value to the researcher or must be so directed as to lead to something which will pass into the store of educational material, or so as to improve the sum of communicable knowledge in an area which education may cover—education in this last context extending to the formation of literary taste and appreciation'. A majority of the Court of Appeal has decided that the preparation of

law reports is for the advancement of education, in spite of the commercial use to which they are put — see *Incorporated Council of Law Reporting* v. *Attorney-General* (1971). The holding of conferences with 'a political flavour' was upheld in *Re Koeppler's* (1986). An educational trust must be for the public benefit within the terms outlined by Lord Simonds in *Oppenheim* v. *Tobacco Securities Trust Co. Ltd* (1951):

(i) the possible beneficiaries must not be numerically negligible; and

(ii) the quality that distinguishes them from other members of the community must be a quality which does not depend on their relationship to a particular individual.

(c) *Trusts for the advancement of religion* Cross J, said in the case of *Neville Estates Ltd* v. *Madden* (1961), 'As between different religions the law stands neutral, but it assumes that any religion is at least likely to be better than none'. Again, there must be some element of public benefit. In *Gilmour* v. *Coats* (1949), a trust for the benefit of a Carmelite convent of strictly cloistered and purely contemplative nuns was found not to be charitable. However, it does not seem to be necessary that the religious group is small — see *Re Watson* (1973).

(d) *Trusts for other purposes beneficial to the community* Other purposes within the 'spirit and intendment' of the 1601 preamble are charitable: for example, relief of the aged, repair of churches, the preservation of places of historic interest. Other worthy and improving purposes may be charitable, but there are three conditions they must meet:

(i) *non-political object* A trust whose main object requires legislation is not charitable as its purpose is primarily political — see *National Anti-Vivisection Society* v. *IRC* (1948);

(ii) *charitable purpose primary* A trust for a police athletic association is not charitable as its main purpose is merely recreational — see *IRC* v. *Glasgow City Police Athletic Association* (1953);

(iii) *public benefit* It was said *obiter* by Lord Simonds in *IRC* v. *Baddeley* (1955) that 'A trust cannot qualify as a charity within the fourth class in Pemsel's case if the beneficiaries are a class of persons not only confined to a particular area but selected from within it by reference to a particular creed'.

15. Advantages of charities

The great advantage to a trust in qualifying as a charity is that it is exempt from income and other taxes. This is why so many of the relevant cases involve the IRC (*see* 23: **14**(d)). There are a number of other advantages attaching to charitable status:

(a) *certainty of objects* If the settlor's general intention appears to be charitable, the gift will not fail merely because the particular object named has ceased to exist. (The *cy-près* rule will apply — *see* 23: **16**).

(b) *perpetuity* A charitable trust will fail if it does not vest within the perpetuity period — *see Re Lord Stratheden and Campbell* (1894), but, on the other hand, if a gift is made to Charity A with provision for the property to pass to Charity B if the first charity ceases to exist, the gift over will be valid even though it may not vest within the perpetuity period.

(c) *inalienability* — charities are not subject to the rule against inalienability.

(d) *purpose trusts* — charitable trusts are valid purpose trusts (*see* 23: **18**).

16. *Cy-près*

If the particular object of the trust fails but the donor has shown a general charitable intention, the court will apply the property to some similar charitable object. This is called application *cy-près* . The doctrine *cy-près* applies where two conditions are met.

(a) *general charitable intention* This is 'a paramount intention on the part of a donor to effect some charitable purpose which the court can find a method of putting into operation' and it is contrasted with a particular charitable disposition to take effect if, but only if, it can be carried into effect in a particular specified way — *see* Buckley, J., in *Re Lysaght* (1966). The Charities Act 1960, s. 14, deems a general charitable intention to exist whenever:

   (*i*) the donor of property cannot be identified or found, for example because he donated to a collecting box; or

   (*ii*) the donor of property has disclaimed in writing all rights to the return of the property if the object of the trust fails;

(b) *failure of original purpose* This is now defined in the Charities Act 1960, s. 13 (as extended by the Charities Act 1985). Trust property may be applied *cy-près* in any of the following situations:

   (*i*) when the original purpose has been fulfilled or is incapable of fulfilment;

   (*ii*) when the original purpose required only part of the property;

   (*iii*) when the property can more efficiently be used in

conjunction with other property applicable for similar purposes;

(iv) when the original purpose was defined by reference to a geographical area or class of persons that is no longer appropriate;

(v) when the original purpose has been adequately provided for by other means or has ceased to be regarded as charitable.

17. Administration

Most charities have to be registered with the Charity Commissioners, who, as constituted under the Charities Act 1960, have general powers of supervision over the administration of such trusts. This power is shared with the courts. Registration is conclusive proof of charitable status. The enforcement of charitable trusts could formerly only be at the suit of the Attorney-General, but the Charities Act 1960 enables the Charity Commissioners to authorise the trustees and certain other persons to commence proceedings for enforcement where necessary.

Purpose trusts

18. Purpose trusts

Public charitable trusts are purpose trusts. An express private trust can never be a purpose trust for three reasons. In the case of a purpose trust:

(a) there is no certainty of objects (*see* 23: 12);

(b) there are no beneficiaries and therefore there is no one able to enforce the trust under the rule in *Saunders* v. *Vautier* (1841) (*see* 23: 22);

(c) the court can control the exercise of the trust, 'for an uncontrollable power of disposition would be ownership, and not trust'.

These three reasons were given by Sir William Grant, MR, in *Morice* v. *Bishop of Durham* (1804).

A number of old cases, however, have allowed non-charitable purpose trusts. Trusts for the maintenance of tombs and monuments, which lack the element of public benefit necessary to be charitable, or for the maintenance of animals have been allowed where they have arisen 'under wills and are intimately connected with the deceased'. Such trusts, said Roxburgh, J in *Re Astor's Settlement Trusts* (1952), can 'properly be regarded as anomalous and exceptional and in no way destructive of the proposition that traces its descent from or through Sir William Grant'.

Sir William Grant's proposition has recently been amended in two types of case:

(a) *Purpose for ascertainable beneficiaries* In *Re Denley's Trust Deed* (1968), land was conveyed to trustees 'for the purpose of a recreation or sports ground for the benefit of the employees of the company'. Recreational purposes are not charitable (*see* 23: **14**(d)(ii)). Goff, J, decided that the trust was nevertheless valid. The beneficiaries, as employees of the company, were sufficiently ascertainable. The court could control the trust by restraining any improper use of the land. 'Where the trust, though expressed as a purpose, is directly or indirectly for the benefit of an individual or individuals, it seems to me that it is in general outside the mischief of the beneficiary principle'. (Compare *R. v. District Auditor, ex parte West Yorkshire Metropolitan County Council* (1986).)

(b) *Unincorporated associations* — in *Neville Estates* v. *Madden* (1961), Cross, J distinguished three types of gift to an unincorporated association:

 (i) a gift to the present members as joint tenants so that any member can sever his share and take it if he ceases to be a member;

 (ii) a gift to the present members subject to their contractual rights and liabilities towards each other, then a member cannot sever this share and, on his death or resignation, it will accrue to the then existing members;

 (iii) a gift for the purposes of the association — Cross, J thought that a gift in this category would fail unless the association were a charity, but, in *Re Lipkinski's Will Trusts* (1977), however, Oliver, J found otherwise and he decided, in the case of a gift for the construction of new buildings for an association, that such a gift was valid where it was for a purpose within the association's powers — here the members were the beneficiaries and, as such, were 'able to enforce the trust or, indeed, in the exercise of their contractual rights, to terminate the trust for their own benefit.'

Resulting trusts

19. Resulting trusts

A resulting trust is one where the court infers that the settlor intended to create a trust in favour of himself or of his heirs or nominees and the benefit results to the donor. This is sometimes called an *implied* trust.

A resulting trust arises in four situations.

(a) *Failure to exhaust beneficial interest* The problem in *Re West Sussex Constabulary's Fund Trusts* (1970) arose out of the amalgamation of the Sussex police forces: what was to be done with the money remaining in the West Sussex Widows, Children and Benevolent Fund, which was not a charitable trust? Goff, J, distinguished between:

(*i*) money raised by collecting boxes, raffles and sweepstakes — here the donor's intention was to part with the money absolutely and, as the trust was not a charity, the *cy-près* rule (*see* 23: **16**) could not apply, so the money would go to the Crown as *bona vacantia*.

(*ii*) money representing donations and legacies — this was given for a purpose that had failed and would be held on resulting trust for the donors and their estates (compare *Re Bucks Constabulary Fund (No. 2)* (1979)).

(b) *Failure of trust* If A vests property in B as trustee for an object that fails, for example because the beneficiary is dead, B will hold the property as trustee for A or his heirs.

(c) *Purchase in the name of another* If A buys property with his own money but has it conveyed to B, it will be presumed that he intended not to make a gift to B, but that B should hold the property as trustee for A or his heirs. Where B is the wife or child of A, the *presumption of advancement* arises. That is, that A intended to advance the interests of his wife or child, and the purchase will be treated as an absolute gift to B unless there is clear evidence to the contrary.

(d) *Voluntary transfer* In *Vandervell* v. *IRC* (1967), the issue was whether the trust was completely constituted (*see* 23: **13**). The settlor directed the trustees of a trust he had established to transfer shares to X with an option for the trustees of a second trust, in favour of the settlor's children, to re-purchase. Before the option was exercised, a high dividend was to be declared on the shares and this would constitute the benefit to X. No doubt the transfer was effective to give X the legal estate in the shares. The IRC, however, maintained that the settlor had failed to transfer the beneficial interest as he had not executed a document under the Law of Property Act 1925, s. 52(1)(c), and that there must be a resulting trust in favour of the settlor on which he could be taxed. By a majority, the House of Lords rejected this: 'If the intention of the beneficial owner in directing the trustee to transfer the legal estate to X is that X should be the beneficial owner, I can see no reason for any further document or further words in the document assigning the legal estate also expressly transferring the beneficial interest: the greater includes the less', said Lord Upjohn.

Constructive trusts

20. Constructive trusts

'A constructive trust is one that arises when a stranger to a trust already constituted is held by the court to be bound in good faith and in conscience by the trust in consequence of his conduct and behaviour.' It is 'a trust to be made out by circumstances' said Bowen, LJ, in *Soar* v. *Ashwell* (1893). A constructive trust arises by operation of law in the following circumstances:

(a) *Vendor's lien* If the vendor of land transfers possession to the purchaser before the purchase price is wholly paid, he has a lien over the land until he is paid in full. Until then, the purchaser holds the land as constructive trustee for the vendor.

(b) *Purchaser's lien* A similar situation arises where a purchaser has paid a deposit on land and the sale is called off for some reason other than the purchaser's default. Here the purchaser has a lien over the land for his deposit and the vendor is a constructive trustee for that amount.

(c) *Trustee profiting from his trust* Trustees must not profit from their trust and, if one receives a benefit for himself as a result of his position he can be compelled to hold the benefit as constructive trustee on the same trusts as if it were part of the express trust — see *Keech* v. *Sandford* (1726) (*see* 23: **29**).

(d) *Mortgagee's power of sale* A mortgagee who exercises his power to sell the mortgaged property holds any surplus monies, after deducting the amount of his loan plus interest, on constructive trust for the mortgagor (*see* 22: **8–10**).

(e) *Transferee of trust property* Where a person buys trust property from a trustee *knowing* that it is being sold in breach of trust, he holds the property on constructive trust for the beneficiaries. Similarly, if trust property is transferred to an agent, such as a solicitor, with notice of the trust, he will hold on constructive trust and will be liable if he misapplies funds — *see Soar* v. *Ashwell* (1893).

(f) *Fraudulent conveyance of property* If property is conveyed with an oral arrangement that X can continue to live there it may be held on constructive trust to allow X to remain there — *see Bannister* v. *Bannister* (1948).

21. Secret trusts

Secret trusts are a form of constructive trust in that they are imposed by the courts. The principle was explained by Lord Sumner in *Blackwell* v. *Blackwell* (1929): 'A court of conscience finds a man in the position of an absolute legal owner of a sum of money, which has been bequeathed to him under a valid will, and it declares that, on proof of certain facts relating to the motives and actions of the testator, it will not allow the legal owner to exercise his legal right to do what he will with his own. This seems to be a perfectly normal exercise of general equitable jurisdiction'. This will arise in two types of case:

(a) *fully secret trusts*, where no trust is disclosed at all;
(b) *half secret trusts* where the fact of a trust is disclosed but not the nature of the trust nor the identities of the beneficiaries.

A secret trust arose in *Ottaway* v. *Norman* (1971). T lived with his housekeeper H. T's son by his former wife, S, often visited them. T told S that when he died the house would go to H and on her death, she would leave it to S. T duly left the house to H and died. Later, H also died, but she left the house to X. Brightman, J, decided that X was bound by a secret trust in favour of S. 'It will be convenient to call the person on whom such a trust is imposed the "primary donee" and the beneficiary under that trust the "secondary donee". The essential elements that must be proved to exist are:

(a) the intention of the testator to subject the primary donee to an obligation in favour of the secondary donee;
(b) communication of that intention to the primary donee; and
(c) the acceptance of that obligation by the primary donee either expressly or by acquiescence'.

Variation of trusts

22. Variation before 1958

Under the rule in *Saunders* v. *Vautier* (1841), the beneficiaries entitled to the whole beneficial interest if all of full age can join together to put an end to the trust. Apart from this rather drastic step, it is possible in some circumstances to vary the terms of a trust while keeping it in existence. The main power to vary is contained in the Variation of Trusts Act 1958 (*see* 23: **23**). There are four other powers of variation that, although not repealed or limited by the 1958 Act, have, in practice, been superseded by it (there is also a power to vary trusts on divorce under the Matrimonial Causes Act 1973):

(a) *common law* The common law jurisdiction to vary trusts was reviewed by the House of Lords in *Chapman* v. *Chapman* (1954) and it may arise in four exceptional circumstances:

    (*i*) to allow *conversion* (*see* 23: **4**(*a*)) of the property of a beneficiary who is a minor;

    (*ii*) to allow *salvage* in cases 'not foreseen or anticipated by the author of the trust where the trustees are embarrassed by the emergency that has arisen': Romer, LJ, in *Re New* (1901);

    (*iii*) to allow the property to be used for the *maintenance* of a beneficiary;

    (*iv*) to approve a *compromise* arrangement where there is genuine dispute about rights.

(b) *Trustee Act 1925, s. 57* This allows the court to give trustees (other than the trustees of a settlement: *see* (c)) power to sell, lease, mortgage or purchase property where this is desirable for the 'management or administration' of the property if the court thinks this expedient but the trust does not give the trustee such power: 'The object of s. 57 was to ensure that trust property should be managed as advantageously as possible in the interests of the beneficiaries, and, with that object in view, to authorise specific dealings with the property' said Lord Evershed, MR, in *Re Downshire's Settled Estates* (1953);

(c) *Settled Land Act 1925, s. 64* This enables the court to authorise any transaction concerning settled land (*see* 20: **25**) 'which in the opinion of the court would be for the benefit of the settled land';

(d) *Trustee Act 1925, s. 53* This enables the court to order the conveyance of property to which a minor is beneficially entitled 'for the maintenance, education or benefit' of the minor.

23. Variation of Trusts Act 1958

The Variation of Trusts Act 1958 enables the court to approve any variation. There are three aspects to consider.

(a) *Extent of the Act* The Act applies to:
    (*i*) any property, real or personal;
    (*ii*) any trust arising before or after the passage of the Act;
    (*iii*) any will, settlement or other disposition.

(b) *Extent of the variation* The Act applies to 'any arrangement (by whomsoever proposed, and whether or not there is any other person beneficially interested who is capable of assenting thereto) varying or revoking all or any of the trusts, or enlarging the powers of the trustees of managing or administering any of the property subject to the trusts'.

(c) *Extent of the approval* The court may approve on behalf of:
    (*i*) a beneficiary who is a minor or other person incapable of assenting;
    (*ii*) any person, whether ascertained or not, who may at some future date become a beneficiary;
    (*iii*) any unborn person;
    (*iv*) any person with an interest under a protective trust. (A protective trust is a trust under the Trustee Act 1925 s. 33, whereby on the bankruptcy or other default of the principal beneficiary the property is held on a discretionary trust.)

Except under (*iv*), the court may not approve a variation on behalf of any person unless it is for the benefit of that person.

Under the rule in *Saunders* v. *Vautier* (1841) (*see* 23: **22**), beneficiaries of full age and understanding acting together can revoke the trust. The Act authorises the court to give approval either to revoke or to vary the trust on behalf of beneficiaries who are not of full age and understanding or who are not ascertained. The Act is used to vary trusts in order to reduce liability to taxation. It gives the courts a discretion whether or not to approve any proposed variation and, although they normally allow schemes to avoid tax, they may decline to do so if the variation is not otherwise advantageous to the beneficiaries. In *Re Weston's Settlements* (1969), Lord Denning, MR, summarised the court's attitude:
    (*i*) In exercising its discretion, the function of the court is to protect those who cannot protect themselves: it must do what is truly for their benefit;
    (*ii*) it can give its consent to a scheme to avoid death duties or other taxes;

(*iii*) the court should not consider merely the financial benefit to the minors or unborn children, but also their educational and social benefit.

In that case, a proposal to transfer the trust to Jersey, although it would avoid English taxes, was found to be not sufficiently advantageous. 'There are many things in life more worthwhile than money. One of these things is to be brought up in this our England, which is still "the envy of less happier lands". I do not believe it is for the benefit of children to be uprooted from England and transported to another country simply to avoid tax . . . Children are like trees: they grow stronger with firm roots.'

Appointment and retirement of trustees

24. Capacity
A trustee may be:

(a) *Any sane person of full age* Appointment of a minor is void.

(b) *A trust corporation* A trust corporation means the Public Trustee or any corporate body empowered by law to conduct trustee business (Trustee Act 1925, s. 68). The *Public Trustee* is a state official established by the Public Trustee Act 1906 as a corporation sole. If he accepts appointment he can be sole trustee or one of several. The advantages of the Public Trustee are:

(*i*) being a trust corporation it never dies;
(*ii*) the state is responsible for any breach of trust.

The disadvantages of the Public Trustee are:

(*i*) it cannot act for a charitable trust;
(*ii*) it cannot run a trust business without the consent of the Treasury.

In trusts of personalty there may be any number of trustees. In trusts of land the maximum number is four and in practice receipts must be given by at least two (Trustee Act 1925, ss. 14 and 34).

25. Appointment
This is done in the following ways:

(a) *Under the trust* The settlor usually appoints the first trustees when the trust is created. Once the trust is established, he has no further power of appointment, unless such a power is expressly reserved in the trust instrument. The trust instrument may alternatively give express power to some other person.

(b) *Under the Trustee Act 1925, s. 36* Trustees are usually appointed under this statutory power. It is exercised by:

    (*i*) the person nominated by the trust instrument; or

    (*ii*) the last surviving trustee or his personal representatives.

The statutory power can be exercised to replace a trustee who:

    (*i*) is dead;

    (*ii*) remains out of the United Kingdom for more than 12 months;

    (*iii*) desires to be discharged;

    (*iv*) refuses to act;

    (*v*) is unfit to act, for example, owing to bankruptcy;

    (*vi*) is incapable of acting, for example, owing to age or insanity;

    (*vii*) is a minor;

    (*viii*) is removed under a power in the trust instrument.

(c) *By the court* The court has two powers to appoint trustees:

    (*i*) *Trustee Act 1925, s. 41* — the court can appoint a new trustee when it is found 'inexpedient, difficult or impracticable so to do without the assistance of the court' and application to the court may be made by any beneficiary or trustee (s. 58);

    (*ii*) *Judicial Trustees Act 1896* — here the court appoints some court official, such as the Official Solicitor, to act as a judicial trustee under the supervision of the court.

26. Termination of trusteeship

This is achieved in the following ways:

(a) *disclaimer* — a trustee may always disclaim a trust provided he has not already done something to signify his acceptance, such as taking possession of part of the trust property, and a disclaimer is usually effected by deed;

(b) *retirement* — a trustee can retire:

    (*i*) under a court order;

    (*ii*) with the consent of the beneficiaries if they are all of full age and capacity;

    (*iii*) under a power in the trust instrument;

    (*iv*) under the Trustee Act 1925, s. 39. — to retire under these provisions, the trustee must execute a deed and leave a trust corporation or two persons to carry on the trust; obtain the consent by deed of his co-trustees; and sign a vesting declaration transferring the property to the new or continuing trustees;

(c) *replacement: see* 23: **25**(b);
(d) *removal: see* 23: **25**(c).

Duties and powers of trustees

27. Duties

The trustees are under a duty to obey the court when it intervenes and, in certain circumstances (*see* 23: **22**), to obey the directions of the beneficiaries. The trustees are also subject to certain general duties:

(a) *to obtain control of the trust property;*
(b) *to take care of the trust property* There are two elements to this:
  (*i*) trustees must take such care as an ordinary prudent man would take of his own property and they are liable for losses occasioned by breach of such duty; the standard will be higher for 'professional' trustees, such as trust corporations — *see Bartlett* v. *Barclays Bank Trust Co. Ltd (N.I.)* (1980);
  (*ii*) trustees must invest in securities authorised by the Trustee Act 1925 and the Trustee Investments Act 1961 — *see British Museum* v. *AG* (1984) and *Steel* v. *Wellcome Trustees Ltd* (1988).
(c) *to sell wasting assets* — under the rule in *Howe* v. *Dartmouth* (1802), it is presumed that the settlor's intention was for his trustees to convert (*see* 23: **4(a)**) wasting assets and hazardous or otherwise unauthorised investments;
(d) *to keep accounts* (*see* 23: **5(f)**);
(e) *to distribute the trust property to those entitled;*
(f) *not to delegate performance of their duties* (*see* 23: **28**);
(g) *not to profit from the trust* (*see* 23: **29**).

28. *Delegatus non potest delegare* ('a delegate must not delegate')

A trustee cannot delegate his duties. He can, however, in certain circumstances, perform those duties through agents:

(a) where authorised by the *trust instrument*;
(b) where this is necessary in the *ordinary course of business*, for example employing a builder to do necessary repairs;
(c) where authorised by *statute*:
  (*i*) *professional services* — a trustee may employ professional people, such as solicitors, accountants, bankers and stock-brokers, for specialised work and he is not liable for their

default provided he has selected them with care (Trustee Act 1925, s. 23);

(*ii*) *surveyors* — where a trustee lends money on the security of a mortgage, he may employ a surveyor to value the property and, if it is later found that the value of the mortgage advance exceeds the true value of the property, the Trustee Act 1925, s. 8, provides that the trustee will not be liable if he lent the money on the advice of the surveyor and he did not lend more than two-thirds of the valuation;

(*iii*) *deputies* — a trustee going overseas for more than one month may by power of attorney, appoint a deputy to act for him in his absence, but he remains personally liable for the acts or default of such a deputy (Trustee Act 1925, s. 28).

29. Duty not to profit from the trust

Profit must be distinguished from indemnification and remuneration:

(a) *profit* — a trustee must not make any profit from his office, unless expressly authorised by the trust instrument, and can be made to refund any unauthorised profit — *see Guinness PLC* v. *Saunders* (1988);

    (*i*) a trustee cannot generally buy trust property — *see Fox* v. *Mackreth* (1788);

    (*ii*) a trustee cannot obtain renewal of a trust lease for his own use — *see Keech* v. *Sandford* (1726);

    (*iii*) if a trustee speculates in unauthorised investments (*see* 23: 27(b)(ii)), the trust is entitled to any profit while the trustee is personally liable to make good any losses — *see Docker* v. *Somes* (1834);

(b) *indemnification* — a trustee may reimburse himself for expenses properly incurred in performance of his duties (Trustee Act 1925, s. 30(2));

(c) *remuneration* is either:

    (*i*) under the trust instrument; or

    (*ii*) awarded by the court;

The principles of remuneration were discussed by the Court of Appeal in *Re Duke of Norfolk's Settlement Trusts* (1979):

    (*i*) the court's jurisdiction to award remuneration is wholly exceptional, to be exercised sparingly;

    (*ii*) normally the court only awards remuneration when this is necessary to obtain the services of a particular trustee or of some particular kind of trustee, such as a trust corporation,

and the Public Trustee has a statutory right to charge for his
services;

(*iii*) possibly the court will award remuneration where an implied
promise to pay on behalf of the beneficiaries is found;

(*iv*) if the level of remuneration is fixed by the trust instrument
the court will not alter it;

(*v*) the court is reluctant to award remuneration unless
application is made promptly.

30. Powers of trustees

The Trustee Act 1925 gives trustees various powers that they can
exercise at their discretion.

(a) *maintenance* — trust money may be used for the maintenance,
education or benefit of a beneficiary who is a minor (s. 31).

(b) *advancement* — trust money can also be used for purposes such as
the purchase of a house for a beneficiary (s. 32);

(c) *sale* or *mortgage* of trust property (ss. 13 and 16);

(d) *insurance* of trust property up to three-quarters of its value (s. 19);

(e) *settlement of claims* by or against the trust (s. 15), but, before
distributing trust property, the trustees should advertise for
claimants in the *London Gazette* and a local newspaper giving at least
two months' notice of the last date for submission of claims and they
will then be under no liability to claimants coming forward after that
date (s. 27);

(f) *investment* authorised by the Trustee Act 1925 and the Trustee
Investments Act 1961.

31. Breach of trust

A trustee is liable to compensate the trust for his own or his
agent's breach of trust. He is only liable for the breach of a co-trustee
if he has contributed to it by his own wilful default (Trustee Act 1925,
s. 30(1)). A trustee is in wilful default if 'he knows that he is
committing, and intends to commit, a breach of his duty, or is
recklessly careless in the sense of not caring whether his act or
omission is or is not a breach of his duty' said Romer, J, in *Re City
Equitable Fire Insurance Co. Ltd* (1925). Thus, a trustee would be liable
for loss occasioned by improperly leaving it — *see Townley* v. *Sherborne*
(1634). Where a breach has been committed, beneficiaries have two
remedies:

(a) to sue the trustees personally for damages for breach of trust;

(b) to obtain a tracing order to pursue and recover trust property wrongfully held by any person — *see Re Diplock* (1950) — but land cannot be recovered from a bona-fide purchaser for value without notice (*see* 23: **3**).

Under normal principles of contribution, a trustee who has compensated the trust may claim for contribution from his co-trustees. In addition, a trustee must indemnify others where:

(a) all are made liable for a breach that he alone committed;
(b) he was a solicitor and counselled the breach; or
(c) he was a beneficiary as well as a trustee — *see Chillingworth* v. *Chambers* (1896).

A trustee may be relieved from liability where:

(a) the court so orders using its powers under the Trustee Act 1925, s. 61;
(b) the Limitation Act 1980 (as amended) debars an action; or
(c) an adult beneficiary releases the trustee from liability with full knowledge of the facts.

Progress test 23

1. Define the nature and scope of equity. **(1, 3)**

2. Briefly summarise the maxims of equity and illustrate the modern working of the maxims by discussing a case in which one of the maxims applied. **(2)**

3. What are the equitable doctrines? **(4)**

4. In what circumstances will the remedy of specific performance be awarded for a breach of contract? **(6)**

5. In what situations is an injunction available? **(7)**

6. Distinguish a trust from a power of appointment. **(9)**

7. What are the requisites of an express private trust? **(10–13)**

8. What is a charitable trust? **(14, 15)**

9. Describe the operation of the *cy-près* doctrine. **(16)**

10. In what circumstances can a purpose trust exist?   **(18)**

11. A buys Blackacre and has it conveyed into the joint names of his solicitor X and Mrs A. What trust will arise here?   **(19)**

12. What is a secret trust?   **(21)**

13. In what circumstances may trusts be varied?   **(22, 23)**

14. Who can be a trustee? How are trustees appointed?   **(24, 25)**

15. What duties are imposed on trustees by law, in the absence of anything to the contrary in the trust instrument?   **(27–29)**

16. What powers are given to trustees by the Trustee Act 1925?   **(30)**

17. When is a trustee liable for breach of trust?   **(31)**

Part six

Law of succession

Law of succession

Requisites of a valid will

1. Characteristics of a will

A will is a declaration made by a person during his lifetime of his intentions concerning the disposal of his property after his death. The maker of the will is called the *testator*. The basis of the modern law is the Wills Act 1837, as amended by the Administration of Justice Act 1982.

A will has certain characteristics:

(a) *ambulatory* — a will has no effect until the death of the testator;

(b) *revocable* — a testator cannot make his will irrevocable;

(c) *sole expression of testamentary wishes* —

> 'The law, on a man's death, finds out what are the instruments which express his last will. If some extant writing be revoked, or is inconsistent with a later testamentary writing, it is discarded. But all that survive this scrutiny form part of the ultimate will or effective expression of his wishes about his estate. In this sense it is inaccurate to speak of a man leaving two wills; he does leave, and can leave, but one will' said Lord Atkinson in the case of *Douglas-Menzies* v. *Umphelby* (1908).

A will may, however, be rectified by court order, so as to give effect to a testator's intentions (where the court is satisfied that it fails to express those due to a clerical error or a failure to understand his instructions: Administration of Justice Act 1982, s. 20). A supplement to a will is called a *codicil*.

(d) *proper law of the will* —

    (*i*) wills of land are governed by the law of the country in which the land is situated, i.e. the *lex situs*;

    (*ii*) wills of personal property, i.e. moveables, must be made in accordance with the law of the testator's domicil at his death;

a will is not necessarily revoked by a change of domicil after its execution (Wills Act 1837, s. 3).

2. Testamentary capacity

By virtue of the Wills Act, 1837, s. 7, and later Acts, any person of full age and sound mind may make a valid will provided it is made in the proper form (*see* 24: **3, 4**).

The only exception to this is that the will of a soldier or sailor 'being in actual military service' is valid even though the soldier or sailor is under age or his will is not in proper form (Wills Act 1837, s. 11). This provision is explained and extended to airmen by the Wills (Soldiers and Sailors) Act 1918. A soldier, sailor or airman is on 'actual military service' if he is serving with forces who are or have been engaged in military operations or who are believed to be about to so engage. Seamen on shore-leave and airmen training overseas for military operations are therefore included — *see Re Wingham* (1949). The court can order a *statutory* will for an adult patient under the Mental Health Act 1983, s. 96.

3. Formalities of a valid will

The Administration of Justice Act 1982, s. 17, has relaxed the formal requirements for making wills, previously provided for in the Wills Act 1837, s. 9. The new provisions are as follows. No will shall be valid unless:

(a) it is in writing and signed by the testator or by some other person in his presence and by his direction; and
(b) it appears that the testator intended by his signature to give effect to the will; and
(c) the signature is made or acknowledged by the testator in the presence of two or more witnesses present at the same time; and
(d) each witness either:

    (*i*) attests and signs the will; or
    (*ii*) acknowledges his signature in the presence of the testator (but not necessarily in the presence of any other witness) but no form of attestation shall be necessary.

So, a will must be written down somewhere, usually in a formal document (although in *the Goods of Barnes* (1926) it was written on an eggshell). Further, it must be signed and it cannot be signed first and written later — *see Wood* v. *Smith* (1991).

4. Witnesses

The testator's signature must be attested by at least two witnesses who must be present when the testator signs or acknowledges his signature — *see Re Olding* (1842).

A blind person cannot witness a will or codicil, as he cannot actually see the signature — *see Re Gibson* (1949) — but an illiterate person can be a witness, as he can see the signature even if he cannot read it.

The testator must be in such a position that he can see the witnesses sign if he wishes to do so — *see Newton* v. *Clarke* (1839) — and he must be aware of what they are doing, e.g. not so near death that he cannot understand — *see Jenner* v. *Ffinch* (1879). 'What could possibly be the object of the legislature, except that the witnesses should see and be conscious of the act done, and be able to prove it by their own evidence; if the witnesses are not to be mentally, as well as bodily, present, they might be asleep, or intoxicated, or of unsound mind' — in *Hudson* v. *Parker* (1844).

If any beneficiary, or the husband or wife of a beneficiary, attests a will, the attestation is valid, but the gift to the witness or his spouse will fail and is void (Wills Act 1837, s. 15). However, if there are sufficient (i.e. two) qualified witnesses apart from the beneficiary or beneficiary's spouse then the gift will not fail (Wills Act 1968, s. 1).

Property that may be disposed of by will

5. Disposable property

Under the Wills Act 1837, s. 3, a will can dispose of all the real and personal property to which the testator is entitled at his death, either in law of equity, and which if not so disposed of would descend upon his heirs or upon his executors or administrators.

In the case of a testator who dies domiciled in England, if the will fails to make reasonable provision for his dependants, the court has power to make provision for those dependants under the Inheritance (Provision for Family and Dependants) Act 1975 (*see* 24: **13**).

Dispositions are either:

(a) *devises*, which are dispositions of freehold land; or
(b) *legacies or bequests* which are dispositions of personalty including leases (*see* 24: **6**).

A general devise of all the testator's lands is presumed to include leasehold land — *see Prescott* v. *Barker* (1874).

6. Legacies
Legacies are of four kinds:

(a) *general legacies* — no particular thing is given, e.g. *a* diamond ring or a gift of £1,000 or *a* horse or *a* thousand shares in ICI;

(b) *specific legacies* — a particular thing is given, e.g. *my* diamond ring, *my* shares in ICI, *my* Rolls-Royce, *my* Picasso;

(c) *demonstrative legacies* — a gift that is directed to be taken from a particular source, e.g. £1,000 *out of* my deposit account;

(d) *a residuary gift* — a gift of the residue of the estate after payment of debts and funeral expenses and the distribution of legacies and devises.

Differences between them are shown by the rules relating to abatement (*see* 24: **7**) and ademption (*see* 24: **8**).

7. Abatement of legacies
The testator's debts must be paid before his estate is distributed, and sometimes the property given by his will must also be used wholly or partly for this purpose. The rule is that general legacies are subject to abatement before specific or demonstrative legacies can be called upon. If a demonstrative legacy is abated in this way — by the fund out of which it is to be paid being used to pay debts — it is transformed into a general legacy to be paid out of any available residuary property.

8. Ademption of specific legacies
If a specific thing given to a legatee is not in the testator's possession at his death, the gift is *adeemed*, i.e. the legatee gets nothing. Here it is presumed that the testator has shown an intention to revoke the gift.

Ademption of a specific legacy will also occur where the thing given has been substantially changed before the testator's death, e.g. where the gift is of 'my collection of valuable stamps' and the testator has sold his stamps and bought a collection of valuable books. A mere change in name or form, however, will not lead to ademption, e.g. where shares are specifically left and the company subsequently changes its name or undergoes reconstruction — *see Re O'Brien* (1946). General legacies are not liable to ademption and demonstrative legacies, if adeemed, are turned into general legacies.

9. Lapsed gifts
Where a legatee or devisee dies before the testator, the gift made

to him lapses and the property so given falls into residue for the benefit of the residuary legatee.

Lapse does not occur in the following:

(a) *Where there is a devise of an entailed interest and the devisee predeceases the testator but is survived by issue capable of inheriting the entailed interest* Here the gift endures for the benefit of such issue subject to a contrary intention in the will (Wills Act 1837, s. 32). For example, where the gift is 'to A and his heirs male', if A dies before the testator but leaves a son, the son will get the land.

(b) *Where there is a devise or bequest to a child or remoter descendant of the testator, and the intended beneficiary dies before the testator, but leaves issue surviving the testator* Then, unless a contrary intention appears in the will, the bequest will take effect for the benefit of the issue.

Similarly, where a devise or bequest to a number of children or remoter descendants of the testator is made, but one of that number predeceases the testator, leaving issue, then, unless a contrary intention appears, the bequest will take effect as if the surviving issue were included in the number. (Wills Act 1937, s. 33, as amended by Administration of Justice Act 1982, s. 19). Thus, for example:

(*i*) A bequeathes money to his son, B, who dies before him, leaving a son and daughter: here, the grandchildren will inherit.

(*ii*) X leaves his estate to his three children, A, B and C, but C predeceases him, but has a son, Z: A, B and Z inherit.

Revocation of wills

10. Wills Act 1837, s. 20

'No will or codicil, or any part thereof, shall be revoked otherwise than as aforesaid i.e. s. 18: *see* 24: **11**, or by another will or codicil, executed in manner hereinbefore required, or by some writing declaring an intention to revoke the same, and executed, or by the burning, tearing, or otherwise destroying the same by the testator, or by some person in his presence and by his direction, with the intention of revoking the same.'

This section provides three ways in which a will can be revoked.

(a) *Subsequent will or codicil* A will usually commences with a clause revoking all former wills (e.g. 'I hereby revoke all other wills and testamentary dispositions heretofore made by me'). If such a clause is not inserted, the later will (or codicil) does not revoke the former will, except in so far as it is inconsistent therewith.

If a testator revokes his will, intending to make a new one, but then fails to make a new will or makes a will that is void for any reason, the original will remains valid. Here the revocation of the first will is regarded as being dependent on the validity of the later one — *see Re Finnemore (dec'd)* (1991). Similarly, if a man destroys his will under the mistaken belief that all his property will pass automatically to his wife at his death and that a will leaving all his property to her is therefore unnecessary, a copy of the will can be admitted to probate — *see In the Estate of Southerden* (1925).

(b) *Writing executed like a will* A will may be revoked by a writing that, though not a will itself, is signed and attested and shows a clear intention to revoke all former wills, e.g. a letter, signed by the testator and attested by two witnesses, requesting the addressee to destroy the will — *see In the Goods of Durance* (1872).

(c) *Destruction* There are three elements:

    (i) *intention to revoke at the time of the revocation (animus revocandi)* If a will is lost and the court is not satisfied that it was destroyed with intention to revoke, verbal evidence may be given as to its contents, e.g. by a witness who read the will and remembers the contents — *see Sugden* v. *Lord St Leonards* (1876);

    (ii) *Sufficient act of destruction* It is insufficient to write 'cancelled' across the will — *see Stephens* v. *Taprell* (1840) — or to cancel the signature and throw the will in a waste-paper basket — *see Cheese* v. *Lovejoy* (1877);

    (iii) *By the testator* or in his presence and by his direction.

11. Revocation by marriage

The Wills Act 1837, s. 18 (as amended by the Administration of Justice Act 1982, s. 18), provides that, subject to certain exceptions, a will is automatically revoked by the testator's marriage. However:

(a) where, at the time of making the will, the testator was expecting to marry and he intended that the will should *not* be revoked by the marriage, it shall take effect; and

(b) where, after a testator has made a will, his marriage is dissolved, annulled or declared void by a court, the will shall take effect, except that any devise or bequest to his former spouse shall lapse, unless the contrary intention appears in the will (Wills Act 1837, s. 18(a), as inserted by AJA 1982, s. 18) — *see Re Sinclair* (1985)).

12. Mutual wills

The doctrine of mutual wills is an equitable doctrine developed to prevent an unconscionable revocation. For the doctrine to operate, three requirements must be met:

(a) there must be an arrangement between two people, usually husband and wife, to execute mutual wills making provision for each other with remainder to a third party, usually a child;
(b) there must be an agreement that the survivor would not revoke this arrangement;
(c) on the death of one party leaving his will unrevoked, the arrangement becomes binding.

The survivor holds the property on implied (*see* 23: **19**) or constructive (*see* 23: **20**) trust for the third party. 'The instrument itself is the evidence of the agreement; and he that dies first does by his death carry the agreement on his part into execution. If the other then refuses, he is guilty of a fraud, can never unbind himself, and becomes a trustee of course for no man shall deceive another to his prejudice. By engaging to do something that is in his power, he is made a trustee for the performance and transmits that trust to those that claim under him', said Lord Camden in *Dufour* v. *Pereira* (1769).

Maintenance of dependants

13. Inheritance (Provision for Family and Dependants) Act 1975

Formerly a testator could dispose of his property by will in any way he chose, but the Inheritance (Family Provision) Act 1938 gave the court power to vary a will at the request of the testator's dependants if he fails reasonably to provide for them. The 1938 Act was extended to cover cases of total intestacy by the Intestates Estates Act 1952.

In respect of a person who died in England or Wales after 31 March 1976, the court's powers are now contained in the Inheritance (Provision for Family and Dependants) Act 1975. Under the 1975 Act there are two things to consider:

(a) dependants who may apply to the court (*see* 24: **14**).
(b) the order of the court (*see* 24: **15**).

The 1975 Act gives the court powers to prevent evasion by ordering a donee to return property to the estate where it was given by the deceased with the intention of defeating the Act and not for full consideration.

14. Dependants

The following dependants of the deceased may apply to the court under s. 1 of the Act.

(a) *a wife or husband of the deceased*;

(b) *a former wife or husband who has not remarried* — a former wife or husband is one whose marriage to the deceased was annulled or dissolved — *see Re Fullard* (1982);

(c) *a child of the deceased* — this includes a child of any age whether married or not and also extends to an adopted or illegitimate child — *see Re Coventry* (1980);

(d) *a person treated by the deceased as a child of the family* — this includes a child who is not the deceased's child — *see Re Leach* (1985);

(e) *A dependant of the deceased* — this includes an elderly relative and also a person living with but not married to the deceased.

Application is made to the High Court or, if the deceased's property does not exceed £30,000, to the county court and must normally be made within six months from the date on which representation of the deceased's estate is taken out (*see* 24: **18**).

15. The order

The court considers the will of the deceased to see whether it makes reasonable financial provision for the applicant (*see* (a)). If the court considers that it does not, then the court goes on to consider what provision it should order (*see* (b)):

(a) *circumstances in which the order may be made* — the Act provides two tests:

(*i*) for a surviving spouse, the test is reasonable financial provision, whether or not the provision is needed for the spouse's maintenance, and it seems that the court will take the same kind of approach as it would had the couple been parted by divorce rather than death — *see Moody* v. *Stevenson* (1991);

(*ii*) for other dependants, the provision must be such as would be reasonable for the applicant's maintenance;

In all cases, the court applies an objective standard; the views and conduct of the deceased are irrelevant and, in deciding whether reasonable financial provision has been made, s. 3 of the Act requires the court to consider a number of guidelines including:

(i) the applicant's resources and needs;
(ii) the obligations of the deceased to the applicant;
(iii) the size of the deceased's estate;
(iv) any physical or mental disability of the applicant;

Further guidelines are laid down in relation to specific applicants, for example, the court must consider:

(i) in the case of a surviving spouse, the age of the applicant and the duration of the marriage;
(ii) in the case of a child of the deceased, the manner in which the applicant expected to be educated or trained;

(b) *the court's order* — if the court decides that reasonable financial provision has not been made in the deceased's will, then it can order provision to be made out of the net estate of the deceased, which is widely defined under s. 25, and the order can be:

(i) periodical payments;
(ii) lump sum payment;
(iii) transfer of property;
(iv) settlement of property;
(v) acquisition of property for transfer or settlement;
(vi) variation of marriage settlement.

Under s. 6, only an order for periodical payments can be varied. The need for certainty in other cases is obvious.

Personal representatives

16. Executors and administrators

The persons who wind up and distribute a deceased's estate are called his personal representatives. Personal representatives are of two kinds:

(a) *Executors* An executor is appointed by the testator in his will. The testator may appoint anyone as his executor and may appoint any number, but probate (*see* 24: **18**) will not be granted to more than four executors, neither will it be granted to a minor until he comes of age (Supreme Court Act 1981). Under the Administration of Estates Act 1925, s. 7, if a last-surviving executor dies testate, then his executors will take his place, but if a last-surviving executor dies intestate, then the court will appoint an administrator *de bonis non administratis* to take over his duties as executor.

(b) *Administrators* An administrator is a personal representative appointed by the court under a variety of circumstances including:

    (*i*) *administrator cum testamento annexo*. Where a will fails to appoint an executor or an appointment of an executor fails (e.g. because the person appointed is incapacitated or refuses to act), the court will appoint a person to administer the estate 'with the will annexed', i.e. to administer in accordance with the will, as though he were an executor. Such an administrator is called an administrator *cum testamento annexo*.

    (*ii*) *administrator on intestacy*;

    (*iii*) *administrator pendente lite* — where legal proceedings concerning the validity of the will are pending, the court may appoint an administrator *pendente lite* (pending litigation) to safeguard but not distribute the estate.

Except in the case of an administrator *pendente lite*, the court appoints up to four administrators from the legatees of good character having the highest priority under the Non-contentious Probate Rules 1987 (amended in 1991).

17. Executor *de son tort*

A person not named in the will to be an executor may be compelled by law to act as an executor if he interferes with the deceased's property before the proper executors take charge of it, e.g. a person who sells property belonging to the deceased, even if by mistake, would be compelled to hold the proceeds of sale as though he were an executor, i.e. in accordance with the terms of the will. Such a person is called an executor *de son tort* (executor by his own wrongdoing).

18. The grant

The court grants either:

(a) *probate*, which confirms the authenticity of the will and the authority of the executor; or

(b) *letters of administration*, which confer authority on the administrator, which is either:

    (*i*) administration with the will annexed; or

    (*ii*) simple administration on an intestacy.

The word 'probate' is often used to cover both probate *and* letters of administration.

Probate is of two kinds:

(a) *non-contentious* business is assigned to the Family Division (*see* 3: 17) and the will is proved in common form.

(b) *contentious* business is assigned to the Chancery Division (*see* 3: 16) and the will is proved in solemn form — contentious business is of three kinds:

  (*i*) questioning the validity of the will;
  (*ii*) disputing the interest of a person claiming to be entitled to letters of administration;
  (*iii*) seeking the revocation of probate or letters of administration.

A party who wishes to object to a will enters a *caveat*; probate will then not be granted without notice to the caveator.

19. Duties of personal representatives

The position is governed primarily by the Administration of Estates Acts 1925 and 1971:

(a) to collect all the assets, e.g. by suing for debts if necessary;

(b) to pay all the deceased's debts in the following order:

  (*i*) *preferred debts* — funeral and testamentary expenses, rates and taxes for the last 12 months, wages of servants for the last four months and not exceeding £800;
  (*ii*) *ordinary debts* (whether special or simple contracts) — in the order in which they were incurred (subject to the personal representatives' right to prefer one debt over another in certain cases);
  (*iii*) *deferred debts* — loans owing to a spouse, etc.;

the order of payment of debts is only important where the estate is insolvent. The property that the executors use to pay debts is generally undisposed of property or residue and then general legacy funds. Specific legacy funds are left to the last.

(c) to distribute the remaining property among beneficiaries.

Intestacy

20. Intestacy

Whilst there are, as we have seen, many rules concerned with the creation and execution of wills, a report by NOP Market Research in the early summer of 1992 revealed that 62% of people in Great

Britain have not made a will, and that it would take a major event, such as the death of a close relative or a serious illness to focus their attention on the matter! Eighty-two% of those interviewed who were married believed that if they died without having made a will, their property would automatically pass to their husband or wife. To die without having made a will is to die *intestate*. Intestacy is of two kinds:

(a) *Total*

(b) *Partial* Where a testator has failed to dispose of all his property by his will, he is said to die partially intestate. The property undisposed of will be distributed by his executors according to the intestacy rules.

The intestate's property all vests in his personal representatives upon trust for sale (with power to postpone indefinitely) for distribution of the proceeds of sale according to the rules laid out below (*see* 24: **21–23**). Before distributing any property among beneficiaries, the personal representatives have to ascertain whether the deceased has left enough property to pay his debts in full. If there is insufficient property, the estate is insolvent. In this case, the personal representatives have to pay as many of the debts as they can in a prescribed order of priority.

The rules governing the order in which debts are payable are the same as those applying in cases of bankruptcy (*see* 24: **27**). Indeed, the only difference from the order of payment in bankruptcy is that the personal representatives have to pay the funeral and testamentary expenses before all other debts.

21. Where the intestate leaves a surviving spouse

The rights of the intestate's widow or widower depend largely on whether there are any children of the marriage or not:

(a) *no issue and no surviving parents, brothers or sisters of the whole blood* — the estate passes absolutely to the surviving spouse;

(b) *issue* — the surviving spouse takes:
    (*i*) personal chattels, e.g. personal jewellery; and
    (*ii*) £75,000 free of death duty with interest until payment; and
    (*iii*) a life interest in one half of the residue;

The remaining property then going to the issue upon the *statutory trusts* (*see* 24: **23**).

(c) *no issue, but a surviving parent, brother or sister of the whole blood* — the surviving spouse takes:
    (*i*) personal chattels; and

(*ii*) £125,000 free of duty with interest until payment; and
(*iii*) half the residue absolutely;
The remaining property, if there are parents, going to the parents of the intestate absolutely; if there are no parents, then to the brothers or sisters on the statutory trusts.

22. Where the intestate leaves no surviving spouse

If, however, he or she leaves:

(a) *issue* — the residue is held for them on the statutory trusts after paying debts, etc.;
(b) *no issue but one or both parents* — the property passes to the parents absolutely;
(c) *no issue or parents but other relatives* — the property is distributed in the following order:

    (*i*) brothers and sisters (or their issue) of the whole blood;
    (*ii*) brothers and sisters (or their issue) of the half blood;
    (*iii*) grandparents absolutely (if there are none of class (i) and (ii) above;
    (*iv*) uncles and aunts (or issue) of the whole blood;
    (*v*) uncles and aunts (or issue) of the half blood;

in cases (i), (ii), (iv) and (v) the property is held on the statutory trusts (*see* 24: **23**).
(d) *no relatives at all* — the property goes to the Crown absolutely as *bona vacantia* (unowned goods), but the Crown may make provision for any dependant or other person for whom the intestate could have reasonably been expected to provide.

23. The statutory trusts

The statutory trusts are set out in the Administration of Estates Act 1925, as amended. The statutory trust to be carried out by the administrators is to divide the property equally among the persons entitled at the age of 18, or on prior marriage.

If a beneficiary under the above tables has predeceased the testator, his share goes to his issue; if there is no issue, then it falls into the common fund.

Bankruptcy

24. Bankruptcy

Bankruptcy refers to court proceedings, whereby an order is made for the distribution of the property of an insolvent debtor among his creditors. Initially, such proceedings lay only against commercial traders but, since 1861, any individual can be 'declared bankrupt'. The Insolvency Act 1985 introduced a new scheme, whereby voluntary arrangements may be made among an insolvent's creditors, which, though involving a court order, do not amount to proceedings in bankruptcy. This scheme, as well as the other provisions, have been re-enacted in the Insolvency Act 1986 (IA 1986), which now effectively codifies the law on bankruptcy.

25. Insolvency

The basic grounds for proceedings under the IA 1986 (whether for voluntary arrangements or an order in bankruptcy) are the insolvency of the debtor:

(a) under the old law, bankruptcy proceedings could only be begun if an 'act of bankruptcy' was committed by the debtor — such acts included fleeing or hiding or attempting to dispose of assets in order to avoid payment of debts;

(b) the IA 1986 has rejected the requirement for an act of bankruptcy as the basis of proceedings (though such acts might now amount to criminal offences relating to bankruptcy — IA 1986, ss. 356–362) and, instead, the basis of proceedings or for an order enforcing voluntary arrangements is the debtor's insolvency which essentially means simply his inability to pay his debts (IA 1986, s. 268).

26. Bankruptcy proceedings

These are begun by a petition for a bankruptcy order, usually made to the county court, although, in some circumstances, to the High Court.

(a) A petition may be made by the debtor himself or one or more of his creditors or by the supervisor of voluntary arrangements that have not been kept (*see* 24: 24), or by the Official Petitioner (in cases of criminal bankruptcy). A petition may only be made in respect of an insolvent person.

(b) While the procedures differ slightly according to who the petitioner is, the next stage (if the petition is accepted) is the making of a bankruptcy order by the court (IA 1986, ss. 267–277). An order will not be granted on a creditor's petition if a reasonable offer to settle debts has been made (s. 27).

In the case of a debtor's petition, the court may appoint an insolvency practitioner, who reports to the court, before deciding whether to make an order. The insolvency practitioner's task is to make such arrangements as he can and these may include voluntary arrangements that the court has power to enforce (s. 274). In any case, no order should be granted unless the total amount involved in the debts falls below a certain level, to be fixed from time to time by separate rules.

(c) When a bankruptcy order is made, arrangements must be made for the administration of his property. The bankrupt person must make a statement of his affairs to the Official Receiver (an officer of the Department of Trade) to whom he must deliver possession of his estate and all books relating to it. The actual administration of the estate is the responsibility of a trustee in bankruptcy; he is appointed by the creditors or by the court. Certain property is not normally subject to such a procedure, including tools and clothing. Property is sold or distributed among the creditors in accordance with procedures laid down in the IA 1986.

27. Priority of debts

It is the duty of the trustee in bankruptcy to pay, as far as possible, all debts. This will normally be impossible. Accordingly, he must follow a prescribed order of priorities, laid down in the IA 1986, s. 328. This creates a list of 'preferential debts' that must be given priority over other debts. The preferential debts are, broadly:

(a) money owed to the Inland Revenue for income tax deducted at source;

(b) VAT owed to the Customs and Excise;

(c) social security and pension scheme contributions;

(d) wages and salaries owed to employees.

No priority exists between these. Preferential debts, however, must be paid before others (IA 1986, s. 326). Only those entitled to payment of the bankruptcy costs and expenses rank higher. After preferential debtors come ordinary creditors but, of course, it is highly unlikely that the bankrupt's estate will be sufficient to meet his indebtedness.

28. Undischarged bankrupts

An undischarged bankrupt cannot:

(a) act as a Director of any company or take part, directly or indirectly, in the management of any company without the permission of the court;

(b) unless appointed by court order, he cannot act as the receiver or manager of the property of any company on behalf of the debenture holders;

(c) he cannot be elected to either House of Parliament;

(d) he cannot be appointed as a magistrate or a member of a local authority or other public body;

(e) he cannot act as a solicitor;

(f) he cannot obtain credit of more than £250 without declaring his status (and, presumably, severely reducing his chances of receiving it).

29. Discharge

A bankrupt may be discharged (released from all debts payable in bankruptcy, except money owed to the Crown or the court itself) in two ways:

(a) *by order of the court* — this applies to criminal bankrupts or to persons who have been undischarged bankrupts during the previous 15 years (IA 1986, s. 279).

(b) automatically, at the end of the relevant period (usually 3 years, although 2 is deemed to be long enough enough where the debts owed were less than £20,000).

Progress test 24

1. What is a will?   (**1**)

2. What is meant by the ademption and abatement of legacies and to what forms of legacies do these terms apply?   (**6–8**)
T by his will leaves half his property to his son, B, and the other half to 'C and the heirs male of his body'. B and C are killed in a plane crash and T dies on hearing the news. Will the gifts lapse? (**9**)

3. How may a will be revoked?   (**10–12**)
T, a soldier, aged 20 in 1944, orally made a will leaving 'all my things to my mother'. In 1946 T married X, by whom he had two children. In 1948 T made a will in favour of X. X died in 1952 and in 1956 T married Y. T has now died. How will his property be distributed?   (**2, 9, 13–15, 21**)

4. How may personal representatives be appointed by or for a deceased person? What is meant by (a) *cum testamento annexo*, (b) *pendente lite* and (c) *de bonis non administratis*? **(16, 17)**

5. You are appointed the sole executor of the will of T. On examining T's estate you discover (a) that he was insolvent, (b) that his will disposes of only half his property, and (c) that the will makes no provision for his wife and his mentally defective son, aged 28. What rules should guide you in administering his estate? **(20, 22)**
Also, what may be the effect of T's insolvency on general and specific legacies contained in his will? **(6–8)**

6. What are the main purposes of bankruptcy? Who may petition for a bankruptcy order? What are the grounds for petitioning for a debtor's bankruptcy? **(24–26)**

7. You are appointed trustee in bankruptcy for X, a debtor. In what order should you pay his debts? **(27)**

8. Explain 'discharge' in bankruptcy. **(29)**

Part seven

Criminal law

Criminal liability

Crime and criminal liability

1. The nature of crime

There is no statutory definition of crime, and it is even conceded that it 'is not possible to discover a legal definition of crime which can be of value for English law' — J W C Turner in *Kenny's Outlines of Criminal Law*. For practical purposes, a crime may be defined as a public wrong whose commission will result in criminal proceedings, which may in turn result in the punishment of the wrongdoer.

2. Public wrong

It is the chief characteristic of crimes that, unlike torts or breaches of contract, it is not left to the individual affected to bring an action in court — though he may initiate such an action by reporting the commission of offences to the police. A criminal prosecution (as opposed to a civil action for damages) is therefore usually brought by the state represented by the Crown (though private prosecutions are still possible in some cases). The corollary is that, whereas the plaintiff to a civil action may, if he so wishes, withdraw from his action, a criminal action can neither be terminated nor compromised (that is, the parties concerned cannot agree to stay proceedings).

3. Criminal proceedings

A clear distinction can be made between criminal and civil proceedings. In relation to the more serious offences, at least, a criminal case will involve a judge and jury, whereas in a civil action, the judge will normally sit alone. There is a presumption, in a criminal trial, that the accused person is innocent and it is the task of his prosecutors to produce evidence that convinces the jury of his guilt 'beyond all reasonable doubt'. No such presumption exists in civil actions, the burden of proof being to establish one's case 'on the balance of probabilities'.

4. Punishment

Whereas the outcome of a successful civil action is usually the award of damages, the purpose of which is to compensate the injured party, a successful prosecution normally results in punishment. This may involve imprisonment, a fine, supervision orders or a combination of these. A prison sentence may be 'suspended' or the accused may be discharged either absolutely or conditionally upon good behaviour. While these are not exactly 'let-offs', they do seem to depart from the traditional notion of punishment. There is a school of thought that criminal 'punishments' should not be punitive at all, but should serve to deter others, or the offender himself, from committing similar crimes by setting an example. In practice, judges seem to comply with both punitive *and* deterrent theories.

5. Crimes that are also torts

Some crimes may also be torts, e.g. assault and battery, public nuisance, libel. In fact, the requirements for criminal prosecutions often differ slightly from those necessary for civil liability, e.g. a public nuisance must affect a 'class of Her Majesty's subjects', to be criminal. Whether the wrong is a tort or a crime will depend on the nature of the proceedings that are taken. Thus, we may speak of a person being guilty of the crime of assault if he is successfully prosecuted in a criminal court; the same person will be liable for the tort of assault if the action is brought in the civil court (*see* 15: **5**).

6. Classification of crimes

The earliest classification involved only felonies. These were the more serious offences, which were regarded as putting good order in jeopardy and included murder, rape, etc. The most serious offences of all, in that they were directed at the state itself, constituted treason. A wrong that was in 'breach of the King's peace', but which fell short of a felony, was normally categorised as a trespass, which explains why several torts today either actually are crimes as well or are similar to crimes in their nature (*see* 25: **5**).

From time to time, however, other offences were created to maintain order. These were often less serious and were generally created by statute, though a number were introduced by the Court of Star Chamber, between 1487 and 1641. They were known generally as misdemeanours. This distinction between felonies and misdemeanours was important, because a person convicted of a felony was liable to forfeiture of his property and, in some cases, to the loss of his life (neither of these measures applied to misdemeanours). In 1870, forfeiture was abolished and the death penalty removed for felonies other than murder but the distinction between felonies and misdemeanour persisted until 1967.

7. Modern classification

In 1967 the old scheme of classifying offences, according to whether they were felonies or misdemeanours, was abolished with the Criminal Law Act 1967 (CLA 1967), s. 1. Whereas the old classification was based, in theory at least, purely on the seriousness of the offence concerned, the newer classification reflected also certain practical considerations. These were:

(a) whether or not the offence was an arrestable one (*see* 25: **8**); and
(b) whether or not the offence was an indictable one (*see* 25: **10**).

8. Arrestable offences

The CLA 1967 classified all offences into two categories — those offences in respect of which a power of summary arrest (arrest without warrant) lay and those in respect of which no such power existed.

The basic system has now been incorporated into the Police and Criminal Evidence Act (abbreviated as PACE) 1984, ss. 24–25. The exact definition of an arrestable offence, as well as the circumstance in which the power of summary arrest may be exercised, however, has been changed by the 1984 Act. The modern law is set out below:

(a) *arrestable offences* — these are defined in PACE as:
  (*i*) offences where the penalty is fixed by law (e.g. murder, which carries a mandatory life sentence);
  (*ii*) offences for which an offender aged 21 years or more may be sentenced to five years or more or that involve criminal damage to property (other than arson);
  (*iii*) certain named offences listed in the Act and including customs offences and some sexual offences;
(b) *general powers of summary arrest* — powers of summary arrest (arrest without warrant) are possessed by both private citizens and police constables, but the citizen's powers of arrest are unchanged by PACE and are as follows:

  (*i*) anyone may arrest, without warrant, any person who is in the act of committing an arrestable offence or whom he has reasonable grounds for believing to be in the act of committing an arrestable offence;

(*ii*) where an arrestable offence has been committed, any person may arrest anyone who is guilty of the offence or whom he suspects, on reasonable grounds, of being guilty of that offence; and as *anyone* enjoys these powers, they are enjoyed not only by private citizens, but also by police constables, although a constable enjoys considerable additional and 'extended' powers of arrest under PACE.

9. The constable's powers of arrest
These are:

(a) As well as the powers of arrest enjoyed by citizens generally, the police constable has the important power of arresting on suspicion of an arrestable offence, which is defined in PACE as follows:
  (*i*) where a constable suspects, on reasonable grounds, that an arrestable offence has been committed, he may arrest, without warrant, anyone whom he reasonably believes to be guilty of the offence; and
  (*ii*) a constable may arrest, without warrant, anyone whom he suspects, on reasonable grounds, to be about to commit an arrestable offence.

(b) As well as the general powers possessed by a constable given above, PACE provides for certain 'extended powers' of arrest that can be employed by a constable in certain circumstances, for example, a constable can arrest a person whom he suspects to be guilty of an offence that is not, normally, an arrestable offence if this is necessary for one of a number of reasons, these reasons being embodied in a number of 'generally arrest conditions'. If a constable is to use his extended power of arrest, at least one of these conditions must be satisfied:
  (*i*) the suspect's name is unknown and cannot be ascertained so that a summons can be served (e.g. he refuses to give it or is unconscious);
  (*ii*) the suspect fails to give a satisfactory address;
  (*iii*) the constable reasonably suspects that the name or address given are false;
  (*iv*) arrest is necessary for the protection of property or a person (including the suspect himself).

Once the arrest has been made, the Code of Practice (which came into force in April 1991) spells out the procedures equired to comply with PACE.

10. Indictable and summary offences

Offences can also be classified according to the mode of trial employed (*see* 3: **25**). There are now three categories of offences thus classified, though one of these ((c) below) is really a 'hybrid':

(a) *indictable offences* — the word 'indictment' refers to the process whereby a person is accused of a criminal offence and actually tried before a judge and jury and, generally speaking, this occurs in relation to the more serious offences, such as murder and armed robbery — we refer to such offences as indictable;

(b) *summary offences* — these are offences that can be dealt with summarily, that is, by the magistrates (*see* 3: **26**) and they tend to be the less serious offences, such as many traffic violations;

(c) *offences that are triable 'either way'* — it has, for many years, been possible for the accused himself to have a say in the mode of trial to be followed in connection with certain offences, in other words, where he is charged with an offence that is 'triable either way' the accused may consent to having the case tried by the magistrates otherwise he will be tried by a judge and jury.

11. Offences that are 'triable either way'

What is meant by 'triable either way' is given in 10 above. Which offences may be thus classified and the factors that determine which mode of trial is employed, are stated in the Magistrates Courts Act (MCA) 1980, ss. 16–23:

(a) *Offences that are triable either way* are:

   (*i*) all those offences specifically given in Schedule 1 of the MCA 1980 as being triable either way; or

   (*ii*) those, by virtue of any other Act of Parliament, that are so triable. Such offences are many and include, for example, public nuisance, certain offences against the person, such as threatening to kill and assault with intent to resist arrest and some sexual offences, such as unlawful intercourse with a girl under 16 (MCA 1980, s. 16).

(b) *Mode of trial* It is the right of the accused to elect for trial by a judge and jury or not. However, before the final decision is made by him, the magistrates must determine which mode of trial is, in their view, most suitable. In so determining, the court must cause the charge to be written down and read out and give both the prosecution and the accused the opportunity to make representations as to which mode of trial is most suitable. In 1992, certain guidelines were published by a working party chaired by Farquharson, LJ.

The court should also take into consideration such things as the seriousness of the case, the circumstances in which the offence was committed and whether or not the powers available to them are sufficient to deal with the accused, if he is found guilty (e.g. where he is charged with a summary offence, but has been convicted of the same offence several times before).

The court having decided which mode of trial it considers suitable, must advise the accused.

If it has decided that summary trial is most suitable, the magistrates court must advise the accused that he may be tried summarily only if he so consents. If it has decided that trial by jury is suitable, then the accused has no choice. If the accused elects trial by jury, then the magistrates act only as examining magistrates and do not actually try the case against the accused (MCA 1980, ss. 19–23).

If the case is being prosecuted by one of the law officers (e.g. the Attorney-General) and he directs that the case is to be tried on indictment, then the accused has no choice in the matter.

12. Elements of a crime

The maxim *actus non facit reum, nisi mens sit rea*, which means the act itself does not give rise to guilt unless done with a guilty intent, applies to crimes generally. The prosecution must, therefore, prove beyond all reasonable doubt that the accused committed a prohibited act (*actus reus*) with a guilty intent (*mens rea*). Some offences do not require a guilty intent, as such and are, accordingly, referred to as crimes of strict liability (*see* 25: **15**). Such offences are invariably the creation of statutes.

13. *Actus reus*

This may consist in an act or omission. It also includes the consequences, and such 'surrounding circumstances', if any be required, as are material to the definition of the crime. The following may serve as examples.

(a) to be murder or manslaughter, the accused's blow or deed must result in the death of the victim; to be guilty of bigamy it is necessary that the accused is already married when undergoing a ceremony of marriage (Offences against the Person Act 1861, s. 57);

(b) some offences do not require an act as such; a person may be convicted on the basis of 'surrounding circumstances' alone.

Example

In *R.* v. *Larsonneur* (1933), D had been forbidden entry to the UK, but was arrested in Ireland, and brought into the country in custody. It was held that she was guilty of an offence, 'being an alien, to whom leave to enter has been refused . . . found in the UK'. The offence consisted of 'being found', not of the *act* of entering.

(c) on the other hand, if an act be required, then the act must be a voluntary one, but an act may be involuntary as the result of an illness — see *R.* v. *Quick* (1973) or an accident depriving D of his consciousness or faculties of volition — see *Watmore* v. *Jenkins* (1962). It may even be involuntary if, through no fault of the driver, he loses control of his car due to mechanical failure — see *Burns* v. *Bidder* (1967) or because he has been stung by a bee — *obiter* in *Hill* v. *Baxter* (1958) (*see* 26: **7, 12**); duress, by depriving a man of choice, also renders his act involuntary;

(d) liability for omissions, as in tort, arises where there is a positive duty to act. Such a duty may arise:

(*i*) by contract — see *R.* v. *Pittwood* (1902);

(*ii*) in a parent and child, or similar relationship, e.g. *R.* v. *Stone and Dobinson* (1977) where a man and his mistress allowed his disabled sister to starve to death (and see *R.* v. *Gibbins and Proctor* (1918);

(*iii*) where the defendant himself creates a dangerous situation.

14. *Mens rea*

The term *mens rea* is usually translated as 'guilty mind'. It refers to the mental element that must accompany the *actus reus* if the accused is to be convicted of a criminal offence. The exact mental element required will vary according to the offence charged. Accordingly, *mens rea* might take any of the following forms, in descending order of seriousness:

(a) *intention* In certain offences, it is necessary that the accused actually intended to bring about the prohibited consequences (i.e. the *actus reus* or part of it) — see *R.* v. *Moloney* (1985). Thus a person is guilty of theft only if it can be shown that he intended to permanently deprive his victim of his property. Merely taking it, intending to return it, is not enough.

(b) *recklessness* Recklessness is normally regarded as the deliberate taking by the accused of an unjustifiable risk. Thus, a person who can foresee that his conduct is likely to cause prohibited consequences, but chooses to continue with his action without intending these consequences, may be said to be reckless. It is sometimes the case that a person charged with a crime requiring proof of intent can, if he lacks that intention, be convicted of a lesser offence requiring only recklessness. Thus, a person charged with *murder* (which normally requires proof of intention to kill or cause serious bodily harm) may be convicted instead of *manslaughter* (which requires only recklessness) if that intent cannot be proved.

(c) *negligence* This amounts to a failure by the accused to foresee the consequences of his act in circumstances where a reasonable man would have foreseen them. Sometimes this is sufficient to constitute the mental element in a crime, e.g. careless driving. There is, however, an overlap between negligence and the kind of recklessness that is seen where a person takes a risk of which he ought to have been aware but was not — an 'inadvertent risk-taker' as seen in *R.* v. *Caldwell* (1981).

15. Strict liability
Certain offences are said to be crimes of *strict liability*.

An offence of strict liability is one where no *mens rea* is required and such offences are invariably the creation of statute. Thus, in *Pharmaceutical Society* v. *Storkwain* (1986), a pharmacist dispensed a forged prescription. This was held to amount to an offence under the Medicines Act 1968, s. 58(2). There was no suggestion or finding that the defendant had acted dishonestly, improperly or even negligently. On the other hand, the House of Lords ruled in *Sweet* v. *Parsley* (1970) that a person who did not know that her tenants were taking drugs should not be convicted of 'being concerned in the management of premises' where drugs were used. Whether or not a statute will be interpreted as creating an offence of strict liability will seemingly depend in part on public policy. Only if the statute expressly, or by necessary implication, rules out the requirement for *mens rea*, will the court interpret it as creating an offence of strict liability.

16. Modes of participation in crime
It is not only the person who actually 'does the deed' (i.e. whose conduct is immediately connected with the *actus reus*) who is guilty of an offence. The Accessories and Abettors Act 1861, s. 8, as amended by the Criminal Law Act 1977 — 'Whosoever shall aid, abet, counsel or procure the commission of any indictable offence whether the same be an offence at common law or, by virtue of any act passed or to be passed, shall be liable to be tried, indicted and punished as a principal offender'.

The Criminal Law Act 1967, abolished the distinction between felonies and misdemeanours (*see* 25: **7**), so the 1861 Act now applies to all indictable (and some summary) offences. The Criminal Law Act 1967, ss. 4, 5, established further offences relating to assisting and concealing offenders after the offence; persons guilty of such activities were formerly known as 'accessories after the fact'.

A participant in an offence may be the following:

(a) *the principal offender* The person who commits the *actus reus* (with the necessary *mens rea*) or instigates an innocent agent to do so.

(b) *an aider and abettor* A person who is present, assisting and encouraging the commission of an offence. Mere presence is not enough — *see R. v. Coney* (1882) — though applauding an unlawful performance probably is — *see Wilcox v. Jeffrey* (1951).

(c) *a counsellor or procurer* That is, one who, prior to the commission of an offence, incites its commission or renders assistance for its commission. There is authority that such a person must be aware of the nature of the offence he is counselling and procuring — *see R. v. Bainbridge* (1960), but it is no defence that he did not want it to occur. Thus, a person who lends a gun to a villain, knowing he is going to use it in a robbery, cannot escape liability on the grounds that he hoped no robbery would occur — *see R. v. Bullock* (1955). If the villain killed someone, the lender of the gun would not be guilty of murder unless he actually contemplated that the gun would be used to cause grievous bodily harm or death. He may, however, be guilty of manslaughter — *see R. v. Betty and Ridley* (1930).

This last point applies equally to aiders and abettors. The general rule is that a secondary party (aider and abettor or counsellor and procurer) is guilty only to the extent of his own *mens rea*; thus, in a 'gang-fight', D was not guilty of any offence, other than common assault, when his friend killed a boy with a knife of which he had no knowledge — *see Davies v. DPP* (1954). Had he known of the knife, and contemplated its use to threaten, he would have been guilty of manslaughter (which requires recklessness) and murder if he had contemplated use of the knife to inflict injury — *see R. v. Betty* (1963).

(d) *one who impedes the arrest of an offender* This category of offender was created by the Criminal Law Act 1967, s. 4 — 'Where a person has committed an arrestable offence, any other person who, knowing or believing him to be guilty of the offence . . . does without lawful authority or reasonable excuse any act with intent to impede his apprehension shall be guilty of an offence'. The offence replaced the old mode of participation whereby D could be an 'accessory after the fact'.

(e) *a concealer* 'Where a person has committed an arrestable offence, any other person who, knowing or believing that the offence . . . has been committed, . . . accepts consideration for concealing information which might assist in securing the prosecution or conviction if the offender is guilty of an offence' (Criminal Law Act 1967, s. 5). (No prosecutions for this offence can be instituted without the consent of the Director of Public Prosecutions).

17. Inchoate offences

'Inchoate' means 'incomplete'. These crimes are only incomplete in the sense that, apart from being themselves criminal offences, they are also steps towards the commission of another, complete offence or in contemplation of such an offence. There are three varieties of 'inchoate' offences — attempt, incitement and conspiracy.

18. Attempts

Most of the law concerning attempts is now to be found in the Criminal Attempts Act 1981 — 'If, with intent to commit an offence to which this section applies, a person does an act which is more than merely preparatory to the commission of the offence, he is guilty of attempting to commit the offence' (s. 1(1)).

The question of whether or not the act is more than preparatory is one of fact for the jury — *see DPP* v. *Stonehouse* (1978). The intention for the offence of attempt will usually be the same as that for the complete offence — *see R.* v. *Whybrow* (1951). In cases such as murder, however, where an intention to commit grievous bodily harm is enough, for attempted murder there must have been an intent to kill.

'A person may be guilty of attempting to commit an offence to which this section applies even though the facts are such that the commission of the offence is impossible' (s. 1(2)). So, if you dip your hand hopefully into an empty pocket, you can still be charged with attempted theft and, if you bring what you think are drugs through customs, but the stuff turns out to be 'a vegetable material akin to snuff', you are nevertheless *attempting* a crime — *see R.* v. *Shivpuri* (1986). On the other hand, if there is no offence to commit, then no attempt has been made. So, if a man comes to England from a country where adultery is criminal and he believes it to be here, too, he cannot be attempting that crime in England whatever he does, because there is no such crime in England — *see R.* v. *Taaffe* (1984).

19. Incitement

It is an offence to incite another to commit a crime (other than conspiracy) whether or not the crime is actually committed — *see R.* v. *Higgins* (1801). For example, D posts a letter of incitement to X, but it is intercepted by the police. D is guilty of attempted incitement — *see R.* v. *Banks* (1873). Incitement consists of any form of influence brought to bear on someone, in order to procure the commission of a crime including threats — *see Race Relations Board* v. *Applin* (1973). As in attempts, an act can only be a criminal incitement if the act incited, if done, is itself criminal.

20. Conspiracy

At common law, an agreement to do an unlawful act, or a lawful act by unlawful means, was a conspiracy. The offence was a common law misdemeanour (*see* 25: **6**), which originated in Star Chamber (*see* 1: **34**). The Criminal Law Act 1977 has resulted in a reclassification of conspiracies. Section 1 of that Act (as substituted by the Criminal Attempts Act 1981) created a new offence of statutory conspiracy. Section 1(1) states,

> 'Subject to the following provisions of this part of this Act, if a person agrees with any other person or persons that a course of conduct shall be pursued which, if the agreement is carried out in accordance with their intentions either:

(a) will necessarily amount to or involve the commission of any offence or offences by one or more of the parties to the agreement; *or*
(b) would do so but for the existence of facts which render the commission of the offence or any of the offences impossible; he is guilty of conspiracy to commit the offence or offences in question.'

Thus, as with attempt, a person can be convicted for conspiring to commit the impossible (but not conspiring to do an act that is not actually a criminal offence).

Section 2 of the Act exempts from liability a person who 'conspires' *only* with:

(a) his or her spouse;
(b) a person lacking criminal capacity (such as a small child); or
(c) his intended victim.

Section 3 provides that a person convicted of statutory conspiracy must not be sentenced to a term of imprisonment greater than that which would have been imposed if he had been convicted of the offence conspired at. Section 5(1) provides for the abolition of the offence at common law, subject to s. 5(2), which provides for the retention of the common law offence so far as it relates to conspiracy to *defraud*. This has been confirmed by the Criminal Justice Act 1987.

Progress test 25

1. Define a crime. How would you distinguish a crime from a civil wrong? **(1–5)**

2. What was meant by a felony? What categories of offences now exist and to what extent is there overlap? **(6–11)**

3. What is meant by *actus reus*? Can a person be guilty of an offence by omitting to act? **(12–13)**

4. Define *mens rea*. When might *mens rea* be dispensed with by the courts? **(14)**

5. In what ways may a person participate in a crime?
A and B go to visit C where B asks for the loan of C's pistol while A is in the bathroom. Later, they stop P in the street and ask for his wallet. When P refuses, B produces the gun and shoots P dead. Both A and B then hide in D's house. Discuss. **(16)**

6. What is meant by an 'inchoate' offence? Discuss the main varieties of inchoate offences. **(17–20)**

7. Nasty and Dirty are heard discussing the security arrangements at Dick's shop. Later Dirty is found outside Dick's shop with a crowbar. Discuss. **(18–20)**
Would your answer be different if, due to the nylon stocking he uses as a mask, Dirty has difficulty seeing and is, in fact, outside his own shop by mistake?

Limitations on criminal responsibility

Types of limitation and how they relate to criminal responsibility

1. General

A number of issues arise in relation to criminal responsibility, quite apart from the considerations of *actus non facit reum, nisi mens sit rea*. Where an offence has been committed, there may be some reason why its perpetrator cannot be held responsible. There are three categories of such reasons:

(a) jurisdictional limitations;
(b) incapacity or exemption;
(c) general defences.

2. Jurisdictional limitations

These are:

(a) *Lapse of time* Generally, lapse of time is no bar to criminal prosecution (contrast tort and contract: *see* Chapters 9 and 14). The Limitation Acts do not, generally, apply to crimes, but in some cases, particular statutes bar prosecution for certain offences after prescribed periods, for example:

    (*i*) summary offences generally — six months; Magistrates Courts Act 1980;

    (*ii*) offences against the Trade Descriptions Act 1968 — three years from the offence, or one year from its discovery.

(b) *Territorial limits* Generally, a person cannot be tried in British courts for an offence committed on land abroad. Again, particular statutes create exceptions, whereby an offence committed by a British subject abroad is triable in this country, e.g. treason, murder, bigamy. Even where an offence has been committed in Britain, where the offender is residing in a foreign country, or has fled there, it is necessary to resort to extradition in order to bring him back to stand trial. This is a process that only exists between states who have agreed an extradition treaty; if no such treaty exists between Britain and the country of refuge, the offender is effectively outside the scope of our jurisdiction. In the case of extradition from the UK the various Acts implementing the treaties generally preclude extradition for 'offences of a political nature'.

3. Incapacity and exemptions

Certain persons may be either incapable of criminal responsibility, or exempt, by virtue of belonging to a class of persons who are subject to special rules or privileges:

(a) *incapacity* The only persons who are effectively 'incapable' of committing crimes are children under the age of 10 years under the Children and Young Persons Act 1969, s. 16. Even if such a child commits an act that would otherwise be an offence, no offence has been committed. Thus, where a seven-year-old child 'stole' a tricycle, his parents could not be guilty of receiving stolen goods when they took it from him. As the child could not steal, the tricycle was not stolen — *see Walters* v. *Lunt* (1951).

Children between the ages of 10 and 14 are capable of criminal acts, but they are exempt unless it can be shown:

    (*i*)   they committed an *actus reus* with *mens rea*; and

    (*ii*)   they did so with a 'mischievous discretion', i.e. knowledge that they were doing wrong, for example, in a case of manslaughter, it was said that the child must know he was doing something 'gravely wrong' — *see R.* v. *Gorrie* (1918).

A boy below the age of 14 years cannot be convicted of rape or attempted rape but he can be convicted of indecent assault.

Children over the age of 14 have full responsibility. They are, however, subject to different treatment to that of adult offenders, so that care orders, etc. may be utilised by the youth court, where most of the offenders between 14 and 17 are tried.

(b) *exemptions* Certain other persons are exempted from criminal liability:

    (*i*)   the Sovereign: 'the Queen can do no wrong' (though those who advise the Sovereign may be responsible for their acts);

    (*ii*)   foreign heads of state and diplomats under the (Diplomatic Privileges Act 1964 and State Immunity Act 1978.

4. Employers and corporations

While neither of these categories are completely exempt or incapable, in practice, circumstances may be such that they cannot be responsible:

(a) *employers* — a master is not, generally, liable for the crimes of his servant (for tortious liability *see* 14: **9**) but he may be liable if:

  (*i*) he counselled or abetted the offence; or
  (*ii*) the servant's act can be attributed to the master in law, e.g. only the master can 'sell' goods, legally or otherwise, as only he has legal ownership of the goods, so an absent master was liable for the fraudulent sale of hams by his servant — *see Coppen* v. *Moore* (1898); or
  (*iii*) the master has delegated the running of his business to the servant;

Example
_____

In *Allen* v. *Whitehead* (1930), D ran a café, which was managed in his absence by X. Unknown to him, X permitted prostitutes to meet there: D was guilty of an offence under the Metropolitan Police Act 1859, which forbade persons from 'permitting such meetings'.

_____

  (*iv*) where the offence is one of strict liability (*see* 25: **15**);

(b) *corporations* — they are generally liable for crimes, but limitations are, in fact, dictated by their artificial nature, so a corporation cannot commit certain offences (e.g. rape or burglary) and cannot be subject to certain punishments (e.g. death or imprisonment) — *see* generally *R.* v. *P & O European Ferries (Dover) Ltd* (1991).

5. General defences

There are several such defences. They differ considerably in that some may amount to a lack, possibly temporary, of volition (therefore no *actus reus* can have voluntarily been committed); others may entail the absence of *mens rea*; others may arise from other factors.

6. Insanity

This is a complete defence, provided that the accused can show that, at the time the offence was committed, he was 'labouring under such defect of reason, from disease of the mind, as not to know the nature and quality of his act or, if he did know it, that he did not know he was doing what was wrong' — *see R.* v. *M'Naghten* (1843).

(a) Everyone is presumed sane. It is up to the accused to prove insanity, but the burden of proof is not the same as that required of the prosecution in proving guilt (i.e. beyond all reasonable doubt). To justify a verdict of 'not guilty by reason of insanity' (*see* (e)) the accused must prove he was (or is) insane on a balance of probabilities (i.e. more likely than not).

(b) There must be some actual disease of the mind. This is a legal, not a medical question. Accordingly neither external factors nor mere stupidity will suffice — *see R.* v. *Kemp* (1957).

(c) D must be in such a condition as not to know the nature and quality of his acts or not to know they are wrong. Strong impulse, even if uncontrollable is not enough, though it might amount to another defence such as automatism (involuntary conduct). If the case is one of murder, a plea of diminished responsibility (Homicide Act 1957, s. 2), if successful, would mitigate so as to make the accused guilty only of manslaughter (*see* 27: **5**).

(d) Partial delusions may be sufficient, but only to the extent that D is to be judged 'as if the facts with respect to which the delusion exists were real'. Thus, if D kills P thinking P to be attacking him, he may be acquitted. If, on the other hand, he does so thinking he has been 'divinely ordained', he is guilty.

(e) If proven, a plea of insanity results in a verdict of 'not guilty by reason of insanity' under the (Criminal Procedure (Insanity) Act 1964, s. 1. The Criminal Procedure (Insanity and Unfitness to Plead) Act 1991 provides the power for the Court to make guardianship or supervision or treatment orders or, indeed, to give an absolute discharge. In cases of murder, however, the only order available is admission to a special hospital.

7. Automatism

An act is not punishable if it is done involuntarily — *see* generally *Hill* v. *Baxter* (1958). Such involuntariness may be the result of a recognised disease of the mind — thus, where a disease of the mind induces loss of control, we sometimes speak of 'insane automatism'.

Such automatism scarcely differs from the defence of insanity and in *Bratty* v. *A-G for Northern Ireland* (1963) HL, it was suggested that, if D raised a defence based on a disease of the mind and the jury rejected the defence of insanity, then 'there could be no room for the alternative defence of automatism'. The better view, therefore, is that, where D raises evidence of a disease of the mind, then the proper defence is insanity — *see now R.* v. *Burgess* (1991).

In cases where the defence raises the defence of diminished responsibility (and possibly also in cases involving the defence of automatism, where it depends upon some abnormality of mind) it is now open to the prosecution to lead evidence of insanity — Criminal Procedure (Insanity) Act 1964, s. 6.

Automatism is not available where the state of unconsciousness is self-induced. For example, a driver charged with manslaughter when he fell asleep at the wheel of his car could not plead automatism as he could have stopped the car when he felt too sleepy to drive — see *Kay* v. *Butterworth* (1945).

8. Intoxication

This includes both drunkenness and intoxication by drugs — *see R.* v. *Lipman* (1970). Neither of these is a defence in itself. It might be the case, however, that the accused, through intoxication, is denying that he had *mens rea*. It is unlikely that he could establish automatism through intoxication though, if intoxication is prolonged it might cause a disease of the mind such as would form the basis of the defence of insanity.

The rules may be summarised as follows:

(a) *Involuntary* intoxication. An example is where D's drink is 'laced' without his knowledge. This is a defence if it means that D has no *mens rea* — *see Ross* v. *H.M. Advocate* (1991) where a can of lager was laced with drugs.

(b) *Voluntary intoxication*:

    (*i*) where the intention to commit the offence is formed before intoxication, this is obviously no defence — *see A-G for Northern Ireland* v. *Gallagher* (1963) HL;

    (*ii*) intoxication and 'specific intent': self-induced intoxication may serve as a partial defence and in *DPP* v. *Majewski* (1976) HL, it was held that when D was charged with an offence involving a 'specific intent', then, by reason of his intoxication through drink and drugs, he should be acquitted of that offence, but should be convicted of a crime of 'basic intent' only, if the facts permitted. 'Specific intent' is a novel concept in the law, and certainly crimes involving ulterior intent (e.g. burglary), or crimes whose definition involves a particular intent (e.g. 'malice aforethought' in murder), fall within its scope;

    (*iii*) where, on the other hand, a crime of 'basic intent' (such as manslaughter) is charged and D attempts to deny *mens rea*, then evidence of intoxication is likely to be fatal to his defence, as the intention to take the drink or drugs may, in itself, be sufficient *mens rea* — *see R.* v. *Lipman* (1970). 'Basic intent' has been defined as 'the intention to do no more than the act which brings about the *actus reus*' i.e. no need to intend or foresee any consequences) said Lord Elwyn-Jones, LC, in *DPP* v. *Majewski* (1976), but intoxication is not, generally, a defence to a crime of recklessness — *see R.* v. *Caldwell* (1981).

9. Duress

It is a defence to show that the accused committed the offence against his will and under compulsion that deprived him of choice (in other words, made his act effectively involuntarily):

(a) *superior orders are not,* in themselves, *sufficient* to amount to duress.

(b) *where the compulsion amounts to threats,* then these must be of physical violence, such as leaves D with no choice. It is traditional to maintain that threats to someone other than the accused himself (including his family) are not enough; more recently this has been doubted — *see Abbott* v. *R.* (1976)). The violence must also be to the person — destruction of property is not enough.

(c) *duress in murder cases* The traditional view is that duress is not available as a defence to murder, nor to attempted murder — *see R.* v. *Gotts* (1992). In *Abbott* v. *R.* (1976), the PC held that duress could not be relied upon by a principal offender. It was relatively recently held by the House of Lords that duress is not available as a defence to a charge of aiding and abetting murder either — *see R.* v. *Howe* (1987).

(d) *duress and treason* The old rule is that duress is no answer to treason. There are, however, various offences of treason, and duress has been allowed as a defence to several of these, such as supplying food to the enemy — *see Oldcastle's* case (1419) — and helping the enemy with propaganda — *see R.* v. *Purdy* (1946).

(e) *marital coercion* This is a defence akin to duress, whereby a wife can show that her offence was committed in the presence of and under the orders of her husband under the Criminal Justice Act 1925, s. 47 — *see R.* v. *Ditta* (1988).

10. Necessity

This means the commission of an offence to prevent some graver occurrence or offence. It is usually only a defence in certain well-defined situations, such as that in the Criminal Law Act 1967, s. 3, where 'reasonable force' may be used in preventing crimes (which would include self-defence) or making an arrest.

In *Buckoke* v. *GLC* (1971), however, it was said that if a fire-engine driver 'shot' the traffic lights in order to hasten to a dangerous fire, he should not be punished. Also *see* Road Traffic Act 1988, s. 34. It is possible that an emergency may provide grounds for upholding the defence of necessity in cases of merely 'technical' offences that do not themselves endanger people or property. In *R.* v. *Martin* (1989) it was held that the defence of necessity is available if, from an objective standpoint, the accused can be said to have acted reasonably in order to avoid a threat of death or serious injury.

The defence is probably not available to murder, on the ground that killing one person enables others to survive — *see R.* v. *Dudley and Stephens* (1884).

Duress may, in some cases, be regarded as a modified form of the defence of necessity.

Statutes have occasionally adopted a modified form of the defence of necessity in circumstances not involving self-defence. For instance, the Abortion Act 1967 permits the carrying out of an abortion when it is thought necessary, two medical practitioners having to certify that they consider the operation necessary for (*inter alia*) the safety of the mother (*see* 27: **8**) (in other circumstances the operation would be a criminal offence).

11. Mistake

It is now settled that, where a mistake of fact is such that it prevents D from having the required *mens rea*, then it is a defence.

Three situations may arise.

(a) *where the law requires intention or recklessness as to some element in the actus reus* — here, a mistake will be a good defence, so, in the case of *DPP* v. *Morgan* (1976) HL, where D persisted in having sexual intercourse with a woman, believing her to be consenting whereas in fact she was not, he was not guilty of rape and the Sexual Offences (Amendment) Act 1976, s. 1, made this rule part of statute law;

(b) *where the offence may be committed negligently* — here, to be a defence, a mistake must be a reasonable one — *see R.* v. *Tolson* (1889).

(c) *strict liability* — here, mistake is no defence at all — *see R.* v. *Woodrow* (1846).

Mistake of law, on the other hand, is no defence to crime — *see R.* v. *Bailey* (1800).

12. Accident

This is only a defence in circumstances where D is not charged with a crime of negligence; neither is it a defence that D intended to commit an offence, but his intended victim is not the person who is, in fact, affected. Thus, where A intended to strike B, but missed and struck C instead, he was still guilty of assault (known as the 'doctrine of transferred malice') — *see R.* v. *Latimer* (1886). Similarly, if D is mistaken as to the identity of his victim, this is no defence (*see* 26: **11** above). On the other hand, if no crime whatsoever is intended, as when D shoots at a rabbit, but hits A, he is not guilty of any crime (unless, in so doing, he was reckless or negligent).

Progress test 26

1. What (a) jurisdictional limitations and (b) incapacities and exemptions might limit criminal responsibility? **(1–4)**

2. What is meant by (a) insanity; and (b) automatism? When might each provide a defence to a criminal charge? **(6, 7)**

3. Soak goes out with his friends, A and B, for a drink. Soak is an alcoholic, but he has been trying to keep his consumption down. While he is in the lavatory and, unknown to him, A slips neat spirit into his beer. Later, when all three are asked to leave, Soak goes berserk and assaults the barman. Discuss. **(6–8)**

4. What is meant by duress? What would be the case if A forces B to take drugs, causing B to completely lose consciousness of what he is doing and, while in that state kill C? **(8, 9)**

5. In what circumstances might necessity be a good defence to a criminal charge? Where would it be true to say that necessity is sometimes known by other names, thus creating specific defences based on necessity? **(9, 10)**

6. When might a mistake be a good defence to a criminal charge? X goes out with his gun, seeking to injure A. He mistakes B for A and shoots at him. Unfortunately he misses and kills C. Discuss. **(11, 12)**

27
Offences against the person

Fatal offences

1. Fatal offences

As the name suggests, fatal offences are those that involve the causing of death.

The relatively recent problem of legalised abortion has given rise to a (somewhat artificial) two-fold classification of such offences.

(a) *offences involving a life in being* — there are two main offences in this category: murder and manslaughter; the general term for such offences is homicide.

(b) *offences involving an unborn child* — these take the form of child destruction, or, abortion.

2. Homicide

This is the general term given to the unlawful killing of a person. Usually, it takes the form either of murder or manslaughter and these offences are normally dealt with separately, though they have certain elements in common.

The common elements are:

(a) *the killing must be unlawful* — killing an enemy soldier in war-time, for instance, is not criminal, whether done intentionally or not.

(b) *to be homicide, the victim must be a 'life in being'* — to 'kill' a fetus in the womb is not homicide, though it might be an offence (*see* 27: 8). The test as to whether a 'life in being' exists in the case of a child is whether or not it enjoys an existence independent of its mother — *see R. v. Brain* (1834).

(c) *for a person to be convicted of murder or manslaughter, it must be shown that his action actually caused or brought about the death of the victim* and that death occurred within a year and a day of his action. Thus, where a person was stabbed and died shortly afterwards, the fact that adequate medical care was not available could not be relied upon by the defendant, even though such care, if available, would probably have saved the victim's life. So long as the stab wound remained an operative cause of death, the defendant was guilty of murder — *see R.* v. *Smith* (1959).

On the other hand, when a defendant wounded a person who later died as a result of a drug that was administered during treatment, and to which he was intolerant, he was not guilty of murder — *see R.* v. *Jordan* (1956).

3. Murder

Murder is defined as the unlawful killing of a reasonable creature in being under the Queen's peace, done with malice aforethought.

As well as those elements that apply to homicide generally, the following points should be noted.

(a) *the Queen's peace* The killing of any person, other than an enemy alien, might be murder and the offence is not confined to British subjects. Nor is it confined to British territory as the British courts have jurisdiction over murders (or manslaughter) committed abroad, so long as the defendant is a British citizen. If an alien commits murder, then British courts have jurisdiction only where this occurs in British territory, though that includes British ships and aeroplanes.

(b) *malice aforethought* This is the *mens rea* of murder. Murder is an offence of *specific intent*, i.e. it must be shown that some consequences, over and above the action involved, were intended. It is not, however, necessary to show that the defendant intended death as such. Thus, malice aforethought might involve the following:

(*i*)   the intention to cause the death of the victim;

(*ii*)   the intention to do serious bodily harm to the victim.

The problem is, of course, that these relate to a state of mind, which must normally be inferred and cannot often be actually proved as such. Accordingly, the law has, from time to time, attempted to formulate the circumstances in which such an intention may be inferred. The latest such attempt was in *R.* v. *Hancock and Shankland* (1986), in which the House of Lords held that the intention to kill or cause serious bodily harm could not be inferred simply because death was the natural consequence of the accused's action. The most one could say was that, where death or serious bodily harm were probable consequences, the greater the likelihood that one or another were foreseen by the accused — the higher the degree of foresight, the greater the likelihood that the consequences were intended.

(c) *penalties for murder* Prior to the Murder (Abolition of Death Penalty) Act 1965, the penalty for certain kinds of murder was death.

It is now a mandatory sentence of life imprisonment. This does not, however, mean that a convicted person will necessarily remain in prison until he dies.

4. Manslaughter

This is unlawfully causing the death of another but without malice aforethought (the same rules relating to causation in murder apply here).

5. Voluntary manslaughter

This is the term used for a situation where D may even intend to kill someone, but nevertheless be guilty only of manslaughter. There are three such situations:

(a) where D acts under provocation (Homicide Act 1957, s. 3);
(b) where D is suffering from diminished responsibility (Homicide Act 1957, s. 2);
(c) where D kills in pursuance of a suicide pact (Homicide Act 1957, s. 4).

Let us look at provocation and diminished responsibility more closely:

(a) *Provocation* The Homicide Act 1957, s. 3, allows the question of provocation to be put to the jury where there is evidence of provocation by things done or said, or both; formerly, words alone were not normally regarded as sufficient. The question for the jury is whether, as a result of what was said or done, a reasonable man would have lost his self-control, and done as D did:

    (i) 'cooling-off' time i.e., if D has had sufficient time to 'cool-off' after being provoked, and before killing, it may be murder, not manslaughter — *see R. v. Hayward* (1833);
    (ii) whatever the rule before, it is now clear that provocation need not be given by the person killed; nor need it be directed at D — *see R. v. Davies* (1975);
    (iii) 'reasonable man' is now to be interpreted as meaning a reasonable person of the age of the accused — *see R. v. Camplin* (1978) HL.

What matters is that D has actually lost his self-control at the time of killing, and that a reasonable man would have done likewise.

(b) *Diminished responsibility* This is defined in the Homicide Act 1957, s. 2, as, 'such abnormality of mind . . . as substantially impairs his mental responsibility for his acts and omissions'. Unlike insanity the cause need not be a disease of the mind, but might include external factors, such as injury, as well as 'irresistible impulse' — *see R.* v. *Byrne* (1960) — but not, it seems, self-administered alcohol — *see R.* v. *Tandy* (1987).

6. Involuntary manslaughter

This covers cases where killing is not intended and includes the following.

(a) *Constructive manslaughter* This is the intention to commit an unlawful and dangerous act from which death results. In the case of *DPP* v. *Newbury* (1977), D threw stones over the side of a railway bridge and one struck the guard of a passing train, killing him. In *R.* v. *Mahal* (1991), the victim was pushed through an open window, 22 feet from the ground.

(b) *Gross negligence* Where an act, though otherwise lawful, is done with such disregard for the lives and safety of others as to amount to an offence — *see Andrews* v. *DPP* (1937).

(c) *An unlawful omission*, such as neglecting to feed a child — *see R.* v. *Lowe* (1973) — or dependent adult — *see R.* v. *Stone and Dobinson* (1977). (This is similar to gross negligence in that there must be obvious disregard for others; it differs, however, in that liability for any consequences of omissions can only occur where D is under a legal duty to act (*see* 25: **10**).)

7. Infanticide

Where a woman wilfully causes the death of her child while it is under the age of 12 months, but while the balance of her mind is disturbed by the after-effects of birth, she is guilty of infanticide and not of murder under the Infanticide Act 1938, s. 1. Infanticide is punishable as manslaughter.

8. Child destruction and abortion

It is not murder to kill a child as yet unborn. It is an offence, however, to destroy the life of an unborn child, unless the destruction is necessary for the preservation of its mother's life under the Infant Life (Preservation) Act 1929, s. 1.

The Abortion Act 1967 legalises abortion in certain circumstances. By virtue of s. 1, a doctor may terminate a pregnancy where two doctors have certified that:

(a) continuance of pregnancy might endanger the health of the mother or of her existing children; or

(b) there is a real risk that the child, if born, would suffer from such mental or physical abnormality as to be severely handicapped.

This does not affect the offence of child destruction as the Abortion Act 1967 specifically provides that it is not to affect the 1929 Act's provisions. Note that the 1929 Act deals only with an unborn child 'capable of being born alive'.

Non-fatal offences

9. Assault and battery

Assault means any act that D causes P to apprehend as an act of violence upon himself. Battery means actually applying force to another.

There are several degrees of assault and we may speak of some of them as 'aggravated' assaults, by virtue of the fact that they are regarded as more heinous (though not necessarily more dangerous).

Most varieties of assault are defined by the Offences against the Person Act 1861:

(a) common assault (s. 47);
(b) assault occasioning bodily harm (s. 47);
(c) assault causing grievous bodily harm (s. 20);
(d) unlawful or malicious wounding (s. 20);
(e) wounding with intent to do grievous bodily harm (s. 18).

Aggravated assaults include:

(a) assault with intent to avoid arrest (s. 38);
(b) assaulting a clergyman in the discharge of his duties (s. 37).

10. Sexual offences

These are:

(a) *Rape* This is now defined by the Sexual Offences (Amendment) Act 1976:

> A man commits rape if he has unlawful sexual intercourse with a woman who, at the time, does not consent to it and, at the time, he knows she does not consent, or is reckless as to whether she consents to it.

This effectively codifies the decision in *DPP* v. *Morgan* (1976) HL. As the definition requires 'unlawful sexual intercourse', it was long thought that a husband cannot be guilty of raping his wife, unless husband and wife are judicially separated — *see R.* v. *Clarke* (1949). However, in *R.* v. *R.* (1991), the House of Lords made it perfectly clear that there is no marital exemption to the crime of rape. Further, if he uses unreasonable force to obtain intercourse with his wife, a man may be guilty of another offence, such as assault — *see R.* v. *Miller* (1954) and *R.* v. *Kowalski* (1988).

(b) *other offences* involving sexual intercourse. It is an offence:

(*i*) to have intercourse with a girl under 16 years of age (Sexual Offences Act 1956, s. 6). A man is not guilty, however, if he reasonably believes the girl to be over 16, so long as she is, in fact, over 13, provided he has not been charged with 'a like offence' previously and is under 24 years of age;

(*ii*) to administer drugs to obtain intercourse under the Sexual Offences Act 1956, s. 4(1);

(*iii*) to procure intercourse by threats or false pretence in s. 2 of the Act;

(*iv*) to procure, for the purposes of intercourse with a third party, a girl under 21 years in s. 23(1) of the Act;

(*v*) to have intercourse with mental defectives or to procure defectives;

(*vi*) to commit incest, i.e. to have intercourse with blood relatives.

(c) *indecent assault* Such an assault, upon either a man or a woman, is an offence under the Sexual Offences Act 1956, ss. 14 and 15. Homosexual acts between consenting males over 21 years of age in private are no longer criminal (Sexual Offences Act 1967, s. 1).

(d) *Other sexual offences* include:

(*i*) offences connected with prostitution;

(*ii*) unnatural offences such as buggery;

(*iii*) indecent exposure (Vagrancy Act 1824, s .4);

(*iv*) abduction of women.

11. Bigamy

It is an offence if anyone, being married 'shall marry any other person during the life of the former husband or wife . . .' under the Offences against the Person Act 1861, s. 57:

(a) 'Being married'. No offence is committed if the previous marriage was, in fact, void or if D has obtained a divorce.

(b) It is a defence to show that the accused's spouse has been continuously absent for seven years or more and that, during that time the accused did not know that such spouse was alive (Offences against the Person Act 1861, s. 57). Note that, under the Matrimonial

Courts Act 1973, s. 19, it is possible to secure a court decree of presumption of death and dissolution of marriage.

(c) It is also a defence if, on reasonable grounds, the accused believes the former spouse to be dead. For example, D was reliably informed that her husband had died after five years of their living apart. She was acquitted of bigamy when, acting in good faith on this advice, she married X — see R. v. Tolson (1889).

This defence of 'honest and reasonable mistake' has been extended to include a belief that the previous marriage was dissolved — see R. v. Gould (1968).

12. Motoring offences

Many offences under the Road Traffic Acts (1988 and 1991), of course, are not offences against the person. The principal offences that are, however, are the following:

(a) *causing death by dangerous driving* The Road Traffic Act 1991 makes it an offence to cause the death of another person by driving a motor vehicle on a road dangerously.

(b) *reckless driving* The Road Traffic Act 1988 makes it an offence to drive a motor vehicle recklessly on a road.

(c) *driving without due care and attention,* or *driving without due consideration for other persons using the road* under the Road Traffic Act 1988. These are separate heads of liability, though it is common to refer to both as 'careless driving'.

(d) a motorist whose driving causes death may be convicted of manslaughter — see *Andrews* v. *DPP* (1937).

Progress test 27

1. Define and distinguish between murder and manslaughter. What is meant by 'malice aforethought' in the former?   (1–5)

2. Distinguish 'voluntary' and 'involuntary' manslaughter. Try to define these by reference to the origins of the offences involved. (4–6)

3. A and B are man and wife. Eight months after the birth of their child, B kills the infant. On arriving home, A is so shocked that he immediately shoots B and, when their neighbour, C, arrives to investigate the noise, he punches him in the eye, blinding him. Later A drinks 15 whiskies and drives to London. Discuss. (5, 7, 9, 12)

4. Distinguish between assault and battery. What is meant by 'aggravated assault'? (Give examples.) (9)

5. Define rape. What other offences involving sexual intercourse are there? (10)

6. What is the general nature of the crime of bigamy? What technical defences might be available to a person charged with bigamy? (11)

7. Outline the main offences connected with road traffic that may be said to constitute offences against the person. (12)

Offences against property

Theft Acts 1968 and 1978

1. Introduction

The law relating to offences now covered by the Theft Acts of 1968 and 1978 was formerly contained in the Larceny Acts 1827, 1861 and 1916.

The Theft Act 1968 substituted the offence of theft for that of larceny and redefined and renamed many of the allied offences relating to frauds, etc. It was found, however, that one particular offence, that of 'obtaining a pecuniary advantage by deception' (Theft Act 1968, s. 16) remained unnecessarily complicated; the Theft Act 1978 has replaced this section with other provisions.

Offences relating to forgery are under the Forgery and Counterfeiting Act 1981 (*see* 28: **16**).

2. Theft

A person is guilty of theft if he 'dishonestly appropriates property belonging to another with the intention of permanently depriving that other of it' (Theft Act 1968, s. 1(1)).

The maximum punishment for theft is ten years imprisonment (Theft Act 1968, s. 7).

3. *Actus reus* of theft

The *actus reus* of theft is the 'appropriation of property belonging to another':

(a) *Appropriation* This is defined in s. 3 as 'any assumption by a person of the rights of an owner' — *see R.* v. *Morris* (1984):

    (i) it is no longer necessary to move the property — to destroy P's goods *in situ* would amount to an appropriation;

    (ii) if D comes by the property innocently, but later decides to keep it, then he 'appropriates' it at that later time — *see Stein v. Henshall* (1976);

(*iii*) it is not necessary that *all* of the rights of an owner are assumed; an assumption of only some such rights is enough; thus, in *R.* v. *Morris* (1984), a person who changed the price tags on goods in a supermarket, intending to pay the lower price, was guilty of theft, as was a man who presented stolen cheques — *see R.* v. *Gomez* (1991).

(b) *property*:

(*i*) section 4(1) defines property as 'money and all property real or personal, including things in action and other intangible property';

(*ii*) things forming part of the land (such as plants) cannot be stolen, normally, unless 'severed' from the land, so picking wild flowers, mushrooms, fruit or foliage is not theft, unless done for sale or commercial purpose (s. 4(2));

(*iii*) wild creatures, on the other hand, may be stolen (s. 4(2));

(c) *belonging to another* — the Theft Act 1968, s. 5(1), states that 'property shall be regarded as belonging to any person having possession or control of it, or having any proprietary right or interest':

(*i*) while, normally, property is stolen from its owner, in *R.* v. *Turner (No.* 2)(1971), where T had taken his car to a garage for repairs, it was held to be theft when he went back one night and removed it, using spare keys, to avoid paying the repair bills, but an owner cannot normally be guilty of theft. Indeed, where D removed his own car from a police pound, this was not theft — *see R.* v. *Meredith* (1973) — as this was because the garage could refuse to return the vehicle (i.e. had control, as well as possession) until the repair bills were paid while the police did not have such a right;

(*ii*) any proprietary right or interest will suffice, thus goods may be stolen from P while they are in the possession of X (though it is likely that the goods are effectively stolen from X, too, as he is in possession) and more significant, perhaps, is the case where D sells goods to P and then fails to deliver them. This is theft from P, who, when he purchased the goods acquired a proprietary interest and it is also theft where a partner appropriates to his own use partnership property — *see R.* v. *Bonner* (1970);

(*iii*) property held for another, which is received for a particular purpose, may be stolen by the holder or receiver in that it still belongs to that other person (s. 5(3)) — it is not enough that by receiving the money, D merely becomes indebted to P — *see R. v. Hall* (1972);

(*iv*) property obtained by mistake is regarded as belonging to any person entitled to restoration, and a failure to make restoration amounts to theft (s. 5(4)), though not every case involving such a mistake involves an obligation to make restoration, but, if the mistake is induced by D, an offence under s. 15 may have been committed (*see* 28: **9**);

(*v*) trust property, for the purposes of the Theft Act 1968, belongs to the person who is entitled to enforce the trust: s. 5(2).

4. *Mens rea* of theft

This is twofold: the appropriation must be both dishonest *and* accompanied by an intention permanently to deprive the person to whom the property belongs (s. 1(1)):

(a) *dishonest* — dishonesty is not defined in the Act, instead, three examples of where an appropriation is *not* to be regarded as dishonest are cited, though s. 2(2) makes it clear that a person's appropriation may be dishonest even if he is willing to pay for the property appropriated, so the following are not dishonest appropriations:

(*i*) where D believes he had a right in law to deprive the other of the property;

(*ii*) where he believes that the other would have consented had he known of the circumstances — *see R. v. Holden* (1991) — he thought taking scrap tyres home was permitted;

(*iii*) where he believes that the person to whom the property belongs cannot be discovered by taking reasonable steps, e.g. where D finds goods that are apparently abandoned;

(b) *the intention permanently to deprive* — a temporary borrowing of property, even if done dishonestly, does not amount to theft, unless it is done in circumstances 'making it equivalent to an outright taking or disposal'.

Example

D takes P's season ticket for the opera and uses it for the remainder of the season, intending to return it afterwards. These would be 'circumstances equivalent to an outright taking'.

On the other hand, where D picked up a lady's handbag in the cinema to ascertain whether it contained anything he would have been interested in stealing, this was not theft, as it was only a 'conditional' taking — *see R.* v. *Easom* (1971).

(c) while it is not theft if there is no intention permanently to deprive anyone, in the event that certain types of property are involved, other offences may be committed without such an intention, as follows:

(*i*) *taking a conveyance without authority* (s. 12). conveyance here includes cars, motor-cycles, or anything constructed for the purpose of conveying persons by land, sea or air and taking them without authority is an arrestable offence (taking a bicycle is a separate summary offence (s. 12(5)).

(*ii*) *removal of articles from a place open to the public* (s. 11) — the place must be a building or part of a building to which the public have access (if no access is permitted the remover may be guilty of burglary (*see* 28: **6**)) and this offence carries a maximum penalty of five years' imprisonment;

(*iii*) *dishonestly abstracting, wasting or diverting electricity* (s. 13) — this offence is punishable by up to five years' imprisonment.

5. Robbery

'A person is guilty of robbery if he steals and, immediately before or at the time of doing so, and in order to do so, he uses force on any person, or puts or seeks to put any person in fear of being then and there subjected to force' states the Theft Act 1968, s. 8(1).

(a) It is necessary that he steals — *see Corcoran* v. *Anderton* (1980). Robbery is, therefore, a form of 'aggravated theft'. (As such, an offender risks life imprisonment.) It is not robbery, then, if D has any of the defences that would be available to him on a charge of theft. For example D demands the repayment of a debt, emphasizing his point with a knife, believing he has a right to the money — *see R.* v. *Robinson* (1977).

(b) Force means more than mere physical contact. A well-executed pickpocketing is therefore not robbery, though a clumsy one may be. It is certainly necessary that force be used or threatened in order to steal. Where some boys surrounded a young man threateningly, and the young man, in fear for his safety, offered money that was accepted, this was not robbery as the threat was made gratuitously and not with a view to stealing — *see R.* v. *Bruce* (1975).

6. Burglary

A person is guilty of burglary (punishable by 14 years' imprisonment) if:

(a) he enters any building or part of a building as a trespasser and with intent to steal, inflict grievous bodily harm or commit rape therein or to do any unlawful damage to the building or anything therein; or

(b) having entered as a trespasser, he steals or attempts to steal or inflicts or attempts to inflict any grievous bodily harm (Theft Act 1968, s. 9).

7. Entry as a trespasser
Some important issues are:

(a) It is crucial to determine whether, at the time of entering, the accused was a trespasser.

Example
_____
In the case of *R.* v. *Collins* (1972), D climbed up a ladder to a girl's bedroom window with the intention of having intercourse with her (regardless of whether she consented). He was on the window-sill when he was beckoned in by the girl. It was held that it was *not* burglary because he had *not* effectively entered the house (not having crossed the window-sill) before the invitation to enter was made.
_____

(b) If D is given permission to enter for a particular purpose, but in fact enters for the purpose of stealing or some other purpose, he is a trespasser — see *R.* v. *Jones and Smith* (1976). It is the same if his entry is made under false pretences. If, for example, D pretends to be a gas man who has come to read the meter and, once inside, steals — *see R.* v. *Boyle* (1954).

(c) It is irrelevant what time of day or night the offence is committed.

(d) If a person commits any burglary and has with him any firearm, offensive weapon or explosive (or imitation firearm), he is guilty of aggravated burglary and liable to imprisonment for life (s. 10) — *see*, e.g. *R..* v. *Stones* (1989).

8. Offences involving deception
These were contained in the Theft Act 1968, ss. 15 and 16. They were defined as:

(a) dishonestly obtaining property by deception (s. 15, *see* 28: **9**);

(b) dishonestly obtaining a pecuniary advantage by deception (s. 16, *see* 28: **10**).

Section 16 has now been repealed by the Theft Act 1978. Section 15 of the Theft Act 1968, though, remains in force.

9. Obtaining property by deception

This offence is committed by anyone who 'by any deception dishonestly obtains property belonging to another with the intention of permanently depriving that other of it'. It carries a penalty of up to ten years' imprisonment under the Theft Act 1968, s. 15(1).

The offence is similar to theft except that, instead of an appropriation, an obtaining by deception must take place. For example, in *R.. v. Ashbee* (1989), passports were obtained and used by means of a fraudulent application for them. Both offences may be committed on the same set of facts. In *R. v. Lawrence* (1971) HL, a taxi driver took a foreign student from Victoria Station to West London; the student, who did not understand English money, held out his wallet for the driver to take the correct fare, but the driver took considerably more. It was held that, while this was an offence under s. 15, it might also have been charged as theft:

(a) deception includes any deception whether by words or conduct: in *R. v. Lawrence* (1971), the conduct of the driver in taking an excessive amount constituted a deception (the taking, of course, also amounted to theft) and such a deception may also involve a 'deception as to present intention' (s. 15(3));

(b) to constitute an offence, it must be shown that the deception was operative;

Example
In *R. v. Laverty* (1970), D, having acquired a stolen car, changed its number plates and offered it for sale to P, who bought it. It was held that as P did not buy the car in reliance on the representation as to the registration number, no offence had been committed (though, had it been proved that P had purchased the car *only* on the understanding that D was its owner, there might have been).

(c) money counts as property for the purposes of this section;
(d) 'obtaining' includes the obtaining for oneself or for another (s. 15(2));
(e) the defences to theft (that D is not, in fact, 'dishonest' (s. 2(1)); or does not, in fact, intend to permanently deprive (s. 6) apply — *see R. v. Feely* (1973).

10. The Theft Act 1978
This Act was passed to replace the offence of 'obtaining a pecuniary advantage by deception' formerly contained in the Theft Act 1968, s. 16. The new offences are as follows:

(a) by deception, dishonestly obtaining any services (s. 1(1)) which carries up to five years' imprisonment and, s. 1(2) states that 'it is an obtaining of services where the other person is induced to confer a benefit, by doing some act, or causing or permitting some act to be done, on the understanding that the benefit has been or will be paid for';

(b) evading, by any deception, any liability (s. 2(1)), which includes:
  (i) the remission, in whole or in part, of any existing liability to make a payment — see R. v. Jackson (1983) and R. v. Modupe (1991) but contrast R v. Attewell-Hughes (1991);
  (ii) with intent to default on payment, in whole or in part, inducing a creditor to wait for, or forgo payment;
  (iii) dishonestly obtaining any exemption or abatement of liability where 'liability' is defined as 'any legally enforceable liability' (s. 2(2)) — gambling debts are thereby still excluded. It is still an offence to proffer a cheque, in order to induce a creditor to defer the date when payment of a liability falls due (s. 2(3)) (offences under this section carry a penalty of up to five years' imprisonment);

(c) dishonestly making off without making payment, in circumstances where payment for any goods supplied or service done is expected or required on the spot (s. 3(1)). Thus, in R. v. Allen (1985), a man was convicted when, having stayed for ten nights in a hotel, he left without paying (this offence carries a penalty of up to two years' imprisonment).

11. False accounting

This is proscribed by the Theft Act 1968, s. 17 and is committed 'where a person dishonestly and with a view to gain for himself or with intent to cause loss to another:

(a) destroys, defaces, conceals or falsifies any account or any record or document made or required for any accounting purpose — see Edwards v. Toombs (1983); or
(b) produces such a document in furnishing information for any purpose which, to his knowledge, is or may be misleading, false or deceptive in a material particular'.

This offence carries a maximum penalty of seven years' imprisonment.

Related offences are:

(a) false statements by company directors, etc. (s. 19), for which the penalty is seven years imprisonment;

(b) suppression of documents, done dishonestly with a view to gain (s. 20), incurring seven years imprisonment.

12. Blackmail

This is dealt with by the Theft Act 1968, s. 21, which states that a person is guilty of blackmail if, with a view to gain for himself or intent to cause loss to another, he makes an unwarranted demand with menaces. The offence carries a sentence of up to 14 years' imprisonment (s. 21(3)).

A demand with menaces is unwarranted unless the person making it believes:

(a) that he has reasonable grounds for making the demand; and
(b) that the use of menaces is a proper means of reinforcing the demand:

  (i) *the thing demanded* — the nature of thing demanded is irrelevant; it need not be money;
  (ii) *the menaces need not involve physical violence* — if they do, however, the offence of robbery may also be committed (*see* 28: **4**) (a 'menace' was defined by Lord Wright in *Thorne* v. *Motor Trade Association* (1937) as 'a threat of any action detrimental to or unpleasant to the person addressed';
  (iii) 'gain' here includes keeping what one has, as well as getting what one has not and 'loss' includes loss of an expectation, as well as losing what one already has (s. 34(2));
  (iv) blackmail is committed as soon as the demand is made and, accordingly, it is improbable that a person could be convicted of *attempted* blackmail (*see* 25: **13**) as either his act is too remote or the offence of blackmail itself is committed.

13. Handling stolen goods

A person is guilty of handling stolen goods if (otherwise than in the course of stealing), knowing or believing them to be stolen, he dishonestly receives the goods, or dishonestly undertakes or assists in their retention, removal, disposal or realisation by or for the benefit of another person, or if he arranges to do so: Theft Act 1968, s. 22(1). (This offence carries a maximum penalty of fourteen years' imprisonment.)

(a) Stolen goods include property that is obtained by theft, blackmail or deception: s. 24(4).
(b) Goods cease to be stolen if they are returned to their lawful

possessor or to other lawful custody: s. 24(3), but whether goods have been so reduced is a question of fact for the jury to decide;

(c) evidence that the accused has been involved in handling the goods within 12 months or has them in his possession at the time is admissible for the purpose of proving that he knew or believed the goods were stolen (s. 27(3)), but it is not *conclusive* evidence — *see R. v. Sloggett* (1972);

(d) an allied offence is contained in s. 23, which makes it an offence to publish an advertisement for the return of stolen goods that states that no questions will be asked or that the person returning the goods will be safe from apprehension or inquiry and a person guilty of such an offence is liable to a fine of £100 on summary conviction.

14. Going equipped for stealing

Under the Theft Act 1968, s. 25, it is an offence for any person to have, when not at his place of abode, any article for use in the course of or in connection with any burglary, theft or cheat (s. 25(1)). Proof that D had an article made or adapted for such a use is proof that he had it with him for such a use (s. 25(2)). It has been held that, where D had innocuous implements (screwdrivers and gloves) it was necessary to prove that they were to be used in the future; it was *not* enough that D was in possession of articles after a robbery and was trying to get rid of them — *see R. v. Ellames* (1974).

15. Husband and wife

As the Theft Act 1968 came into force, a husband can be prosecuted for stealing from his wife, and vice versa under s. 30 of the Act.

Other offences

16. The Forgery and Counterfeiting Act 1981

Forgery is defined (s. 1) as the making of a false instrument with the intention that it shall be used to induce somebody to accept it as genuine and, by reason of so accepting it, do or do not do some act to his own or any other person's prejudice.

(a) 'instrument' is defined in s. 8 as any document; any stamp used by the Post Office or Inland Revenue; any disc, tape, sound track or other device on or in which information is recorded or stored by mechanical, electronic or other means (but *see R. v. Gold and Schifreen*

(1987)); a currency note; or any mark used by the Post Office as an alternative to a stamp;

(b) an instrument is 'false' if it purports:

    (*i*) to have been made in the form or terms in which it is made by or on the authority of a person who did not in fact make it or authorise it in that form or terms; or

    (*ii*) to have been altered in any respect by or on the authority of a person who did not in fact alter it or authorise the alteration; or

    (*iii*) to have been made or altered on a date or at a place or in circumstances in which it was not in fact made or altered; or

    (*iv*) to have been made or altered by a person who does not in fact exist, where it is purported by the instrument that he does exist (s. 9);

(c) a person is induced to act (or not to act) to his prejudice if it is intended that he should suffer loss of property (whether temporary or permanent) or the loss of some opportunity to gain financially; or that someone should be given the opportunity to gain a financial advantage, whether by way of remuneration or otherwise, from him (s. 10);

(d) it is also an offence to use a false instrument, or a copy of a false instrument with the intention of inducing somebody to accept it as genuine and, by reason of accepting it, to do or not to do some act to his own or any other person's prejudice (ss. 4 and 5);

(e) the Act also makes it an offence for a person to have in his custody or control any money order, postal order, UK postage or Inland Revenue stamp, share certificate, passport, cheque or travellers' cheque, cheque or credit card or birth or marriage certificate, knowing or believing it to be false (s. 5).

A person guilty of any of the above offences is liable to a fine of up to £2,000 or 6 months' imprisonment on summary conviction, or on indictment, to a term of up to 10 years.

17. The Criminal Damage Act 1971

This Act now governs the main offences concerning damage to property. This Act therefore replaces the Malicious Damage Act 1861 and simplifies the law (as the 1968 and 1978 Theft Acts do in relation to the old Larceny Acts 1827–1916)).

Under the Criminal Damage Act 1971, it is an offence punishable by up to ten years' imprisonment, without lawful excuse, to destroy or damage any property belonging to another, intending to destroy or damage that property or being reckless as to whether any such property might be destroyed or damaged:

(a) property, to be damaged, has to be material — intangible • property is (of course) excluded (compare theft), whereas (again unlike theft) land is included (s. 10(1)) but, interestingly, 'hacking' into computer disks constituted criminal damage in *R. v. Whiteley* (1991);

(b) damage does not necessarily involve breaking: a completed jig-saw puzzle could be damaged by being dismantled, a pavement is damaged by paint — see *Hardman* v. *Chief Constable of Avon and Somerset* (1986).

(c) lawful excuse includes 'claim of right', similar to the denial of dishonesty in a charge of theft (*see* 28: **4**(a)), but also includes the defence that the accused destroyed or damaged the property in order to protect property or a right to property belonging to himself or another (for the defence of necessity *see* 26: **10**);

(d) the statute covers the offence known as arson, which is to destroy or damage property by fire;

(e) it is also an offence to threaten to destroy or damage property without lawful excuse (s. 2), which might also constitute blackmail, if done with a view to gain or causing loss and if an unwarranted demand is made.

Progress test 28

1. Define theft. What is meant by 'property belonging to another'?   (**2, 3**)

2. Shifty comes across Happy's mackintosh in a cloakroom. He decides to try it on to see if it will fit him. In fact, it is far too small. Has Shifty committed any offence?   (**4**)

3. Distinguish between robbery and blackmail.   (**5, 12**)

4. In how many ways might burglary be committed? Outline the differences between them.   (**6, 7**)

5. Which offences involving deception arise under the Theft Acts? What are their main features?   (**8–10**)

6.   Sly sells goods cheaply to Stupid. The police raid Stupid's home and he is charged with handling, the goods having been the proceeds of a lorry hi-jacking. Stupid denies the offence, but has in fact, been involved in a similar matter three months previously. Is he guilty?   **(13)**

7.   Define forgery. Explain the phrase 'a false instrument'.   **(16)**

8.   Outline what is involved in the offence of criminal damage. **(17)**

29

Offences against state security and public order

Offences against state security

1. Treason

Treason is still a capital offence. Various statutes have created a number of ways in which it can be committed, the most important of which are the following:

(a) compassing the death of the Sovereign or levying war against the Sovereign in his realm or giving aid and comfort to the Sovereign's enemies in the realm or elsewhere (Statute of Treasons 1351);

(b) compassing or imagining or intending the Sovereign's death, destruction, wounding or imprisonment (Treason Act 1795);

(c) expressing intention to depose the Sovereign, incite invasion or intimidate either House of Parliament (Treason Felony Act 1848).

2. Misprision of treason

This means concealing treason (without concurring in it) and is punishable by imprisonment for life.

3. Official Secrets Acts 1911–1920 and 1989

These Acts seek to protect the secrecy surrounding much information of an 'official' character. They are not confined to matters relating to defence or national security. Thus, various activities are prohibited:

(a) it is an offence for any person, for any purpose prejudicial to the interests of the state, to enter any prohibited place (OSA 1911, s. 1), including military establishments: in *Chandler* v. *DPP* (1964), it was held that when protesters entered an airfield, they were guilty, even though their aim was the promotion of peace, as interfering with the airfield's activities was prejudicial to the interests of the state, it being government policy to maintain such airfields;

(b) the OSA 1989 was passed as a reflection of government concern following the 'Spycatcher' affair (*Attorney-General* v. *Guardian Newspapers* (1987) and (1988)) and as a settled view that members of the security services are, or should be, under a duty of life-long confidentiality about their work (there had also been many criticisms made of the overly broad OSA 1911, s. 2); the 1989 Act defines various categories of official information, the unauthorised disclosure of which is a crime. They include security and intelligence, defence, international relations, information obtained in confidence from other states or international organisations, but disclosure by those outside Crown service or government contractors will not be criminal unless a 'test of harm' can be satisfied; for those within these categories, harm will be assumed and there is no 'public interest' defence.

4. Perjury

This occurs where any person knowingly makes a false statement on oath in any judicial proceeding (Perjury Act 1911, s. 1). Related offences include the making of false statements relating to births, marriages or deaths (whether under oath or not) and procuring some other person to commit perjury (sub-ornation of perjury).

All forms of perjury are punishable by fine or imprisonment for up to seven years or both.

5. Sedition

This means any practices (short of treason) intended to promote disaffection among subjects, either against the state or among themselves, or to bring the Sovereign or government into hatred.

Offences against public order

6. Offences against public order

For the most part, these now fall under the Public Order Act 1986 (POA 1986). This Act abolished the old common law offences of riot, rout, unlawful assembly and affray and replaced them with a number of statutory offences. It also changed the existing law on threatening, abusive and insulting behaviour and incitement to racial hatred (formerly contained in the Public Order Act 1936, ss. 5 and 5(a) and created a number of brand new offences, as well as introducing increased police powers to deal with public disorder. The offences now contained in the POA 1986 are summarised below.

7. New offences
The new offences in the POA 1986 are as follows.

(a) *riot* — this replaces the old common law offence: where 12 or more persons use or threaten violence for a common purpose, in circumstances where a reasonable person would fear for his safety, they are guilty of riot (s. 1);
(b) *violent disorder* — a new offence, this consists of the use or threat of violence by three or more people that causes a reasonable person to fear for his safety (s. 2).

8. Threatening, abusive or insulting words or behaviour
The POA 1986, ss. 4–5, replaces those offences found previously in s. 5 of the Act of 1936 with two new offences. They consist of using threatening, abusive or insulting words or behaviour or written notices where:

(a) their use is intended or likely to cause fear of violence, or provoke the use of violence (s. 4); *or*
(b) their use is likely to cause harassment, alarm or distress to any person (s. 5) (it is enough for this offence if conduct is disorderly; it does not necessarily have to be threatening, abusive or insulting).

Both of these offences may be committed in private as well as public places.

9. Incitement to racial hatred
The POA 1986 creates new offences relating to racial hatred (*see* 4: **27, 28**).

10. Failure to comply with police regulations, prohibitions and orders
The POA 1986 confers upon the police the power to make regulations and orders and to prohibit processions in certain circumstances for the purpose of preventing public disorder or disruption to the community or violence. Failure to comply with any of these is an offence. The main examples of such powers are as follows:

(a) regulations as to the route, time and size, etc., of processions and other assemblies;
(b) the prohibition of processions that threaten disorder or intimidation;

(c) orders excluding individuals from football matches, where they have committed certain specified offences (s. 31).

11. Public mischief

It is an offence, punishable summarily, to cause wasteful employment of the police by means of false reports (Criminal Law Act 1967, s. 5(2)).

Generally, however, there is no duty to report offences at all; the offence applies only where reports are volunteered, which are in fact false, and where this is done knowingly (Criminal Law Act 1967, s. 5(2). For an important exception in cases of terrorism *see* 29: **12**.

12. Terrorism

The Prevention of Terrorism (Temporary Provisions) Act 1989 includes the following offences:

(a) belonging to a proscribed organisation;
(b) supporting a proscribed organisation;
(c) the commission, preparation or instigation of acts of terrorism;
(d) remaining in the UK having become subject to an exclusion order made by the Home Secretary.

13. Criminal eviction and harassment

It is an offence:

(a) to unlawfully deprive the residential occupier of any premises in his occupation;
(b) to carry out acts calculated to interfere with the peace or comfort of the residential occupier or persistently withdraw or withhold services (if done with intent to cause the residential occupier to give up occupation, or to refrain from exercising any rights thereto) under the Protection from Eviction Act 1977, s. 1(2), (3).

14. Conspiracy

Sometimes this is regarded as an offence against the state. Certainly this is true historically, but for the modern law on conspiracy *see* 25: **20**.

15. Unlawfully entering or remaining on property

There are now various offences connected with entry to land or premises and remaining there unlawfully. These arise under the Criminal Law Act 1977 and Public Order Act 1986:

(a) *the Criminal Law Act 1977* This Act creates two distinct offences of entering or remaining on premises:

(*i*) it is an offence to use or threaten violence for the purpose of unlawfully securing entry to any premises where there is someone opposed to such entry and the person using or threatening violence knows this (s. 6(1)), the maximum penalty for which is six months' imprisonment.

(*ii*) it is an offence if a person who has entered premises as a trespasser fails to leave them on being requested to do so (s. 7(6)), this offence also carrying a six-month prison sentence;

(b) *the Public Order Act 1986* This Act, in s. 39, creates a new offence as follows:

(*i*) a senior police officer is empowered to order people off land, where, having entered as trespassers, they take up (or intend to take up) residence there and either cause damage or use threatening, abusive or insulting words or behaviour or bring 12 or more vehicles on to the land, but the power only arises if the occupier himself has been unable, by taking reasonable steps, to remove the trespassers;

(*ii*) if the trespassers do not comply with such an order or, if they return within three months, the police have the power to arrest them, whereupon they may be tried summarily and, if convicted, fined or imprisoned for three months (*see* 15: **17**).

16. Public nuisance and obstruction of the highway

This may also constitute a tort (*see* 15: **26**). Unlike the tort of private nuisance, public nuisance can take the form of an isolated event 'if it is done under such circumstances that the public right to condemn it should be vindicated' — *see R. v. Mutters* (1864).

17. Criminal libel

Libel is also a tort (*see* Chapter 18). Criminal proceedings are rare. While it was formerly an offence to spread false reports concerning a magnate (*Scandalum Magnatum* 1275), it is nowadays thought proper to bring a criminal action for libel only where the libel is a particularly serious one and it is in the public interest to bring such an action. It is not, however, necessary (for a libel to be criminal), that it should tend to provoke a breach of the peace — *see Goldsmith* v. *Pressdram Ltd* (1977). Criminal libel differs from the tort of libel in that:

(a) justification (truth) is no defence (although it is a defence if the article is true, *and* it is in the public interest that it be published) under the Libel Act 1843, s. 6;

(b) fair comment may not be a defence — *see Goldsmith* v. *Pressdram Ltd* (1977);

(c) publication need not be to a third party; publication to the defamed person himself is enough as a breach of the peace may be thereby provoked;

(d) libelling a class of persons may be criminal (though not tortious).

18. Blasphemy

It is an offence at common law to publish blasphemous matter. Matter is blasphemous if it denies the truth of the Christian religion or vilifies Christ. It is said that blasphemy is criminal because it tends to 'shake the fabric of society generally' said Lord Sumner in *Bowman* v. *Secular Society Ltd* (1917). Also *see R.* v. *Chief Metropolitan Stipendiary Magistrate, ex parte Choudhury* (1991) In *R.* v. *Lemon* (1979) HL, three of the law lords agreed that:

(a) it is not necessary that the publication should tend to provoke a breach of the peace; and

(b) it is not necessary that the accused should actually intend to blaspheme — it is enough that he intends publication.

This last point was the main area of dissent, though it was also suggested that in modern society, where many people subscribe to faiths *other* than Christianity, to protect the Christian faith specifically was wrong. The offence is under review by the Law Commission (*see* Working Paper No. 79 (1981)).

Progress test 29

1. Define and distinguish between the various forms of treason. (1)

2. What is meant by (a) perjury, (b) sedition and (c) public mischief? (4, 5, 11)

3. Outline the major offences contained in the Public Order Act 1986. (6, 7, 8, 9, 10)

4. What are the rights enjoyed by a residential occupier with respect to (a) a troublesome landlord and (b) a would-be squatter? **(15)**

5. Define (a) criminal libel and (b) blasphemy. Outline the chief elements of these offences. **(17, 18)**

Appendices

Appendix 1
Bills of exchange and cheques for banking students

In this appendix, statutory references are to the Bills of Exchange Act 1882 unless otherwise indicated.

Bills of exchange

1. Bills of exchange

A bill of exchange is 'an unconditional order in writing, addressed by one person to another, signed by the person giving it, requiring the person to whom it is addressed to pay on demand, or at a fixed or determinable future time, a sum certain in money, to, or to the order of, a specified person, or to bearer' under the Bills of Exchange Act 1882, s. 3(1).

A cheque is a bill of exchange:

(a) drawn on a banker, and

(b) payable on demand (s. 73).

There are three characteristics of *negotiability* common to every bill of exchange, cheque and promissory note:

(a) valuable consideration is presumed and there is no need to state it;

(b) it can be transferred from A to B by:
   (i) indorsement; or
   (ii) delivery, so that B can sue on it in his own name;

(c) B, provided he takes in good faith and for value, obtains a good title in spite of any defect in A's title.

2. Bills of Exchange Act 1882

This Act codified the law relating to cheques and bills of exchange that had been developed from the customs of merchants and bankers over preceding centuries.

The law relating to cheques is contained partly in the Bills of Exchange Act and partly in the Cheques Act 1957.

Most of the rules of law applied by the BEA to bills generally also apply to cheques, except that, as cheques are bills payable on demand, the rules relating to presentation for acceptance do not apply.

3. Working of a bill

A bill can be issued by a businessman and drawn on his debtor (or by a customer on a bank). For example, where A is owed £1,000 by B, A may draw a bill on B, ordering him to pay the money (or part of it) to C or in accordance with C's instructions. C, the payee, may then sell ('negotiate') the bill to D for value and D may then give it to E. The ultimate recipient of the bill will then be entitled to present it to B for payment and, if B has accepted liability, he is contractually bound to pay the person who presents the bill to him.

Where bills are drawn between private persons (or companies) the drawee will generally be under no liability to a payee or later holder unless he first 'accepts' the bill. Until acceptance, the drawee's contractual duties are to the drawer only.

There are, therefore, three necessary parties:

(a) X, who gives the order and signs it, is the *drawer*;
(b) Y, to whom the order is given, is the *drawee*;
(c) Z, to whom the money is to be paid, is the *payee*.

4. Order and bearer bills

A bill may be drawn payable to bearer or to the order of the drawer, payee or, sometimes, the drawee:

(a) *order bills*, i.e. payable to a named payee or some person designated by him, and a bill is an order bill if:
  (*i*) the bill itself so states; or
  (*ii*) it is payable to a specific person without further words prohibiting transfer, e.g. 'pay X or order' or, simply, 'pay X', but a bill payable to 'X only' is not an order bill;
(b) *bearer bills* occur where:
  (*i*) the bill itself so states, or
  (*ii*) the last or only indorsement is in blank (*see* Appendix 1: 17(f)); or
  (*iii*) the bill is payable to a fictitious or non-existent person.

A *non-existent* person is one who has never existed or, at least, does not exist at present. A *fictitious* person is one who *does* exist but was not the person intended by the drawer to receive payment — *see Bank of England* v. *Vagliano Bros.* (1891).

5. **Inland and foreign bills**
    The differences are:

(a) *an inland bill* is one that is or purports to be:
    (*i*) both drawn and payable within the British Isles; or
    (*ii*) drawn within the British Isles upon some person resident there.

(b) *other bills* are called '*foreign bills*', but, unless the contrary appears on the face of the bill, a holder may treat it as an inland bill.

6. **Bills in a set**
    A set of bills means a bill executed in duplicate, triplicate, etc. The payment of one 'part' of a bill in a set discharges the other parts.
    However, if the drawee mistakenly accepts two parts, or more, he will be liable on each part accepted as if it were a separate bill. Similarly, a holder who indorses several parts is liable on each.
    It is common practice to draw foreign bills in a set to avoid delay or loss in transit.

7. **Inchoate instruments**
    Where a person signs a blank piece of paper with intention that it may be converted into a bill, it operates as authority to fill it up as a complete bill for any amount using the signature already on it as that of drawer, acceptor or indorser (s. 20).

    NOTE: The paper must be delivered with this intention, not stolen — *see Baxendale* v. *Bennett* (1873).

    Similarly, if a person obtains a bill that is incomplete (inchoate) in any way, he has implied authority to rectify the omission in any manner he thinks fit (s. 20(1)). So, where A hands B a blank cheque (one with no sum mentioned), B or any later transferee may insert any value he thinks fit and A will be liable on the cheque, even though it is completed fraudulently — *see Lloyds Bank* v. *Cooke* (1907).

8. **Time of payment**
    A bill must be payable on demand or at a fixed or determinable future time (s. 3(1)):

(a) *payable on demand* — a bill is so payable if:
  (*i*) it is expressed to be payable 'on demand' or 'at sight' or 'at presentation'; or
  (*ii*) where no time for payment is expressed; or
  (*iii*) where accepted or indorsed when overdue;
(b) *determinable future time* — a bill is so payable when expressed to be payable:
  (*i*) at a fixed period 'after sight or date'; or
  (*ii*) on or at a fixed period after the occurrence of some event that is certain to happen, though the time of happening may be uncertain, e.g. 'the death of X', but not 'the marriage of X', as X might never marry (an instrument payable at a determinable future time is called a *time bill*; the period of time is called the *usance*);
(c) *computation of time* — a bill may stipulate that it is to be paid at a fixed period after issue or after acceptance, e.g. 'three months after acceptance' (in such cases, 'month' means calendar month), and time then begins to run from the day after issue or from the date of acceptance respectively and, if the time for acceptance expires on a non-business day, the period is extended until the next business day (s. 14(1)).

9. Acceptance of bills

The drawee is under no liability on the bill until he accepts it by signing the bill in such a way as to signify acceptance of liability to pay the money stated in the bill (s. 17), e.g. not by signing that he will give goods to the value of the bill instead of money.

Acceptance may be made before signature by the drawer or, more usually, after. It may also be accepted when overdue or when previously dishonoured by non-acceptance or non-payment.

Acceptance may be either *general* (unqualified) or it may be *qualified*. Qualified acceptance may be:

(a) *conditional*, e.g. 'accepted subject to deduction for expenses';
(b) *partial*, e.g. for part only of the sum specified;
(c) *local*, i.e. payable *only* at a particular place (merely naming a place for payment is generally acceptance, unless it is to be made *only* at the place named);
(d) *qualified as to time*, e.g. 'accepted payable in six months' where the bill specified three months;
(e) *qualified as to drawee*, i.e. accepted by some of the drawees but not by all.

NOTE: The holder is entitled to demand general acceptance, and may treat the bill as dishonoured if qualified acceptance only is offered (s. 44).

10. Presentment for acceptance (s.39)
This is necessary only where:

(a) the bill is payable some time 'after sight' or 'after demand', as presentation will enable calculation of the period after which the bill will be payable;

(b) there is an express stipulation for presentment; or

(c) the bill is payable elsewhere than at the residence or place of business of the drawee, e.g. at a bank (the drawee, for his convenience, may nominate his bank or some other place as the place of payment; in which case, the bill is said to be *'domiciled'* and domiciling a bill is not qualified acceptance unless it is done in such a way as to prohibit the holder from seeking payment anywhere else).

Presentment is excused (and the bill may be treated as dishonoured) where:

(a) the drawee is dead, bankrupt, lacks capacity or is a fictitious person; or

(b) presentment is impossible; or

(b) acceptance is refused.

Presentment must be at a reasonable hour on a business day and joint drawees must all be approached. Where a drawee is dead, presentment should be to his personal representatives (s. 41).

11. Referee in case of need
The drawer or any indorser who fears that a bill may not be accepted on presentment may designate some person other than the drawee as 'referee in case of need', to whom a holder may apply for payment, if he wishes, in the event of dishonour by the drawee (s. 15). This practice is less common in England than on the Continent.

A referee in case of need (or any other person) who accepts a bill after it has been dishonoured in this way is giving 'acceptance for honour' of the drawer or any indorser on whose behalf he intervenes.

12. Presentment for payment
A bill *not* payable on demand must, after it has been accepted, be presented for payment on the day it falls due (s. 45). A bill *payable on demand* must be presented within a *reasonable* time. A bill not

presented within due time is not invalidated, but cannot be enforced against persons who drew or indorsed it (unless that indorsement was added within a reasonable time).

Presentment must be made at a reasonable hour on a business day. It may be dispensed with:

(a) where, after reasonable diligence, it cannot be effected;
(b) where the drawee is a fictitious person;
(c) where presentment is waived (s. 46).

13. Notice of dishonour

When a bill is dishonoured by non-acceptance or non-payment, notice must be given to the drawer and any indorsers whom the holder may wish to make liable. An indorser who is sued himself may, similarly, notify the drawer and any previous indorser, so making them also liable. No special form of notice is required (it may be oral or written providing it clearly identifies the bill). Return of a dishonoured bill to the drawer is sufficient notice. Notice must be given within a reasonable time of dishonour.

Where a foreign bill is dishonoured, formal notice of dishonour must be given by the process of *noting and protesting*, i.e. a notary public is instructed to present the bill for payment and to note upon it the answer obtained. The notary then issues a formal certificate of dishonour called the protest. If a notary public cannot be found, any householder may serve instead.

14. Lost instruments

Where a bill is lost before it is overdue, the holder may apply to the drawer for a replacement and the drawer can be compelled to comply. However, the drawer is entitled to demand security from the holder against the possibility of the lost bill being found, the drawer thus becoming liable on both bills.

15. Discharge of bills

This is effected by:

(a) *payment in due course*, i.e. to a bona fide holder without notice that the title is defective;
(b) *an acceptor becoming the holder* at or after maturity of the bill;
(c) *renunciation by the holder* of all rights against the acceptor (renunciation must be in writing unless the bill is delivered up to the acceptor);
(d) *intentional cancellation* by the holder or his agent;

(e) *material alteration* of the bill or the acceptance, without the consent of all parties liable upon it, e.g. by alteration of the date, sum payable, time of payment, or substituting a qualified for a general acceptance.

NOTE: If the alteration is not apparent on the face of the bill, a holder, in due course, may enforce the bill as though it had not been altered, i.e. with the alteration deleted — *see Scholfield* v. *Londesborough* (1896).

Negotiation of bills

16. Meaning of negotiation

A bill is negotiated when it is transferred in such a way as to constitute the transferee the holder of the bill, i.e. by mere delivery of a bearer bill or by delivery plus indorsement of an order bill.

Negotiation *may be prohibited* by means of clear words written on the face of the bill, e.g. 'not negotiable'. (In the case of an ordinary bill of exchange, the words, 'not negotiable' prohibit its transfer entirely, but in the case of a cheque (*see* Appendix 1: **27**) they merely mean that the bill ceases to be a negotiable instrument and becomes an ordinary assignable chose in action, i.e. the transferee of such a cheque will get no better title than his transferor had — *see Wilson & Meeson* v. *Pickering* (1946).)

17. Indorsements (s. 32)

Indorsement has the following requirements:

(a) *must be written on the bill* (usually on the back) and the signature of the indorser alone is sufficient, without further words indicating transfer;

(b) *manner of indorsement* should correspond with the drawing, e.g. if the payee's name is misspelt, he should indorse in the misspelt version (adding the correct version if he wishes);

(c) *partial indorsement is ineffective* — the indorsement must relate to the total value of the bill;

(d) *where there are several payees, all* should indorse, unless one has authority to indorse on behalf of the others, e.g. a partner on behalf of his firm;

(e) *indorsement by an agent* — he should sign in such a way as to show he accepts no personal liability and signs merely as agent as if he fails to do so, he is personally liable (the usual form of agent's signature is 'J Smith *per pro* Brown & Co.';

(f) *blank and special indorsements* — if the indorser merely signs his own name, without specifying the name of the transferee (*blank indorsement*), the bill becomes payable to bearer and any subsequent holder can convert it back into an order bill by indorsing himself and adding the name of the person to whom he transfers it (*special indorsement*) (s. 34).

Where a named indorsee is a fictitious or non-existent person the bill is treated as payable to bearer.

18. Restrictive and conditional indorsements
The features of these are:

(a) *restrictive indorsement* — one that *prohibits* further transfer or *limits* transferability, e.g. 'Pay X only, signed: J. Smith', or, similarly, an indorsement indicating that the transferee is to receive payment only as agent for the indorser (s. 35);
(b) *conditional indorsement* — one that restricts the indorser's liability on the bill, e.g. *sans recours* (without recourse), indicating that the indorser disowns all liability; or an indorsement *sans frais* (without expenses), indicating that the indorser will accept liability for the value of the bill, but not for the expenses of enforcing it (an indorsee is entitled to refuse any such indorsement, but if he accepts it, he is bound by its terms (s. 33);
(c) *facultative indorsement* — one that restricts the holder's liability on the bill, e.g. 'Notice of dishonour waived', indicating that the indorser will accept liability on the bill, even though the holder fails to notify him properly if dishonour occurs.

19. Position of holder
A payee, indorsee or bearer of a bill is a holder and his rights depend on whether he is a holder for value or a holder in due course (a payee cannot be a holder in due course):

(a) *holder in due course* — a person who has taken a bill:
    (*i*) complete and regular on the face of it;
    (*ii*) before it was overdue and without notice that it was dishonoured (if such was the case);
    (*iii*) in good faith and for value; and
    (*iv*) without notice of any defect in the transferor's title (s. 29);
A holder in due course is entitled to sue on the bill in his own name and to defeat any defences depending on defects of title or arising from the relations of the parties prior to his taking the bill and is

presumed to be a holder in due course until the contrary is proved, e.g. by showing positively that he took the bill with knowledge that it was obtained by fraud or for an illegal consideration;

(b) *holder for value* — a holder of a bill for which value has, at some time been given (not necessarily by the holder himself), e.g a person to whom the payee or holder in due course gives a bill as a present. A holder for value is entitled to sue in his own name, but takes the bill subject to any defects in title arising through fraud, illegality, etc. and, therefore, receives no better title than the person who transferred the bill to him, so, if he obtains a bill from a holder in due course, he will normally have a perfect title.

> NOTE: A holder of a bill for which value has not been given cannot generally enforce it at all, but, by s. 30, value is presumed to have been given for any bill and a person seeking to defeat the claim of any holder on this ground must prove positively that value was not given.

20. Liability of drawer

By drawing the bill he engages:

(a) that it will be duly paid on presentment; and

(b) that, if it is dishonoured, he will compensate the holder or any indorser for any loss suffered thereby.

As against a holder in due course, he is precluded from denying the existence and capacity of the payee.

21. Liability of drawee

This consists of:

(a) *before acceptance* — he is not liable to any holder (though he may be personally liable to the drawer if he dishonours a bill properly drawn upon him).

(b) *after acceptance* — he becomes the person primarily liable on the bill, and engages that he will pay the bill according to the terms (if any) of his acceptance, as against a holder in due course he cannot deny:

    (*i*) the existence, capacity and signature of the drawer;

    (*ii*) the existence and capacity of the payee of an order bill (though he may deny the validity or genuineness of the payee's indorsement).

> NOTE: Once the bill has been accepted, the drawee (acceptor) becomes the person primarily liable upon the bill, and the drawer and the

indorsers are merely guarantors for him, and therefore are liable only if the acceptor fails to pay.

22. Liability of indorser

Any person who indorses a bill engages that it will be duly paid upon presentment and that, if dishonoured, he will compensate the holder (or any person who indorses the bill subsequently to his own indorsement) who is compelled to pay it.

He is precluded from denying:

(a) *to a holder in due course* — the genuineness of the drawer's signature and of all indorsements prior to his own; and

(b) *to a later indorser* — the validity of the bill or of his own title when he indorsed it.

23. Indorsement by a stranger

Any person who signs a bill otherwise than as drawer or acceptor incurs the liability of an ordinary indorser towards a holder in due course, even though he himself may be a stranger to the bill (i.e. not a party to it, but signing merely at the request, for example, of the drawer, to add his credit to the bill).

24. Forgeries

When a signature on a bill is forged (or placed on it without the authority of the person whose signature it purports to be), the signature is *wholly inoperative*. No rights whatsoever can be acquired in the bill through such a signature (s. 24).

Note, however, that the drawee, after accepting the bill, cannot later deny the genuineness of the drawer's signature, even though it was, in fact, forged (s. 54). An indorser who has once signed a bill is similarly estopped from raising the defence of forgery of the drawer's or any earlier indorser's signature (s. 55).

Cheques

25. Definition

A cheque is a bill of exchange drawn on a banker and payable on demand (s. 73).

It is not necessary that the words 'on demand' should appear on the cheque, as all bills are treated as payable on demand where no time appears for payment (s. 10).

26. Crossed cheques

The object of crossing a cheque is to convey instructions that it is not to be paid otherwise than through a bank or to make some other stipulation as to the manner of payment:

(a) *general crossing* — this is done by drawing two transverse lines across the face of the cheque   with or without the addition of the words '& Co.' between the lines, and the *effect* of this is to make the cheque payable *only* through a collecting banker, i.e. it prevents payment over the counter (*see* Appendix 1: **27**).

(b) *special crossing* — this is done by adding the name of a particular banker, with or without the addition of the two transverse lines of the general crossing.

27. Forms of general crossing

In addition to the ordinary general crossing indicating payment through a banker, the following additional instructions may be added.

(a) *not negotiable* This deprives the cheque of its negotiability and it becomes an ordinary chose in action, i.e. it can be assigned, but the assignee will get no better title than the assignor had. Thus, where a clerk took a blank cheque from his employer that was already crossed 'not negotiable', and fraudulently made it payable to P, it was held that the employer could recover the amount of the cheque from P, as the clerk had no title to the cheque and P could get no better title than the clerk had — *see Wilson & Meeson* v. *Pickering* (1946).

(b) *account payee only* This was not a statutory crossing, but was recognised and obeyed by bankers' custom. Now the Cheques Act 1992 provides that a cheque crossed 'account payee' or 'account payee only' shall be non-transferable. This alters the previous practice, that the collecting bank was merely put on enquiry if it was asked to collect for someone other than the payee.

28. Duty of bankers as to crossed cheques

The banker is liable to the true owner for any loss occasioned where:

(a) *he pays a cheque crossed specially to more than one banker* (unless the additional special crossing merely indicates that one of the bankers named is to collect as agent for the other); or

(b) *he pays a cheque crossed generally otherwise than to a bank*; or

(c) *he pays a cheque crossed specially otherwise than to the banker named* in the crossing, or his agent.

29. Alteration of a cheque

Generally a *visibly altered* bill is void against all parties who have not assented to the alteration (*see* Appendix 1: **15**).

However, a banker who pays a cheque that has been altered, where the alteration is not apparent, is protected against liability to his customer by reason of such payment, if the alteration or forgery was facilitated by the negligence of his customer — *see London Joint Stock Bank* v. *Macmillan* (1918). Where a customer signs a series of blank cheques that have been obtained by a rogue and used to obtain money from the bank, the bank is not liable for the customer's loss — *see Welch* v. *Bank of England* (1955).

30. Protection of paying banker

The drawee bank is protected by statute against liability if it pays in the following circumstances:

(a) *cheques with forged indorsements* — provided they are paid:
- (*i*) in good faith; and
- (*ii*) in the ordinary course of business;
- (*iii*) without negligence (s. 60);

NOTE: The section applies to forged indorsements, and gives no protection where it is the *drawer's* signature that is forged.

(b) *no indorsement or irregular indorsement* — provided the cheque;
- (*i*) is drawn on the banker; and
- (*ii*) is paid in good faith and in the ordinary course of business (Cheques Act 1957, s. 1);

(c) *crossed cheques* — provided the bank pays a cheque drawn upon it:
- (*i*) in good faith and without negligence;
- (*ii*) if crossed generally, to a banker, and if crossed specially, to the banker to whom it is crossed (s. 80).

31. Protection of collecting banker

A collecting banker is protected from liability where he receives payment for a customer who has no title or defective title where he does so in good faith and without negligence (whether or not the cheque is crossed) (Cheques Act 1957, s. 4).

NOTE: The section applies only to *customers*. A person becomes a customer as soon as he opens an account, i.e. where the bank obliges someone, not having an account, by cashing his cheques from time to time, this does not make that person a customer — *see Commissioners of Taxation* v. *English, Scottish & Australian Bank Ltd* (1920).

A collecting bank loses protection if it is negligent, e.g.:

(a) if it opens an account for someone without making reasonable inquiries — *see Hampstead Guardians* v. *Barclays Bank* (1923);

(b) if it collects payment of a cheque made out to the customer's employer, without making enquiries as to the circumstances — *see Underwood Ltd* v. *Martins Bank* (1924);

(c) if it pays into a customer's private account a cheque payable to him only in his official capacity — *see Ross* v. *London County Bank* (1919);

(d) if it receives payment for a customer of cheques clearly indicating that they are payable to the customer only as agent for someone else — *see Bute (Marquess)* v. *Barclays Bank* (1955).

32. Relation of bank and customer

The relationship is basically that of debtor and creditor (as long as the account is in credit). The bank is under a duty to cash all cheques properly drawn on the customer's account, provided they do not exceed the amount of the customer's credit. If a bank wrongfully dishonours a cheque, it is liable:

(a) *for nominal damages*, for the mere fact of dishonour; and

(b) *for any special damage* that the customer can prove the dishonour caused him, e.g. by injury to his reputation in business (special damage is presumed in favour of a trader or businessman whose business cheque is dishonoured).

The customer must exercise reasonable care in drawing his cheques and must compensate the bank for any loss caused by his negligence, e.g. if this facilitates fraud — *see London Joint Stock Bank* v. *Macmillan* (1918). However, in the absence of negligence, there is no duty on the customer to take precautions against forgery — *see Kepitigalla Rubber Estates Ltd* v. *National Bank of India* (1909).

A banker can use the Limitation Act 1980 against a customer who tries to draw a cheque on an account six years after the last demand for payment — *see Joachimson* v. *Swiss Bank Corpn* (1921).

33. Termination of banker's authority

A banker's authority to pay a cheque drawn by his customer is terminated by:

(a) *countermand of payment*, oral or written;

(b) *notice of the customer's death*;
(c) *notice* of the presentation of a *bankruptcy petition* against the customer;
(d) *the making of a bankruptcy order* against the customer.

Progress test Appendix 1: negotiable instruments

1. What is a bill of exchange? How does it differ from a cheque? **(1)**

2. Distinguish between order and bearer bills. What is, and what is the effect of, an inchoate instrument?   **(4, 7)**

3. Explain briefly (a) an inland bill, (b) bills in a set and (c) qualified acceptance.   **(5, 6, 9)**

4. When is presentment of a bill for acceptance necessary and when is it excused? When is presentment for payment necessary? **(10, 12)**

5. How may a bill of exchange be discharged?   **(15)**

6. Explain briefly (a) referee in case of need, (b) notice of dishonour, (c) special indorsement and (d) holder for value.   **(11, 13, 17, 19)**

7. How may an indorser of a bill (a) prohibit transfer, (b) restrict his own liability and (c) increase his own liability?   **(18)**

8. Explain the liability of (a) the drawer and (b) the drawee of a bill.   **(20, 21)**

9. How far is it true to say that a person who signs a bill otherwise than as drawer or drawee accepts liability as a guarantor of the bill?   **(22, 23)**

10. What are the effects of (a) forgery, (b) material alteration and (c) loss of a bill of exchange?   **(14, 15, 24)**

11. What is a holder in due course of a bill of exchange and what are his rights?   **(19)**
A pays a gambling debt to B by cheque, payable to B or order. B indorses the cheque to C for value without telling him how it was obtained. Can C enforce the cheque against A?

12. What is the effect of crossing a cheque and what kinds of crossing are there?   **(26–28)**

13. State the provisions of the Bills of Exchange Act and of any other statute, protecting (a) a paying banker and (b) a collecting banker.   **(30, 31)**

14. What is the relationship of a banker to his customer? When does a person become a customer of a bank and how does the banker's authority on behalf of his customer terminate?   **(31–33)**

15. The X Bank frequently cashes cheques to oblige Y, a commercial traveller, employed by Z. X Bank cashes a cheque made out to 'Y, agent for Z'. It is now discovered that Y was defrauding his employer. Explain the position of the X Bank. **(32, 33)**

Appendix 2
Examination technique

The first point concerning examination technique, perhaps, is that it is something that, so far as is possible, should be learnt *before* taking any examinations in law. The tutorial system, particularly, is designed to assist to that end, but there are some things a student can do alone to ensure that he uses his material to the best advantage.

A revision programme could well include the following.

(a) It is useful to go through your notes and essential source-materials making précis notes of these.

One good way of doing this is to attempt to summarise each topic according to the legal principle involved, adding only such information as is vital to your understanding of that principle, possibly in a different colour ink.

(b) Having reduced your materials to the essentials, read through your notes, noting how much you understand. If necessary, compress the notes further so that all the material can be reduced into clear, well-understood statements of principles.

(c) Then, tackle some specimen questions. Try to do this without the use of notes, referring to these only after you have attempted the question. It is helpful, also, to make a summary of those principles you feel are applicable to the question, as well as the main cases you wish to cite, before embarking on your answer.

There are several kinds of examination question and each requires a slightly different technique.

There are, however, several general rules applicable to all of these:

(a) plan your answer before commencing;

(b) keep to the point of the question and state the principles you use clearly;

(c) make sure you explain yourself — do not assume that the examiner knows what it is you are getting at;

(d) make sure you time your answers so as to be certain of completing the examination;

(e) above all, always cite authorities, in the form of relevant judicial decisions and statutes, to support each main point you make.

The kinds of examination questions you can expect to meet are as follows:

(a) *problems* These are very common in law examinations, though some subjects do not lend themselves to problem questions as much as others (e.g. the English legal system).

An example of a problem question might be: 'A, a minor, obtains a radio on hire purchase from B. Being unable to afford the payments A sells the radio for cash to C. Advise B.'

Such a problem involves several distinct issues and your job is, first, to identify these. Thus, you should initially make a note of the issues raised, which here are:

    (*i*) capacity of minors to contract;

    (*ii*) liability to pay for purchase of necessaries;

    (*iii*) conversion (Torts (Interference with Goods) Act 1977);

    (*iv*) *nemo dat quod non habet* rule.

You should then state the legal principles applicable to these issues (for example: '(*i*) capacity — a minor is generally *not* liable in contract'), listing the main cases and statutes, thus building up a complete answer.

(b) *straightforward 'textbook' questions* For example 'How far is English law judge-made'? These are designed to test your memory, and your ability to organise your information.

While it is obvious that this question is testing your knowledge of judicial law-making (and in particular the doctrine of precedent), you should be careful to present a balanced answer — thus, for example, judges might 'make' law by interpreting statutes; on the other hand, the limitations upon the judges' ability to make law (implicit in the doctrine of Parliamentary sovereignty) should be mentioned, too.

(c) *'quotation' questions* For example 'The categories of negligence are never closed', said Lord Macmillan in *Donoghue* v. *Stephenson* (1932). Discuss. While these are often similar to textbook questions, they call for a slightly different approach. They are often a little more difficult in so far as it is necessary, first and foremost, to decide what the quotation is saying — what does it mean? You may disagree with what the person quoted is saying, in which case you should present authorities supporting your opposing point of view.

Index

abortion, 45, 385, 387, 390–1
accessories after the fact, 374–6
Act of God, 192, 206–7, 221, 255, 259
actus non facit reum nisi mens sit rea,
  372, 379
actus reus, 372–3, 374, 375, 381, 395–7
administrative law, 27
administrative tribunals, 52–6
Admiralty Court, 14–15, 39, 42
adoption, 44, 46, 73, 81
adultery, 78, 79, 80
agency, 111, 165–76
  creation, 168–70
  duties of principal and agent, 172–3
  estoppel, 169
  implied, 168–9
  ratification, 169–70
  termination, 170–2
agents
  authority, 174–6
  bills of exchange, 420
  definition, 165
  del credere, 94, 166
  duties, 172–3
  mercantile, 166
  special, 165
  vicarious liability, 173, 216–17
  warranty of authority, 174
aliens, 73, 75, 113
animals, 82, 192, 229, 256–7, 258
animus manendi, 72
arbitration, 61–4
arrestable offences, 369–70
assault and battery, 224, 225–7, 368,
  375, 385–6, 391–2
assize courts, 8–9, 17, 24, 36, 44
Attorney-General, 41, 66–7, 323, 372
auctioneers, 98, 167
audi alterem partem, 54
automatism, 382, 382–3

bailment, 190–3, 232
bankers, 21, 167, 181, 340–1, 417–18,
  426–30
bankruptcy, 43, 46, 47, 171, 172, 275
  acquisition of ownership, 272
  conditional bills of sale, 311
  discharge, 150, 362
  express private trusts, 326
  priority of debts, 361
  proceedings, 360–1
  quasi-contract, 161
  undischarged bankrupts, 361–2
barristers, 24, 33, 50–1, 57–8
  Court of Appeal, 37
  Crown Court, 44
  House of Lords, 37
  inferior courts, 45, 48
  special courts, 55–6
beneficiaries, 10, 323–4, 349, 351–5,
  358, 359
  certainties, 325, 326–7
  duties and powers of trustees,
    341–2, 342, 343
  equitable doctrines and remedies,
    320, 321–2, 323
  law of property, 272–3, 282, 288–9
  purpose trusts, 332
  quasi-contracts, 161
  resulting trusts, 333–4
  secret trusts, 335
  trustees as, 334
  variation of trusts, 336
bequests, 349, 351
bigamy, 372, 392–3
bills of exchange, 21, 93, 108, 115,
  180–1, 404, 417–30
  acceptance, 420–21, 422–3, 425
  bearer bills, 418–19
  cheques, 21, 115, 133, 181, 404,
    417–18, 426–30

discharge, 422–3
dishonour, 422, 424
foreign bills, 419
forgeries, 426
holders, 182, 423, 424–5
indorsements, 423–6, 428
liabilities, 425–6
negotiation, 423–6
order bills, 418–19
presentment, 421–2
time of payment, 419–20
bills of sale, 93, 184, 276, 310–11, 313
blackmail, 402, 405
blasphemy, 84, 412
breach of contract, 85, 118, 120–1,
122–3, 125, 322, 323
discharge, 153–4
fundamental, 127
misrepresentation, 134
quasi-contract, 162–3
remedies, 155–8
torts, 202–3, 212, 212–13, 215
British citizenship, 73–4
brokers, 166–7
burglary, 381, 398–9, 403

capacity
contracts, 82, 112–16
crime, 82, 377, 380
testamentary, 348
torts, 82, 211–18
trustees, 338
care, duty of, 172, 311, 340
negligence, 225, 239, 240, 240–1,
244, 246, 249–50, 251
case law, 27–34
certiorari, 43
champerty, 141
Chancery Division of the High Court,
17, 41, 43–4, 357
charities, 328–32, 338
administration, 331
advantages, 329–30
cy-pres doctrine, 330–1
definition, 328–29
cheques, 21, 115, 133, 181, 404,
417–18, 426–30
choses in action, 274
children, 44, 45, 46, 47–8, 49
criminal law, 377, 380, 387, 390–1
entails, 288
equity and trusts, 317, 324, 336,
337–8, 338

law of contract, 113, 114–15, 138,
190
law of person, 72, 73, 80, 80–2
law of succession, 351, 353–5, 358,
359
torts, 212–13, 213, 214, 250–1
variation of trusts, 336
choses in action, 150, 274, 275, 276,
313, 423, 427
mercantile law, 178, 179–80
choses in possession, 274
circuit judges, 24, 42, 44–5, 45–6, 51
codicils, 347, 349, 351–2
codification of law, 24, 28, 417
collective agreements, 95
Commercial Court, 42
common law, 4–16, 27, 32, 33, 83, 84,
184, 317
barristers' immunity, 58
blasphemy, 412
conspiracy, 377–8
the Crown, 212
employers' breach of duty, 215
history, 5–16
illegal or void contracts, 140–1
lien, 195–6
marriage, 78, 140–1
participation in crime, 374
property, 272, 296, 299
riot, 409
securities, 307, 311
variation of trusts, 336
common law courts, 8–9
companies, 66–9
competition law, 144–5
conciliar courts, 15
consensus ad idem, 95–7
consideration, 91, 93, 105–10, 119,
160, 161
adequacy, 106
characteristics, 106–8
definition, 105–6
quasi-contract, 160, 161
conspiracy, 15, 44–5, 212, 377–8, 409
constables, 370
constitutional law, 83–6
constitutional monarchy, 83
contra proferentem rule, 124, 126–7
contracts, 8, 10, 24, 42, 43, 85, 91–196
acceptance, 91, 99–102
agency, 165–76
capacity to contract, 112–16
certainty of terms, 101

competition law, 144–5
conditions, 118, 121–2, 154, 184–5
consensus ad idem, 95–7
consideration, 91, 93, 105–10, 119, 160, 161
construction of terms, 123–4
counter-offers, 100–1
damages for breach, 155–8
determinable, 123
discharge by agreement, 149–50
discharge by breach, 153–4
discharge by frustration, 151–3
discharge by operation of law, 150
discharge by performance, 147–9
duress, 129, 137
equitable remedies, 322, 323
exclusion clauses, 124, 125–7
express terms, 118–19
formalities, 92–4
frustration of, 151–3
guarantee, 94
illegal, 129, 139–41, 160
implied terms, 119–20, 185–6, 188, 194
indemnity, 94
innominate terms, 118, 122–3
intention to create legal relations, 94–7
invalid, 129–45
limitation of action, 155
mercantile law, 111, 178–96
minors' contracts, 82, 114–16
misrepresentation, 106, 119, 129, 132–3, 133–6
mistake in, 119, 124, 129, 130–3, 161, 321
offers, 91, 97–8, 100–3
privity, 106, 110–12
quasi-contracts, 160–3
rectification of, 119, 124, 129
remedies for breach, 155–8
restraint of trade, 141–3
restraints of sale of business, 143
restraints upon employees, 142–3
sale of land, 93, 283
simple, 91, 357
solus agreements, 142, 143
standard form, 124–5
synallagmatic, 122
termination of offer, 102–3
terms, 118–27, 185–6
under seal, 92–3
undue influence, 129, 137–8

unenforceable, 129
unilateral, 122
void, 93, 115–16, 129, 139–44, 160, 161–2, 184, 213
voidable, 115, 123, 129, 136
warranties, 120–1, 134, 154, 174, 185–6
written, 93, 119, 283
contractual duty, 110
conversion, 320
conveyancing, 24, 59, 189, 274, 277, 283, 335
copyhold, 277, 281
coroners' courts, 49
corporations, 66–7, 211, 380–1
chartered, 66–7
contracts, 113–14
statutory, 67
Council on Tribunals, 54
counsellors, 375
county courts, 30, 43, 45–7
appeals from, 39, 44
jurisdiction, 46–7
Court of Appeal, 16, 17, 29–30, 36, 39–41, 58
Civil Division, 39–40
Criminal Division, 40–1
Court of Chancery, 4, 10, 12, 17, 280–1, 281–2
courts martial, 55–6
courts merchant, 13–14, 14
covenants, 294–7, 320–1
crimes, 10
attempts, 376
classification, 368–69
definition, 367
elements of a crime, 372
inchoate offences, 376
incitement, 376–7
modes of participation, 376–7
and torts, 202, 216, 368
criminal law, 4, 8, 24, 367–412
abortion, 385, 387, 390–1
accident, 385–6
actus reus, 372–3, 374, 381, 395–7
arrestable offences, 369–70
assault and battery, 368, 385–6, 391–2
automatism, 382, 382–3
bigamy, 372, 392–3
blackmail, 402, 405
blasphemy, 412
burglary, 398–399

child destruction, 390–1
conspiracy, 377–8, 410
corporations, 380–1
Criminal Damage Act 1971, 404–5
criminal liability, 367–78
criminal proceedings, 367
deception, 399–400, 400–1
defences, 381–6
employers, 380–1
exemptions, 380
false accounting, 401–2
fatal offences, 387–91
forgery, 403–4
handling stolen goods, 402–3
homicide, 387–8
incapacity, 380
incitement to racial hatred, 407, 408
indictable offences, 371
infanticide, 390
insanity, 381–2, 382
intoxication, 383–4
jurisdictional limitations, 379–80
limitations on criminal
    responsibility, 379–6
manslaughter, 372, 374, 375, 382,
    383, 387, 389–90, 393
mens rea, 372, 373–4, 375, 381, 388,
    397–8
mistake, 385
motoring offences, 374, 384–5, 393
murder, 372, 374, 375, 382, 384,
    385, 387–89
necessity, 384–5
non-fatal offences, 391–2
offences against the person, 387–93
offences against property, 395–405
offences against public order,
    406–11
offences against state security, 406–7
offences triable either way, 371–2
Official Secrets Acts, 406–7
perjury, 407
punishment, 368
rape, 368, 380, 381, 385, 391–2, 399
riot, 407, 408
robbery, 398
sedition, 407
sexual offences, 371, 372
summary offences, 371, 372
terrorism, 409
theft, 395–8
Theft Act 1978, 395–403
treason, 406

violent disorder, 408
Crown Court, 17, 24, 30, 36, 39, 44–5,
    45, 48
Crown Prosecution Service, 60–1
Crown, the, 6, 14, 23, 25, 83–6, 367
    appointment of judiciary, 50–1
    intestacy, 358
    torts, 23, 212
custom, 20–1, 83
cy-pres doctrine, 330–1

damages, 40, 43, 134–5, 194, 215, 273,
    342
    breach of contract, 135, 154, 155–8,
        174
    criminal law, 368
    equitable remedies, 321
    trespass, 230, 233
damnum sine injuria, 204–5
deception, 399–401
deeds, 92–3, 187, 274, 275, 278, 327
    interests in land, 286, 287
    mortgages, 303, 304, 309
defamation, 40, 261–7
    defences, 264–7
    definition, 261
    fair comment, 265, 412
    innuendo, 262–3
    justification, 264–5
    libel, 261–2, 267, 411–12
    limitation, 267
    privilege, 265–7
    publication, 263–4, 412
    reference to plaintiff, 263
    slander, 261–2, 267
delegated legislation, 24–6, 38
    control, 26–7
    criticism, 25–6
delegatus non potest delegare, 172, 340–1
deportation, 74, 75
devises, 349, 351
diplomatic immunity, 113, 212, 380
Director General of Fair Trading, 144
Director of Public Prosecutions, 60–1,
    376
dishonesty, 397
divorce, 13, 17, 44, 46, 47, 72, 79–80
domestic tribunals, 56, 69
domicile, 72, 72–3
dominant tenement, 286, 297, 298, 300
donatio mortis causa, 188, 189
duress, 129, 137, 373, 384, 385

easements, 277, 286, 297–300
  extinguishment, 300
  prescription, 299–300
EC nationals, 75
ecclesiastical courts, 8, 13, 39, 55
ecclesiastical law, 12–13, 13
election, 320–1
equitable interests
  land, 281–2, 284, 287–8, 303–9
  property, 272–3, 277–8, 319
equity, 4, 8, 27, 46, 47, 317–23
  advantages and disadvantages, 11
  choses in action, 273
  equitable doctrines, 316, 320–1
  equitable protection, 319–20
  equitable remedies, 317, 321–3
  formalisation, 11
  history, 10–12
  importance, 12
  injunctions, 321, 322–3
  maxims, 317–19
  nature and scope of, 317
  origins, 10
  restrictive covenants, 296, 296–7
  specific performance, 321, 322
escrow, 92
estate agents, 166, 167–8
estates, 13, 43, 355–61
  law of property, 273, 276–8, 280–5
estoppel, 93, 109, 150, 169, 183, 317, 318
European Convention on Human Rights 1950, 63–4, 84
European Court of Justice, 29, 32, 36, 38, 62–3
ex turpi causa non oritur actio, 139
executors, 213, 355–6, 356, 356–7
expressio unius est exclusio alterius, 33
extradition, 379–80

factors, 166–7
facts, 5, 130, 161, 240, 385
false accounting, 401–2
Family Division of the High Court, 17, 41, 44, 82, 357
  President, 39–40, 44
fee simple, 281, 282, 283–4, 287
felonies, 368–9, 374–5
feudal system, 6, 7, 276, 277–8, 280–1
fire, 190, 253–4, 255, 256, 405
foreclosure, 305, 307–8
forgery, 15, 45, 395, 426, 428, 429
freedom of assembly, 85

freedom of speech, 26, 84–5
freehold, 273, 275, 280, 281, 282–3

General Medical Council, 56
gifts, 188–90, 274, 283, 320, 332, 349
  lapsed, 350–1
guardians, 46, 48, 81, 81–2

habeas corpus, 43, 84
handling stolen goods, 402–3
High Court, 8, 14–17, 24, 30, 36, 39–40, 41–7
  appeals from, 38, 39, 40
  appeals to from tribunals, 54
  defamation, 267
  guardians, 81–2
  judiciary, 50–1
hire purchase, 93, 101, 183, 193–5, 213
homicide, 387–8
House of Commons, 22, 23, 26
House of Lords, 12, 16, 19, 22–3, 29–30
  Appeals Committee, 37–8, 39, 50
  judicial system, 36–8, 39, 50–1, 56, 57, 58, 60

immigration, 74–5
in alieno solo, 286
in consimili casu statute, 7–8
incorporation, 66–9
indictable offences, 48–9, 371
industrial tribunals, 52
infanticide, 45, 390
injunctions, 322–3
injuria sine damno, 205
innkeepers, 192–3
Inns of Court, 57
innuendos, 262–3
insanity, 381–2, 382, 383
insolvency, 275, 360
intestacy, 272, 275, 277, 290, 307, 357–59
  no surviving spouse, 359
  partial, 358
  statutory trusts, 359
  surviving spouse, 358
  total, 353, 358
intoxication, 113, 213, 349, 383–4

joint tortfeasors, 215
Judge Advocate General, 55–6
judges, 5, 7, 24, 28, 30, 33, 184, 202

criminal offences, 371
judicial system, 37, 40, 42–5, 50–1,
    55, 57, 61
Judicature Acts 1873–75, 9, 11, 12,
    14–15, 16, 16–17, 28–9
    legal and equitable interests, 272–3
judicial protection, 84
judicial review, 42–3
judicial system, 36–64
    arbitration, 61–4
    Court of Appeal, 39–41
    High Court, 41–5
    House of Lords, 36–8, 39, 50–1, 56,
        57, 60
    inferior civil courts, 45–8
    judiciary, 50–1
    legal aid, 60–1
    legal profession, 57–60
    Privy Council, 38–9
    special courts, 51–6
judiciary, 50–1
    immunity, 51
    length of appointment, 51
jura in re aliena, 275
jura in re propria, 275
jurists, 27, 33, 73
jury, 5, 48, 49, 202, 371, 376
justices of the peace, 24, 50
juvenile courts, 44, 47–8, 49, 380

land, 43, 46, 69, 98, 280–90, 409–10
    co-ownership, 284–5
    easements, 286
    equitable doctrines, 320
    equitable interests, 281–2, 287–8
    fee simple, 282, 282–3
    freehold, 281, 282–3
    imperfect gifts, 189
    leases, 292–300
    legal estates in, 282–4
    legal interests, 281, 285–6
    mortgages, 303–10
    proper law of the will, 347
    real and personal, 271, 273, 273–4,
        277
    rentcharges, 286
    sale of, 93, 283
    strict settlement, 288–9
    trusts for sale, 289, 290
Land Tribunal, 40, 52–3, 297
law merchant, 12–13, 13–14, 184
law reporting, 33–4
Law Society, 58

leasehold, 271, 273, 282–3, 349
leases, 273, 274, 287, 292–300
    covenants, 294–7
    creation of, 293
    definition, 292
    determination of, 293–4
    discharge of covenants, 297
    easements, 297–300
    minors, 115
    profits, 297–300
    protection against forfeiture, 294
    restrictive covenants, 295–7
    tenancies, 292–3
    term of years absolute, 284
legacies, 250–1, 342, 349, 357
legal advice, 60
legal aid, 24, 60–1
legal duty, 110
legal executives, 59–60
legal profession, 57–60
legislation, 21–7
legitimation, 13, 73, 80–1
libel, 84, 260–1, 368, 410–11
liens, 167, 186, 195–6, 303, 311, 334
light, 300
limitation of action, 155, 222, 267
loans, 115–16, 213, 357
Lord Chancellor, 7, 10, 15, 24, 27
    judicial system, 37–40, 42–3, 45–8
Lord Chief Justice, 37, 39–40, 40, 42,
    50
Lords of Appeal in Ordinary (Law
    Lords), 16, 37, 50–1
Lords Justices of Appeal, 37, 39–40, 51

magistrates' courts, 44, 47–8, 51, 60,
    361, 371, 371–2
Magna Carta, 8, 22, 37, 83
maintenance, 47, 49, 141, 336, 341,
    353–5
    purpose trusts, 331–2
malice, 203–4, 218, 264, 265, 266,
    383, 385–6, 388
mandamus, 42
manslaughter, 45, 372, 375, 382, 387,
    388, 389–90
    involuntary, 390
    voluntary, 389–90
marriage, 8, 13, 49, 76–80, 115, 140–1
    bigamous, 372, 392–3
    coercion, 384
    criminal liability, 377, 391–2, 403
    gifts, 189

joint tenancies, 285
law of succession, 349, 352–3, 353, 354, 354–5, 358
legal consequences, 78
magistrates jurisdiction, 49, 80
nullity, 78
polygamous, 74–5
torts, 213, 227
voidable, 78–9
Master of the Rolls, 37, 39–40, 50, 56
medieval courts, 8
mens rea, 372, 373–4, 375, 381, 388, 397–8
mental disorder, 79, 113, 213
criminal responsibility, 381–3, 389, 389–90
law of succession, 348, 349, 355
mercantile law, 113, 178–96
assignment, 178–9
bailment, 190–3
hire-purchase, 193–5
liens, 195–6
negotiable instruments, 179–82
minors,
adoption, legitimacy and guardianship, 44, 46, 80–2
capacity, 212–13, 380
contracts, 113, 114–16, 189, 213
incapacity, 82, 380
torts, 212–13
trusts, 336, 338
mischief rule, 31, 32
misdemeanours, 368–9, 374–5, 377
misrepresentation, 106, 119, 129, 132–3, 213
mistake
in contracts, 119, 124, 129, 130–3, 161, 321
criminal responsibility, 385, 386
trusts, 326
mortgages, 43, 46, 187, 275, 277, 302–13, 342
bills of sale, 310–11
consolidation, 306–7
equitable, 303, 304–5, 306
land, 303–10
legal, 303, 304, 305–6
personalty, 310–12
pledges, 302, 311–12
priority, 309
puisne, 309
redemption, 307–8, 308–9
remedies of mortgagees, 305–6, 306

motoring offences, 246, 371, 374, 384–5, 393
murder, 44–5, 372, 375, 382, 384, 385, 387–9

National Health Service tribunals, 52
nationality, 23, 71–2, 73–6
natural justice, 54–5
naturalisation, 74
nec vi, nec clam, nec precario, 20, 299
negligence, 202, 203, 206–7, 213, 215, 239–52, 334
barristers' immunity from liability, 58
common duty of care, 249–50
contributory, 246
criminal law, 374, 385–6, 390
defamation, 267
defective chattels, 246, 248
defective premises and land, 248
definition, 239
economic loss, 242
exclusion clauses, 126–7
innkeeper's liability, 192
involuntary manslaughter, 390
legal duty of care, 239, 240
mistake and misrepresentation, 133, 134, 135
occupiers' liability, 248–52
pledges at common law, 311
proof, 245
public policy, 244–5
specific duties, 242
standard of care, 240–1
statements, 241, 243–4
strict liability, 253, 259, 374
trespass and nuisance, 225, 231–2
negotiable instruments, 179–82, 274
bills of exchange, 180–1, 181
cheques, 181
position of holders, 182
nemo dat quod non habet, 182–4
nervous shock, 246, 247
non est factum, 93, 133
novation, 150
novus actus interveniens, 207–8
nuisance, 202, 225, 234–7, 368, 411

obiter dicta, 30
occupiers' liability, 248–52
defences, 250
liability to trespassers, 250–1
offences against the person, 387–93

fatal, 387–91
non-fatal, 391–3
offences against property, 396–405
offences against public order, 407–11
offences against state security, 406–7
Official Secrets Acts, 44–5, 406–7
Orders in Council, 15, 25, 38
ownership, 161, 271–3, 319, 395–6
  co-ownership of land, 284–5, 285
  fee simple, 283, 284
  pledges at common law, 311
  treasure trove, 49

Parliament, 21–3, 26, 51, 62, 361
Parliamentary Commissioner for
  Administration (Ombudsman), 86
parol evidence rule, 119
part performance, 147, 287, 293, 305
partnerships, 43, 70–1, 115
patents, 46, 274, 275
pawn, 195, 276, 302, 310
perjury, 408
personal action, 273
personal freedom, 84
personality, 183–4, 273, 273–4, 276,
  277, 336, 338
  mortgages, 310–13
persons, legal, 66–86
  corporations, 66–7
  marriage, 76–80
  minors, 80–2
  registered companies, 67–80
  status, 71
  unincorporated associations, 69
"pie powder" courts, 14, 36
pledges, 187, 195, 302, 310, 311, 312,
  312–13
  real and personal property, 275,
  276
possession, 227, 233, 270–1, 286, 292
powers of arrest, 227, 369–70, 370
precedent, 9, 27–9, 30–1
  hierarchy, 29–30
principals, 165, 166, 168, 169–70, 172,
  173
  authority of agent, 174–5, 175,
  175–6
private law, 3–4
privilege, 165, 265, 265–6
privity of contract, 110–12, 178
  acquisition of rights and liabilities,
  111–12
Privy Council, 15, 35, 38

Judicial Committee, 38–40, 50–1
probate, 24, 44, 46, 113, 352, 356–7
procedural law, 4–5
processions, 409
procurers, 375
professional incompetence, 262
profits à prendre, 286, 297
prohibition, 43
property, 8, 10, 85, 271–313
  bankruptcy, 272, 275, 311
  choses in action, 274, 313
  choses in possession, 274
  disposal by will, 349–51
  equitable interests, 272–3, 281–2,
  287–8
  estates, 280–90
  leases, 292–300
  legal interest, 272–3, 285–6
  minors, 115
  ownership, 271, 272, 284–5, 285
  personalty, 273, 273–4, 276
  possession, 271–2
  Property Acts 1925, 276–7, 277,
  277–8
  realty, 273, 276
  securities, 275–6, 302–13, 348–9
  succession upon death, 275, 355
  transfer *inter vivos*, 274, 289
  trusts, 336, 341
proximate cause, 207
public inquiries, 26
public interest, 265
public law, 3–4
puisne judges, 42, 44, 51

quantum meruit action, 147, 162–3
quasi-contracts, 160–3
Queen's Bench Division of High
  Court, 14–15, 39, 40, 41–3, 44, 54
Queen's Counsel, 57

race relations, 46, 75–6, 84–5, 407, 408
rape, 45, 368, 380, 381, 385, 391–2,
  399
ratio decidendi, 30
real action, 273
realty, 273, 276, 277, 284, 336
reasonable foresight, 207
receiver, 306
recklessness, 342, 373–4, 375, 385
rectification, 119, 131, 321
references, 267
Registrar of Companies, 67, 68, 312

remoteness of damage in tort, 208,
208–9, 209–10
Rent Assessment Committees, 53
rentcharge, 277, 286
res ipsa loquitur, 245
rescission, 131, 133, 134, 135, 135–6,
150, 317, 321
resale prices maintenance, 144
restraint of trade, 141–3
Restrictive Practices Court, 40, 55, 144
right of survivorship, 285
rights of citizens, 83–4
riot, 85, 408
robbery, 45, 190, 375, 403
Roman law, 4
royal courts, 8, 15, 201
rule of law, 83–4

sale of goods, 184–7
ascertained and unascertained
goods, 184–5
implied conditions and warranties,
185–6
rights of seller, 186–7
Scrutiny Committee, 26
seat belts, 246
securities, 275, 302–13, 317
mortgages, 302–13
sedition, 45, 84, 408
self-defence, 84, 226–7, 384
servient tenement, 286, 298, 300
sex discrimination, 75
sexual offences, 82, 371, 385, 391–2
slander, 261–2
Social Security Commissioner, 52
Social Security tribunals, 52
solicitors, 24, 44, 46, 50, 57–9, 340–1,
362
Solicitors Disciplinary Tribunal, 56
solus agreements, 142, 143, 308
Special Commissioners of Income
Tax, 53
special courts, 51–6
specific intent, 388
specific performance, 131, 287, 321,
322, 323
"spent" convictions, 264–5
stare decisis, 29–30
status, 71
statute law interpretation, 31–2, 32–3
statutes, 24, 31, 285, 286, 340–1, 385
statutory instruments, 25

statutory trust for sale, 285
strict liability, 206–7, 215, 218, 221,
236–7, 253–9
animals, 256–7, 257–258
crimes, 372, 374, 381, 385
dangerous objects, 253–4
defences, 255, 259, 385
definition, 253
fire, 255–6
Ryland v. *Fletcher*, 253–5
statutory torts, 258–9
strict settlement, 288–90
subordinate legislation, 24–6
subsidiary systems of law, 12–15
substantive law, 4–5
succession, 272, 275, 317, 347–62
bankruptcy, 359–62
intestacy, 357–9
maintenance of dependants, 353–5
personal representatives, 355–7
property disposable by will, 349–51
requisites of valid will, 347–49
revocation of wills, 351–3
summary offences, 48–9, 371, 372
supply of goods and services, 187–8
Supreme Court of Judicature, 12, 16,
17, 36, 50

tacking, 307
tenancies, 292–300
tenders, 101–2
terrorism, 410
theft, 45, 395–403, 405
time immemorial, 21
tort, 8, 10, 42, 82, 136, 201–67, 323
capacity, 211–15
causation, 207, 207–8
crimes, 368, 411
defamation, 261–7, 411
defences, 218–22, 237, 253, 259,
264–7
definition, 201
fault, 206–7
history, 201–2
intention, 205–6, 253
malice, 205–6
minors, 82
motive, 205–6
negligence, 206–7, 213, 215, 239–52
nuisance, 225, 234–7
remoteness of damage, 208, 208–9,
209–10

statutory, 258–9
statutory authority, 221–2, 255
strict liability, 206–7, 218, 236–7,
    253–9
trespass, 224–34
vicarious liability, 173, 206, 215,
    216–18
volenti non fit injuria, 218–20
wrongful interference with goods,
    231–4
trade unions, 56, 69, 69–70, 212
treason, 44–5, 384, 406
treasure trove, 49
Treaty of Rome, 19
trespass, 8, 9, 202, 224–34, 271
    defences, 226–7, 231
    remedies, 230–1, 233–4
    to goods, 232
    to land, 227–31
    to the person, 225–7
trespassers, 228–9, 230, 231, 250–1,
    410
    criminal law, 398–399, 399, 411
trust instrument, 289, 340
trustees, 138, 272–3, 285, 289, 323,
    338–43
    appointment, 277, 338–40
    breach of trust, 335, 342–3
    capacity, 338
    delegation, 340–1
    duties, 277, 340–2
    powers, 336, 340
    remuneration, 341–2
    retirement, 277, 339–40
trusts, 10, 43, 46, 272–3, 317, 323–43
    breach of, 203, 215, 338, 342–3
    certainties, 325–6, 326, 326–7, 330
    completely constituted, 327
    constructive, 334–5
    discretionary, 324–5, 337
    express private, 325–7
    express public (charities), 328–31
    incompletely constituted, 327
    powers of appointment, 324–5
    precatory, 326
    purpose, 331–2
    resulting, 333–4
    secret, 335
    variation of, 336–8

trusts for sale, 284, 284–5, 285, 289,
    290, 320

uberrimae fidei, 134, 136
ubi remedium ibi jus, 7
ultra vires doctrine, 22, 25–6, 26, 27,
    55, 66–7, 69, 113–14
undue influence, 129
unfair dismissal, 85
unincorporated associations, 69–79,
    332

vesting deed, 275, 289
violent disorder, 409
visitors, 250

wagers, 140
wardship, 81–2
warranties, 120–1, 134, 136, 154, 172,
    174, 185–6
    ex post facto, 187
wills, 13, 73, 188, 189, 272, 275, 307,
    347–57
    administrators, 355–6
    appointment of guardians, 81
    bequests, 349
    capacity to make, 348
    characteristics of, 347–8
    codicils, 349, 351–2
    devises, 349
    disposable property, 349–51
    estates and interest in land, 283,
        286, 287, 289, 290
    executors, 349, 355–6
    formalities of, 348
    intestacy, 357–59
    legacies, 349, 350, 350–1
    maintenance of dependants, 353–5
    minors, 82
    mutual, 353
    personal representatives, 355–7
    probate, 357
    revocation of, 347, 351–3
    trusts, 337, 342
    witnesses, 348, 349
writ system, 7, 10, 66–7

youth courts, 47–8, 49, 380